MW01489726

GEOMETRY
for Christian Schools®

Teacher's Edition

GEOMETRY

for Christian Schools®

Second Edition

Ron Tagliapietra, Ed.D.
Kathy D. Pilger, Ed.D.
Larry Hall, M.S.
Larry Lemon, M.S.

Teacher's Edition

 Bob Jones University Press
Greenville, South Carolina 29614

Barnes & Noble Books: *Flatland* by Edwin A. Abbott. © 1963. Used by permission.

Note:
The fact that materials produced by other publishers may be referred to in this volume does not constitute an endorsement of the content or theological position of materials produced by such publishers. Any references and ancillary materials are listed as an aid to the student or the teacher and in an attempt to maintain the accepted academic standards of the publishing industry.

GEOMETRY for Christian Schools® Teachers Edition
Second Edition

Ron Tagliapietra, Ed.D.	**Design (Student and Teacher)**	**Typesetting**
Kathy D. Pilger, Ed.D.	**Preface, Inc.**	**Melba Clark**
Larry Hall, M.S.	**Editor**	
Larry Lemon, M.S.	**Suzette Jordan**	

Produced in cooperation with the Bob Jones University Department of Mathematics of the College of Arts and Science, the School of Education, and Bob Jones Academy.

for Christian Schools is a registered trademark of Bob Jones University Press.

© 1999 Bob Jones University Press
Greenville, South Carolina 29614
First Edition © 1985 Bob Jones University Press

Printed in the United States of America
All rights reserved

ISBN 1-57924-237-5

15 14 13 12 11 10 9 8 7 6

Contents

8 Area

Area

God has given some insects fantastic skills as nest builders. Nests of hornets are nearly spherical while the mud dauber builds a conelike nest. Wasps and honeybees are master builders of hexagon-shaped nests.

The hexagon shape eliminates wasted space. It provides the maximum storage area using the least amount of material. This shape also produces an amazingly strong construction because each cell is reinforced by the cells around it. God has given His creatures the ability to build geometric nests.

God used hornets to drive out enemies of Israel (Josh. 24:12). Yet God describes death for a Christian as a wasp without its stinger—a little bug making a lot of noise.

"O death, where is thy sting? O grave, where is thy victory? The sting of death is sin; and the strength of sin is the law. But thanks be to God, which giveth us the victory through our Lord Jesus Christ" (I Cor. 15:55-57).

After this chapter you should be able to

1. define area.
2. state and use the postulates for area.
3. prove area formulas for various triangles and quadrilaterals.
4. prove and apply the Pythagorean theorem.
5. develop the formula for the area of a regular polygon.
6. develop the formula for the area of a circle.
7. find the surface areas of cylinders, cones, and spheres.
8. define the Platonic solids and find their surface areas.

309

Overview

Most of your students will enjoy this chapter, which offers a study of areas of various plane figures and the surface area of common three-dimensional figures. Many formulas will be developed throughout this chapter. Students should understand that *area* is the number of square units needed to cover a polygon or surface. Since students often confuse *area* and *volume,* these two concepts are covered in separate chapters.

Bulletin Board Idea

Place one of each of the six main figures (with their interior) whose area will be found in this chapter. They are the trapezoid, parallelogram, rectangle, triangle, regular polygon (use pentagon or hexagon), and circle. Draw the altitude on the trapezoid, parallelogram, and triangle; the apothem on the regular polygon; and the radius on the circle. Title the board *Area.*

Presentation

This chapter develops formulas for the areas of common geometric figures. Students should memorize the formulas and be able to apply them to numerical problems. This material is very useful to all students for practical problems in everyday life. The proofs help students see why the formulas are correct; however, you need not assign any proofs to students on the intuitive track (though you may still want to work through some proofs in class).

Please Note. The dimensions of some regular polygons have been rounded to decimal values (usually tenths). While the sides determine the radius and apothem, the radicals are more convenient in rounded form.

Please Note. Answers to area problems often include π or square roots. The advantage is that the answer is exact. The disadvantage is that such answers are less familiar and require further work to interpret. We try always to include an exact answer for those who prefer this. Those encouraging calculator use can easily calculate up to ten significant digits from the exact answer.

Calculator answers always involve rounding off. When calculators are used, the greatest accuracy comes from using the π button and not rounding until the final answer. If you want students to use 3.14, they will get less exact answers. Answers given are as accurate as possible to help all teachers evaluate answers

regardless of calculator policies. A problem may occur using π to find a circumference that is then used to find the surface area of a cone. Students who round π to 3.14, then round the circumference, and finally round the surface area will obtain an answer with a wide margin of error since each calculation is less precise and the errors are being multiplied. ■

Meaning of Area

Objectives

1. To define and illustrate area concepts and postulates.
2. To prove and apply the area formula for rectangular regions.
3. To apply the Area Addition Postulate to regions reducible to rectangular regions.

Vocabulary

area of a region
Area Addition Postulate
Area of Square Postulate
Area Postulate
Congruent Regions Postulate

Assignment

• Intuitive: 1-22, 26-30
• Standard: 1-30
• Rigorous: 1-15 odd, 18-30

Resource

• *Visual Packet,* Perimeter, Area, Volume. This poster distinguishes area from perimeter.

8.1 Meaning of Area

Every believer should look forward to his future residence, the Holy City. In Revelation 21 God inspired John to give us a glimpse of the city whose residents' names are written in the Lamb's Book of Life (v. 27). Read Revelation 21 carefully. Notice that the measurement of the city is of great importance, for two entire verses are devoted to telling us about these measurements. From verses 16 and 17, we can find the volume of the city and the surface area of the city. Both surface area and volume are built on the basic concept of *area.*

What does *area* mean? On a line, which has one dimension, each segment corresponds to a number called the length of the segment. Likewise, in a plane, which has two dimensions, each region corresponds to a number called the *area.*

To find the length of a segment, you choose an arbitrary segment as a unit segment, and you measure segments with this arbitrary measure. When finding an area, you choose an arbitrary region to measure the area of a polygon. Any region can be chosen as the unit region. A triangular region, a rectangular region, or a hexagonal region can be used, but usually a square region is used. You can find the area by seeing how many square units will cover a given region.

The area of the rectangular region is the number of square units required to completely cover the region.

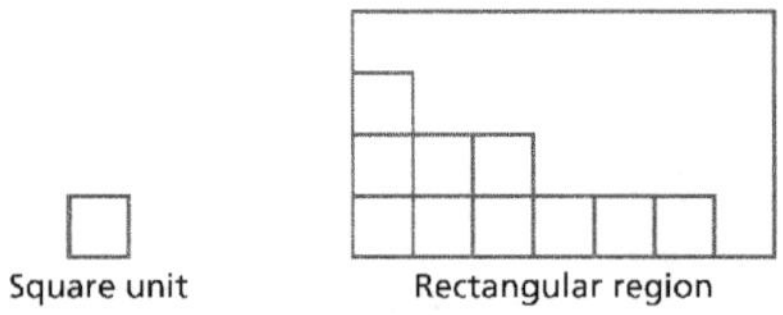

Square unit   Rectangular region

Figure 8.1

Notice that it is the rectangular region—not the rectangle itself—that you are finding the area of. Remember that a region is the union of the simple closed curve and its interior. What is the area of the rectangular region in figure 8.2?

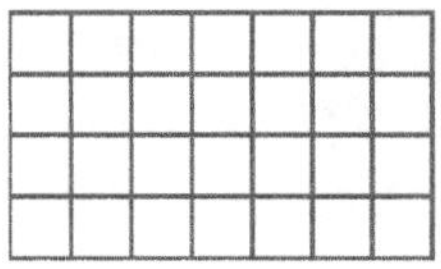

Figure 8.2

Read the opening part of this section and the biblical references. Discuss the significance of the size of the Holy City.

Common Student Error. Students often confuse the concepts of perimeter and area. This shows up when they are asked to find the area of a rectangle and come up with the perimeter instead. If we consider the two rectangles in the figure, which of them is larger? (*b*) is taller, but (*a*) is wider. So the issue has to do with what we mean by larger. Measure the distance around (perimeter) and (*b*) is larger ($p = 16$). If we compare area, we find each has an area of 12 square units. Any shape that we can use to cover the figures might be chosen as a standard unit of area. Since we use squares,

students should be reminded that units of area such as square inches can be written as in.² but should be called "square inches."

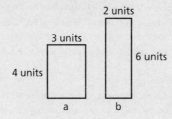

In distinguishing perimeter and area, try to connect the idea of a line with perimeter. Students should be able to take the sides of a figure and make a line out of them. It is actually a segment composed of four smaller segments when the figure is a rectangle. Area, on the other hand, needs to be thought of as a piece of paper that covers the figure. All of the interior of the figure and none of the exterior is covered. The baseboard of your room can be used as an example requiring perimeter measure, and the carpet or tile floor can be used as an example requiring area measure.

Also, you can draw a "square yard" on the blackboard and divide it to show that it contains nine square feet.

The **area of a region** is the number of square units needed to cover it completely.

Postulate 8.1
Area Postulate. Every region has an area given by a unique positive real number.

Postulate 8.2
Congruent Regions Postulate. Congruent regions have the same area.

Postulate 8.3
Area of Square Postulate. The area of a square is the square of the length of one side: $A = s^2$.

The three postulates above give us a starting point for our study of area. The first one permits us to look for areas of regions. The second guarantees that the number will make sense. The Area of Square Postulate is the first postulate that tells us how to find an area without counting squares.

EXAMPLE 1	Find the area of square *ABCD*.
Answer	The area of this square region is $A = s^2$ $A = (4)^2$ $A = 16$ square units

Figure 8.3

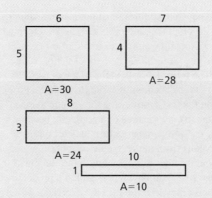

The web press at BJU Press prints 608,000 pages per hour for textbooks. This means that 3500 square feet of paper pass through the press every minute. Since it stores 292 square feet, it can continue printing while a new roll of paper is being installed.

Flash

Rolls of paper for printing presses are measured in square feet and require the rectangle formula. Storing enough paper to run continuously and cutting and folding the paper into pages all hinge on area.

Reading and Writing Mathematics

Have the students write a paragraph explaining in words

1. what area is. **the number of square units required to cover a region**
2. the difference between area and perimeter. **Area is the space enclosed by a boundary while perimeter is the length of the boundary.**
3. the kind of units used to measure area. **square units**

Additional Problems

1. Find the area of a rectangle that measures 6 ft. wide by 12 ft. long. **72 ft.²**
2. Find the area of a square with side 5 mm. **25 mm²**
3. Find the area of the region in the figure. **69 m²**

4. Find the area of the region in the figure. **92 units²**

5. A rectangle has a base of 16 ft. and an area of 128 sq. ft. What is the height of the rectangle? **8 ft.**

Motivational Idea. A loop of string can be used to illustrate how perimeter can be kept fixed while area changes. Use your thumb and first finger on each hand to form a rectangle with the string. You can make the rectangle long and narrow or roughly square. You can easily show how the area can be made very small (very narrow).

Motivational Idea. Give each student a piece of graph paper and a separate worksheet with several rectangles and other polygons that can be divided into rectangular pieces. Then have the students find the area of each diagram by cutting the graph paper to fit the figures and then counting the squares.

Review the definition of region. A region is the union of a simple closed curve and its interior. The Area Postulate guarantees that every region has an area. Notice that when we speak of the area of a rectangle, we actually mean the area of the rectangular region that the rectangle bounds. Read through the Congruent Regions Postulate and the Area of Square Postulate, being sure that your students understand these ideas.

Postulate 8.4

Area Addition Postulate. If the interiors of two regions do not intersect, then the area of the union is the sum of their areas.

This postulate tells us how to find the area of rectangle *ABPQ*.

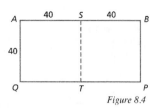

The squares *ASTQ* and *SBPT* both have areas of 1600 square units according to Postulate 8.3. The Area Postulate tells us that

Area *ABPQ* = Area *ASTQ* + Area *SBPT*
= 1600 + 1600
= 3200 square units

Figure 8.4

This computation was much faster than counting the 3200 squares, but you know that there is a simpler formula for areas of rectangles. $A = bh = 40 \cdot 80 = 3200$. Let's try to prove this formula.

Theorem 8.1

The *area of a rectangle* is the product of its base and height: $A = bh$.

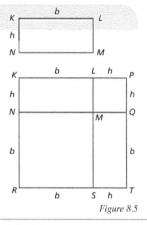

       Given: Rectangle *KLMN*

Auxiliary lines: Mark *P* on $\overrightarrow{KL}$ so *LP* = *h*
               Mark *Q* on $\overrightarrow{NM}$ so *MQ* = *h*
               Mark *R* on $\overrightarrow{KN}$ so *NR* = *b*
               Mark *S* on $\overrightarrow{LM}$ so *MS* = *b*
               Mark *T* where $\overrightarrow{RS}$ intersects $\overrightarrow{PQ}$

       Prove: Area of *KLMN* = *b* · *h*

Figure 8.5

STATEMENTS	REASONS
1. Rectangle *KLMN*	1. Given
2. *LP* = *PQ* = *MQ* = *LM* = *ST* = *KN* = *h* and *NR* = *MS* = *QT* = *NM* = *RS* = *KL* = *b*	2. Auxiliary constructions
3. *LPQM*, *NMSR*, and *KPTR* are squares	3. Definition of square
4. *MQTS* is a rectangle	4. Definition of rectangle Continued ▶

Tips

The Area Addition Postulate is important to the development and proofs of the area formulas. Look at the simple example of this concept illustrated after the statement of the postulate.

The formula for the area of a rectangle, $A = bh$, is Theorem 8.1. Go through the proof using the text proof as a guide. Students need to understand the area of a rectangle because they can prove the area formulas for other polygons from the rectangle formula.

Go through example 2 with the students. Make sure that they understand this procedure because they will use it in the exercises. Do some of those exercises (or Additional Problems 3-4) as a class activity.

Ex. 20. Students must use the unit conversion that one furlong is 606.75 feet given in Chapter 3 (p. 113). Remember that a furlong in ancient Greece was not the same as the modern furlong, so a dictionary will not help (unless it is a Bible dictionary). Students using modern versions may see the measurements in *stadia*, which are the same as furlongs (emphasizing the stadium at Olympus). ■

5. *MQTS* and *KLMN* are congruent	5. Definition of congruent rectangles
6. Area *KPTR* = Area *KLMN* + Area *LPQM* + Area *NMSR* + Area *MQTS*	6. Area Addition Postulate
7. Area *KPTR* = $(b + h)^2 = b^2 + 2bh + h^2$ Area *LPQM* = h^2 Area *NMSR* = b^2	7. Area of Square Postulate
8. Area *KLMN* = Area *MQTS*	8. Congruent Regions Postulate
9. $b^2 + 2bh + h^2$ = Area *KLMN* + $h^2 + b^2$ + Area *KLMN*	9. Substitution (steps 7 and 8 into 6)
10. $2bh = 2 \cdot$ Area *KLMN*	10. Addition property of equality
11. bh = Area *KLMN*	11. Multiplication property of equality

Sometimes you will want to find the area of a polygonal region that is not convex or that has no special formula. To do this, you should separate the polygon into portions for which you can easily find the areas. After finding those areas, add them together to find the total area of the region. Notice how helpful the Area Addition Postulate is.

EXAMPLE 2 Find the area of the given polygonal region.

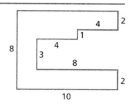

Answer
1. Separate the figure into rectangular regions.

2. There are four regions marked off in this concave polygon.

3. Find the area of each region.
   $A_A = (8)(2) = 16$
   $A_B = (2)(8) = 16$
   $A_C = (4)(1) = 4$
   $A_D = (8)(2) = 16$

4. Add the four areas together to find the total area of the region.
   $A = A_A + A_B + A_C + A_D$
   $= 16 + 16 + 4 + 16$
   $= 52$ square units

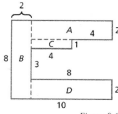

Figure 8.6

Answers

1. $A = 225$ sq. yd.
2. $A = 44.89$ sq. in.
3. $A = 144$ sq. cm
4. $s = 18$ ft.
5. $s = 5.7$ m
6. $A = 36$ sq. in.
7. $A = 72$ sq. ft.
8. $A = 42$ sq. yd.
9. $A = 26.16$ sq. cm
10. $h = 5.33$ ft.
11. $b = 5.47$ yd.
12. $h = 15$ m
13. 52 sq. units
14. 369 sq. units
15. 108 sq. units
16. 287 sq. units

▶ A. Exercises

Complete the following tables.

Square with side s		
	s	A
1.	15 yd.	
2.	6.7 in.	
3.	12 cm	
4.		324 sq. ft.
5.		32.49 sq. m

Rectangles			
	b	h	A
6.	3 in.	12 in.	
7.	8 ft.	9 ft.	
8.	12 yd.	3.5 yd.	
9.	2.4 cm	10.9 cm	
10.	9 ft.		48 sq. ft.
11.		32 yd.	175 sq. yd.
12.	27 m		405 sq. m

Find the area of each polygonal region.

13.
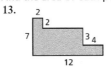

15.
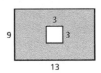

14.
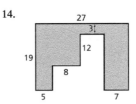

16.
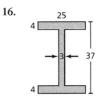

▶ B. Exercises

17. Find the area of your classroom floor in square feet and in square yards.
18. Find the area of your bedroom in square feet.
19. How many 8-inch square tiles would be needed to cover the floor of a room that is 12 by 15 feet?
20. Find the area, in square feet, of the foundation of the Holy City, according to Revelation 21:16.

Find the area of each rectangle.
21. $b = \sqrt{5}$ $h = \sqrt{7}$
22. $b = x$ $h = x + 5$
23. $b = x + 7$ $h = x - 7$
24. $b = y + 5$ $h = y + 7$

▶ C. Exercises

25. The inner square has its vertices at the midpoint of the sides of the outer square. Prove that the area of the outer square is double the area of the inner square.

■ Cumulative Review

Find the perimeter of each region.
26. Rectangular region of exercise 19
27. Polygonal region of exercise 14
28. Circular region with diameter of $\sqrt{3}$ in.

29. Give bounds for the measure of angle x.

30. Give bounds for s.

17. Answers will vary.
18. Answers will vary.
19. 405 tiles
20. 53,012,961,000,000 sq. ft.
21. $\sqrt{35}$ sq. units
22. $x^2 + 5x$ sq. units
23. $x^2 - 49$ sq. units
24. $y^2 + 12y + 35$ sq. units
25.

1. $A_{inner} = a^2$	1. Area of Square Postulate
2. $A_{outer} = 4b^2$	2. Area of Square Postulate
3. $a^2 = b^2 + b^2$ $= 2b^2$	3. Pythagorean theorem
4. $A_{inner} = 2b^2$	4. Transitive property of equality
5. $A_{outer} = 2\,A_{inner}$	5. Substitution

26. 54 ft. [3.4]
27. 124 units [3.4]
28. $\pi\sqrt{3} \approx 5.44$ in.^{2} [3.4]
29. $0° < x < 60°$ [6.5]
30. $1 < s < 11$ [7.5]

Other Polygons

Objectives

1. To derive and prove formulas for the area of triangles and special quadrilaterals.
2. To apply the formulas to calculate areas of regions enclosed by them.

Assignment

• Intuitive: 1-16, 26-30
• Standard: 1-23, 26-30
• Rigorous: 7-30

Resources

• *Visual Packet,* Area. This poster compares the main area formulas.
• *Activities Manual,* Perimeter and Area in Brief. Develops a further understanding of area and perimeter and their relationship to congruence.
• *Test Packet,* Quiz 1, Chapter 8 covers Sections 8.1 and 8.2.

Flash

All seven systems of crystals are shown in this chapter. Classification of crystals depends on the lengths of their axes and the angles of intersection. The most basic specimens are shown for each system and can be described easily (see captions). Point out that the prefix *ortho* means "perpendicular" in math (as in the term *orthocenter*).

Crystal System	Axes	Simplest Form
isometric	3 perp., 3 equal	cube (all faces sq.)
tetragonal	3 perp., 2 equal	right sq. prism (2 sq. faces)
orthorhombic	3 perp., 0 equal	right rect. prism (no sq. faces)
monoclinic	2 of 3 perp.	right prism (parallelogram base)
triclinic	0 of 3 perp.	oblique prism (parallelogram base)
rhombohedral	1 perp. to other 3	oblique prism (rhombic base)
hexagonal	1 perp. to other 3	hexagonal prism

8.2 Other Polygons

Now that you understand the meaning of *area,* your next goal should be to find the area of familiar polygonal regions quickly.

This dolomite crystal from Monroe County, New York, has faces that are rhombi (rhombohedral).

This natrolite crystal from Bound Brook, New Jersey, is a right prism with rectangular bases (orthorhombic).

Presentation

This section introduces and proves the basic area formulas for triangles and common quadrilaterals. First, prove the formula for the area of a right triangle. This formula is a steppingstone for proving the remaining formulas.

Most students will already know the formula for the area of a triangle, and some will find this long proof useless. Remind them that they have never tested the truth of the rule they have been using. This may be an ongoing battle with some students, but try to help them desire to know why statements are true rather than just accepting them without proof.

Continue through the area formulas for triangles, parallelograms, trapezoids, and rhom-

bi. The proofs should help the students learn the formulas without memorizing them. After seeing why $A = bh$ works for parallelograms as well as rectangles, the students should be able to look at a triangle and picture it as half of a parallelogram. This enables them to use $A = \frac{1}{2} bh$ without really memorizing it.

The section ends by posing the question "Do you think the formula for the area of a trapezoid will work for other quadrilaterals?" (*yes*) You can easily repeat examples 1 and 4 by using the trapezoid formula and showing that the same answer is obtained. Point out that this key formula can rescue them if they forget one of the other formulas. Tell them that they must know the area formulas for all

Theorem 8.2

The *area of a right triangle* is one-half the product of the lengths of the legs.

Given: Right △ABC with right angle at C

Draw: Auxiliary lines at A and B perpendicular to $\overleftrightarrow{AC}$ and $\overleftrightarrow{BC}$ respectively, thus forming quadrilateral ACBD

Prove: Area = $\frac{1}{2}bh$

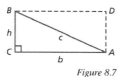

Figure 8.7

STATEMENTS	REASONS
1. △ABC with ∠C as the right angle	1. Given
2. $\overleftrightarrow{BC} \perp \overleftrightarrow{AC}$	2. Definition of perpendicular
3. $\overleftrightarrow{AC} \parallel \overleftrightarrow{BD}$; $\overleftrightarrow{BC} \parallel \overleftrightarrow{AD}$	3. Two lines perpendicular to the same line
4. $\overleftrightarrow{BD} \perp \overleftrightarrow{AD}$	4. Line perpendicular to one of two parallel lines is perpendicular to the other
5. ∠D, ∠CAD, ∠CBD are right angles	5. Definition of perpendicular
6. ACBD is a rectangle	6. Definition of rectangle
7. $\overline{BC} \cong \overline{AD}$, $\overline{AC} \cong \overline{BD}$	7. Opposite sides congruent
8. △ABC ≅ △BAD	8. LL (or SAS)
9. Area △ABC = Area △BAD	9. Congruent Regions Postulate
10. Area ACBD = Area △ABC + Area △BAD	10. Area Addition Postulate
11. Area ACBD = 2(Area △ABC)	11. Substitution (step 9 into 10)
12. Area ACBD = bh	12. Area of Rectangle Theorem
13. bh = 2(Area △ABC)	13. Substitution (step 12 into 11)
14. $\frac{1}{2}bh$ = Area △ABC	14. Multiplication property of equality

The formula for the area of a rectangle is $A = bh$. Likewise the formula for the area of a parallelogram region is $A = bh$, where b is the length of the base and h is the height of the parallelogram. The height, h, is always the perpendicular distance between the base and the opposite side.

Notice that the area of the right triangles will be helpful in proving this area formula.

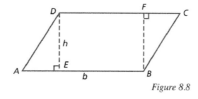

Figure 8.8

Reading and Writing Mathematics

Ask the students to consider a unit circle (radius = 1) as the basic unit of measure for area.

1. Have them draw a rectangle 4 units by 2 units and sketch unit circles in it.

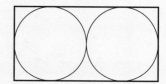

2. Have them sketch a circle of diameter 4 units and put 3 unit squares in it.

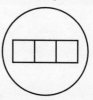

3. Have them express an opinion as to why we use square units of measure. *Answers will vary.*

Additional Problems

Find the area of each of the following figures.

1. **28 cm²**

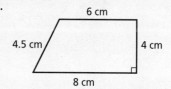

2. **48 m²**

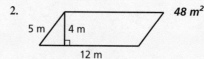

3. **96 in²**

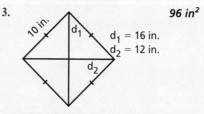

$d_1 = 16$ in.
$d_2 = 12$ in.

4. Find the area of the dart, given CE = 2 cm, DB = 3 cm. **6 cm²**

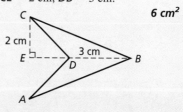

5. Two sides of a tract of land are parallel and measure 20 km and 30 km. How wide is the property between these parallel sides if the area is 850 km²? **34 km**

five special quadrilaterals but should work hard on the trapezoid since it is the most general. Students (except those in the intuitive track) should also be able to prove each formula.

Students who have difficulty retaining the six formulas should list them on a summary sheet. Such students will need plenty of calculation work so that they learn the formulas through practice. Make a worksheet with a dozen polygons for practice in calculating areas.

One-on-one. If the sides and altitude of a parallelogram are given (this should be done so that they have to discriminate between the sides and the altitude), some student may use

the side length instead of the altitude. Use a box with the ends removed to help this student. With one side on the floor, you can lean the box at various angles to form parallelograms. As the box gets flatter, the decreasing area will become apparent. Ask that student if the sides have changed (*no*). So, using the two sides would yield the same number as the original rectangle no matter how small the parallelogram's area becomes. Point out that the altitude does decrease.

Theorem 8.3

The *area of a parallelogram* is the product of the base and the altitude: *A = bh*.

> **Given:** Parallelogram *ABCD*
> **Draw:** Altitudes from *B* and *D* to $\overline{CD}$ and $\overline{AB}$ respectively
> **Prove:** *A* = *bh*

STATEMENTS	REASONS
1. Parallelogram *ABCD*	1. Given
2. $\overline{BC} \cong \overline{AD}$	2. Opposite sides congruent
3. $\angle A \cong \angle C$	3. Opposite angles congruent
4. $\overleftrightarrow{DE} \perp \overleftrightarrow{AB}$; $\overleftrightarrow{BF} \perp \overleftrightarrow{CD}$	4. Definition of altitude
5. $\angle AED$ and $\angle CFB$ are right angles	5. Definition of perpendicular
6. $\triangle ADE \cong \triangle CBF$	6. HA (or SAA)
7. Area $\triangle ADE = \frac{1}{2}(AE)h$	7. Area of Right Triangle Theorem
8. Area $\triangle CBF = \frac{1}{2}(AE)h$	8. Congruent Regions Postulate
9. Area *BEDF* = (*BE*)*h*	9. Area of Rectangle Theorem
10. Area *ABCD* = Area $\triangle ADE$ + Area $\triangle CBF$ + Area *BEDF*	10. Area Addition Postulate
11. Area $ABCD = \frac{1}{2}(AE)h + \frac{1}{2}(AE)h + (BE)h$	11. Substitution (steps 7, 8, and 9 into 10)
12. Area *ABCD* = (*AE* + *BE*)*h*	12. Distributive property
13. *AE* + *BE* = *AB* = *b*	13. Definition of betweenness
14. Area *ABCD* = *bh*	14. Substitution (step 13 into 12)

EXAMPLE 1   What is the area of parallelogram *ABCD*?

Answer   *A* = *bh*
A = (25)(10)
A = 250 sq. in.

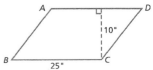

Figure 8.9

Tips

Ex. 20. The proof requires the theorem that says that the diagonals of a rhombus are perpendicular (Additional Problem 2 in Section 7.2). Students may still need a reminder. If you have not previously covered this theorem, you may wish to prove it now or to skip this exercise.

Ex. 21. Students will need this algebra skill to solve the next two exercises.

Ex. 22. Let *x* = the height. Since the bases are *x* + 1 and *x* + 3,
$A = \frac{1}{2}(x + 1 + x + 3)x = 63$. Multiply both sides by 2 to get rid of fractions and combine like terms in parentheses to get $(2x + 4)x = 126$. Multiply out the left and subtract 126 from both sides to obtain 0 on the right:

$2x^2 + 4x - 126 = 0$. Factor to obtain $2(x + 9)(x - 7) = 0$. (If you divided both sides by 2 first, you will get an alternative form with no 2 in front.) Since *x* represents height, the negative solution (−9) is irrelevant, and *x* = 7 inches is the answer.

Ex. 23. With height *x*, the base is *x* + 3.
$A = x(x + 3) = \frac{22}{9}$. Obtain $9x(x + 3) = 22$ by clearing fractions. Distribute the left and subtract 22 from both sides to obtain standard form: $9x^2 + 27x - 22 = 0$. Next, factor $(3x + 11)(3x - 2) = 0$. Of the two solutions, $-\frac{11}{3}$ and $\frac{2}{3}$, only the latter is positive and is therefore the height. ∎

Thus 250 square-inch units could fit into this parallelogram region. What about the area of a triangular region? Look at the following triangle.

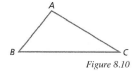

Figure 8.10

You have already learned the formula for the area of a right triangle, $A = \frac{1}{2}bh$. This formula works for all triangles.

> **Theorem 8.4**
> The *area of a triangle* is one-half the base times the height: $A = \frac{1}{2}bh$.

What kind of figure is polygon *ABCD*?

You know that the formula for the area of a parallelogram is $A = bh$. Notice that a diagonal such as $\overline{AC}$ divides the parallelogram into two congruent triangles, and thus the

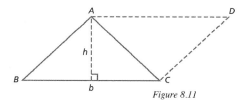

Figure 8.11

area is cut in half. So the area of a triangle is simply one-half the area of a parallelogram. The formal proof is exercise 18 and is similar to the proof of the area of a right triangle.

EXAMPLE 2   Find the area of △*XYZ*.

    Answer $A = \frac{1}{2}bh$

             $A = \frac{1}{2}(12)(9)$

             $A = 54$ square feet

Figure 8.12

Notice that the height (altitude) must be perpendicular to the base and must intersect the opposite vertex. Similarly, the height of a trapezoid must be perpendicular to both of its bases.

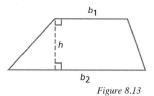

Figure 8.13

You will prove the formula for the area of a trapezoid in the exercises.

Theorem 8.5
The *area of a trapezoid* is one-half the product of the altitude and the sum of the lengths of the bases: $A = \frac{1}{2}h(b_1 + b_2)$.

EXAMPLE 3 Find the area of trapezoid *ABCD*.

Answer $A = \frac{1}{2}h(b_1 + b_2)$

$A = \frac{1}{2}(7)(18 + 10)$

$A = \frac{1}{2}(7)(28)$

$A = 98$ square millimeters

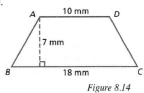

Figure 8.14

Notice that $\frac{1}{2}(b_1 + b_2)$ averages the lengths of the bases. For the trapezoid above, the average base length is $\frac{18 + 10}{2} = 14$. For the area, simply multiply this average by the height: $A = 14 \cdot 9 = 98$.

Since a rhombus is a parallelogram, you already know how to find its area.

EXAMPLE 4 Find the area of rhombus *FGHI*.

Answer $A = bh$

$A = 4(3)$

$A = 12$ square units

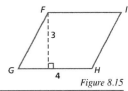

Figure 8.15

Here is another formula for the area of a rhombus.

In rhombus *ABCD* the lengths of the diagonals are d_1 and d_2. The area of the rhombus is $A = \frac{1}{2}d_1d_2$.

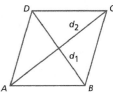

Figure 8.16

Theorem 8.6

The *area of a rhombus* is half the product of the lengths of the diagonals: $A = \frac{1}{2}d_1 d_2$.

EXAMPLE 5 Find the area of rhombus PQRS.

Answer $A = \frac{1}{2}d_1 d_2$

$A = \frac{1}{2}(12)(8)$

$A = 48$ square units

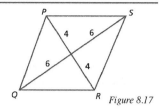

Figure 8.17

The trapezoid is sometimes called the "grandfather" of special quadrilaterals because rectangles, parallelograms, and squares are trapezoids. The formula for the area of a trapezoidal region should work for these other quadrilaterals. Do you think it does? Try it on one.

► A. Exercises

Make a summary table for the area formulas learned thus far.

	Figure	Formula
1.	Rectangle	
2.	Square	
3.	Triangle	
4.	Parallelogram	
5.	Trapezoid	
6.	Rhombus	

Find the area of each figure.

7.

8.

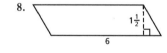

Answers

1. $A = bh$
2. $A = s^2$
3. $A = \frac{1}{2}bh$
4. $A = bh$
5. $A = \frac{1}{2}h(b_1 + b_2)$
6. $A = bh$ or $A = \frac{1}{2}d_1 d_2$
7. 35 sq. units
8. 9 sq. units
9. 28 sq. units
10. 16 sq. units
11. 153 sq. units
12. 672 sq. units
13. 72 sq. units
14. 225 sq. units
15. 175.5 sq. units
16. 575 sq. units
17. In a parallelogram $b_1 = b_2 = b$, $A = \frac{1}{2}(b_1 + b_2)h = \frac{1}{2}(b + b)h = \frac{1}{2}(2b)h = bh$
18.

1. $\triangle ABC$	1. Given
2. Construct $l \parallel \overleftrightarrow{AB}$ through C, $m \parallel \overleftrightarrow{BC}$ through A, intersecting l at D	2. Auxiliary lines
3. $ABCD$ is a parallelogram	3. Definition of parallelogram
4. $\overline{AB} \cong \overline{DC}$; $\overline{AD} \cong \overline{BC}$	4. Opposite sides of parallelogram congruent
5. $\overline{AC} \cong \overline{AC}$	5. Reflexive property of congruent segments
6. $\triangle ABC \cong \triangle CDA$	6. SSS
7. Area $\triangle ABC =$ Area $\triangle CDA$	7. Congruent Regions Postulate
8. Area $ABCD =$ Area $\triangle ABC +$ Area $\triangle CDA$	8. Area Addition Postulate
9. Area $ABCD =$ 2(Area $\triangle ABC$)	9. Substitution (step 7 into 8); distributive property
10. Area $ABCD = bh$	10. Area of parallelogram
11. $bh =$ 2(Area $\triangle ABC$)	11. Transitive property of equality
12. $\frac{1}{2}bh =$ Area $\triangle ABC$	12. Multiplication property of equality

19.

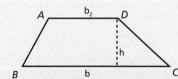

1. Trapezoid $ABCD$ with diagonal $\overline{AC}$	1. Given
2. Area $ABCD =$ Area $\triangle ABC +$ Area $\triangle ADC$	2. Area Addition Postulate
3. Area $\triangle ABC = \frac{1}{2}h(BC)$; Area $\triangle ADC = \frac{1}{2}h(AD)$	3. Area of triangle
4. Area $ABCD = \frac{1}{2}h(BC) + \frac{1}{2}h(AD)$	4. Substitution
5. Area $ABCD = \frac{1}{2}h(BC + AD)$	5. Distributive property

20.

1. Rhombus *PQRS* with diagonals $\overline{PR}$, $\overline{QS}$, intersecting at *E*	1. Given
2. $PR \perp QS$ at *E*	2. Diagonals of a rhombus are perpendicular
3. A = Area *PQRS* = Area $\triangle PQR$ + Area $\triangle PRS$	3. Area Addition Postulate
4. $PE = RE$, $QE = SE$	4. Diagonals of rhombus bisect each other
5. Area $\triangle PQR$ = $\frac{1}{2}d_1$ (QE) Area $\triangle PRS$ = $\frac{1}{2}d_1$ (SE)	5. Area of triangle
6. $A = \frac{1}{2}d_1(QE) + \frac{1}{2}d_1(SE)$	6. Substitution (step 5 into 3)
7. $A = \frac{1}{2}d_1(QE + SE)$	7. Distributive property
8. $QE + SE = QS = d_2$	8. Definition of betweenness
9. $A = \frac{1}{2}d_1d_2$	9. Substitution

21. $(x + 5)(x - 3) = 0$; $x = -5$ or $x = 3$
22. $\frac{1}{2}h[(h + 1) + (h + 3)] = 63$; $h = 7$ in.
23. $x(x + 3) = \frac{22}{9}$; $\frac{2}{3}$ inch
24.

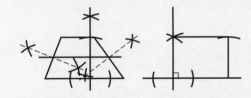

25. Since the median bisects the side at the midpoint, $AD = BD$ and the bases of the two triangles have equal length. Since the triangles also have the same height, *h*, the areas ($\frac{1}{2}$ base times height) must be the same.

26. [2.5]

27. [2.7]

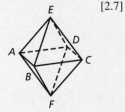

---

9. 10. 11.

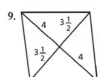 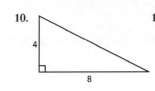 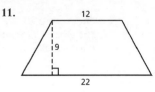

▶ **B. Exercises**

Find the area of the following:

12. A triangle with base 56 and height 24
13. A parallelogram with base 12 and height 6
14. A square with side 15
15. A rhombus with one diagonal equal to 27 and the other diagonal equal to 13
16. A trapezoid with bases equal to 32 and 14 and height measuring 25
17. Show how the formula for the area of a parallelogram can be obtained from the formula for the area of a trapezoid.
18. Prove Theorem 8.4: Area of triangle = $\frac{1}{2}bh$
19. Prove Theorem 8.5: Area of trapezoid = $\frac{1}{2}h(b_1 + b_2)$
20. Prove Theorem 8.6: Area of rhombus = $\frac{1}{2}d_1d_2$
21. Use the factoring method (from algebra) to solve the following quadratic equation: $x^2 + 2x - 15 = 0$.
22. The bases of a trapezoid are one and three feet longer than the height respectively. If the area is 63 square feet, find the height.
23. The base of a parallelogram is three more than the height. The area is $\frac{22}{9}$ square inches. Find the height.

▶ **C. Exercises**

24. Construct a rectangle with the same area as a given trapezoid.
25. Explain why a median of a triangle divides the triangular region into two regions of equal area.

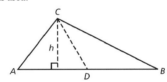

28. [2.4]

29. [2.7]

30. [2.6]

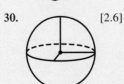

Sketch an example of each.

26. Octagon with two nonintersecting diagonals
27. Octahedron with vertices labeled
28. Closed curve that is not simple
29. Hexahedron that is a pyramid and has a concave base
30. Sphere with three radii, each perpendicular to the other two

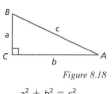

8.3 Pythagorean Theorem

The Pythagorean theorem should be familiar to you. You have studied this relationship among the sides of a right triangle in previous math classes. Remember that this theorem works only with a right triangle.

Figure 8.18

$$a^2 + b^2 = c^2$$

The theorem is named after the ancient Greek mathematician Pythagoras, who first proved it.

The second baseman at Memorial Stadium in Baltimore, Maryland, throws a ball to force a runner out at home. The distance thrown can be calculated from the baseline distances using the Pythagorean theorem.

8.3
Pythagorean Theorem

Objectives
1. To prove the Pythagorean theorem.
2. To apply the Pythagorean theorem to right triangles.
3. To develop a formula for the area of an equilateral triangle.

Vocabulary
Pythagorean theorem

Assignment
- Intuitive: 1-19, 26-27
- Standard: 1-23, 26-30
- Rigorous: 7-30

Resource
- *Activities Manual,* Pythagorean Theorem in Principle. Looks at alternate ways to prove the Pythagorean theorem.

Reading and Writing Mathematics
Have the students sketch a square of side *s*. Connect the midpoints of the sides to inscribe a second square in the first. Find the area of the inner square. If this is repeated, what would be the area of the third square? Show all work. ***Work will include the Pythagorean theorem and the Area of a Square formula. Final answers will be $\frac{s^2}{2}$ and $\frac{s^2}{4}$.***

Presentation

Remind students about the need to test all things. Although students already know the Pythagorean theorem, few have tried to prove it. Discuss the proof in the text. Several other famous methods of proof are shown in the Pythagorean theorem activity found in the *Activities Manual.*

Motivational Idea. A good way to introduce this material is to illustrate the relationship with some concrete materials. Make eight congruent right triangles with sides *a* and *b*. Make two squares with sides *a* + *b*. Using an overhead projector, you can show the area relationship: area of an *a* by *a* square plus the area of a *b* by *b* square equals the area of a *c* by *c* square.

Emphasize that the Pythagorean theorem works only for right triangles. Do some practical application problems similar to those in the exercise section. Students will need to spend plenty of time on #20-24. Review the definition of an isosceles trapezoid in preparation for #21. Exercise 23 is very important and students should memorize the result. The 30-60 right triangle relationships are not introduced until Chapter 14 and several problems prior to then require this knowledge.

Challenge them not to give up easily on the problems. Exercise 24 is especially important since this proof requires the use of the Pythagorean theorem and completes the proofs of the area theorems for the basic polygons

from Section 8.2. Theorem 8.8 gives a convenient formula for finding the area of an equilateral triangle. This formula will be used frequently, so make sure your students understand how to apply it.

Common Student Error. Students may get comfortable with $c^2 = a^2 + b^2$ and make mistakes when the letters used to label the triangle are different, especially when a given triangle has a hypotenuse labeled *a*. They are better off thinking of the relationship as hypotenuse² = leg² + leg².

Additional Problems

1. Determine whether the three given values can be the sides of a right triangle.
   a) 18, 34, 39 **no**
   b) 8, 6, 10 **yes**
   c) 20, 30, 50 **no**
   d) 52, 39, 65 **yes**
   e) 25, 60, 65 **yes**

2. Find the altitude of the equilateral triangle with a side of 6 yd. **$3\sqrt{3}$ yd.**

3. A screen door measures 36 inches by 80 inches. Find the length of a diagonal brace for this screen door. **Brace should be 7 ft. 3 $\frac{3}{4}$ in., or 87 $\frac{3}{4}$ in. long (and the ends will be mitered to fit).**

4. *Given:* $BC = 8$, $CA = 6$, $AB = 12$,
   $\overline{CD} \perp \overline{AB}$

   Find: CD

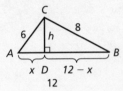

$\dfrac{\sqrt{455}}{6}$ **or 3.56**

(Area = $\sqrt{455}$ by Heron's formula; then use $A = \frac{1}{2}bh = \frac{1}{2}(12)h$ and solve for h.)

Proof requires testing a statement against standards of truth. Math must be tested against Scripture and against God's laws of reasoning. In everyday life we must likewise prove everything to make sure that it is true (I Thess. 5:21). To do so, we must daily go to the Word of God (Acts 17:11).

Figure 8.19 illustrates the Pythagorean theorem.

$$a^2 + b^2 = c^2$$
$$3^2 + 4^2 = 5^2$$
$$9 + 16 = 25$$
$$25 = 25$$

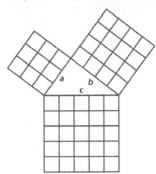

Figure 8.19

> **Theorem 8.7**
> *Pythagorean Theorem.* In a right triangle, the sum of the squares of the lengths of the legs is equal to the square of the length of the hypotenuse: $a^2 + b^2 = c^2$.

One proof of the Pythagorean theorem uses figure 8.20.

Find the areas of each part using formulas for the area of a rectangle ($A = bh$) and the area of a triangle ($A = \frac{1}{2}bh$).

Figure 8.20

$$A_{\text{lg. square}} = (a + b)(a + b) = a^2 + 2ab + b^2$$
$$A_{\text{sm. square}} = c \cdot c = c^2$$
$$A_{\text{triangle}} = \frac{1}{2}ab$$

The sum of the areas of the four triangles and the smaller square equals the area of the larger square.

$$A_{\text{lg. square}} = 4A_{\text{triangle}} + A_{\text{sm. square}}$$
$$a^2 + 2ab + b^2 = 4(\tfrac{1}{2}ab) + c^2$$
$$a^2 + 2ab + b^2 = 2ab + c^2$$
$$a^2 + b^2 = c^2$$

Tips

Ex. 20. When solving the equation, students should write $c = \pm a\sqrt{2}$ and then reject the negative value since the distances must be positive.

Ex. 22. Students must remember that each diagonal of a rhombus is a perpendicular bisector of the other. Thus, halves of each diagonal (12 and x) form the legs of a right triangle with a hypotenuse of 13 ($\frac{1}{4}$ of the perimeter).

$$13^2 = x^2 + 12^2$$
$$169 = x^2 + 144$$
$$x^2 = 25$$

So $d_2 = 10$

$$A = \tfrac{1}{2}d_1 d_2$$

$$A = \tfrac{1}{2} \cdot 10 \cdot 24$$
$$A = 120 \text{ units}^2$$

Ex. 29. The sides are $4x$ and $5x$. $A = 20x^2 = 5120$. Thus, $x = 16$, so the sides $4x$ and $5x$ are 64 and 80.

Ex. 30. Each square has an area of $\frac{968}{8} = 121$, so its sides are 11 cm long. The figure consists of 18 of these lengths, so $P = 18 \cdot 11$. ∎

The converse of this theorem is also true. The converse states, "If the sum of the squares of the lengths of two sides of a triangle equals the square of the length of the third side, then the triangle is a right triangle." You will prove this in the exercises, and you can always determine whether a triangle is a right triangle by using this theorem.

The Pythagorean theorem helps in the proof of a special formula for the area of an equilateral triangular region.

Answers
1. 4
2. 12
3. $\sqrt{85}$
4. $\sqrt{109}$
5. $\sqrt{5}$
6. 24
7. $2\sqrt{13}$
8. $2\sqrt{209}$
9. $\sqrt{x^2 + 25}$
10. 9

Theorem 8.8

The *area of an equilateral triangle* is $\frac{\sqrt{3}}{4}$ times the square of the length of one side: $A = s^2 \frac{\sqrt{3}}{4}$

EXAMPLE   Find the area of equilateral $\triangle LMN$.

Answer $A = s^2 \dfrac{\sqrt{3}}{4}$

$A = 7^2 \dfrac{\sqrt{3}}{4}$

$A = \dfrac{49\sqrt{3}}{4}$ square centimeters

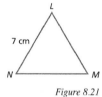

7 cm

Figure 8.21

▶ A. Exercises

Complete the following table. Consider $\triangle ABC$ to be a right triangle with c as the hypotenuse.

	a (units)	b (units)	c (units)
1.		3	5
2.		5	13
3.	9	2	
4.	3	10	
5.	$\sqrt{2}$	$\sqrt{3}$	
6.		32	40
7.	6	4	
8.	8		30
9.	x	5	
10.		x	$\sqrt{x^2 + 81}$

8.3 PYTHAGOREAN THEOREM   **325**

11. no
12. yes
13. yes
14. no
15. $\dfrac{5\sqrt{39}}{2}$ sq. inches

16. $5\sqrt{15}$ sq. units
17. $h = \sqrt{119}$ units; $A = 15\sqrt{119}$ sq. units
18. $h = 6\sqrt{2}$ units; $A = 156\sqrt{2}$ sq. units
19. $\dfrac{25\sqrt{3}}{4}$
20. $a^2 + a^2 = c^2$
    $2a^2 = c^2$
    $a\sqrt{2} = c$
21. $h = 4$, $A = 36$ sq. in.
22. 120 sq. units

Tell which of the following triangles are right triangles.

11.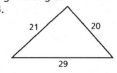

13.

12.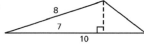

14.

▶ **B. Exercises**

Find each area. (*Hint:* Find the height first if necessary.)

15. A right triangle has a leg measuring 5 inches and a hypotenuse measuring 8 inches.

16.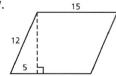

18.

17.

19.

20. Show that for an isosceles right triangle $c = a\sqrt{2}$.
21. The bases of an isosceles trapezoid are 6 inches and 12 inches. Find the area if the congruent sides are 5 inches.
22. The perimeter of a rhombus is 52 and one diagonal is 24. Find the area.

Prove the next two formulas. Use paragraphs or derivations instead of a two-column proof.

23. The altitude of an equilateral triangle is given by $h = \dfrac{\sqrt{3}}{2}s$ where s is the length of one side.

24. Theorem 8.8: $A = s^2 \dfrac{\sqrt{3}}{4}$ (*Hint:* Substitute result of exercise 23 into area of triangle formula.)

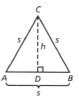

► C. Exercises

25. Prove the converse of the Pythagorean theorem: If the sum of the squares of two sides of a triangle equals the square of the third side, then the triangle is a right triangle.

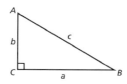

■ Cumulative Review

Find the area of each rectangle.

26.

27.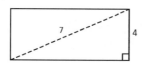

28. Give bounds for c if $b < 5$.

29. The consecutive sides of a rectangle have a ratio of 4:5. If the area is 5120 m², what are the dimensions of the rectangle?

30. The figure is made up of 8 congruent squares and has a total area of 968 cm². Find the perimeter.

23. $\triangle CDA \cong \triangle CDB$ by HL since the equilateral triangle has congruent sides and the altitude is congruent to itself. Thus, $\overline{AD} \cong \overline{BD}$ and D is midpoint of AB; $(AD)^2 + h^2 = s^2$ by Pythagorean theorem (on $\triangle ACD$). So $(\tfrac{1}{2}s)^2 + h^2 = s^2$ and $h^2 = s^2 - \tfrac{1}{4}s^2 = \tfrac{3}{4}s^2$ or $h = \dfrac{\sqrt{3}}{2}s$.

24. Area $\triangle ABC = \tfrac{1}{2}bh = \tfrac{1}{2}s\dfrac{\sqrt{3}}{2}s = s^2\dfrac{\sqrt{3}}{4}$

25.

1. $(AC)^2 + (BC)^2 = (AB)^2$	1. Given
2. Draw $\triangle DEF$ with $DF = AC$, $EF = BC$, and $m\angle F = 90°$	2. Auxiliary lines
3. $(DF)^2 + (EF)^2 = (DE)^2$	3. Pythagorean theorem for $\triangle DEF$
4. $(AC)^2 + (BC)^2 = (DE)^2$	4. Substitution (step 2 into 3)
5. $(AB)^2 = (DE)^2$	5. Transitive property of equality
6. $AB = DE$	6. Square root on both sides
7. $\overline{AC} \cong \overline{DF}$; $\overline{BC} \cong \overline{EF}$; $\overline{AB} \cong \overline{DE}$	7. Definition of congruent segments
8. $\triangle ABC \cong \triangle DEF$	8. SSS
9. $\angle ACD \cong \angle DFE$	9. Definition of congruent triangles
10. $\angle ACB$ is a right angle	10. Angle congruent to a right angle is right
11. $\triangle ABC$ is a right triangle	11. Definition of right triangle

26. $A = 21$ [8.1]
27. $4\sqrt{33}$ [8.2]
28. $7 < c < \sqrt{74}$ [7.4-7.5]
29. 64 m × 80 m [8.1]
30. 198 cm [8.1]

Heron of Alexandria

Objectives

1. To identify Heron of Alexandria as an important ancient mathematician.
2. To distinguish between pure and applied mathematics, stressing the importance of both.

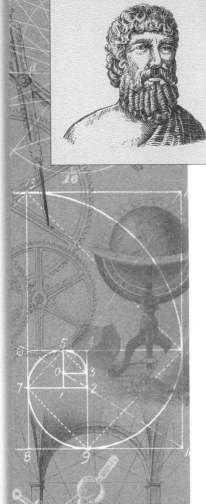

Geometry Through History

HERON OF ALEXANDRIA

Heron, also called Hero, was an ancient geometer who proved an amazing formula as you will soon see. Exactly when Heron lived is unknown, but guesses from 80 B.C. to A.D. 100 have all been proposed. For present purposes, you will most easily understand his circumstances by relating him to the time of Christ and the apostles (ca. 10 B.C. to A.D. 70). However, he probably lived in Alexandria, Egypt.

Heron considered math a very practical subject. All four of his books make use of math in practical ways. *Geometrics* presents calculations of perimeter, area, and volume—necessary for weights and measures in business. In *Pneumatics* he applied geometry to hydraulic engineering to design steam engines and water pumps. His book on optics, *Catoptrics*, applies geometry to show that the angle of incidence equals the angle of reflection and that light follows the shortest distance between two points. *Automata* explains the design of small machines and mechanical toys. Heron learned mathematics well from his teacher Ctesibus.

This practical application approach to geometry is called geodesy, while the earlier theoretical approach of Euclid, stressing reasoning, is called classical geometry. Heron, however, included proofs for some of his formulas

Presentation

Be sure that students understand the four branches of mathematics as the classical Greeks conceived them. We now use algebra as the name for what the ancients called arithmetic. This should make sense since they were interested in the theoretical relations between the numbers, which is what we study in algebra.

	Theoretical	Applied
Classical Algebra	Arithmetic	Logistics
Classical Geometry	Geometry	Geodesy

Point out that only the theoretical topics were required in school; it was assumed that educated people would be able to apply the subject on their own. Since both theoretical subjects were among the seven liberal arts, students studied both arithmetic and geometry throughout their education. ∎

and applications. His famous book *Metrica* contains the proof of the area formula, now named in his honor.

Heron's formula: The area A of a triangle is

$$A = \sqrt{s(s-a)(s-b)(s-c)}$$

where a, b, c are the lengths of the sides and the semiperimeter $s = \frac{(a+b+c)}{2}$.

Heron's geodesy has obvious benefits, but you should see that Euclid's geometry developed the theory that permitted Heron to accomplish his work. Geometry develops reasoning skills; geodesy applies those skills to specific problems. Classical geometry continued to flourish in Greek culture after Euclid until the time of Hipparchus of Nicaea (180-125 B.C.). No theoretical advances were made after Hipparchus until the time of Ptolemy (A.D. 100-168). During the interim, geodesy displaced classical geometry and works such as Heron's filled an important role.

The same tension between the theoretical and the practical occurs in other branches of math also. Classical arithmetic investigated the theoretical aspects of numbers, while logistics applied arithmetic to business problems. Are you surprised? In the Bible you can read epistles that begin with theory (doctrine) and end with practical applications (Ephesians, Galatians, Philippians, and Romans). Theory and practice go together. You should seek to develop a balance of theory and practice in all you do. Appreciate the classical geometers for their careful reasoning, but learn from Heron the value of applying what you know to life. Heron learned all he could and then he set about to use it. Will you?

His famous book Metrica *contains the proof of the area formula, now named in his honor.*

Heron's Formula

Objectives

1. To state and prove Heron's formula for the area of a triangle.
2. To apply Heron's formula to find the area of various triangles.

Vocabulary

Heron's formula
semiperimeter

Assignment

- Intuitive: 1-5
- Standard: 1-5
- Rigorous: 1-5

Resource

- Appendix J. Proof of Heron's Formula.

Additional Problems

1. Find the area of a triangle whose sides measure 12 yds., 18 yds., and 20 yds.
   106.65 yd²
2. Find the area of the piece of property shown in the figure. If an acre is 43,560 ft.², how many acres are in the property?

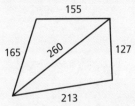

Area is 25,555.8 ft.² or 0.59 acres (Use Heron's formula on the two triangles separately and add the areas: 12,116.621 + 13,439.196.)

Heron's Formula

Heron's formula is used to find the area of a triangle when only the lengths of the sides are known. If you know the length of the altitude of a triangle, you can find the area by the formula $A = \frac{1}{2}bh$. But if you do not know the height, you can use Heron's formula to find the area. The formula uses a number called the semiperimeter.

Definition

The **semiperimeter** of a triangle is one-half of the perimeter of a triangle: $s = \frac{a + b + c}{2}$.

Heron's Formula

If $\triangle ABC$ has sides of lengths a, b, and c and semiperimeter s, then the area of the triangle is $A = \sqrt{s(s - a)(s - b)(s - c)}$.

EXAMPLE Find the area of the triangle shown.

Answer $s = \frac{(3 + 6 + 7)}{2} = 8$

$A = \sqrt{s(s - a)(s - b)(s - c)}$

$= \sqrt{8(8 - 3)(8 - 6)(8 - 7)}$

$= \sqrt{8 \cdot 5 \cdot 2 \cdot 1}$

$= \sqrt{80}$

$= 4\sqrt{5}$

Presentation

This lesson can best catch the students' interest if you spend a little time with the biographical sketch. The balance of useful methods against careful theory is an important point to note about Heron's mathematics.

Motivational Idea. This formula is practical for surveyors, who need to calculate areas of parcels of land. Even though the calculations are now done on computers, the methods programmed into those computers depend on Heron's formula. Work several examples with the students so that they will see the important role that the semiperimeter plays. This is definitely an exercise in which calculators should be used. See if the students recognize that the Area Addition Postulate is needed to complete #5.

A proof of the formula is provided in Appendix J. Outline the major steps to help students comprehend the development: 1) Drop altitude h, 2) use the Pythagorean theorem on both right triangles, 3) solve both equations for h^2 and set them equal, 4) find x and replace it in the factored form of the simpler expression for h^2 and simplify, 5) substitute using semiperimeter s, 6) solve for ch, and 7) substitute into $A = \frac{1}{2} ch$.

Notice that the diagram in the text assumes that the altitude h from C intersects $\overleftrightarrow{AB}$. This assumption that $\overline{AB}$ divides into x and $c - x$ fails if $\triangle ABC$ is obtuse and c is not the longest side. As the teacher, you have three choices:

1. Tell the students that c must be the longest side. This matter of labeling vertices does not interfere with the theorem's applicability.
2. Ignore the special case. The theorem is in fact true when c is a short side of an obtuse triangle, even though our proof does not show it.

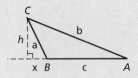

You can prove this formula using analytic geometry. The proof is based on the figure shown.

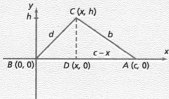

▶ Exercises

Find the area of each triangle that has the given side measures. Round your answers to the nearest tenth.
1. 3 units, 8 units, 9 units
2. 6 units, 18 units, 21 units
3. 27 units, 13 units, 18 units

Find the areas of the figures below. Round your numbers to the nearest tenth.

4.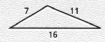

5.

3. Use Heron's formula to find the area of an equilateral triangle with each side *a* units long. $\frac{a^2\sqrt{3}}{4}$
4. Find the area of the triangle with sides 14, 32, and 26. $24\sqrt{55} \approx 178$
5. Find the area of the following figure. $6\sqrt{10} + 2\sqrt{14} \approx 26.46$

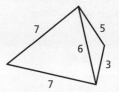

Answers
1. 11.8 sq. units
2. 50.1 sq. units
3. 101.0 sq. units
4. 31.9 sq. units
5. 357.8 sq. units

Tips

3. Point out the problem and tell the students to do the proof as homework, following the steps in the book but beginning with the obtuse picture. Due to the length of the proof, this is not recommended unless you have plenty of time and excellent students.

   Your main goal should be to help them understand Heron's theorem. They should not memorize the proof. The example should be studied carefully to achieve this goal (whether or not the proof is presented).

Ex. 5. Find the two areas separately (101.8 and 256) and add. (Note use of Area Addition Postulate.) ■

8.4

Regular Polygons

8.4 Regular Polygons

Objectives

1. To define terms related to regular polygons.
2. To derive and apply a formula for the area of regular polygons.
3. To find relationships between the apothem, altitude, and side of an equilateral triangle.

Vocabulary

apothem of a regular polygon
center of a regular polygon
central angle of a regular polygon
radius of a regular polygon

Assignment

• Intuitive: 1-13, 21-25
• Standard: 1-17, 21-25
• Rigorous: 1-13 odd, 14-25

Resources

• *Activities Manual*, Bible Activity: Sin—The Corruption of Truth.
• *Test Packet,* Quiz 2, Chapter 8 covers Sections 8.3 and 8.4.

Reading and Writing Mathematics

Have students discuss the advantages and disadvantages of triangles as basic units of area (instead of squares).

Every polygon has an area. The area can be obtained by subdividing the polygon into triangles (as you did for finding angle sums in Chapter 4). Then add the areas of the triangles according to the Area Addition Postulate.

You have already learned to find areas of two regular polygons: the equilateral triangle and the square. You should remember that these figures can be inscribed or circumscribed in a circle. In fact, every regular polygon has both an inscribed and a circumscribed circle. Both circles are shown for the regular heptagon in figure 8.22. Notice that the circles have a common center. The incenter and circumcenter are the same point.

Figure 8.22

These amethyst quartz crystals from Idaho Springs, Colorado, are classified as hexagonal because of the cross sections.

Presentation

Circumscribe a circle about a regular polygon. Draw the radii to the vertices of the polygon and draw at least one other radius of the circle. Point out that since the vertices of the polygon are on the circle, it makes sense to talk about the center, radius, and central angles of the circle as the center, radius, and central angles of the polygon too. Point out, though, that the circle has radii (and central angles) that are not radii of the polygon. This will help students understand three of the new terms without having to memorize anything.

Next, draw all the radii of a regular octagon. This drawing will illustrate Theorem 8.9 and aid your discussion of example 1.

Ask students what is true about the triangles formed. (*congruent*) To find the area of these triangles, use the side of the polygon as the base. The height of each triangle is also needed to find the area, and it has a special name, *apothem.* Thus, each triangle has an area of half the side (base) times the apothem (height). To find the area of the entire polygon, multiply the area of such a triangle by the number of triangles (number of sides of the polygon): $A = n\left(\frac{1}{2}\right)as$. Since ns is the perimeter of the polygon, you can also write $A = \frac{1}{2}ap$, which is Theorem 8.10. The students are asked to develop this formula in #20, so discussing the plan of the proof will get them headed in the right direction.

After developing the formula, go through example 2, which illustrates the use of this theorem. The values used for the side and apothem have been rounded. A side of 10 for the octagon would require an apothem of about 12.07 units, which has been rounded to 12.

The regular hexagon conveniently divides into six equilateral triangles. Example 3 shows that the apothem, radius, and side of a regular hexagon can all be calculated if any one of them is known. Students will not learn the relations among these three values for other types of polygons until the end of Chapter 14.

Emphasize the fact mentioned in step 3 of example 3. The apothem (altitude) always bisects the side of the regular polygon. This

These apophyllite crystals from Paterson, New Jersey, form square-based right prisms (tetragonal).

Additional Problems

1. How many degrees does each central angle measure in a regular dodecagon? What is the angle measure of each interior angle of a regular dodecagon? What is the total angle sum of the interior angles of a regular dodecagon?   *30°, 150°, 1800°*

2. Find the area of each of the following regular polygons.

a) *1176√3 sq. units ≈ 2037 sq. units*
b) *5576 sq. units*

Find the apothem and area of each regular polygon inscribed in a circle of radius 10.

3. triangle with $s = 17.3$ *a = 5.02, A = 130 (values may vary from 129.6 to 130.3, depending on formulas used and rounding)*

4. pentagon with $s = 11.76$ *a = 8.09, A = 237.8*

5. decagon with $s = 6.18$ *a = 9.51, A = 293.9*

Definitions

The **center of a regular polygon** is the common center of the inscribed and circumscribed circles of the regular polygon.

The **radius of a regular polygon** is a segment that joins the center of a regular polygon with one of its vertices.

The **apothem of a regular polygon** is the perpendicular segment that joins the center with a side of the polygon.

These three special parts of a regular polygon are illustrated in figure 8.23. The center is C, the radius is r, and the apothem is a. The angle formed by two radii drawn to consecutive vertices has a special name.

Figure 8.23

Tips

means that for a given side of the polygon, the apothem is the median of the triangle formed by the central angle. The apothem is also the angle bisector and the perpendicular bisector of the side of the triangle.

If you plan to assign any of #18-20, you may wish to read #18 and use it to prove the following statement as an example.
Prove: Each radius of a regular *n*-gon bisects an interior angle.

1. $\triangle CPQ \cong \triangle CRQ$	1. Exercise 18
2. $\angle CQP \cong \angle CQR$	2. Definition of congruent triangles
3. $\overrightarrow{QC}$ bisects $\angle PQR$	3. Definition of angle bisector

Ex. 18. The *n*-gon context appears hard, but the proof is easy. The radii are congruent and the central angles are congruent (Theorem 8.9). This gives SAS.

Ex. 19. Exercise 18 proves the six triangles congruent. The triangles therefore have the same area (Congruent Regions Postulate). Multiply the formula for the area of an equilateral triangle by 6 and reduce.

Ex. 20. Step 7 also uses commutative and associative properties of multiplication. These steps can be shown separately. ∎

Definition

A **central angle of a regular polygon** is the angle formed at the center of the polygon by two radii drawn to consecutive vertices.

$\angle RPQ$ is a central angle of the octagon. Notice that there are eight central angles in all, one for each side.

Figure 8.24

Theorem 8.9

The central angles of a regular n-gon are congruent and measure $\frac{360°}{n}$.

EXAMPLE 1   What are the measures of the central angles and the base angles of the regular octagon?

Answer   1. By Theorem 8.9, the eight central angles divide the circle into eight congruent parts.

$$m\angle RPQ = \frac{360°}{8} = 45°$$

2. $\triangle RPQ$ is isosceles because the radii are congruent. Since the base angles must be congruent, each angle measures half of the remaining $180° - 45° = 135°$ in the triangle.

$$m\angle PRQ = m\angle PQR = \frac{135°}{2} = 67.5°$$

The next theorem enables you to find areas of regular polygons.

Theorem 8.10

The *area of a regular polygon* is one-half the product of its apothem and its perimeter: $A = \frac{1}{2}ap$.

Theorem 8.11

The apothem of an equilateral triangle is one-third the length of the altitude: $a = \frac{1}{3}h$.

Theorem 8.12

The apothem of an equilateral triangle is $\sqrt{3}$ times one-sixth the length of the side: $a = \dfrac{\sqrt{3}}{6}s$.

EXAMPLE 2 Find the area of the following regular octagon.

Answer 1. To use the formula $A = \frac{1}{2}ap$, you must find the perimeter:
$p = ns = 8 \cdot 10 = 80$.

2. Use the formula to find the area:
$A = \frac{1}{2}ap$.

$A = \frac{1}{2}(12)(80)$

$A = 480$

Figure 8.25

EXAMPLE 3 Find the area of the regular hexagon.

Answer 1. Since the hexagon has six sides, each having a length of 4 units,
$p = 6 \cdot 4 = 24$ units.

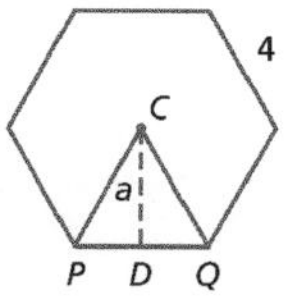

2. The central angle is $\dfrac{360°}{6} = 60°$;

the base angles are $\dfrac{180 - 60}{2} = 60°$ also.

So $\triangle CPQ$ is equiangular and therefore equilateral: $CP = CQ = PQ = 4$

Figure 8.26

3. You can see that the apothem always bisects the side of a regular polygon (use HA): $PD = QD$.

4. To find the apothem, use the Pythagorean theorem:

$2^2 + a^2 = 4^2$

$a^2 = 16 - 4 = 12$

$a = \sqrt{12}$ or $2\sqrt{3}$

5. To find the area, use the formula

$A = \frac{1}{2}ap$.

$A = \frac{1}{2}(2\sqrt{3})(24)$

$A = 24\sqrt{3}$ (or $A \approx 41.6$ square units)

Answers

1. ∠AHG, ∠GHF, ∠FHE, ∠EHD, ∠DHC, ∠CHB, ∠BHA
2. 51.4°
3. 84 sq. units
4. 336 sq. units
5. 2784 sq. units
6. 2457 sq. units
7. 64 sq. units
8. $216\sqrt{3}$ sq. units ≈ 374
9. 6, $6\sqrt{2}$, 144
10. 13, 15, 585
11. 11.7, 233
12. 26.3, 2000.7
13. $\sqrt{3}$, $2\sqrt{3}$, $9\sqrt{3}$

As you calculate areas of regular polygons, remember that the apothem is always the perpendicular bisector of a side and that the radius always bisects an angle.

▶ A. Exercises

1. Name the central angles in this heptagon.
2. How many degrees are in a central angle of a regular heptagon?

Find the area of each regular polygon using Theorem 8.10.

3.

5.

7.

4.

6.

8.

▶ B. Exercises

Complete the following table.

	Number of sides of a regular polygon	Length of apothem (units)	Length of side (units)	Length of radius (units)	Area (sq. units)
9.	4		12		
10.	6			15	
11.	5	8		9.9	
12.	9		18		
13.	3		6		

Prove the formulas in exercises 14-16. However, use derivations with formulas rather than two-column proofs.

14. Prove Theorem 8.10 for the case of a regular quadrilateral by showing that the formula for the area of a regular quadrilateral reduces to the formula for the area of a square.

15. Theorem 8.11. Use the two formulas for the area of a triangle to show that $a = \frac{h}{3}$ for an equilateral triangle.

16. Theorem 8.12. For an equilateral triangle $a = \frac{s\sqrt{3}}{6}$. (*Hint:* Exercise 23 in section 8.3 may help.)

17. Each central angle of a regular polygon forms a triangle with a side of the polygon. Why must the base angles of these triangles be congruent?

Use the portion of the regular n-gon shown at the right to help you complete the following proofs.

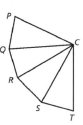

18. The triangles formed by the central angles of a regular n-gon are congruent. (Prove $\triangle CPQ \cong \triangle CRQ$.)

19. Use exercise 18 and example 3 to find a formula for the area of a regular hexagon.

▶ **C. Exercises**

20. Prove Theorem 8.10 that for any n-gon its area can be found by the formula $A = \frac{1}{2}ap$. (*Hint:* Form n congruent triangles in the n-gon; then find the area of each triangle.)

■ **Cumulative Review**

Give the name for each.
21. A cylinder with polygonal bases
22. A cone with a polygonal base
23. A pair of lines that are neither parallel nor intersecting
24. The form of argument shown

$p \rightarrow q$
p
Therefore q.

25. Adjacent angles in which the noncommon sides form opposite rays

14. Substitute $a = \frac{1}{2}s$ and $p = 4s$ into the regular polygon area formula.

$A = \frac{1}{2}ap$
$= \frac{1}{2}(\frac{1}{2}s)(4s)$
$= s^2$

15.

$A = \frac{1}{2}bh = \frac{1}{2}sh$ and $A = \frac{1}{2}ap = \frac{1}{2}a(3s) = \frac{3as}{2}$. Therefore: $\frac{1}{2}sh = \frac{3}{2}as$ or $sh = 3as$ or $h = 3a$ or $a = \frac{h}{3}$.

16. $a = \frac{1}{3}h = \frac{1}{3}(\frac{\sqrt{3}}{2}s) = \frac{\sqrt{3}}{6}s$

17. Since the radii are congruent, the triangles are isosceles. The base angles are congruent by the Isosceles Triangle Theorem.

18.

1. $\overline{PQ} \cong \overline{RQ}$	1. Definition of regular n-gon
2. $\overline{CP} \cong \overline{CR}$	2. Radii congruent
3. $\overline{CQ} \cong \overline{CQ}$	3. Reflexive property of congruent segments
4. $\triangle CPQ \cong \triangle CRQ$	4. SSS

19. $A_{hexagon} = 6A_{triangle}$
$= 6(s^2\frac{\sqrt{3}}{4})$
$= 3\frac{\sqrt{3}}{2}s^2$

20.

1. Regular n-gon with all radii drawn	1. Given
2. The n triangles formed are congruent	2. Exercise 18
3. The n triangles have the same area, $A_{triangle}$	3. Congruent Regions Postulate
4. $A_{triangle} = \frac{1}{2}as$	4. Area of triangle
5. Total area is $A = A_{triangle} + A_{triangle} + A_{triangle} + \ldots + A_{triangle}$	5. Area Addition Postulate
6. $A = nA_{triangle}$	6. Distributive property
7. $A = n(\frac{1}{2}as) = \frac{1}{2}a(ns)$	7. Substitution (step 4 into 6)
8. $P = ns$	8. Perimeter formula
9. $A = \frac{1}{2}ap$	9. Substitution (step 8 into 7)

21. prism [2.7]
22. pyramid [2.6]
23. skew [1.4]
24. modus ponens [5.6]
25. linear pairs [4.4]

Circles

Objectives

1. To derive the formula for the area of a circle from the formula for the area of a regular n-gon.
2. To apply the formula to calculate areas of circles.

Assignment

- Intuitive: 1-18, 21-25
- Standard: 1-25
- Rigorous: 8-25 and Mind over Math

Resources

- *Visual Packet,* Area. Focus on the portion of the poster about area of circles.
- *Activities Manual,* Construction Skills. An extension of previous construction work.
- *Test Packet,* Quiz 3, Chapter 8 covers Section 8.5.

Reading and Writing Mathematics

Discuss what kind of triangle might make a good unit of area.

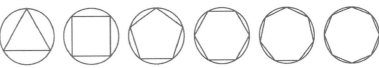

8.5 Circles

In the last section you learned that the formula for the area of a regular polygon is $A = \frac{1}{2}ap$, where a is the apothem and p represents the perimeter. Look at a regular polygon and a circle that is circumscribed about the polygon.

The use of pivot irrigation in this aerial view of a farm in Texas results in circular fields.

Figure 8.27

As you look from the left to the right, notice that the length of the apothem gets closer to the radius of the circle and that the perimeter gets closer to the circumference of the circle. Furthermore, the area of the polygon approaches the area of the circumscribed circle. This relationship enables us to predict the formula for the area of a circle from the formula for the area of the inscribed regular polygon.

In summary,

$a \rightarrow r$ (apothem approaches radius)

$p \rightarrow c$ (perimeter approaches circumference)

$A_{n\text{-gon}} \rightarrow A_{circle}$ (area of n-gon approaches area of circle)

So the formula $A_{n\text{-gon}} = \frac{1}{2}ap$ becomes $A_{circle} = \frac{1}{2}rc$. To simplify, substitute the formula for circumference, $c = 2\pi r$.

$$A = \frac{1}{2}rc$$

$$A = \frac{1}{2}r(2\pi r)$$

$$A = \pi r^2$$

338 CHAPTER 8 AREA

Remind students that the more sides a regular polygon has, the closer its shape approaches the circumscribed circle. This idea was used to find the circumference of circles in Chapter 3 and is used again in this section. This method is important in higher mathematics, particularly calculus.

If you wish to introduce a term from calculus, tell students that as the number of sides of the polygon increases, its shape becomes more nearly circular and that the area of the circle is the *limit* of the area of the regular polygons. This discussion, then, helps students develop concepts of limits for *calculus* (and you can tell them this). Encourage them to go as far as possible in their study of mathematics.

Go through the development of this formula carefully. As the drawings in the text show, the difference between the lengths of the chords (sides of the polygon) and lengths of the arcs of the circle grows smaller. While the number of sides of the polygon increases without bound, the polygon and the circle become practically indistinguishable at a relatively small number of sides. (For example, a 360-gon inscribed in a circle of radius 6 has an apothem of 5.999, a side of 0.1047, and an area of 113.091; the area of the circle is 113.097. Some of these calculations require trigonometry; see Chapter 14.)

Encourage your students to have an overall plan for working exercises like 11 through 18.

For example, in #11 the plan would be the following: Required area = area of square minus area of four circles.

$$A = A_{square} - 4A_{circle}$$
$$A = s^2 - 4\pi r^2$$
$$A = (12)^2 - 4\pi(3)^2$$
$$A = 144 - 36\pi$$

Work through several of the exercises in this section in class. This section should be easy for most of your students.

Theorem 8.13
The *area of a circle* is pi times the square of the radius: $A = \pi r^2$.

▶ A. Exercises

Complete the table.

	c (units)	r (units)	d (units)	A (sq. units)
1.		9		
2.		7		
3.			4	
4.	π			
5.			1.6	
6.				0.04π
7.	30π			
8.		22		
9.				25π
10.				0.56π

▶ B. Exercises

Find the area of the shaded portion.

11.

14.

12.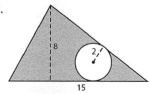

15.

13.

8.5 CIRCLES **339**

Additional Problems

Find the area of the shaded portion in each figure.

1. The polygon is regular with $s = 2$ meters.
   $(\frac{4}{3}\pi - \sqrt{3})$ m² ≈ 2.46 m²
2. The triangle is equilateral with side 4 cm.
   $4\sqrt{3} - \frac{4\pi}{3}$ ≈ 2.74 cm²
3. The triangle is equilateral with side 6 inches.
   $(9\sqrt{3} + \frac{3\pi}{2})$ in.² ≈ 20.3 in.²
4. The radius of the circle is 5 cm.
   $25\pi - 3\sqrt{91}$ ≈ 49.9 cm²

Answers

1. $18\pi, 18, 81\pi$
2. $14\pi, 14, 49\pi$
3. $4\pi, 2, 4$
4. $0.5, 1, 0.25\pi$
5. $1.6\pi, 0.8, 0.64\pi$
6. $4\pi, 0.2, 0.4$
7. $15, 30, 225\pi$
8. $44\pi, 44, 484\pi$
9. $10\pi, 5, 10$
10. $1.5\pi, 0.75, 1.5$
11. $144 - 36\pi$ sq. units (≈ 30.9)
12. $60 - 4\pi$ sq. units (≈ 47.4)
13. 128π sq. units (≈ 402.1)
14. $50\pi - 100$ sq. units (≈ 57.1)
15. 21π sq. units (≈ 66.0)

Tips

Ex. 18. For the pentagon, $p = ns = 5 \cdot 34 = 170$, $a = \sqrt{29^2 - 17^2} = 23.5$, and $A = \frac{1}{2}ap = \frac{1}{2}(23.5)(170) = 1997.5$.
$A_{circle} = \pi r^2 = \pi \cdot 29^2 \approx 2642.1$
$A_{shaded} = A_{circle} - A_{pentagon} = 2642.1 - 1997.5 \approx 644.6$

Ex. 19. This problem is important because an annulus will be used in deriving the volume of a sphere in Section 11.5.

Ex. 20. Methods will vary. One method requires three steps. 1) Find the area of two white pieces by subtracting the area of a circle (two semicircles) from the area of the square: $10^2 - \pi5^2 = 100 - 25\pi$, 2) double this to find the area of the white space inside the square: $200 - 50\pi$ (or about 42.92), and 3) subtract the area of the white space from the area of the square to get the shaded area: $100 - (200 - 50\pi) = 50\pi - 100$ (or about 57.08). ■

16. $30 + 16 + \frac{1}{2}\pi \cdot 2^2 = 46 + 2\pi \ (\approx 52.3)$
17. $9 \cdot 4 - \frac{1}{2}\pi \cdot 3^2 = 36 - \frac{9}{2}\pi \ (\approx 21.9)$
18. 644.6
19. $A_{\text{outer}} - A_{\text{inner}} = \pi x^2 - \pi y^2 = \pi(x^2 - y^2)$
20. $50\pi - 100 \approx 57.1 \text{ cm}^2$
21. B is between A and C if $\overrightarrow{BC} \cap \overrightarrow{BA} = \{B\}$ and A, B, C are collinear (or) if $AB + BC = AC$ [2.2]
22. a quadrilateral with two pairs of parallel opposite sides [4.5]
23. $\triangle ABC \cong \triangle DEF$ if $\overline{AB} \cong \overline{DE}$, $\overline{AC} \cong \overline{DF}$, $\overline{BC} \cong \overline{EF}$, $\angle A \cong \angle D$, $\angle B \cong \angle E$, $\angle C \cong \angle F$ [6.3]
24. lines that intersect to form right angles [4.3]
25. a segment joining a vertex of the triangle to the midpoint of the opposite side [7.2]

Mind over Math

See Appendix B.

16.

17.

18. Find the shaded area if the pentagon is regular.

19. An *annulus* is the ring formed by two concentric circles with different radii. Derive a formula for the area of an annulus formed by two circles with radii x and y, where $x > y$.

▶ **C. Exercises**

20. Find the shaded area if *ABCD* is a square. (*Hint:* The arcs are semicircles.)

■ **Cumulative Review**

Define each.
21. Between
22. Parallelogram
23. Congruent triangles
24. Perpendicular lines
25. Median of a triangle

1. To double the area of a given rectangle, can you double the lengths of consecutive sides? Explain. What should you do?
2. If you triple the length of a side of a square, what happens to the area?
3. If you multiply the radius of a circle by a factor of five, what happens to the area?
4. What percentage should Bill select on the photocopier to achieve an enlargement of his picture that doubles its area?

8.6 Surface Areas of Prisms and Cylinders

In Chapter 2 you learned that cylinders and cones with polygonal bases are called prisms and pyramids respectively. In fact, prisms and pyramids are classified by their bases. A triangular prism has triangles as bases, while a pentagonal pyramid has a pentagon for a base. Now you will learn to find the surface areas of these three-dimensional solids.

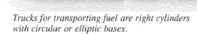

Trucks for transporting fuel are right cylinders with circular or elliptic bases.

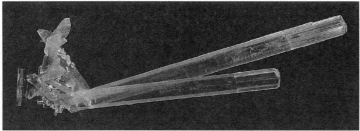

Gypsum from the Cave of Swords, Mexico, forms right prisms with parallelogram bases (monoclinic).

This chalcanthite crystal from Utah forms an oblique prism with parallelogram bases (triclinic).

Surface Areas of Prisms and Cylinders

Objectives

1. To differentiate between surface area and lateral surface area of prisms and cylinders.
2. To derive and apply formulas for calculating the surface area of prisms and cylinders.

Vocabulary
lateral surface area
surface area

Assignment
- Intuitive: 1-10, 13, 21-25
- Standard: 1-17, 21-25
- Rigorous: 5-25

Resources
- *Visual Packet,* Surface Area. Focus on the portion of the poster about cylinders.
- *Activities Manual,* Math History Activity. Focuses on the life and mathematical contributions of Plato.

Flash
The gypsum comes from the state of Chihuahua in Mexico. Monoclinic and triclinic are distinguished by having one *(mono)* or three *(tri)* inclined axes. The resulting shapes can be described as in the table (Section 8.2, Flash) or as oblique rectangular prisms and parallelepipeds respectively (see Chapter 11).

Presentation

Read the first three paragraphs with your students. Discuss the danger of pretending to be a Christian while not possessing true saving faith.

Motivational Idea. Have students cut cardboard and tape the pieces together to form prisms, pyramids, and other three-dimensional figures. Have students cover these with graph paper and then count the number of squares. This will help them associate surface area with the outer surface in contrast to volume (Chapter 11).

Motivational Idea. Students may enjoy making patterns (called *nets*) that can be folded into solid figures. For instance, a square pyramid would look like a square with an equilateral

triangle attached to each side. You can use the nets to form the cardboard figures mentioned above, or you may want to display them in class.

Develop the formulas for the lateral area and surface area of a prism as discussed in the text. The key idea is that surface area of a cylinder (or prism) is given by $S = L + 2B$. This works for any type of cylinder.

For a right prism, the lateral area is found by applying the formula for the area of a rectangle. The formula for lateral area, $L = pH$, is applicable only to right prisms. This means that the lateral edges and lateral faces must be perpendicular to the two bases. The reason that this formula does not work for an oblique prism is that the lateral faces may be different

(some rectangles and some parallelograms). For an oblique prism we can find the lateral area if enough information is given to find the area of each lateral face separately.

After determining the shape, the students can apply the appropriate formula to find B. When teaching, emphasize a few basic facts such as this and most students will remember the methods. Since a cube is a right prism with a square base (perimeter $4s$), the formula for the surface area of a cube can be derived from the formula for the prism ($L = 4s \cdot s$). Thus, $S = 2s^2 + 4s^2 = 6s^2$.

Motivational Idea. Use the circumscribed circle concept (limits) mentioned earlier to find the formula for the surface area of a cylinder.

Reading and Writing Mathematics

Ask the students to research the term *geodesic*, give a definition of it, and explain what the geodesic would be in a plane and on a sphere. ***the shortest distance between two points on a surface; in a plane, a segment; on a sphere, an arc of a great circle***

Additional Problems

1. The base of the following diagram has perimeter 23 m and area 20 m². If the height is 11 m, find the surface area. ***293 m²***

Find the lateral and total surface area of the following solid figures.

2.

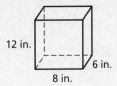

12 in.
6 in.
8 in.

L = 336 in.², S = 432 in.²

3.

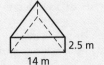

2.5 m
14 m

L = 105 m², S = 105 + 49√3
≈ 189.9 m²

4.

8'
12'

L = 192π ft.², S = 320π ft.²

You already know that the word *area* describes the number of squares needed to cover a region. Similarly, *surface area* is the number of square units needed to cover the outer shell of a solid in space.

Just what does the word *surface* mean? Mathematically, *surface* means "the boundary of a three-dimensional figure." Another meaning of *surface* is "the outward appearance." Are you more than a surface Christian? People who show only an outward appearance of Christianity but do not have a changed heart are not really saved. Surface Christianity is just a pretense. As Romans 10:10 clearly states, true Christianity is an inner change of the heart. "For with the heart man believeth unto righteousness," and man becomes a new creature (II Cor. 5:17). Make sure that you are not just a surface Christian.

To find the surface area of a prism, you must find the number of square units that would cover the two bases and all the lateral faces. Each lateral face is a parallelogram, and the height of a prism is always the perpendicular distance between the two bases.

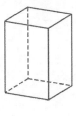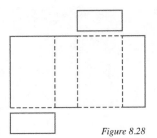

Figure 8.28

For a right prism, the height *H* of the prism is the same as the length of a lateral edge. This makes it easy to derive a formula for surface area. The sum of the areas of all the lateral faces is called the lateral surface area (*L*). In figure 8.28, the bases were cut out by cutting along the perimeter *p* of the base, and then an edge of the prism was slit and laid open. The union of all the lateral faces forms one large rectangle. The base of this rectangle is the perimeter *p* of the base of the prism. The height of the rectangle is the height *H* of the prism. The base times the height gives the lateral area.

$L = pH$

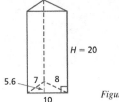

$H = 20$

5.6
7
8
10

Figure 8.29

Emphasize the fact that the basic formulas for the lateral surface area and the total surface area for a right prism and a right cylinder are identical.

Ex. 6. Students must recognize that the bases are right triangles to find their areas.

Ex. 12. The easiest method is to name the length of a side of the base *x*, which makes the height 3*x*. Each square base has an area of *x²*, and the lateral surface area is $L = 12x^2$. Thus, $2x^2 + 12x^2 = 224$ or $14x^2 = 224$. Divide to obtain $x^2 = 16$, or $x = 4$. Since the side is 4, the height is 12 ft.

Ex. 13. Equation: $6s^2 = 1350$. Divide both sides by six and take square roots.

Ex. 14. Set up a quadratic equation. Using *h* as the height and *h* − 7 as the radius, you obtain $2\pi(h-7)^2 + 2\pi(h-7)h = 1248\pi$. This equation can be solved correctly, but

many students will forget to FOIL. If they FOIL correctly and simplify, they will obtain $2h^2 - 21h + 49 = 624$. You can avoid having to FOIL by naming the radius and using *r* + 7 as the height: $2\pi r^2 + 2\pi r(r+7) = 1248\pi$. After you simplify, the equation becomes $2r^2 + 7r - 624 = 0$. Solve by factoring (or the quadratic formula): $(2r + 39)(r - 16) = 0$. The solutions are $r = \frac{-39}{2}$ and $r = 16$, but the radius must be positive, so the answer is 16 feet.

Ex. 16. $S = L + 2B$, so $500 = 320 + 2B$. Thus, $2B = 180$ and $B = 90$ square feet.

The perimeter of the base of the triangular prism shown is $p = 10 + 8 + 7 = 25$. The lateral surface area is as follows.

$$L = pH$$

$$L = 25(20)$$

$$L = 500 \text{ square units}$$

To find the total surface area, add the area of the two bases to the lateral surface area. This results in the following formula, where B represents the area of each base.

$$S = L + 2B$$

Now how do you find the area of the bases? The bases are triangles, so use the triangle formulas that you have learned.

$$B = \frac{1}{2}bh$$

Remember that h (lowercase) here represents the height of the triangle, not the height of the prism.

$$B = \frac{1}{2}(10)(5.6)$$

$$B = 28 \text{ square units}$$

The surface area of this triangular prism is calculated below.

$$S = L + 2B$$

$$S = 500 + 2(28)$$

$$S = 500 + 56$$

$$S = 556 \text{ square units}$$

This means that you could cover the triangular prism with 556 square units.

> **Theorem 8.14**
>
> The *surface area of a prism* is the sum of the lateral surface area and the area of the bases: $S = L + 2B$.
>
> The lateral surface area of a right prism is the product of its height and the perimeter of its base: $L = pH$.

A cube is a special case of a rectangular prism. Since a cube has six congruent faces, you should be able to apply this theorem to show that the surface area of a cube is $6s^2$ (see exercise 17). Another special case is that of a regular prism. A *regular prism* is a right prism with a regular polygon as its base.

5. Find the dimensions of the square base of a right prism if the height is 24 cm and the lateral surface area is 576 cm².
   6 cm × 6 cm

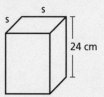

6. A right circular cylinder has the same height as diameter. If the total surface area is 96π in.², what is the size of the cylinder?
   8 in. in diameter and 8 in. high

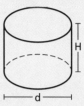

Ex. 20 Total the four surfaces.

$$L_{outer} = 12\pi$$

$$L_{inner} = 9.6\pi$$

$$A_{annulus} = 1.44\pi$$

$$S = L_{inner} + L_{outer} + 2A_{annulus}$$

$$= 24.48\pi \approx 76.9 \text{ cm}^2$$

The development of the formula for the surface area of a right circular cylinder is similar to that of a right prism.

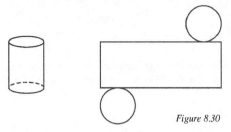

Figure 8.30

When the lateral surface of a cylinder is unrolled and laid out in a plane, you again obtain a rectangle. The base and height of the rectangle still correspond to the perimeter and height of the cylinder. However, the correct term for the perimeter of the base is *circumference* since the base is a circle:

$$L = cH$$

where c is the circumference of the cylinder. Remember that the height (H) is always the perpendicular distance between the two bases.

To find the total surface area of a cylinder, simply add the area of the two bases to the lateral surface area.

EXAMPLE Find the surface area for the circular cylinder in figure 8.31.

Answer
$$S = L + 2B$$
$$S = cH + 2B$$
$$S = 2\pi rH + 2\pi r^2$$
$$S = 2\pi(6)(9) + 2(36)\pi$$
$$S = 108\pi + 72\pi$$
$$S = 180\pi \text{ square units} \approx 565 \text{ square units}$$

Figure 8.31

Theorem 8.15

The *surface area of a cylinder* is the sum of the lateral surface area and the area of the bases: $S = L + 2B$.

The lateral surface area of a right cylinder is the product of its circumference and height: $L = cH$.

▶ A. Exercises

1. Find the lateral surface area of the right prism if the base is a square.

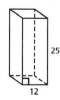

25
12

2. Find the surface area of the right prism shown.

4   4
13
4

Find the lateral surface areas and total surface areas of the following figures. The bases in exercises 3, 5, and 8 are regular.

3.

8
3.5
5

5.

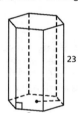

23
8

7.

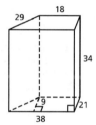

29   18
34
9
21
38

4.

3
6

6.

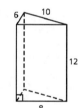

6   10
12
8

8.

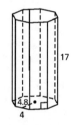

17
4.8
4

8.6 SURFACE AREAS OF PRISMS AND CYLINDERS   **345**

8.6 SURFACE AREAS OF PRISMS AND CYLINDERS   **345**

Answers

1. $L = 1200$ sq. units
2. $S = 156 + 8\sqrt{3}$ sq. units ≈ 170 sq. units
3. $L = 200$ sq. units, $S = 287.5$ sq. units
4. $L = 36\pi$ sq. units ≈ 113 sq. units
   $S = 54\pi$ sq. units ≈ 170 sq. units
5. $L = 1104$ sq. units,
   $S = 1104 + 192\sqrt{3}$ sq. units
   ≈ 1437 sq. units
6. $L = 288$ sq. units, $S = 336$ sq. units
7. $L = 3604$ sq. units,
   $S = 3604 + 504 = 4108$ sq. units
8. $L = 544$ sq. units, $S = 697.6$ sq. units

9. $L = 294\pi$ sq. meters, top = 49π sq. meters
   (no paint needed for bottom), total =
   343π sq. meters ≈ 1077.6 sq. meters
10. L = 868 sq. units
11. 420π sq. in. ≈ 1319 sq. in.
12. base is 4' × 4'; height is 12'
13. 15" × 15" × 15"
14. radius is 16 ft.; height is 23 ft.
15. $270\sqrt{3}\pi$ sq. ft ≈ 1469 sq. ft.
16. 90 sq. ft.

9. The local water tower is a right circular cylinder standing 21 meters high and having a radius of 7 meters. Its exterior needs to be painted. How many square meters of paint will you need for one coat?

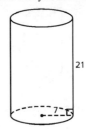

10. The diagram shows a vertical mine shaft from which rocks have been falling. How much sheet metal is needed to cover the sides of the shaft as a safety measure?

▶ **B. Exercises**

11. The diameter of the base of a right circular cylinder is 12 inches, and the height is 29 inches. What is the surface area of the cylinder?

12. The surface area of a right prism is 224 square feet, and the length of a side of the square base is one-third the height. What are the dimensions of the prism?

13. The total area of a cube is 1350 square inches. Find the dimensions of this cube.

14. The total area of a right circular cylinder is 1248π square feet. The radius of the base of the cylinder is 7 feet less than the height. Find the radius and the height of the cylinder.

15. Find the lateral area of a right circular cylinder whose diameter is $10\sqrt{3}$ feet and whose height is 27 feet.

16. The surface area of a cylinder is 500 square feet; the lateral surface area is 320 square feet. Give the area of a base.

17. Prove that the surface area of a cube is $6s^2$.
18. Prove that the surface area of a right circular cylinder is
$S = 2\pi r(H + r)$.

▶ C. Exercises

19. Prove that the surface area of a right prism with bases that are regular n-gons is $ns(H + a)$.
20. Find the surface area of the napkin ring.

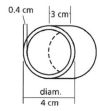

0.4 cm   3 cm

diam.
4 cm

■ Cumulative Review

Define each term.
21. circle
22. tangent
23. supplementary angles
24. congruent angles
25. circumcenter

17.

1. $S = pH + 2B$	1. Surface area of prism
2. $B = s^2$	2. Area of Square Postulate
3. $p = 4s$	3. Perimeter of square
4. $H = s$	4. Definition of cube
5. $S = 4s \cdot s + 2s^2$ $= 6s^2$	5. Substitution

18.

1. $S = cH + 2B$	1. Surface area of cylinder
2. $B = \pi r^2$	2. Area of circle
3. $c = 2\pi r$	3. Circumference of circle
4. $S = 2\pi rH + 2\pi r^2$	4. Substitution
5. $S = 2\pi r (H + r)$	5. Distributive property

19.

1. $S = pH + 2B$	1. Surface area of right prism
2. $B = \frac{1}{2} ap$	2. Area of regular polygon
3. $S = pH + 2(\frac{1}{2}ap)$	3. Substitution
4. $S = pH + ap$	4. Inverse property of multiplication
5. $S = p (H + a)$	5. Distributive property
6. $p = ns$	6. Perimeter of regular polygon
7. $S = ns (H + a)$	7. Substitution (step 6 into 5)

20. 76.9 cm²
21. set of all points a given distance from a given point [2.4]
22. a line that intersects a circle in exactly one point [3.5]
23. two angles for which the sum of angle measures is 180 [4.4]
24. angles having the same measure [4.2]
25. the center of the circumscribed circle [7.2]

Surface Areas of Pyramids and Cones

Objectives

1. To distinguish between the total surface area and the lateral area of pyramids and cones.
2. To derive and apply formulas for calculating the surface area of pyramids and cones.

Vocabulary

altitude of a pyramid or cone
regular pyramid
slant height of a pyramid or cone

Assignment

- Intuitive: 1-16, 22-25
- Standard: 1-19, 22-25
- Rigorous: 5-15 odd, 16-25

Resources

- *Visual Packet,* Surface Area. Focus on the portion of the poster about cones.
- *Activities Manual,* Calculator Skills. Focuses on the use of calculator skills to find areas and introduces the use of the trigonometric function keys.

8.7 Surface Areas of Pyramids and Cones

In Chapter 2 you studied cones and pyramids. Since a pyramid is a special type of cone, we will begin with the pyramid. Before finding its surface area, you must first learn its essential parts.

The conveyor dumps processed materials into the top of the hopper for storage. Tapering at the bottom into a pyramid, the hopper functions like a funnel to dispense the product as necessary.

This triangular pyramid has four faces: three lateral faces and a base. The common point above the base where the lateral faces intersect is the *vertex*. The *altitude* (H) of a pyramid is a segment that extends from the vertex, perpendicular to the plane of the base. The lateral edges are the segments formed by the intersection of the lateral faces. In figure 8.32, $\triangle ABD$ is the base, point C is the vertex, $\overline{AC}$ is a lateral edge, and $\triangle CBD$ is one of the lateral faces. The surface area consists of the lateral surface area and the area of the base: $S = L + B$.

Figure 8.32

A *regular pyramid* is a right pyramid that has a regular polygon as its base. The formula that we will develop for the surface area of a pyramid can be used only for regular pyramids. What kind of figure is each lateral face of a regular pyramid?

For a regular pyramid, you can calculate the base area and the lateral surface area easily. To find the lateral surface area, find the area of one of the congruent isosceles triangles and multiply that area by the number of sides of the base. The slant height is labeled l in figure 8.33. The *slant height* of a regular pyramid is the height of a triangular face of the pyramid.

Figure 8.33

Presentation

Review the relationship between a cone and a pyramid. A pyramid is a special case of a cone in which the simple closed curve that forms the base is a polygon. This means that *cone* may be an alternate correct answer to some questions for which pyramid is a better answer.

In this section, the key idea is that the surface area of a cone is found by $S = L + B$. Define the vocabulary words and show that adding the area of the base to the lateral area gives the surface area for any cone (including pyramids).

For regular pyramids, we can be more specific. In a regular pyramid, the vertex is equidistant from each vertex of the base. A plumb bob hanging from the vertex of a regular pyramid will meet the base at its center. Since the slant height, l, is the altitude of a triangular face, the area of the face can be found by $A = \frac{1}{2}sl$. By adding all these congruent faces and factoring out $\frac{1}{2}l$, the lateral area can be expressed as $L = \frac{1}{2}pl$, where p is the perimeter.

Sometimes the surface area may be found only after some other value is first calculated. Often the Pythagorean theorem will be needed to find this other value (as in example 2, step 3). Draw a diagram of the hexagonal base and point out the equilateral triangles formed by consecutive radii. The apothem divides each equilateral triangle into two right triangles. Find the apothem using the Pythagorean theorem:

$$a^2 + \left(\frac{b}{2}\right)^2 = r^2.$$

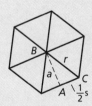

Another frequently used right triangle is formed by the slant height (l), the altitude of the prism (H), and the apothem (a). The equation is $a^2 + H^2 = l^2$.

EXAMPLE 1 Find the surface area of the regular pyramid.

Answer Use the slant height to find the area of a triangular face.

$$A = \tfrac{1}{2}bh$$

$$A = \tfrac{1}{2}(7)(16)$$

$$A = 56$$

Figure 8.34

The lateral surface area consists of five such triangles:

$$L = 5 \cdot 56$$

$$L = 280 \text{ square units}$$

Using the perimeter of 35, find the base area:

$$B = \tfrac{1}{2}ap = \tfrac{1}{2}(4.8)(35) = 84$$

Find the total surface area:

$$S = L + B = 280 + 84 = 364 \text{ sq. units}$$

In general, the formula for the lateral surface area of a regular pyramid is

$$L = \tfrac{1}{2}bln,$$

where b is the length of a side of the base, n is the number of sides of the base, and l is the slant height. Since bn is the same as the perimeter, p, the formula could be written as follows:

$$L = \tfrac{1}{2}pl$$

Theorem 8.16

The *surface area of a pyramid* is the sum of the lateral surface area and the area of the base: $S = L + B$.

By using this theorem and some algebra, we can derive a practical formula for the surface area of a regular pyramid. Notice the use of factoring with the distributive property.

$$S = \tfrac{1}{2}pl + \tfrac{1}{2}ap$$

$$S = \tfrac{1}{2}p(l + a), \text{ where } p \text{ is the perimeter of the base, } l \text{ is the slant height,}$$
and a is the length of the apothem.

In some regular pyramids, you can figure out some of the lengths without being told.

Reading and Writing Mathematics

Have the students look up and write a definition of the following plane curves and sketch them:

1. epicycloid *plane curve traced by a fixed point on a circle as it rolls along the outside of a fixed circle*

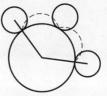

epicycloid

2. hypocycloid *plane curve traced by a fixed point on a circle as it rolls along the inside of a fixed circle*

hypocycloid

Additional information can be found from triangular, square, and hexagonal bases, knowing only the length of a side of the polygon. Other bases, such as pentagonal and octagonal, will require either the apothem or radius (until students learn trigonometry, Chapter 14).

Next, develop the formula for lateral surface area of a right circular cone. This formula is derived from using polygons with increasing numbers of sides. The slant height (l) is again related to radius (r) of the base (circle) and the height (H) of the cone by $l^2 = r^2 + H^2$. Example 3 presents the calculation of the surface area for a specific right circular cone.

Students who understand how the formulas are derived will retain them. In contrast, students who memorize the formulas without understanding them will not be able to apply them appropriately and will forget them right after a test.

Tips

Ex. 18. Only the outside gets painted. $S = L_{pyramid} + A_{frame} + L_{base}$. The area of the frame includes its top (difference in areas of the squares) and its four narrow faces (convert 8" height to 0.67 ft.). The base has four rectangular faces with two triangles removed.

Ex. 20. If x is the slant height of the unsliced cone, then the removed cone has a slant height of $x - 13$. The slant heights and radii of these cones are proportional:

$$\frac{x - 13}{7} = \frac{x}{12} \text{ or } 12(x - 13) = 7x, \text{ so } x = \frac{156}{5}$$
and $x - 13 = \frac{91}{5}$.

$$L = L_{unsliced} - L_{removed} = \pi r_1 l_1 - \pi r_2 l_2 =$$
$$\pi(12)\frac{156}{5} - \pi(7)\frac{91}{5} = \pi \frac{(1872 - 637)}{5} = 247\pi.$$

Additional Problems

Find the lateral and total surface area of the figures in #1 and #2.

1.

$h = 6$

$d = 4$

$L = 4\sqrt{10}\pi, S = 4\pi(\sqrt{10} + 1) \approx 52.3 \text{ in.}^2$

2.

16

8

$L = 96\sqrt{19} \approx 418.5 \text{ cm}^2,$
$S = 96\sqrt{3} + 96\sqrt{19} \approx 584.7 \text{ cm}^2$

3. Find the surface area of a silo with a conical top as shown in the diagram.
$640\pi + 80\pi = 720\pi \approx 2262 \text{ ft.}^2$

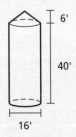

6'

40'

16'

4. Find the total surface area of a regular tetrahedron with the length of the edge 1 meter. $\sqrt{3} \approx 1.73 \text{ m}^2$

EXAMPLE 2   Find the surface area of this regular pyramid.

Answer   **1.** The surface area is the lateral area plus the area of the base.

$S = L + B$

23

12   12   12

Figure 8.35

2. First find the lateral area. The perimeter of the base is six times the side length, 12 units. So $p = (6)(12) = 72$. The slant height is 23 units.

$L = \frac{1}{2}pl$

$L = \frac{1}{2}(72)(23)$

$L = 828$ square units

3. Draw the hexagonal base. Label the apothem a, which is a leg of a right triangle. The other leg is 6 (half the base), and the hypotenuse (radius) is 12. Find the length of the apothem using the Pythagorean theorem.

$a^2 + b^2 = c^2$

$a^2 + 6^2 = 12^2$

$a^2 = 144 - 36$

$a^2 = 108$

$a = 6\sqrt{3}$ or 10.4

4. Find the area of the base.

$B = \frac{1}{2}ap$

$B = \frac{1}{2}(10.4)(72)$

$B = 374.4$ square units

5. Find the surface area.

$S = L + B$

$S = 828 + 374.4$

$S = 1202.4$ square units

Triangular and hexagonal pyramids are classes of pyramids, while pyramids themselves are a type of cone. Classification systems help you organize information. You will classify other figures later in this book, but systems of classification are also important outside mathematics. Christians, for example, should display the fruit of the Spirit (Gal. 5:22-26). They are to be a peculiar class of people so that they can draw other people to Christ (I Pet. 2:9).

Next, find the areas of the circular bases and the total surface area. $A_{\text{bottom}} = \pi \cdot 12^2 = 144\pi$, and $A_{\text{top}} = \pi \cdot 7^2 = 49\pi$. The total surface area is $S = L + A_{\text{top}} + A_{\text{bottom}} = 247\pi + 49\pi + 144\pi = 440\pi \text{ cm}^2$.

Ex. 21. By the Pythagorean theorem, the diagonal of the square is $6\sqrt{2}$ units. Using the right triangle (dotted), the height and radius are each half the length of the diagonal, or $3\sqrt{2}$. For the lateral surface area of the upper cone, $L = \pi rl = \pi(3\sqrt{2})(6) = 18\pi\sqrt{2}$. The surface area of the solid is obtained by doubling, or $S = 36\pi\sqrt{2}$. ∎

Do you recall how the formula to find the area of a circle was developed from the formula for the area of a regular polygon? The same procedure will be used here to develop the formula for the area of a cone. As the number of sides of the base of the regular pyramid increases, the pyramid approaches the shape of a cone. The formulas for surface area are also very similar. Figure 8.36 shows the development and then the essential elements of the cone.

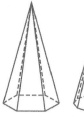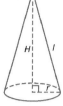

Figure 8.36

In the last figure, H is the height of the cone, l is the slant height, and r is the radius of the circular base. Now compare the surface-area formulas. Remember that perimeter approaches circumference, and apothem approaches radius.

	Pyramid	Cone
Lateral area	$L = \frac{1}{2}pl$	$L = \frac{1}{2}cl$
Surface area	$S = L + B$	$S = L + B$
	$S = \frac{1}{2}pl + \frac{1}{2}ap$	$S = \frac{1}{2}cl + \frac{1}{2}rc$
	$S = \frac{1}{2}p(l + a)$	$S = \frac{1}{2}c(l + r)$

Theorem 8.17

The *surface area of a cone* is the sum of the lateral surface area and the area of the base: $S = L + B$; the lateral surface area of a circular cone is half the product of the circumference and slant height: $L = \frac{1}{2}cl$.

Using the theorem above and some algebra, you can derive a practical formula for the area of a cone. For a circular cone, $c = 2\pi r$ and $B = \pi r^2$.

$$S = L + B$$
$$S = \frac{1}{2}cl + B$$
$$S = \frac{1}{2}(2\pi r)l + \pi r^2$$
$$S = \pi rl + \pi r^2$$

Answers
1. 724.5, 1017.45
2. 126, 184.8
3. 12, 432, 1008
4. 54, 60.3
5. 8, 72, 238.3
6. 5, 167.5
7. 12, 108
8. 2.0, 157.5, 178.7 (or 178.5)
9. 3.2, 3, 184.4 (or 184.8)
10. 13.2, 211.2

EXAMPLE 3   Find the surface area of the cone.

Answer   1. Find the lateral area.

$$L = \pi r l$$
$$L = \pi(6)(18)$$
$$L = 108\pi$$

2. Find the area of the base.

$$B = \pi r^2$$
$$B = \pi \cdot 6^2$$
$$B = 36\pi$$

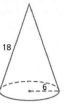

Figure 8.37

3. Add L and B.

$$S = L + B$$
$$S = 108\pi + 36\pi$$
$$S = 144\pi$$

▶ A. Exercises

Complete the following tables.

	Regular Right Pyramids					
	Apothem length (units)	Slant height (units)	Number of sides in the base	Length of one side of the base (units)	Lateral area (sq. units)	Surface area (sq. units)
1.	9.3	23	7	9		
2.	4.2	9	7	4		
3.		9	4	24		
4.	1.4	12	9	1		
5.	$4\sqrt{3}$	3	6			
6.	3.4	10	5		125	
7.	3.7	9		2		152.8
8.		15	3	7		
9.		8		11	132	
10.	4.8		8	4		288

Right Circular Cones				
	Radius (units)	Slant height (units)	Lateral area (sq. units)	Surface area (sq. units)
11.	9	12		
12.	5	4		
13.		6	18π	
14.	10			220π
15.	4		112π	

11. 108π, 189π
12. 20π, 45π
13. 3, 27π
14. 12, 120π
15. 28, 128π
16. 36π√5 = 253 sq. ft., or 4.2 hides;
    5 hides are necessary
17. 16 ½" × 16 ½"
18. S = 368 sq. ft.; 3(368 ÷ 250) ≈ 4.4; 5 gal.

▶ B. Exercises

16. Tepees are made with buffalo hides in the shape of a cone and have dirt floors. One buffalo hide provides 60 square feet of leather. How many hides are necessary to make a tepee that is 12 feet high and 12 feet in diameter?

17. Give the dimensions of the square piece of paper needed to make the dunce's cap shown below.

18. How much paint is needed to paint the steeple of Heritage Bible Church if one gallon covers 250 square feet per coat? The steeple needs three coats.

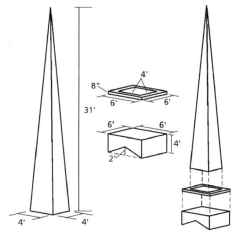

19.

1. $S = L + B,$ $\quad L = \frac{1}{2}pl$	1. Surface area of pyramid
2. $B = s^2$	2. Area of Square Postulate
3. $p = 4s$	3. Perimeter of square
4. $L = \frac{1}{2}(4s)l = 2sl$	4. Substitution (step 3 into 1)
5. $S = 2sl + s^2$	5. Substitution (steps 2 and 4 into 1)
6. $S = s(2l + s)$	6. Distributive property

20. $S = L + A_{bases} = 247\pi + 193\pi = 440\pi$ cm^2

21. Using the right triangle, shown dotted, the height and radius are equal to half the diagonal of the square $H = r = 3\sqrt{2}$; L (2 cones) $= 2\pi rl = 2\pi(3\sqrt{2})(6) = 36\pi\sqrt{2}$ m^2 (the surface area of the solid consists of the combined lateral surface areas [L] of these two cones).

22. B [2.2]

23. C [2.3]

24. A [2.1]

25. D [2.3]

---

19. Derive and prove a factored formula for the surface area of a right pyramid with a square base, where l = slant height and s = length of a side of the square.

▶ C. Exercises

20. Slice a cone parallel to its base to obtain a *frustum* of the cone. Find the total surface area of the frustum. (*Hint:* The part removed is proportional to the whole.)

21. Rotate a square about one of its diagonals to form a conical figure. If one side of the square is 6 m, what is the surface area of the solid?

■ Cumulative Review

Match. Assume that each pair of rays has at least one point in common. Use each answer once.

22. segment   A. union of two collinear rays

23. angle   B. intersection of two collinear rays

24. line   C. union of two noncollinear rays

25. point   D. intersection of two noncollinear rays

8.8 Surface Areas of Polyhedra and Spheres

You are now ready to find surface areas for two more polyhedra and spheres.

Galena crystals from Galena, Kansas, form in cubes (isometric).

Definition

A **sphere** is the set of all points in space equidistant from a given point.

The *center* of the sphere is the given point that is used as a reference to all other points of the sphere. The *radius* of a sphere is a segment that connects the center of the sphere to any point of the sphere. A plane that passes through the center of the sphere intersects it in a *great circle*. The great circle and its sphere have the same radius.

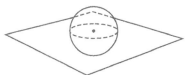

Figure 8.38

Figure 8.39 shows an example of a great circle. Two great circles separate the sphere into four sections, or *lunes*. (You can think of an orange section as a lune.)

Figure 8.39

Objectives

1. To state and apply the formula for surface area of a sphere.
2. To name the regular polyhedra.
3. To state and apply the formulas for surface area of regular polyhedra.

Vocabulary

great circle
lune
Platonic solid
regular polyhedron

Assignment

- Intuitive: 1-16, 25-29, and Practice (*Activities Manual*)
- Standard: 1-20, 25-29, and Platonic Solids in Detail (*Activities Manual*)
- Rigorous: 5-29 and Platonic Solids in Detail (*Activities Manual*)

Flash

Isometric refers to axes of equal (*iso*) length (*metric*). The town of Galena, Kansas, is named for its mineral deposits.

Presentation

Review the various parts of the sphere. The easiest proof of the formula for the surface area of a sphere requires calculus. Since you cannot prove the formula for the students, help them conceptualize the formula in other ways. After explaining the formula, discuss example 1, which shows how to calculate the surface area of a sphere using the formula.

Motivational Idea. Take a soft spherical object (racquetball or foam-rubber ball) and dip it into water. While it is wet, roll it along the chalkboard until it makes one rotation. Then ask the students to tell what type of figure was formed on the chalkboard (*rectangle*). Trace around the rectangle so that you can still see it after the water dries. The width is approxi-

mately the diameter of the sphere, $2r$, and the length is the circumference of the sphere, $2\pi r$. If this rectangle roughly represents the surface area of the sphere, you can find the area by multiplying the length by the width. This is the formula for the surface area of a sphere.

Motivational Idea. Use a rubber ball and cord to compare the surface area of a sphere to the area of four great circles. Cut the ball carefully into two hemispheres. Insert a nail into one of them and wrap the cord around the nail. When the great circle (and its interior) is completely covered, make a mark on the cord with a pen. Step two is to double the length of the cord. Then use the cord to cover the hemisphere. It should exactly cover it, indicating an

area of $2\pi r^2$ for the hemisphere or an area of $4\pi r^2$ for a sphere.

Next, define regular polyhedron. There are three properties that must be satisfied in order for a polyhedron to be classified as regular.

1. It must be convex.
2. The faces must all be congruent polygons.
3. The same number of edges must meet at each vertex.

Students should readily see that a regular polyhedron with n faces has a surface area of $S = nA$, where A is the area of one face.

Resources

- *Visual Packet,* Surface Area. Focus on the portions of the poster about spheres and polyhedra.
- *Activities Manual,* Platonic Solids in Detail. Gives methods for building models of Platonic solids and develops more concepts about them.
- *Activities Manual,* Practice
- *Test Packet,* Quiz 4, Chapter 8 covers Sections 8.6 and 8.8.

Reading and Writing Mathematics

1. Have the student find out what a trihedral angle is and sketch one. ***an angle formed by three planes meeting in one point***

2. What is a central trihedral angle? ***trihedral angle with vertex at the center of a sphere***
3. What kind of intersection will result between a central trihedral angle and the surface of a sphere? ***a spherical triangle***

Additional Problems

1. Find the surface area of a sphere whose diameter is 16 m. ***256π m²***
2. Find the surface area of a sphere whose circumference is 240π cm. ***$57,600\pi$ cm²***
3. Find the surface area of a lune with a central angle of 45 on a sphere of radius 4 feet. ***8π ft.²***

In the diagram, all four lunes are the same size: each is one quarter of the sphere. It can be proved that the area of a great circle is numerically the same as the surface area of one of these four lunes. This proof is beyond the scope of high school geometry. Since the formula for the area of a great circle with radius r is πr^2, the surface area of each of the four lunes is also πr^2. Therefore, the surface area of the sphere is $4\pi r^2$.

Theorem 8.18
The *surface area of a sphere* is 4π times the square of the radius: $S = 4\pi r^2$.

EXAMPLE 1 Find the surface area of the following sphere.

Answer $S = 4\pi r^2$
$S = 4\pi 8^2$
$S = 256\pi$ square units ≈ 804 sq. units

Figure 8.40

Just as a regular polygon can be inscribed in a circle, so a regular polyhedron can be inscribed in a sphere.

Definition

A **regular polyhedron** is a polyhedron with faces bounded by congruent regular polygons and with the same number of faces intersecting at each vertex.

A regular hexahedron is a cube, made up of six congruent regular quadrilaterals (squares). Four other regular polyhedra are shown below.

Regular hexahedron (cube)
Figure 8.41

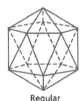

Regular tetrahedron   Regular octahedron   Regular dodecahedron   Regular icosahedron   *Figure 8.42*

Tips

Ex. 21. Another possible answer is $S = 3e^2 \sqrt{25 + 10\sqrt{5}}$. Also, using trigonometry (Chapter 14), $S = 15e^2 \cot 36$.

Ex. 22. The surface areas are $6e^2$ for the cube, $\frac{3}{2}\pi e^2$ (or $4.7e^2$) for the cylinder, and πe^2 (or $3.14e^2$) for the sphere. The sphere has the least.

Ex. 23. $CD = 8 + 5 = 13$ in. Take point E 5 inches above the table on the radius shown in circle C, then $CE = 8 - 5 = 3$ in. Since $x^2 + 3^2 = 13^2$, $x^2 = 160$ and $x = 4\sqrt{10} \approx 12.65$ inches.

Ex. 24. $A_{\text{circle}} = \pi r^2 = 576\pi$. So $r^2 = 576$ or $r = 24$. Thus, $x^2 + 24^2 = 26^2$ by the Pythagorean theorem, and $x^2 + 576 = 676$. Subtracting, $x^2 = 100$, or $x = 10$ inches from the center.

Ex. 29. Circle is incorrect since cylinders may be oval or even square. ■

The five regular polyhedra shown are the only possible regular polyhedra. Each of these polyhedra determines a convex solid called a *Platonic solid*. Since Plato discovered that these were the only regular polyhedra, they were given the name *Platonic solids* in his honor.

Do you remember the formula for the area of a regular polygon? Since all the faces of a regular polyhedron are congruent, it is easy to find the surface area.

Theorem 8.19

The *surface area of a regular polyhedron* is the product of the number of faces and the area of one face: $S = nA$.

EXAMPLE 2	Blake sells calendars in the shape of a regular dodecahedron. To make sure the calendar for a month would fit on a side, he designed the area of one face to cover 3 square inches. Find the total surface area.
Answer	The dodecahedron has 12 sides, so $S = nA = 12 \cdot 3 = 36$ square inches.

▶ **A. Exercises**

Find the total surface area of each sphere.

1.

2.

3.

4. The surface area of a sphere is 676π square feet. What is the length of its diameter?

5. The surface area of a sphere is 320π square yards. What is the length of its radius?

	Regular polyhedron	Number of faces	Number of edges	Number of vertices
6.	tetrahedron			
7.	dodecahedron			
8.	hexahedron			
9.	octahedron			
10.	icosahedron			

4. The surface area of a sphere is 6.4 times $10^7\pi$ mi.^{2}. What is its diameter? What sphere could this be? ***8000 mi., the earth***

5. Find the surface area of a regular octahedron with edge 5 mm. Each face is an equilateral triangle. ***$50\sqrt{3}$ mm^2***

Answers

1. 64π sq. units
2. 400π sq. units
3. 20π sq. units
4. 26 ft.
5. $4\sqrt{5}$ sq. yd. ≈ 8.94
6. tetrahedron, 4, 6, 4
7. dodecahedron, 12, 30, 20
8. hexahedron, 6, 12, 8
9. octahedron, 8, 12, 6
10. icosahedron, 20, 30, 12

11. 80 sq. inches
12. 54 sq. feet
13. $180\sqrt{3}$ sq. cm
14. $9\sqrt{3}$ sq. meters
15. 4620 sq. ft.
16. 249.6 sq. inches
17. 18 cm
18. 75.4 gal.
19.

1. $S = 4\pi r^2$	1. Surface area of sphere
2. $d = 2r$	2. Diameter is twice radius
3. $r = \frac{d}{2}$	3. Multiplication property of equality
4. $S = 4\pi \left(\frac{d}{2}\right)^2 =$ $4\pi \frac{d^2}{4} = \pi d^2$	4. Substitution (step 3 into 1)

20.

1. $S = n \cdot A$	1. Surface area of regular polyhedron
2. $A = \frac{1}{2} ap$	2. Area of regular polygon
3. $S = \frac{1}{2} nap$	3. Substitution

21. tetrahedron: $S = e^2 \sqrt{3}$;
     hexahedron: $S = 6e^2$;
     octahedron: $S = 2e^2 \sqrt{3}$;
     dodecahedron: $S = 6ap$ or $30ae$;
     icosahedron: $S = 5e^2 \sqrt{3}$
22. sphere
23. $4\sqrt{10}$ or about 12.65 inches

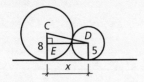

Give the surface area of each regular polyhedron.
11. An octahedron with one face of area 10 square inches
12. A hexahedron with an edge 3 feet long
13. An icosahedron with an edge six centimeters long
14. A tetrahedron with an edge three meters long
15. A dodecahedron with an edge fourteen feet long and an apothem for one face eleven feet long

▶ **B. Exercises**

16. What is the surface area of a soccer ball that has a circumference of 28 inches?
17. What is the diameter of a softball that has a surface area of 324π square centimeters?
18. If the maintenance men are going to paint a spherical water tower whose radius is 30 feet and each gallon of paint covers 150 square feet of metal, how many gallons of paint must they have to give the tower one coat of paint?
19. Prove that for a sphere $S = \pi d^2$.
20. Prove that for a regular polyhedron $S = \frac{1}{2} nap$, where n is the number of faces.

▶ **C. Exercises**

21. For each of the five regular polyhedra, give the simplest formula that you can for its surface area. Use e for the length of one edge.
22. If a cube has edge e, a cylinder has diameter and height e, and a sphere has diameter e, which has the least surface area?
23. Two spherical balls are sitting on a table touching each other. If their radii are 8 inches and 5 inches, how far apart are their points of contact with the table?

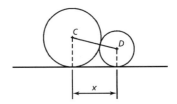

24. If a sphere has a radius of 26 inches, how far from the center should a plane cut through the sphere to give a circle whose area is 576π in.^{2}?

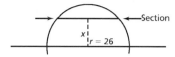

Cumulative Review

Identify each set by name.

25. The intersection of all faces of a polyhedron

26. The intersection of two sides of a triangle

27. The intersection of two faces of a tetrahedron

28. The intersection of a right pyramid with a plane containing the altitude of the pyramid

29. The intersection of the lateral surface of a cylinder with a plane parallel to the bases

24. 10 inches from the center

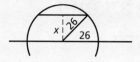

25. $\varnothing$ [2.8]
26. vertex (point) [2.3]
27. edge (segment) [2.7]
28. triangle [2.6]
29. simple closed curve [2.6]

Geometry and Scripture

Objectives

1. To identify area measures given in the Bible and survey methods used to measure land areas in ancient times.
2. To find dimensions for various objects in the tabernacle and to calculate the areas of these items.

Answers

1. 144
2. plowing
3. sowing
4. 275 shekels
5. 12,000 furlongs by 12,000 furlongs; 144,000,000 sq. furlongs

Geometry and Scripture

You know that twelve inches is equal to one foot. However, twelve square inches is not the same as one square foot. This concept is not hard to understand, but it can be confusing when you are converting units.

1. How many square inches are in one square foot?

The Jews measured areas differently depending upon what was being measured. A field was measured by stating either the number of yokes of oxen needed for plowing it or the amount of seed needed for sowing it.

Which method is used in each verse?

2. I Samuel 14:14

3. Isaiah 5:10

4. If a man sanctified a field using five and a half homers of barley, what would the land's value be (Lev. 27:16)?

You can understand why most things could not be measured the way fields were measured. Does a yoke of oxen plow a city or a curtain? Would you sow a city or a curtain with seed? In such cases dimensions were given.

5. Review the dimensions given for New Jerusalem. Give the dimensions of the area that the city will cover. How many square furlongs will that be?

Presentation

This study surveys the concept of area in the Bible. Units of area occur only twice in Scripture as mentioned in the study (#2 and #3). The unit is called an acre in KJV English but is not the same as a modern acre. The word refers to the amount of seed needed for sowing a field or the number of pairs of oxen needed to harvest a field. For measuring plane objects other than fields, people typically stated the length and width in linear units separately. Examples of this method are also given in the study. ■

Read Exodus 36, which describes the curtains for the tabernacle.

6. Give the dimensions of each linen curtain (vv. 8-13).

7. How many square cubits of material were used for each curtain? All together?

8. Give the dimensions of each goat-hair curtain (vv. 14-18).

9. How many square cubits were there in each curtain? All together?

> **HIGHER PLANE:** Convert the dimensions in questions 5, 6, and 8 to modern units (use the table on page 113).

First Samuel 14:14 is a key verse since it defines the term *acre*. It is one of only two Bible verses that use this area measurement. In the context, the purpose of including the measurement is to show the courage and power of Jonathan and his armourbearer in defeating twenty enemies in a small open area. All twenty men had freedom of movement to attack the valiant pair from all sides.

> ### Line upon Line
> AND THAT FIRST SLAUGHTER, which Jonathan and his armourbearer made, was about twenty men, within as it were an half acre of land, which a yoke of oxen might plow.
>
> **I SAMUEL 14:14**

6. 28 cubits × 4 cubits
7. 112 square cubits; 1120 square cubits
8. 30 cubits × 4 cubits
9. 120 square cubits; 1320 square cubits

Higher Plane

New Jerusalem 1379 × 1379 mi. (1,901,641 sq. mi.)

linen curtain 42 × 6 ft. (252 sq. ft.)

goat-hair curtain 45 × 6 ft. (270 sq. ft.)

Review

Objectives

To help students prepare for evaluation.

Vocabulary

See Appendix A.

Assignment

- Intuitive: 1-30
- Standard: 1-30
- Rigorous: 1-30

Resources

- *Activities Manual*, Cumulative Review
- *Activities Manual*, Terms and Symbols
- *Test Packet*, Chapter 8 Exam

Answers

1. 153 sq. units
2. 576 sq. units
3. 7 sq. units
4. $x^3 - 9x^2$ sq. units
5. 72 sq. units
6. 208 sq. units
7. 15 sq. units
8. 228 sq. units
9. $81\sqrt{3}$ sq. units
10. 96 sq. units
11. 102 sq. units
12. 225π sq. units
13. 81π sq. units
14. 36π sq. units
15. $39 + \frac{1}{2}\pi$
16. 139.5 sq. units
17. $2904\sqrt{3}$ sq. units (or 5029.9)
18. 784π sq. units
19. 140 sq. units
20. $144\sqrt{3}$ sq. units

In the following exercises, b = base length, h = height, A = area, H = altitude, L = lateral area, l = slant height, r = radius, c = circumference, d = diameter length, a = apothem, and s = side length.

Draw pictures and find the following areas (measurements are in units).
1. Rectangle with $b = 17$ and $h = 9$
2. Square with $s = 24$
3. Square with $s = \sqrt{7}$
4. Rectangle with $b = x^2$ and $h = x - 9$
5. Parallelogram with $b = 12$ and $h = 6$
6. Parallelogram with $b = 26$ and $h = 8$
7. Triangle with $b = 6$ and $h = 5$
8. Triangle with $b = 19$ and $h = 24$
9. Equilateral triangle with $s = 18$
10. Trapezoid with $b_1 = 10$, $b_2 = 14$, $h = 8$
11. Trapezoid with $b_1 = 24$, $b_2 = 10$, $h = 6$
12. Circle with $r = 15$
13. Circle with $c = 18\pi$
14. Circle with $d = 12$
15.

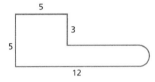

16. Regular pentagon with $s = 9$ and $a = 6.2$
17. Regular hexagon with $s = 44$

Find the surface area of each figure.
18. Sphere with $r = 14$
19. Regular icosahedron with a face covering 7 square units
20. Regular dodecahedron with $s = 2\sqrt{3}$ and $a = 2.4$

Presentation

One important goal of a teacher is to see the students conceptualize the ideas being studied. A student who has the concept clearly in mind will not need to rely on rote memory for definitions or statements of theorems. As a general rule, students with greater mathematical ability will conceptualize rapidly with little drill. In fact, drill will bore them and have a negative effect. They need to be challenged to stretch themselves. At the other end of the mathematical ability spectrum are students who can conceptualize only after much drill.

Motivational Idea. Encourage students to express each idea in their own words or with a sketch. For area formulas, emphasize the value of understanding where the formulas come from. Students should try to explain why a formula works rather than just repeating it. These "big pictures" greatly reduce what must be memorized. ∎

Find the lateral surface area and the total surface area for each surface below.

21. A right prism having a square base with $s = 8$ and $H = 22$
22. A right prism having a rhombus as a base with $H = 29$ and diagonals of lengths 8 and 13
23. A right circular cylinder with $d = 18$ and $H = 36$
24. Equilateral triangular pyramid with $b = 34$ and $l = 43$
25. A right circular cone with $r = 6$ and $l = 13$
26. Give the meaning of area.
27. In any regular polygon, why must the base angles of the triangles formed by consecutive radii be congruent?
28. Prove that for a sphere $S = cd$.
29. Determine the altitude of a regular tetrahedron if the edge has length s.

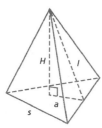

30. Explain the mathematical significance of I Samuel 14:14.

21. $L = 704$ sq. units; $S = 832$ sq. units
22. $L = 885.3$ sq. units; $S = 989.3$ sq. units
23. $L = 648\pi$ sq. units; $S = 810\pi$ sq. units
24. $L = 2193$ sq. units; $S = 2193 + 289\sqrt{3} \approx 2694$ sq. units
25. $L = 78\pi$ sq. units; $S = 114\pi$ sq. units
26. The number of square units needed to cover a region
27. The triangles are isosceles (radii congruent), and the Isosceles Triangle Theorem guarantees congruent base angles.
28.

Statement	Reason
1. Sphere	1. Given
2. $S = 4\pi r^2$	2. Surface area of sphere
3. $S = (2\pi r)(2r)$	3. Associative property of multiplication
4. $c = 2\pi r$	4. Circumference of great circle
5. $d = 2r$	5. Diameter is twice radius
6. $S = cd$	6. Substitution (steps 4 and 5 into 3)

29. For each triangular face, $h = \frac{\sqrt{3}}{2}s$ and $a = \frac{\sqrt{3}}{6}s$. (Also, the slant height of the pyramid [l] is the same as the height of the triangle [h].)

By Pythagorean theorem: $H^2 + a^2 = h^2$
$H^2 = h^2 - a^2 = \left(\frac{\sqrt{3}}{2}s\right)^2 - \left(\frac{\sqrt{3}}{6}s\right)^2 = \frac{3}{4}s^2 - \frac{3}{36}s^2 = \frac{2}{3}s^2, H = \frac{\sqrt{6}}{3}s$

30. This is one of only two verses that use units of area and it is the only one that defines *acre*. It illustrates that the typical work for a yoke of oxen was the common unit for measuring fields in Bible times. It also shows the valor of Jonathan and his armourbearer in defending a half acre against twenty men.

9 Circles

Circles

Umbrellas probably originated in the Orient, perhaps in ancient China.

The earliest ones were constructed of paper and were made waterproof by the application of a substance such as linseed oil. The Chinese decorated their umbrellas with elaborate designs, usually of some scene in nature. In China, umbrellas were actually a sort of status symbol—an indication of a person's rank in society.

Umbrellas are excellent examples of radial symmetry, the geometric concept of an object's having congruent parts around a central axis. Each congruent section of an umbrella radiates from the center of the umbrella to form a circle.

The starfish and the sand dollar also illustrate radial symmetry. These fascinating sea creatures clearly show God's use of geometry in His creation. But such symmetry is only a glimpse into the wonders of God's creation (Isa. 55:8): "For my thoughts are not your thoughts, neither are your ways my ways, saith the Lord." Have you given your Creator complete control of your life?

After this chapter you should be able to

1. define and correctly use terms related to circles.
2. use the Law of Contradiction to do an indirect proof.
3. determine arc measures using central or inscribed angles.
4. determine angle measures between intersecting secant and/or tangent lines.
5. find areas and perimeters of segments and sectors.
6. prove relationships involving circles.
7. construct figures using circles.

365

Overview

This chapter focuses on circles, including related segments (chords) and lines (secants and tangents). After developing theorems about the angles determined by such lines, students learn theorems about arcs and the angles that intercept them. The chapter concludes with a look at constructions related to circles. You may need two days on sections that contain a large amount of material.

Check whether you are on schedule for the year. If you need to catch up, this is a good time to decide what to omit. Count the number of sections you need to make up, and then decide whether you will gain enough time by omitting Chapter 14, and even Chapter 12 if necessary. If you think more cuts will be needed, look through Sections 9.4, 9.5, 9.7, 10.3, 10.4, and 10.8 to identify those portions least important to you. If you decide to omit any portions from Chapter 9, adapt your tests (or do not give a test and just quiz on the parts you cover).

Bulletin Board Idea
Title a bulletin board *The Inspiration of the Circle*. Show photos of such things as a truck with wheels shown prominently, a set of gears, a fan (circular motion), a spool of thread, a fishing reel. Be creative—try to find examples in unusual or unexpected places. Add to the board as students come up with ideas.

Flash
This Oriental umbrella shows circles and radii. The supports form the lateral edge of a pyramid with a regular 44-gon base.

Circles and Chords

Objectives

1. To review sets of points associated with a circle.
2. To identify and prove relationships and theorems for congruent circles and chords.

Vocabulary
congruent circles

Assignment
- Intuitive: 1-16, 26-30
- Standard: 1-20, 22, 26-30
- Rigorous: 5-30

Resources
- *Visual Packet,* Circles. This poster reviews terms from Section 2.4.
- *Activities Manual,* Value of π in Brief. Experiments to determine the value of π.

Reading and Writing Mathematics
Have the students look up the definition of "curvature of a circle," give a definition, and compare curvature to the radius of a circle. *Curvature is defined as $\frac{1}{r}$, where r is the radius. It measures the angular rotation of the tangent line per unit length of arc. The smaller the circle, the higher the curvature.*

9.1 Circles and Chords

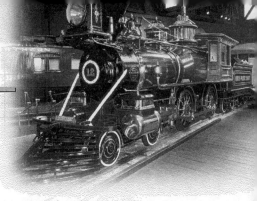

The wheel is one of many applications of circles. If a point revolves around a circle, the point never reaches an end. Circles are often used to represent eternity because the point can continue around forever. You, too, are an eternal being and will spend eternity in heaven or hell. Accept Jesus Christ as your Savior and look forward to a glorious eternity in heaven. First John 5:11-13 explains how you can know for sure that your eternal life will be spent in heaven with God.

The rod joining the back wheels of a locomotive shows a portion of a secant line. The train shown is at the Railroad Museum in Sacramento, California.

Before studying the circle in more detail, review the definitions on page 56 in Chapter 2. Make sure that you understand each definition.

In ⊙C the center is C, and the circle has radius $\overline{CX}$ and a chord $\overline{LM}$. $\overline{QR}$ is a diameter, and $\overset{\frown}{LM}$ is an arc of the circle. From the definition of circle, you can clearly see that all radii of a circle are congruent. What are congruent circles?

Figure 9.1

Definition

Congruent circles are circles whose radii are congruent.

Figure 9.2

Presentation

The section begins with a discussion about eternity and spiritual consequences. Do not neglect this opportunity to discuss eternal issues with your students.

Review the definitions given on page 56 (Chapter 2). It is important that you review these basics since the entire chapter builds on them. Remind students that congruent circles have congruent radii. Concentric circles have the same center but different lengths for their radii, so they are not congruent.

Common Student Error. The radius, the chord, and the diameter are segments associated with a circle but are not part of the circle. They may have endpoints on the circle and hence share a point or two with the circle;

however, the circle is the set of points at a distance equal to the radius from a fixed point called the center. Remember that the area of a circle is short for the area of a circular region. The circle itself is a curve, with no area.

Motivational Idea. Discuss the Chord Postulate and then illustrate Theorem 9.1 by having the students construct several circles with compasses. Instruct them to draw in several chords that are perpendicular to a radius of the circle. Have them measure a chord and observe that it is bisected by the radius if constructed in this manner. This type of activity is not a proof but is an illustration of the concept. Illustrations usually make the statement more believable and easier for students to remember.

If you know that $\overline{HI} \cong \overline{LM}$, then you know that $\odot H \cong \odot L$. In this section we will examine one postulate and three theorems about chords and circles.

Postulate 9.1
Chord Postulate. If a line intersects the interior of a circle, then it contains a chord of the circle.

Theorem 9.1
In a circle, if a radius is perpendicular to a chord of a circle, then it bisects the chord.

> **Given:** $\odot O$ with radius $\overline{OC}$ and chord $\overline{AB}$; $\overline{OC} \perp \overline{AB}$
> **Prove:** $\overline{OC}$ bisects $\overline{AB}$

Figure 9.3

STATEMENTS	REASONS
1. $\odot O$ with radius $\overline{OC}$ and chord $\overline{AB}$; $\overline{OC} \perp \overline{AB}$	1. Given
2. Draw radii $\overline{OA}$ and $\overline{OB}$	2. Auxiliary lines
3. $\angle ODA$ and $\angle ODB$ are right angles	3. Definition of perpendicular lines
4. $\triangle ODA$ and $\triangle ODB$ are right triangles	4. Definition of right triangles
5. $\overline{OA} \cong \overline{OB}$	5. Radii of a circle are congruent
6. $\overline{OD} \cong \overline{OD}$	6. Reflexive property of congruent segments
7. $\triangle ODA \cong \triangle ODB$	7. HL
8. $\overline{AD} \cong \overline{BD}$	8. Definition of congruent triangles
9. $AD = BD$	9. Definition of congruent segments
10. D is the midpoint of $\overline{AB}$	10. Definition of midpoint
11. $\overline{OC}$ bisects $\overline{AB}$	11. Definition of segment bisector
12. If $\overline{OC} \perp \overline{AB}$, then $\overline{OC}$ bisects $\overline{AB}$	12. Law of Deduction

Additional Problems

1. Given $\odot M$ with radius 6 cm and $\odot N$ with radius 4 cm as shown in the diagram, complete each statement:

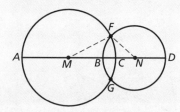

a) If $BC = 1$ cm, then find CN. **3 cm**
b) If $BC = 1$ cm, then find the perimeter of $\triangle MNF$. **19 cm**
c) If $BC = 2$ cm, then find AD. **18 cm**
d) If $BC = 2$ cm, then find AB. **10 cm**

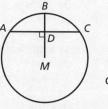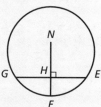

2. *Given:* $AM = GN$, $DM = HN$, $GE = 12$
   Find: AD **6 units**
3. Given $AC = 8$ units, $GE = 8$ units, $DM = 3$ units, $HN = 3$ units, show $AM = GN$. **Radii perpendicular to a chord bisect it; thus, $AD = GH = 4$; by LL $\triangle ADM \cong \triangle GHN$, $\overline{AM} \cong \overline{GN}$, and $AM = GN$**
4. Given $\odot M \cong \odot N$, $DM = HN$, $AD = 5x + 4$ units, $GE = 18$ units, find x. **$2(5x + 4) = 18$; $x = 1$**

(continued)

Tips

This section shows the proofs of two theorems similar to those that the students will be required to prove. Go through these two carefully in class, and make sure that the students understand the procedures used. The theorems about the chords of circles give some useful results that let us apply congruent triangles and the Pythagorean theorem for the solution of problems.

The review questions provide a summary of types of congruence. The summary provides a comparison and shows that congruent segments and angles are the foundation for defining the other types of congruence.

Ex. 30. Some students may state the "triangulation criterion" for congruence rather than the original definition (Section 6.3). If you have deemphasized the actual definition, you may accept this answer. ∎

5. *Prove:* If the center of a circle is equidistant from the sides of an inscribed triangle, the triangle is equilateral.

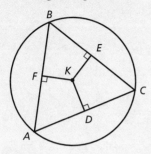

1. Center *K* is equidistant from the sides of inscribed △*ABC*	1. Given
2. *KF* = *KE* = *KD*	2. Definition of equidistant
3. $\overline{AB} \cong \overline{BC}$; $\overline{BC} \cong \overline{AC}$; $\overline{AB} \cong \overline{AC}$	3. In a circle, if two chords are the same distance from the center, they are congruent
4. △*ABC* is equilateral	4. Definition of equilateral triangle
5. If the center of ⊙*K* is equidistant from the sides of △*ABC*, then △*ABC* is equilateral	5. Law of Deduction

Here is another theorem about chords.

Theorem 9.2

In a circle or in congruent circles, if two chords are the same distance from the center(s), the chords are congruent.

Given: ⊙*A* ≅ ⊙*B*; $\overleftrightarrow{AZ} \perp \overleftrightarrow{QR}$; $\overleftrightarrow{BU} \perp \overleftrightarrow{PN}$; *AX* = *BY*
Prove: $\overline{QR} \cong \overline{PN}$

Figure 9.4

STATEMENTS	REASONS
1. ⊙*A* ≅ ⊙*B*; $\overleftrightarrow{AZ} \perp \overleftrightarrow{QR}$; $\overleftrightarrow{BU} \perp \overleftrightarrow{PN}$; *AX* = *BY*	**1.** Given
2. $\overline{AX} \cong \overline{BY}$	**2.** Definition of congruent segments
3. Draw $\overline{AQ}$ and $\overline{BP}$	**3.** Line Postulate
4. $\overline{AQ} \cong \overline{BP}$	**4.** Definition of congruent circles
5. △*AQX* ≅ △*BPY*	**5.** HL
6. $\overline{QX} \cong \overline{PY}$	**6.** Definition of congruent triangles
7. *QX* = *PY*	**7.** Definition of congruent segments
8. $\overleftrightarrow{AZ}$ bisects $\overline{QR}$; $\overleftrightarrow{BU}$ bisects $\overline{PN}$	**8.** A radius perpendicular to a chord bisects the chord
9. *X* is the midpoint of $\overline{QR}$; *Y* is the midpoint of $\overline{PN}$	**9.** Definition of segment bisector
10. $QX = \frac{1}{2}QR$; $PY = \frac{1}{2}PN$	**10.** Midpoint Theorem
11. $\frac{1}{2}QR = \frac{1}{2}PN$	**11.** Substitution (step 10 into 7)
12. *QR* = *PN*	**12.** Multiplication property of equality
13. $\overline{QR} \cong \overline{PN}$	**13.** Definition of congruent segments
14. If $\overleftrightarrow{AZ} \perp \overleftrightarrow{QR}$, $\overleftrightarrow{BU} \perp \overleftrightarrow{PN}$, and *AX* = *BY*, then $\overline{QR} \cong \overline{PN}$	**14.** Law of Deduction

The converse of this theorem is also true. It is stated here, and the proof will be done as an exercise.

> **Theorem 9.3**
> In a circle or in congruent circles, if two chords are congruent, then they are the same distance from the center(s).

▶ **A. Exercises**

Use the figure for exercises 1-4.
1. Name the circle, the center of the circle, and a diameter.
2. Name two chords.
3. Name three radii.
4. Name all the arcs.

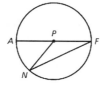

Find the indicated measures. Use the figure for exercises 5-16.

5. *Given:* $\overline{AG} \cong \overline{AC}$; $BE = 12$ units
   Find: IF

6. *Given:* $BE = 18$ units
   Find: BC

7. *Given:* $IF = 16$ units; $BE = 16$ units; $AC = 6$ units
   Find: AG

8. *Given:* $AD = 4$ units
   Find: AH

9. *Given:* $AC = 3$ units; $BE = 8$ units
   Find: AB

10. *Given:* $GH = 6$ units; $IG = 12$ units
    Find: HF

11. *Given:* $\overline{BE} \cong \overline{IF}$; $BC = 4$ units; $AB = 7$ units
    Find: AG

12. *Given:* $\overline{AG} \cong \overline{AC}$; $IG = 10$ units
    Find: BE

13. *Given:* $AI = 8$ units; $AG = 6$ units
    Find: IF

14. *Given:* $\overline{AC} \cong \overline{AG}$; $CE = 3x + 5$ units; $GI = 8$ units
    Find: x

15. *Given:* $\overline{BE} \cong \overline{IF}$; $AC = 2x + 6$ units; $AG = 4x - 10$ units
    Find: AC

16. *Given:* $\overline{AC} \cong \overline{AG}$; $IF = x^2 + 7x - 12$ units; $BE = x^2 + 3x + 8$ units
    Find: BC

Answers
1. $\odot P$, P, $\overline{AF}$
2. $\overline{AF}$, $\overline{NF}$
3. $\overline{PA}$, $\overline{PN}$, $\overline{PF}$
4. $\overarc{AF}$, $\overarc{AN}$, $\overarc{NF}$, $\overarc{ANF}$, $\overarc{AFN}$, $\overarc{FAN}$, $\odot P$
5. 12 units
6. 9 units
7. 6 units
8. 4 units
9. 5 units
10. $6\sqrt{5}$ units
11. $\sqrt{33}$ units
12. 20 units
13. $4\sqrt{7}$ units
14. 1 unit
15. 22 units
16. 24 units
17.

1. $\odot D$ with $\overleftrightarrow{DB} \perp \overleftrightarrow{AC}$; $\overleftrightarrow{DF} \perp \overleftrightarrow{GE}$; $\overline{BD} \cong \overline{DF}$	1. Given
2. $BD = DF$	2. Definition of congruent segments
3. $\overline{AC} \cong \overline{EG}$	3. Chords equidistant from center are congruent
4. $\overline{AD} \cong \overline{DE} \cong$ $\overline{CD} \cong \overline{DG}$	4. Radii of a circle are congruent
5. $\triangle ADC \cong \triangle GDE$	5. SSS
6. $\angle CAD \cong \angle DGE$	6. Definition of congruent triangles

18.

1. $\odot D$ with $\overleftrightarrow{DB} \perp \overleftrightarrow{AC}$	1. Given
2. $\angle ABD$ and $\angle CBD$ are right angles	2. Definition of perpendicular
3. $\triangle ABD$ and $\triangle CBD$ are right triangles	3. Definition of right triangle
4. $\overline{AD} \cong \overline{CD}$	4. Radii of a circle are congruent
5. $\overline{BD} \cong \overline{BD}$	5. Reflexive property of congruent segments
6. $\triangle ADB \cong \triangle CDB$	6. HL

19.

1. $\odot D$ with $\overleftrightarrow{DB} \perp \overleftrightarrow{AC}$; $\overleftrightarrow{DF} \perp \overleftrightarrow{GE}$; $\overline{AC} \cong \overline{GE}$	1. Given
2. $BD = FD$	2. Congruent chords are equidistant from the center
3. $\overline{BD} \cong \overline{FD}$	3. Definition of congruent segments
4. $\overline{CD} \cong \overline{DG}$	4. Radii of a circle are congruent
5. $\angle DBC$ and $\angle DFG$ are right angles	5. Definition of perpendicular
6. $\triangle DBC$ and $\triangle DFG$ are right triangles	6. Definition of right triangle
7. $\triangle DBC \cong \triangle DFG$	7. HL

20.

1. ⊙X with $\overleftrightarrow{XA} \perp \overleftrightarrow{LM}$; $\overleftrightarrow{XB} \perp \overleftrightarrow{MN}$; $\overline{XA} \cong \overline{XB}$	1. Given
2. $XA = XB$	2. Definition of congruent segments
3. $\overline{LM} \cong \overline{MN}$	3. Chords equidistant from center are congruent
4. △LNM is an isosceles triangle	4. Definition of isosceles triangle

21.

1. ⊙M with $\overleftrightarrow{MQ} \perp \overleftrightarrow{PR}$; $\overleftrightarrow{MT} \perp \overleftrightarrow{PS}$; ∠RPM ≅ ∠SPM	1. Given
2. ∠MQP and ∠MTP are right angles	2. Definition of perpendicular
3. △MQP and △MTP are right triangles	3. Definition of right triangle
4. $\overline{MP} \cong \overline{MP}$	4. Reflexive property of congruent segments
5. △MQP ≅ △MTP	5. HA
6. $\overline{PQ} \cong \overline{PT}$	6. Definition of congruent triangles
7. $PQ = PT$	7. Definition of congruent segments
8. $\overline{MQ}$ bisects $\overline{PR}$ (at midpoint Q); $\overline{MT}$ bisects $\overline{PS}$ (at midpoint T)	8. Radius perpendicular to chord bisects chord (definition of segment bisector)
9. $PQ = \frac{1}{2}PR$; $PT = \frac{1}{2}PS$	9. Midpoint Theorem
10. $\frac{1}{2}PR = \frac{1}{2}PS$	10. Substitution (step 9 into 7)
11. $PR = PS$	11. Multiplication property of equality
12. $\overline{PR} \cong \overline{PS}$	12. Definition of congruent segments

22.

1. $\overleftrightarrow{GF}$ is the perpendicular bisector of chord $\overline{LM}$	1. Given
2. $\overline{XL} \cong \overline{XM}$	2. Radii of a circle are congruent
3. $XL = XM$	3. Definition of congruent segments
4. X is on $\overleftrightarrow{GF}$	4. Every point equidistant from the endpoints of the segment is on the perpendicular bisector

Use the diagram for the proofs in exercises 17-19.

17. *Given:* ⊙D with $\overrightarrow{DB} \perp \overleftrightarrow{AC}$; $\overrightarrow{DF} \perp \overleftrightarrow{GE}$; $\overline{BD} \cong \overline{DF}$
    Prove: ∠CAD ≅ ∠DGE
18. *Given:* ⊙D with $\overrightarrow{DB} \perp \overleftrightarrow{AC}$
    Prove: △ADB ≅ △CDB
19. *Given:* ⊙D with $\overrightarrow{DB} \perp \overleftrightarrow{AC}$; $\overrightarrow{DF} \perp \overleftrightarrow{GE}$; $\overline{AC} \cong \overline{GE}$
    Prove: △DBC ≅ △DFG

Prove the following statements.
20. *Given:* ⊙X with $\overleftrightarrow{XA} \perp \overleftrightarrow{LM}$; $\overleftrightarrow{XB} \perp \overleftrightarrow{MN}$; $\overline{XA} \cong \overline{XB}$
    Prove: △LNM is an isosceles triangle

21. *Given:* ⊙M with $\overleftrightarrow{MQ} \perp \overleftrightarrow{PR}$; $\overleftrightarrow{MT} \perp \overleftrightarrow{PS}$; ∠RPM ≅ ∠SPM
    Prove: $\overline{PR} \cong \overline{PS}$

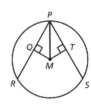

22. *Prove:* The perpendicular bisector of a chord contains the center of the circle.

23.

1. $\overleftrightarrow{AB} \parallel \overleftrightarrow{CD}$; ⊙S; $\overline{CX} \cong \overline{XD}$; $\overrightarrow{PQ} \perp \overline{CD}$	1. Given
2. $\overleftrightarrow{SP} \perp \overleftrightarrow{AB}$	2. Line perpendicular to one of two parallel lines is perpendicular to the other
3. $\overrightarrow{SP}$ bisects $\overline{AB}$	3. A radius perpendicular to a chord bisects the chord

23. *Given:* $\odot S$; $\overline{AB} \parallel \overline{CD}$; $\overline{CX} \cong \overline{XD}$; $\overleftrightarrow{PQ} \perp \overleftrightarrow{CD}$
    Prove: $\overline{SP}$ bisects $\overline{AB}$

24. *Given:* $\overleftrightarrow{AC} \parallel \overleftrightarrow{BD}$, $\overleftrightarrow{CE} \parallel \overleftrightarrow{DF}$, $\overline{AC} \cong \overline{BD}$
    Prove: $\odot E \cong \odot F$

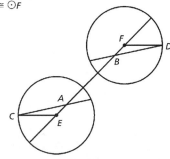

▶ C. Exercises

25. If chords from each of two circles are congruent and are the same distance from the center of their respective circles, then the two circles are congruent.

■ Cumulative Review

Complete each definition.
26. Congruent segments: $\overline{AB} \cong \overline{CD}$ if . . .
27. Congruent angles: $\angle ABC \cong \angle DEF$ if . . .
28. Congruent circles: $\odot A \cong \odot B$ if . . .
29. Congruent triangles: $\triangle ABC \cong \triangle DEF$ if . . .
30. Congruent polygons: . . .

9.1 CIRCLES AND CHORDS **371**

26. $AB = CD$ [3.3]
27. $m\angle ABC = m\angle DEF$ [4.2]
28. The radii are congruent. [6.3]
29. $\overline{AB} \cong \overline{DE}$, $\overline{AC} \cong \overline{DF}$, $\overline{BC} \cong \overline{EF}$, $\angle A \cong \angle D$,
    $\angle B \cong \angle E$, $\angle C \cong \angle F$ [6.3]
30. Two polygons are congruent if they have the same number of sides and corresponding parts (sides and angles) congruent. [6.3]

24.

1. $\overleftrightarrow{AC} \parallel \overleftrightarrow{BD}$, $\overleftrightarrow{CE} \parallel \overleftrightarrow{DF}$, $\overline{AC} \cong \overline{BD}$	1. Given
2. $\angle CAE \cong \angle DBF$	2. Alternate Exterior Angle Theorem
3. $\angle AEC \cong \angle BFD$	3. Parallel Postulate
4. $\triangle ACE \cong \triangle BDF$	4. SAA
5. $\overline{CE} \cong \overline{DF}$	5. Definition of congruent triangles
6. $\odot E \cong \odot F$	6. Definition of congruent circles

25.

1. $\odot O$ and $\odot P$; $\overline{MN} \cong \overline{RS}$; $OF = PT$; $\overline{OF} \perp \overline{MN}$; $\overline{PT} \perp \overline{RS}$	1. Given
2. $MN = RS$	2. Definition of congruent segments
3. $\overline{OF}$ bisects $\overline{MN}$; $\overline{PT}$ bisects $\overline{RS}$	3. A radius perpendicular to a chord bisects the chord
4. F is the midpoint of $\overline{MN}$; T is the midpoint of $\overline{RS}$	4. Definition of segment bisector
5. $FN = \frac{1}{2}MN$, $TS = \frac{1}{2}RS$	5. Midpoint Theorem (Theorem 3.1)
6. $\frac{1}{2}MN = \frac{1}{2}RS$	6. Multiplication property of equality (see step 2)
7. $FN = TS$	7. Transitive property of equality
8. $\overline{OF} \cong \overline{PT}$, $\overline{FN} \cong \overline{TS}$	8. Definition of congruent segments
9. $\angle OFN$ and $\angle PTS$ are right angles	9. Definition of perpendicular
10. $\triangle OFN$ and $\triangle PTS$ are right triangles	10. Definition of right triangle
11. $\triangle OFN \cong \triangle PTS$	11. LL
12. $\overline{ON} \cong \overline{PS}$	12. Definition of congruent triangles
13. $\odot O \cong \odot P$	13. Definition of congruent circles

Analytic Geometry 9

Graphing Circles

Objectives

1. To derive the equation of a circle with center at the origin.
2. To graph circles from their equations.
3. To write equations of circles from the graph.

Vocabulary
standard form for equation of circle

Assignment
- Intuitive: 1-4
- Standard: 1-4
- Rigorous: 1-5

Resource
- *Activities Manual,* Bible Activity: The Holy Spirit—The Guide to Truth.

Additional Problems
Graph.

1. $x^2 + y^2 = 81$

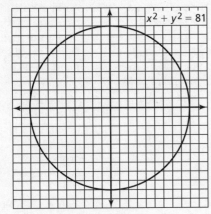

2. $x^2 + y^2 = 16$

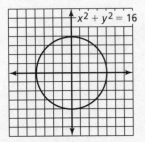

From the given information, find the equation of the circle.

3. center $(0, 0)$ and radius $r = 7$ $x^2 + y^2 = 49$
4. center $(0, 0)$ and passes through $(3, 4)$
   $x^2 + y^2 = 25$
5. center $(0, 0)$ and passes through $(-6, 2)$
   $x^2 + y^2 = 40$

Graphing Circles

A circle is a conic section formed by the intersection of a right circular cone with a plane that is perpendicular to the axis. A circle is also a locus of points that are a given distance from a given point in a plane. From this latter definition we can develop an equation for a circle.

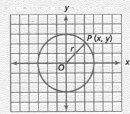

Circle O in the figure above has its center at the origin and radius r. The radius intersects $\odot O$ at P, which has coordinates (x, y). Since a circle is the set of points equidistant from the center O, this set can be described by the distance formula. Substitute the radius for d and the coordinates for the two points.

$$d = \sqrt{(x_1 - x_2)^2 + (y_2 - y_2)^2}$$
$$r = \sqrt{(x - 0)^2 + (y - 0)^2}$$
$$r = \sqrt{x^2 + y^2}$$
$$r^2 = \sqrt{(x^2 + y^2)^2}$$
$$r^2 = x^2 + y^2$$

This is the standard form of the equation of a circle with its center at the origin. Notice that the equation contains the radius rather than the length of the radius itself. Now graph a circle from its equation.

EXAMPLE   Graph $x^2 + y^2 = 16$.

Answer   Use the formula $x^2 + y^2 = r^2$ to find r.

Continued ▶

Presentation

The proof of the equation of a circle emphasizes the relationship between algebra and geometry and shows the value of analytic geometry. Understanding this proof will help students do #4 and Additional Problems 4-5. Those problems require the distance formula or Pythagorean theorem in order to determine the radius of the circle. ∎

By transitivity, $r^2 = 16$ and $r = 4$.

Count four units from the origin along each axis and connect the points with a circle.

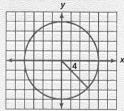

You should also be able to look at the graph of a circle in standard position and write its equation.

▶ Exercises

Graph each:
1. $x^2 + y^2 = 25$
2. $x^2 + y^2 = \frac{1}{4}$

Write the equation of each graph:

3.

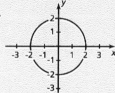

4.

Prove the theorem:
5. The midpoint of the hypotenuse of a right triangle is equidistant from each vertex.

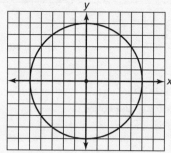

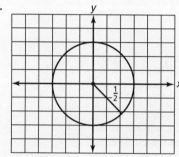

3. $x^2 + y^2 = 4$
4. $x^2 + y^2 = 2$

5.

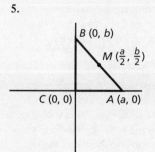

1. Right triangle
2. $M(\frac{a}{2}, \frac{b}{2})$ is midpoint of $\overline{AB}$
3. $MA = \sqrt{(a - \frac{a}{2})^2 + (0 - \frac{b}{2})^2}$

$MB = \sqrt{(0 - \frac{a}{2})^2 + (b - \frac{b}{2})^2}$

$MC = \sqrt{(0 - \frac{a}{2})^2 + (0 - \frac{b}{2})^2}$

4. $MA = \sqrt{\frac{a^2}{4} + \frac{b^2}{4}} = \frac{1}{2}\sqrt{a^2 + b^2}$

$MB = \sqrt{\frac{a^2}{4} + \frac{b^2}{4}} = \frac{1}{2}\sqrt{a^2 + b^2}$

$MC = \sqrt{\frac{a^2}{4} + \frac{b^2}{4}} = \frac{1}{2}\sqrt{a^2 + b^2}$

5. $MA = MB = MC$

1. Given
2. Midpoint formula
3. Distance formula

4. Algebra

5. Transitive property of equality

Tangents

Objectives

1. To identify and define tangents and secants.
2. To prove theorems about tangents and secants.
3. To classify common tangents and tangent circles.
4. To reason through indirect proofs using the Law of Contradiction.

Vocabulary

common external tangent
common internal tangent
common tangent
externally tangent circles
internally tangent circles
point of tangency
secant
tangent
tangent circles

Assignment

• Intuitive: 1-20
• Standard: 1-23, 26-30
• Rigorous: 1-30

Resources

• *Activities Manual,* Indirect Proofs in Detail. Looks at the use of indirect proofs in geometry and how lawyers and detectives use this method in their work.
• *Activities Manual,* Detectives in Brief
• *Test Packet,* Quiz 1, Chapter 9 covers Sections 9.1 and 9.2.

9.2 Tangents

The word *tangent* is derived from the Latin word *tangere,* which means "to touch." This derivation is logical when you think about the relationship between a tangent line and a circle. A tangent line intersects the circle in one and only one point, therefore giving the effect of simply touching the circle. $\overleftrightarrow{FG}$ is tangent to circle *O* at point *F*.

The belts on this 2.5 liter Duratech engine used in Ford vehicles form tangent segments to the circles.

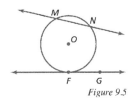

Figure 9.5

$\overline{MN}$ is a chord of $\odot O$, and the line $\overleftrightarrow{MN}$ that contains chord $\overline{MN}$ is called a *secant.*

Definitions

A **secant** is a line that is in the same plane as the circle and intersects the circle in exactly two points.

A **tangent** is a line that is in the same plane as the circle and intersects the circle in exactly one point.

The **point of tangency** is the point at which the tangent intersects the circle.

Presentation

Talk about the word *tangent* and its etymology (word history), which is given in the first paragraph of this section. Read the definitions given in this section and have the students draw several circles on their paper and then draw secant and tangent lines, identifying the point of tangency, chords, and related terms.

Read Theorem 9.4 to your students, explain what it means, and illustrate it. The proof is very important because it is the first indirect proof the students have seen. Go through the reasoning in the paragraphs below the theorem and make sure that the students understand the proof. Have them copy into their notebooks the steps for using this method of proof.

Indirect proof is a very important type of proof. Explain that we all use indirect proof when we accept an opponent's premises for purposes of argument in order to reveal the flaws. Aristotle called it *reductio ad absurdum* (reducing to absurdity). Paul also used it in arguing for the resurrection (I Cor. 15). While you may choose not to stress these proofs, you should discuss the concept.

Be sure that you explain why indirect proof is valid. The Review Exercises (26-29) offer two proofs of the Law of Contradiction, which is the basis of indirect proofs. Either proof of the law can be used in class, but you may need to review some concepts from Chapter 5. If you use the symbolic logic proof, your students will

need to remember modus ponens and modus tollens. If you use the truth table, they should complete the table with you. The truth table method will review the truth values for the various connectives.

One-on-one. In beginning an indirect proof, a student may try to assume what he has to prove. Remind the student that this is circular argument and that the goal of an indirect proof is to rule out alternatives (show that they are false). It is counterproductive to assume what you want to prove and to seek a contradiction.

Common Student Error. Students often misinterpret *opposite.* Emphasize that they must find the negation. Indirect proof is used to

You will study theorems related to circles and tangents in this section. Many of the main ideas of the theorems were developed in several of the exercises in the previous section.

Theorem 9.4

If a line is tangent to a circle, then it is perpendicular to the radius drawn to the point of tangency.

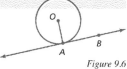

Given: $\overleftrightarrow{AB}$ is a tangent to $\odot O$ at point A
Prove: $\overline{OA} \perp \overleftrightarrow{AB}$

Figure 9.6

This theorem can be proved using indirect proof. This is the first time that you have seen an indirect proof; pay close attention to the method used here so that you can use it in the future.

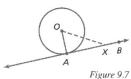

Figure 9.7

Suppose that $\overline{OA}$ is not perpendicular to $\overleftrightarrow{AB}$. Then there must be some other $\overleftrightarrow{OX}$ that is perpendicular to $\overleftrightarrow{AB}$ (where $X \in \overleftrightarrow{AB}$). Since we know that the shortest distance from a point to a line is the perpendicular distance, then $OX < OA$. This implies that X is in the interior of $\odot O$, thus making $\overleftrightarrow{AB}$ a secant, which intersects a circle in two points. But this is a contradiction of the given information that $\overleftrightarrow{AB}$ is a tangent. Thus the assumption that $\overline{OA}$ is not perpendicular to $\overleftrightarrow{AB}$ must be false. Hence $\overline{OA} \perp \overleftrightarrow{AB}$.

This type of reasoning is different from the normal deductive proof that you have been studying. The main steps in an indirect proof are as follows:

1. Assume the opposite of what you are trying to prove.
2. Reason deductively from the assumption.
3. Reason to a conclusion that contradicts the assumption, the given, or some theorem.
4. Conclude that the assumption is false and therefore the statement you are trying to prove is true.

These types of proofs are also called proofs by contradiction, because the Law of Contradiction is used to draw the conclusion from the first three steps. This law will be proved in the review exercises.

Additional Problems

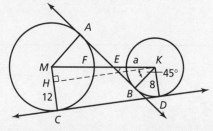

Given: $\odot M$ and $\odot K$ with common tangents $\overleftrightarrow{AB}$ and $\overleftrightarrow{CD}$; $m\angle BKE = 45°$; $KD = 8$; $MC = 12$

Find:

1. *EB* $m\angle BEK = 45$; $\triangle BEK$ isosceles; *EB = 8*
2. *AE* $\triangle AME$ is also an isosceles right $\triangle$; *AE = 12*
3. *EF* by Pythagorean theorem, *ME* $= 12\sqrt{2}$; *EF* $= 12\sqrt{2} - 12$
4. *MK* $20\sqrt{2}$
5. *AB* **20**
6. *CD* **CD = HK**, which by the Pythagorean theorem equals $\sqrt{(MK)^2 - (MH)^2} = 28$
7. *Given:* Perimeter of $\triangle ABC$ is 42, $BX = 8$, and $CX = 6$
   Find: *AB* and *AC* **AC = 13, AB = 15**

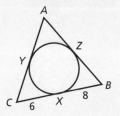

---

rule out every alternative. For this reason, you assume that the negation is true. When you find a contradiction, the negation will be false, and therefore the desired statement will be true. In its most elementary form, the method of indirect proof says to prove a proposition A, you must assume $\sim A$ and arrive at a contradiction.

Common Student Error. Some students may negate correctly and still be unable to progress. They think that they must find a contradiction to the given. However, a contradiction to any postulate, theorem, or previous statement in the proof is also acceptable. The proof of Theorem 9.5 illustrates this. The goal is simply to show that the assumption is incompatible (inconsistent) with the system of geometry.

You may wish to give an indirect proof that is not from geometry.

Example

Show that $x^6 - 2x^3 + 3 = 0$ has no real solutions. Assume that a solution $x = a$, where a is real, exists. Then $a^6 - 2a^3 + 3 = 0$ and $(a^6 - 2a^3 + 1) + 2 = 0$; therefore, $(a^3 - 1)^2 = -2$. But this is a contradiction since the square of any real number is positive. The assumption that real solutions exist is false. Therefore, the equation has no real solutions.

Read and illustrate Theorem 9.6, which is the converse of Theorem 9.4. Then study through Theorem 9.7 and its proof. This proof is direct and should be easy for students to follow.

Motivational Idea. Have your students construct a circle on their paper and use a straightedge to draw two tangent lines from each of several points outside the circle. Then have the students use a ruler to convince themselves of the truth of Theorem 9.7. Prove one or two of the theorems in the exercise section as a class exercise.

Define common tangent lines, both internal and external. Use the diagram in the book and have the students draw these special tangent lines on their paper. Then discuss the idea of tangent circles. Point out that tangent circles can also be either internally tangent or externally tangent.

Theorem 9.5

Law of Contradiction. **If an assumption leads to a contradiction, then the assumption is false and its negation is true.**

Now let us return to Theorem 9.4 and rewrite the proof of it in a two column form, using the Law of Contradiction.

STATEMENTS	REASONS
1. $\overleftrightarrow{AB}$ is tangent to $\odot O$ at A	1. Given
2. $\overleftrightarrow{AB}$ intersects $\odot O$ in exactly one point	2. Definition of tangent
3. Assume $\overrightarrow{OA}$ is not perpendicular to $\overleftrightarrow{AB}$	3. Assumption
4. Draw the line perpendicular to $\overleftrightarrow{AB}$ that passes through O; let X be the point of intersection	4. Auxiliary line
5. $OX < OA$	5. Longest Side Inequality ($\angle X$ is right)
6. X is interior to $\odot O$	6. Definition of interior of a circle
7. $\overleftrightarrow{AB}$ contains a chord of $\odot O$	7. Chord Postulate
8. $\overleftrightarrow{AB}$ intersects $\odot O$ in two points	8. Definition of chord
9. $\overrightarrow{OA}$ is perpendicular to $\overleftrightarrow{AB}$	9. Law of Contradiction (compare steps 2 and 8)

This type of proof makes proofs of some theorems easier. With practice you will learn when to use the indirect type of proof. The converse of Theorem 9.4 is also true. You will be asked to prove this theorem in the exercises.

Theorem 9.6

If a line is perpendicular to a radius at a point on the circle, then the line is tangent to the circle.

In Chapter 3 you studied tangent line segments. If you are given a circle and a point in the exterior of the circle, you can find two line segments that are tangent to the circle. For example, given $\odot P$ and point X, you can find $\overline{XA}$ and $\overline{XB}$ tangent to $\odot P$.

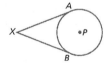

Figure 9.8

Tips

Ex. 21. Indirect proof. It requires the theorem that there is exactly one line through a given point perpendicular to a given line. This theorem is proved in the *Activities Manual* (and uses an indirect proof). You may simply state the theorem for the students to use if you do not use the activity. If you do not state it or prove it, students will not be able to complete this proof.

Ex. 24. Indirect proof. Students may obtain contradictions at least three other ways. Step five could identify $\overline{LQ}$ as a radius and therefore perpendicular to $\overleftrightarrow{AB}$ (which contradicts the unique perpendiculars through point L). Since two lines perpendicular to the same line are parallel, $\overleftrightarrow{LQ} \parallel \overleftrightarrow{LX}$, which contradicts the fact that point L is in common. Finally, $\triangle LQX$ has two right angles (which contradict the 180° in a triangle). ∎

The next theorem proves that such segments are congruent.

Theorem 9.7
Tangent segments extending from a given exterior point to a circle are congruent.

Given: ⊙A with exterior point X; $\overline{XM}$ and $\overline{XN}$ are tangent to ⊙A
Prove: $\overline{XM} \cong \overline{XN}$

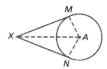

Figure 9.9

STATEMENTS	REASONS
1. ⊙A with exterior point X; $\overline{XM}$ and $\overline{XN}$ are tangent to ⊙A	1. Given
2. Draw $\overleftrightarrow{AM}$, $\overleftrightarrow{AN}$, and $\overleftrightarrow{AX}$	2. Auxiliary lines
3. $\overline{AM} \cong \overline{AN}$	3. Radii of a circle are congruent
4. $\overleftrightarrow{AM} \perp \overleftrightarrow{XM}$; $\overleftrightarrow{AN} \perp \overleftrightarrow{XN}$	4. A radius to the point of tangency is perpendicular to the tangent segment
5. ∠XMA and ∠XNA are right angles	5. Definition of perpendicular
6. △XAM and △XAN are right triangles	6. Definition of right triangles
7. $\overline{AX} \cong \overline{AX}$	7. Reflexive property of congruent segments
8. △XAM ≅ △XAN	8. HL
9. $\overline{XM} \cong \overline{XN}$	9. Definition of congruent triangles

Definitions

A **common tangent** is a line that is tangent to each of two coplanar circles.

Tangent circles are coplanar circles that are tangent to the same line at the same point.

Answers

1. 90
2. right
3. $2\sqrt{65}$ units
4. 8 units
5. 90
6. 23 units
7. $3\sqrt{13}$
8. 24 units
9. $5\sqrt{11}$ units
10. isosceles
11. (e), q
12. a, d
13. b, c, l
14. ⊙L, ⊙M
15. ⊙R, ⊙S
16.

17.

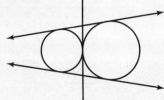

18.

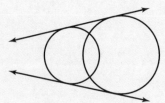

19.

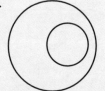

20.

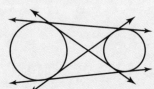

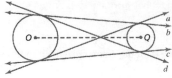

Figure 9.10

Figure 9.10 shows four common tangents of ⊙O and ⊙Q. Common tangents are classified as internal if they intersect the segment joining the centers. In the figure, a and d are common internal tangents. Other common tangents, such as b and c, are common external tangents.

Figure 9.11

Circles can be tangent in two ways. *Internally tangent circles* are tangent circles on the same side of the common tangent. *Externally tangent circles* are tangent circles on opposite sides of the common tangent. ⊙P and ⊙M are externally tangent circles, while ⊙N and ⊙M are internally tangent circles.

▶ A. Exercises

Given: ⊙L with line m tangent to ⊙L at C; $\overline{BF}$ and $\overline{FE}$ are tangent segments; find the indicated information.

1. $m\angle LCD$
2. What kind of triangle is △LBF?
3. If $LC = 8$ units and $CD = 14$ units, find LD (not drawn).
4. If $AC = 16$ units, find LB.
5. $m\angle LBF$
6. If $FE = 23$ units, find BF.
7. If $BL = 6$ units and $EF = 9$ units, find LF.
8. If $BL = 12$ units, find AC.
9. If $LC = 7$ units and $LF = 18$ units, find EF.
10. Consider $\overline{BE}$ (not drawn). What kind of triangle is △BEF?

Consider the following diagrams for exercises 11-15.

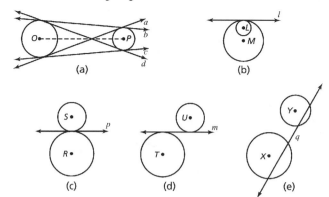

(a)   (b)

(c)   (d)   (e)

11. Which diagram shows a secant? Name the secant.
12. Name two common internal tangents in diagram (a).
13. Name the common external tangents in diagrams (a) and (b).
14. Name all internally tangent circles.
15. Name all externally tangent circles.

▶ B. Exercises

Draw the following figures.

16. Two internally tangent circles, one having a radius that is half the length of the other; show the common tangent line and a line that is a secant of only one of them
17. Two circles having only one common internal tangent and two common external tangents
18. Two circles having two common external tangents and no common internal tangents
19. Two circles for which no common tangent is possible
20. Two circles having two common internal tangents and two common external tangents

Prove the following statements.

21. If a line is perpendicular to a tangent line at the point of tangency, then the line passes through the center of the circle.

21.

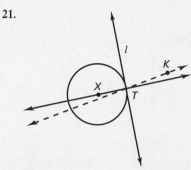

1. $\overleftrightarrow{KT} \perp l$; l intersects $\odot X$ at T	1. Given
2. $\overleftrightarrow{KT}$ does not contain X	2. Assumption
3. Draw $\overline{XT}$	3. Auxiliary line
4. $\overline{XT} \perp l$	4. Tangent is perpendicular to radius at point of tangency
5. $\overleftrightarrow{XT} = \overleftrightarrow{KT}$	5. There is exactly one line perpendicular to a given line at a given point T
6. $\overleftrightarrow{KT}$ contains the center X	6. Law of Contradiction (compare steps 2 and 5)

22.

1. $\odot X$ and $\odot Y$; $\overleftrightarrow{AD}$ and $\overleftrightarrow{EC}$ are common tangents	1. Given
2. $\overline{AB} \cong \overline{EB}$; $\overline{BD} \cong \overline{BC}$	2. Tangent segments from same point are congruent
3. $AB = EB$; $BD = BC$	3. Definition of congruent segments
4. $AB + BD = EB + BC$	4. Addition property of equality
5. $AB + BD = AD$; $EB + BC = EC$	5. Definition of betweenness
6. $AD = EC$	6. Substitution (step 5 into 4)
7. $\overline{AD} \cong \overline{EC}$	7. Definition of congruent segments

23.

1. $\odot M$ and $\odot N$ with common tangents $\overleftrightarrow{XW}$ and $\overleftrightarrow{XZ}$	1. Given
2. $\overline{XY} \cong \overline{XV}$; $\overline{XZ} \cong \overline{XW}$	2. Tangent segments congruent
3. $XY = XV$; $XZ = XW$	3. Definition of congruent segments
4. $XY + YZ = XZ$; $XV + VW = XW$	4. Definition of betweenness
5. $XY + YZ = XV + VW$	5. Substitution (step 4 into 3)
6. $YZ = VW$	6. Addition property of equality ($XY = XV$ by step 3)
7. $\overline{YZ} \cong \overline{VW}$	7. Definition of congruent segments

24.

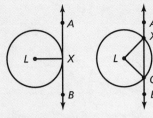

1. $\overline{LX}$ is a radius of $\odot L$; $\overline{LX} \perp \overleftrightarrow{AB}$ at X	1. Given
2. $\overleftrightarrow{AB}$ intersects $\odot L$ in (at least) one point X	2. Definition of radius
3. $\overleftrightarrow{AB}$ intersects $\odot L$ in two points, X and Q	3. Assumption
4. $\angle LXQ$ is a right angle	4. Definition of perpendicular
5. $\triangle LXQ$ is a right triangle	5. Definition of right triangle
6. $\overline{LQ}$ is the hypotenuse of $\triangle LXQ$	6. Definition of hypotenuse
7. $LQ > LX$	7. Hypotenuse is longer than either leg
8. $\overline{LQ} \cong \overline{LX}$	8. Radii of a circle are congruent
9. $LQ = LX$	9. Definition of congruent segments
10. $\overleftrightarrow{AB}$ cannot intersect $\odot L$ in two points	10. Law of Contradiction (compare steps 7 and 9)
11. $\overleftrightarrow{AB}$ is tangent to $\odot L$	11. Definition of tangent line (one point of intersection, steps 2, 10)

25.

1. $\overline{JF} \cong \overline{GI}$; $\odot F$ and $\odot G$ are tangent to line a at L	1. Given
2. $\odot F \cong \odot G$	2. Definition of congruent circles
3. $\overline{FL} \cong \overline{GL}$	3. Radii of congruent circles are congruent
4. $\overline{LK} \cong \overline{LK}$	4. Reflexive property of congruent segments
5. $\overline{FL} \perp a$; $\overline{GL} \perp a$	5. Radius is perpendicular to tangent at point of tangency
6. $\angle FLK$ and $\angle GLK$ are right angles	6. Definition of perpendicular
7. $\triangle FLK$ and $\triangle GLK$ are right triangles	7. Definition of right triangle
8. $\triangle FLK \cong \triangle GLK$	8. LL
9. $\overline{FK} \cong \overline{GK}$	9. Definition of congruent triangles
10. $\triangle FKG$ is isosceles	10. Definition of isosceles triangle

22. *Given:* $\odot X$ and $\odot Y$; common tangents $\overleftrightarrow{AD}$ and $\overleftrightarrow{EC}$
Prove: $\overline{EC} \cong \overline{AD}$

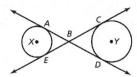

23. *Given:* $\odot M$ and $\odot N$; common tangents $\overleftrightarrow{XW}$ and $\overleftrightarrow{XZ}$
Prove: $\overline{YZ} \cong \overline{VW}$

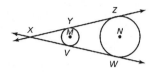

▶ **C. Exercises**

24. *Prove:* Theorem 9.6
25. *Given:* $\overline{JF} \cong \overline{GI}$; $\odot F$ and $\odot G$ are tangent to line a at point L
Prove: $\triangle FKG$ is an isosceles triangle

■ **Cumulative Review**

Justify the steps in the proof of the Law of Contradiction.

	Step	Reason
26.	p	
	q	previously known (given or proved)
27.	$p \rightarrow q$	
	$\sim q$	previously known (given or proved)
28.	$\sim p$	

29. Make a truth table to prove the Law of Contradiction: $[p \rightarrow (q \land \sim q)] \rightarrow \sim p$.
30. Give an alternate symbolic form of the Law of Contradiction.
(*Hint:* Consider exercises 26–28.)

26. assumed [5.6]
27. Law of Deduction [5.6]
28. modus tollens [5.6]
29. [5.4]

p	q	$\sim q$	$q \land \sim q$	$p \rightarrow (q \land \sim q)$	$\sim p$	$[p \rightarrow (q \land \sim q)] \rightarrow \sim p$
T	T	F	F	F	F	T
T	F	T	F	F	F	T
F	T	F	F	T	T	T
F	F	T	F	T	T	T

30. $[(p \rightarrow q) \land \sim q] \rightarrow \sim p$ (Same as modus tollens) [5.6]

9.3 Arcs

An arc was defined earlier to be a curve that is a subset of a circle. How do we measure arcs? Arcs are measured in degrees, just as angles are, but you will need to know more about the relationship between angles and arcs in order to measure them.

Two special types of angles are associated with a circle. These angles are called *central angles* and *inscribed angles*. The figure below shows an example of each. ∠LKM is a central angle; notice that it intersects the circle in two points and has its vertex at the center of ⊙K.

∠UVW is an inscribed angle. It has a point of the circle as a vertex, and it intersects the circle in two other points.

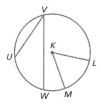

Figure 9.12

Natural features such as Delicate Arch, Utah, also exhibit an arc for support.

Objectives

1. To identify and define relationships between arcs of circles, central angles, and inscribed angles.
2. To identify minor arcs, major arcs, and semicircles and express them using correct notation.
3. To prove theorems relating the measures of arcs, central angles, and chords.

Vocabulary

arc measure
central angle
congruent arcs
inscribed angle
major arc
minor arc
semicircle

Assignment

- Intuitive: 1-13, 22-25
- Standard: 1-19, 22-26
- Rigorous: 5-13 odd, 14-26, and Mind over Math

Resource

- *Test Packet,* Quiz 2, Chapter 9 covers Section 9.3.

Flash

Delicate Arch spans 32 feet and rises 46 feet tall, but it is not the largest of the 2000 arches at Arches National Park. The park has the greatest density of natural arches anywhere in the world.

Presentation

Review the difference between a central angle and an inscribed angle. It may seem like a misnomer to call an angle "inscribed," since there is no way an angle can be placed inside a circle the way a triangle or some quadrilaterals can. Since an angle is made up of two rays with a common endpoint, they quickly cross the circle and extend infinitely. It helps to think of an inscribed angle in much the same way as we talk about the angles of a triangle.

Review the definition of arc and state the definition of arc measure that relates to the measure of a central angle. Go through the material that is presented before the definition of *minor arc,* illustrating the new terms. Explain that one must include a third point in the symbol for a major arc to distinguish it from a minor arc. Ask students how many points would be needed to designate a semicircle (*3, since the ends of a diameter determine two semicircles*).

The difference between $\overarc{AB}$ and $m\overarc{AB}$ is similar to the difference between ∠A and m∠A. Sets of points must not be confused with numbers. Students should not have trouble if you make this comparison.

Define *congruent* arcs and ask whether the arcs can be on the same circle (*yes*). Ask why (*reflexive property of congruent circles guarantees that a circle is congruent to itself and therefore meets the condition of congruent circles*). Explain that any definition or theorem about congruent circles can also apply to figures within the same circle. Figures in the same circle are automatically in congruent circles because the circle is congruent to itself.

Common Student Error. Students may not understand why the definition of congruent arcs requires the arcs to lie on congruent circles. Have them consider the circles on a basketball court (12-foot diameter). Ask them to determine the length in feet of a 90-degree arc (9.4 feet). Next, have them construct a circle with a central angle of 90 degrees. They will realize that this arc is less than one foot long. Emphasize that the arcs have the same measure but are not congruent because they are not the same size (length). The radii of the circles

Reading and Writing Mathematics

A multifoil is a symmetric plane figure with congruent arcs around a regular polygon such that the arcs bisect its sides. The *quatrefoil* is shown. Have the students construct a *trefoil* or a *hexafoil* and calculate the arc measures for each figure.

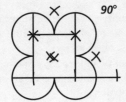

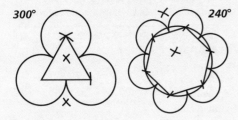

Additional Problems

Use the diagram to answer the following questions. $\overline{AD}$ is a diameter.

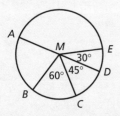

1. Name nine minor arcs using proper notation. **$\overarc{AB}$, $\overarc{AC}$, $\overarc{BC}$, $\overarc{BD}$, $\overarc{BE}$, $\overarc{CD}$, $\overarc{CE}$, $\overarc{DE}$, $\overarc{AE}$**
2. Name three major arcs. **$\overarc{ACE}$, $\overarc{ADC}$, $\overarc{ADB}$ *Answers will vary.***
3. Find $m\overarc{AB}$. **75**
4. Find $m\overarc{AE}$. **150**
5. Find $m\overarc{CD} + m\overarc{DE}$. **75**

A **central angle** is an angle that is in the same plane as the circle and whose vertex is the center of the circle.

An **inscribed angle** is an angle with its vertex on a circle and with sides containing chords of the circle.

Note: Each of these angles determines a pair of arcs of the circle. For example, ∠*LKM* determines $\overarc{LM}$ and $\overarc{LUM}$. Similarly, ∠*UVW* is inscribed in $\overarc{UVW}$ and intercepts $\overarc{UW}$. Here is the basic relationship between the measures of central angles and of the arcs that they intercept.

Arc measure is the same measure as the degree measure of the central angle that intercepts the arc.

Figure 9.13

In ⊙*B*, if the measure of the central angle, ∠ *ABC*, is 60, then $m\overarc{AC} = 60$ also. If an arc is cut off by a diameter, then the arc has a special name—semicircle. The measure of a semicircle is 180°, since it is intercepted by a straight angle, whose measure is 180°. Because a circle is made of two semicircles, the total degree measure of a circle is 360°. There are also some other arcs that have special names.

Definitions

A **minor arc** is an arc measuring less than 180 degrees. Minor arcs are denoted with two letters, such as $\overarc{AB}$, where *A* and *B* are the endpoints of the arc.

A **major arc** is an arc measuring more than 180 degrees. Major arcs are denoted with three letters, such as $\overarc{ABC}$, where *A* and *C* are the endpoints and *B* is another point on the arc.

A **semicircle** is an arc measuring 180 degrees.

---

made the difference in the arc lengths. (Arc length will be addressed further in Section 9.6.)

Motivational Idea. Cut 45° sectors from three or four circles of different radii. The central angles can be superimposed for a good match, but the arcs will not match.

Motivational Idea. To study the Arc Addition Postulate, draw a circle on the chalkboard and mark several points on it. Have the students then state examples of the Arc Addition Postulate from the illustration on the chalkboard.

State and illustrate Theorems 9.8-9.12. Study through the proof of Theorem 9.9 with the students, answering any questions that they

have about this material. The proof illustrates that two parts are necessary for proofs of biconditionals. If time allows, do a few of the exercises as a class activity.

Ex. 1. Any ten: $\overarc{AB}$, $\overarc{AD}$, $\overarc{AE}$, $\overarc{AF}$, $\overarc{AG}$, $\overarc{BC}$, $\overarc{BD}$, $\overarc{BE}$, $\overarc{BF}$, $\overarc{BG}$, $\overarc{CD}$, $\overarc{CE}$, $\overarc{CF}$, $\overarc{CG}$, $\overarc{DE}$, $\overarc{DF}$, $\overarc{DG}$, $\overarc{EF}$, $\overarc{EG}$, $\overarc{FG}$

Ex. 2-3. The middle letter may vary in naming major arcs and semicircles. This makes multiple answers possible, but it also makes it easy to accidentally list the same arc twice ($\overarc{DCA}$ and $\overarc{DFA}$ are the same). ■

The Arc Addition Postulate is similar to the Angle Addition Postulate.

Postulate 9.2

Arc Addition Postulate. If B is a point on $\overset{\frown}{AC}$, then $m\overset{\frown}{AB} + m\overset{\frown}{BC} = m\overset{\frown}{AC}$.

Figure 9.14

This postulate is used often in proving theorems that involve arcs. You will prove as an exercise the theorem below, which shows that there is a relationship between the measures of minor and major arcs. The degree measure of a major arc can be given in terms of its associated minor arc. Look at figure 9.15 and remember that $m\odot P = 360$.

Figure 9.15

Theorem 9.8

Major Arc Theorem. $m\overset{\frown}{ACB} = 360 - m\overset{\frown}{AB}$.

EXAMPLE   If $m\overset{\frown}{AB} = 50$, find $m\overset{\frown}{ACB}$.

Answer   By the theorem, $m\overset{\frown}{ACB} = 360 - m\overset{\frown}{AB} = 360 - 50 = 310$.

Definition

Congruent arcs are arcs on congruent circles that have the same measure.

Figure 9.16

Since $m\overset{\frown}{AB} = 20$ and $m\overset{\frown}{CD} = 20$, you can say that $\overset{\frown}{AB} \cong \overset{\frown}{CD}$.

The next theorem introduces arcs that are subtended (cut off) by chords. Remember that proving a biconditional statement requires two parts.

Given $\odot M$ with diameters $\overline{DB}$ and $\overline{AC}$, $m\overset{\frown}{AD} = 108$. Find each of the following.

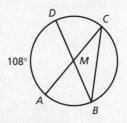

6. $m\angle AMB$ **72**
7. $m\angle BMC$ **108**
8. $m\overset{\frown}{DAB}$ **180**
9. $m\overset{\frown}{DC}$ **72**
10. *Given:* $\odot Q$ with tangent $\overleftrightarrow{CP}$, $m\angle CPQ = x$
    Prove: $m\overset{\frown}{AC} = 90 - x$

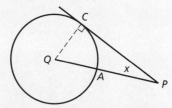

1. $\odot Q$ with tangent $\overleftrightarrow{CP}$; $m\angle CPQ = x$	1. Given
2. $\overline{CQ} \perp \overleftrightarrow{CP}$	2. Radius is perpendicular to a tangent at the point of tangency
3. $\angle QCP$ is a right angle	3. Definition of perpendicular
4. $\triangle CQP$ is a right triangle	4. Definition of right triangle
5. $\angle CQA$ and $\angle CPQ$ are complementary	5. The acute angles of a right triangle are complementary
6. $m\angle CQA + x = 90$	6. Definition of complementary angles
7. $m\angle CQA = 90 - x$	7. Addition property of equality
8. $m\angle CQA = m\overset{\frown}{AC}$	8. Definition of arc measure
9. $m\overset{\frown}{AC} = 90 - x$	9. Substitution (step 6 into 7)

Theorem 9.9
Chords of congruent circles are congruent if and only if they subtend congruent arcs.

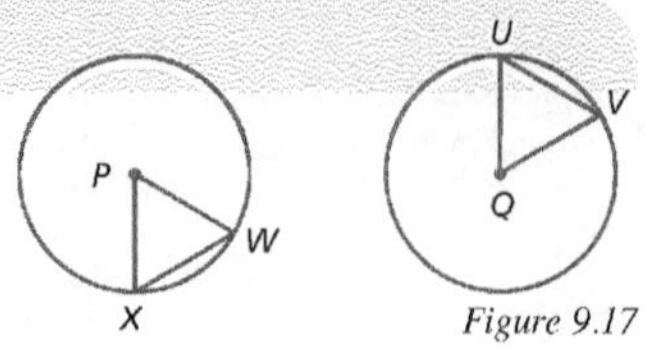

Figure 9.17

STATEMENTS	REASONS
Part 1	
1. $\odot P$ with chord $\overline{WX}$; $\odot Q$ with chord $\overline{UV}$; $\odot P \cong \odot Q$; $\overline{UV} \cong \overline{WX}$	1. Given
2. $\overline{QU} \cong \overline{PX}$; $\overline{QV} \cong \overline{PW}$	2. Radii of a circle are congruent
3. $\triangle UQV \cong \triangle XPW$	3. SSS
4. $\angle UQV \cong \angle XPW$	4. Definition of congruent triangles
5. $m\angle UQV = m\angle XPW$	5. Definition of congruent angles
6. $m\angle UQV = m\overset{\frown}{UV}$; $m\angle XPW = m\overset{\frown}{WX}$	6. Definition of arc measure
7. $m\overset{\frown}{UV} = m\overset{\frown}{WX}$	7. Substitution (step 6 into 5)
8. $\overset{\frown}{UV} \cong \overset{\frown}{WX}$	8. Definition of congruent arcs
9. If $\overline{UV} \cong \overline{WX}$, then $\overset{\frown}{UV} \cong \overset{\frown}{WX}$	9. Law of Deduction
Part 2	
10. $\overset{\frown}{UV} \cong \overset{\frown}{WX}$; $\odot P \cong \odot Q$	10. Given
11. $m\overset{\frown}{UV} = m\overset{\frown}{WX}$	11. Definition of congruent arcs
12. $m\angle UQV = m\overset{\frown}{UV}$; $m\angle WPX = m\overset{\frown}{WX}$	12. Definition of arc measure
13. $m\angle UQV = m\angle WPX$	13. Substitution (step 12 into 11)
14. $\overline{QU} \cong \overline{PX}$; $\overline{QV} \cong \overline{PW}$	14. Radii of a circle are congruent
15. $\triangle UQV \cong \triangle XPW$	15. SAS
16. $\overline{UV} \cong \overline{WX}$	16. Definition of congruent triangles
17. If $\overset{\frown}{UV} \cong \overset{\frown}{WX}$, then $\overline{UV} \cong \overline{WX}$	17. Law of Deduction
Part 3	
18. In congruent circles, chords are congruent if and only if the arcs are congruent	18. Definition of biconditional (see steps 9 and 17)

Three other biconditional theorems follow (exercises 18-21).

Theorem 9.10
In congruent circles, chords are congruent if and only if the corresponding central angles are congruent.

Theorem 9.11
In congruent circles, minor arcs are congruent if and only if their corresponding central angles are congruent.

Theorem 9.12
In congruent circles, two minor arcs are congruent if and only if the corresponding major arcs are congruent.

▶ A. Exercises

Use the diagram for exercises 1-10. In $\odot O$, $\overline{AC}$ is a diameter.

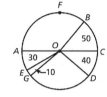

1. Name at least ten minor arcs.
2. Name at least five major arcs.
3. Name all semicircles.

Find each of the following.

4. $m\overset{\frown}{ED}$
5. $m\overset{\frown}{AB}$
6. $m\overset{\frown}{BD}$
7. $m\angle BOD$
8. $m\overset{\frown}{AD}$
9. $m\overset{\frown}{BC} + m\overset{\frown}{BA}$
10. Name all congruent arcs.

17.

1. $\odot O$; E is the midpoint of $\overline{BD}$ and $\overline{AC}$; $\overline{BE} \cong \overline{AE}$	1. Given
2. $BE = AE$	2. Definition of congruent segments
3. $BE = ED$; $AE = EC$	3. Definition of midpoint
4. $ED = EC$	4. Substitution (step 3 into 2)
5. $BE + ED = AE + EC$	5. Addition property of equality
6. $BE + ED = BD$; $AE + EC = AC$	6. Definition of betweenness
7. $BD = AC$	7. Substitution (step 6 into 5)
8. $\overline{BD} \cong \overline{AC}$	8. Definition of congruent segments

Answers

1. Answers will vary.
2. Any 5 of the 20 possible major arcs corresponding to minor arcs in #1
3. $\overset{\frown}{AFC}$, $\overset{\frown}{ADC}$
4. 110
5. 130
6. 90
7. 90
8. 140
9. $m\overset{\frown}{ABC} = 180$
10. $\overset{\frown}{AG} \cong \overset{\frown}{DC}$; $\overset{\frown}{AFC} \cong \overset{\frown}{AGC}$; $\overset{\frown}{GC} \cong \overset{\frown}{DA}$; $\overset{\frown}{ABG} \cong \overset{\frown}{DAC}$
11. 80
12. 12 units
13. They are congruent since congruent central angles subtend congruent chords.
14.

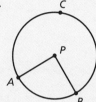

1. $m\overset{\frown}{AB} + m\overset{\frown}{ACB} = m\odot P$	1. Arc Addition Postulate
2. $m\odot P = 360$	2. Degree measure of circle
3. $m\overset{\frown}{AB} + m\overset{\frown}{ACB} = 360$	3. Substitution
4. $m\overset{\frown}{ACB} = 360 - m\overset{\frown}{AB}$	4. Addition property of equality

15.

1. $\odot U$; $\overset{\frown}{XY} \cong \overset{\frown}{YZ} \cong \overset{\frown}{ZX}$	1. Given
2. $\overline{XY} \cong \overline{YZ} \cong \overline{ZX}$	2. Chords are congruent when arcs are congruent
3. $\triangle XYZ$ is an equilateral triangle	3. Definition of equilateral triangle

16.

1. Points M, N, O, and P on $\odot L$; $\overset{\frown}{MO} \cong \overset{\frown}{NP}$	1. Given
2. $m\overset{\frown}{MO} = m\overset{\frown}{NP}$	2. Definition of congruent arcs
3. $m\overset{\frown}{MP} + m\overset{\frown}{PO} = m\overset{\frown}{MO}$; $m\overset{\frown}{PO} + m\overset{\frown}{ON} = m\overset{\frown}{NP}$	3. Arc Addition Postulate
4. $m\overset{\frown}{MP} + m\overset{\frown}{PO} = m\overset{\frown}{PO} + m\overset{\frown}{ON}$	4. Substitution (step 3 into 2)
5. $m\overset{\frown}{MP} = m\overset{\frown}{ON}$	5. Addition property of equality
6. $\overset{\frown}{MP} \cong \overset{\frown}{ON}$	6. Definition of congruent arcs

18.

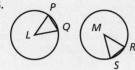

1. ∠PLQ ≅ ∠RMS; ⊙L ≅ ⊙M	1. Given
2. $\overline{PL} \cong \overline{QL} \cong$ $\overline{RM} \cong \overline{SM}$	2. Radii of congruent circles are congruent
3. △PLQ ≅ △RMS	3. SAS
4. $\overline{PQ} \cong \overline{RS}$	4. Definition of congruent triangles
5. If two central angles of congruent circles are congruent, then the chords they subtend are congruent	5. Law of Deduction

19.

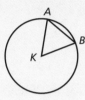

1. $\overline{AB} \cong \overline{CD}$; ⊙K ≅ ⊙P	1. Given
2. Draw radii $\overline{AK}$, $\overline{BK}$, $\overline{CP}$, $\overline{DP}$	2. Line Postulate
3. $\overline{AK} \cong \overline{BK} \cong$ $\overline{CP} \cong \overline{DP}$	3. Radii of congruent circles are congruent
4. △AKB ≅ △CPD	4. SSS
5. ∠AKB ≅ ∠CPD	5. Definition of congruent triangles
6. If two chords in congruent circles are congruent, then the central angles are congruent	6. Law of Deduction

20.

1. $\overparen{AB} \cong \overparen{CD}$; ⊙K ≅ ⊙L	1. Given (part 1)
2. $\overline{AB} \cong \overline{CD}$	2. Chords congruent if and only if arcs congruent
3. ∠AKB ≅ ∠CLD	3. Chords congruent if and only if central angles congruent
4. If minor arcs are congruent, then the central angles are congruent	4. Law of Deduction
5. ∠AKB ≅ ∠CLD	5. Given (part 2)
6. $\overline{AB} \cong \overline{CD}$	6. Chords congruent if and only if central angles congruent
7. $\overparen{AB} \cong \overparen{CD}$	7. Chords congruent if and only if arcs congruent
8. If central angles are congruent, then the minor arcs subtended are congruent	8. Law of Deduction
9. Two minor arcs are congruent if and only if their central angles are congruent	9. Definition of biconditional (steps 4 and 8)

Use the figure for exercises 11-13. ⊙P ≅ ⊙Q.

11. If $\overline{AB} \cong \overline{CD}$ and m∠BPA = 80, find m∠CQD.
12. If m∠APB = m∠CQD and AB = 12, find CD.
13. If m∠APB = 75 and m∠CQD = 75, what is true about $\overline{AB}$ and $\overline{CD}$? Why?

▶ **B. Exercises**

Prove the following theorems.
14. Theorem 9.8
15. *Given:* ⊙U with $\overparen{XY} \cong \overparen{YZ} \cong \overparen{ZX}$
    Prove: △XYZ is an equilateral triangle

16. *Given:* Points M, N, O, and P on ⊙L; $\overparen{MO} \cong \overparen{NP}$
    Prove: $\overparen{MP} \cong \overparen{NO}$

17. *Given:* ⊙O; E is the midpoint of $\overline{BD}$ and $\overline{AC}$; $\overline{BE} \cong \overline{AE}$
    Prove: $\overline{AC} \cong \overline{BD}$

18. Theorem 9.10a. If two central angles of congruent circles are congruent, then the chords they subtend are congruent.

19. Theorem 9.10b. If two chords in congruent circles are congruent, then the central angles that intercept them are congruent.

20. Theorem 9.11

▶ **C. Exercises**

21. *Prove:* Theorem 9.12

■ Cumulative Review

22. State the Triangle Inequality.

23. State the Exterior Angle Inequality.

24. State the Hinge Theorem.

25. State the greater than property.

26. Prove that the surface area of a cone is always greater than its lateral surface area.

MIND OVER MATH

Find the perimeter and area of the shaded region in the marked figure.

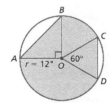

22. The sum of the lengths of any two sides of a triangle is always greater than the length of the third side. [7.5]

23. The measure of an exterior angle of a triangle is always greater than the measure of either remote interior angle. [7.3]

24. If two pairs of sides of two triangles are congruent but the included angle of one is larger in measure than the included angle of the second, then the third side of the first is longer than the third side of the second. [7.4]

25. If $a = b + c$, where $c > 0$, then $a > b$. [7.3]

26.

1. Cone
2. $S = L + B$
3. $B > 0$
4. $S > L$

1. Given
2. Surface area of cone
3. Area Postulate
4. Greater than property

Mind over Math

See Appendix B.

21.

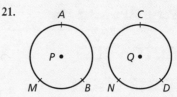

Part 1

1. ⊙P with $\overarc{AB}$; ⊙Q with $\overarc{CD}$; $\overarc{AB} \cong \overarc{CD}$ where both are minor arcs
    1. Given

2. $m\overarc{AB} = m\overarc{CD}$
    2. Definition of congruent arcs

3. $\overarc{AMB}$ and $\overarc{CND}$ are major arcs
    3. Definition of major arc

4. $m\overarc{AMB} = 360 - m\overarc{AB}$
   $m\overarc{CND} = 360 - m\overarc{CD}$
    4. Major Arc Theorem

5. $m\overarc{AMB} = 360 - m\overarc{CD}$
    5. Substitution (step 2 into 4)

6. $m\overarc{AMB} = m\overarc{CND}$
    6. Substitution (step 4 into 5)

7. $\overarc{AMD} \cong \overarc{CND}$
    7. Definition of congruent arcs

8. If minor arcs are congruent, then so are the major arcs
    8. Law of Deduction

Part 2

9. $\overarc{AMB} \cong \overarc{CND}$
    9. Given

10. $m\overarc{AMB} = m\overarc{CND}$
    10. Definition of congruent arcs

11. $m\overarc{AMB} = 360 - m\overarc{AB}$; $m\overarc{CND} = 360 - m\overarc{CD}$
    11. Major Arc Theorem

12. $360 - m\overarc{AB} = 360 - m\overarc{CD}$
    12. Substitution (step 11 into 10)

13. $-m\overarc{AB} = -m\overarc{CD}$
    13. Addition property of equality

14. $m\overarc{AB} = m\overarc{CD}$
    14. Multiplication property of equality

15. $\overarc{AB} \cong \overarc{CD}$
    15. Definition of congruent arcs

16. If the major arcs are congruent, then so are the minor arcs
    16. Law of Deduction

17. Minor arcs congruent if and only if the corresponding major arcs are congruent
    17. Definition of biconditional (see steps 8 and 16)

Geometry and Transportation

Objectives

1. To identify some of the contributions of geometry to the world of transportation.
2. To appreciate the application of mathematics to real-life transportation situations.

GEOMETRY AND TRANSPORTATION

We can hardly imagine the days when people had to walk or ride a horse. The invention of the circular wheel has changed everything. Bicycles, motorcycles, cars, trucks, and trains all rely on these circles. In fact, even airplanes rely on circles for takeoffs and landings. The revolution in transportation has not stopped with the invention of the wheel. Bicycles have been adapted for racing and for mountain trails. Cars have come a long way since the Model T. Commercial jets, fighter planes, and the Concorde would all look strange to Wilbur and Orville Wright.

Those who design vehicles must use the geometry of circles to make sure that the brakes enable the wheels to stop fast enough and to make appropriate gear ratios. Even designing the little wheels or pulleys for trolleys and cable cars requires knowledge of circles. The people who design these vehicles use simple geometric principles, but the calculations can get complicated.

Airplanes cannot fly unless they have enough lift. The force of the air flowing over the wings must create a vacuum or low pressure area above the wings, giving enough upward force to support the weight of the airplane. The Anglo-French supersonic transport, Concorde, has 3856 square feet of wing surface. The maximum takeoff weight is 408,000 pounds, depending on speed, atmospheric pressure, temperature, and altitude. Many supersonic aircraft are equipped with devices on their wings to increase low speed lift, but retracting these allows the plane to fly at supersonic speeds.

Suppose that as the designer of the aircraft you want to increase its maximum takeoff weight by 16,000 pounds. How many square feet will you have to add to the wings to increase the lift by that much?

Radar screens track weather and airplanes on a circular grid.

Presentation

Ask students where the 106 lb./ft.^{2} came from in the denominator of the fraction at the top of page 389 (quotient of 408,000 pounds maximum weight divided by 3856 square feet of wing surface). Tell students that when they read they should ask themselves where numbers come from and use a scratch pad to check. Only textbooks try to show every step; in technical writing, such detail wastes space because much of it is obvious to the technicians. Instead, technicians write the main steps and expect the reader to figure out the details. Detailed thinking in math class will prepare you for reading reports and manuals throughout your life.

Motivational Idea. You may want to discuss whether Archimedes' principle applies to aircraft as well as to things underwater (an object is buoyed up by a force equal to the weight of the water it displaces). Even a small, single-seat private plane weighs far more than the air it displaces. Dirigible airships such as the *Hindenburg* and Goodyear blimp fly because of the displacement of air. Show encyclopedia photos of the *Hindenburg* disaster. Such hydrogen-filled dirigibles caught fire easily. Since then, blimps and weather balloons have been filled with helium instead. The density of helium is about one-seventh that of air. A balloon containing 1000 mg^3 of helium would be buoyed up by a force of more than 1000 kg. In contrast, hot-air balloons rise because heat rises (the hot air is lighter than the cooler air surrounding it). ■

$$\frac{16{,}000 \text{ lb.}}{106 \text{ lb./ft.}^2} = 151 \text{ square feet}$$

Thus you will need to add 151 square feet to the total wing area, or 75.5 square feet to each wing. Because part of the increased capacity will be the structure of the aircraft, the increased carrying capacity will be only part of the 16,000 pounds.

Besides vehicle design, transportation also depends on routing. On the ground, construction crews build roads, tunnels, and bridges. These, too, require geometry. Tunnel builders plan dynamite blasts to clear more tunnel in a certain radius without destroying previous work. Air traffic controllers and submarine captains both use circular range markers. They must be able to read the circular grid (polar coordinates) to locate other planes or vessels in the area.

Some designers are experimenting with solar-powered cars; a solar-powered airplane has already crossed the English Channel. How much of a problem would it be to power a simple golf cart with solar cells?

A cart that travels 25 miles per hour requires about 900 watts of power. Simple solar (or photovoltaic) cells produce 0.084 watts.

$$\frac{900 \text{ watts}}{0.084 \text{ watts per cell}} = 10{,}714 \text{ cells}$$

Since solar cells cost about $10.00 apiece, 10,714 cells would cost $107,140. Since each cell is 5 by 2.5 centimeters, each cell covers $5 \cdot 2.5 = 12.5$ sq. cm. Altogether, they would cover 133,925 cm$^2 \approx 13.4$ m^2 (10,714 cells by 12.5 cm^2/cell).

Thus the cells would cover an area of about 3.7 meters on a side. Do you think your golf cart would look a little top-heavy? Perhaps your solar panel could double as a sail.

Those who design vehicles must use the geometry of circles to make sure that the brakes enable the wheels to stop fast enough and to make appropriate gear ratios.

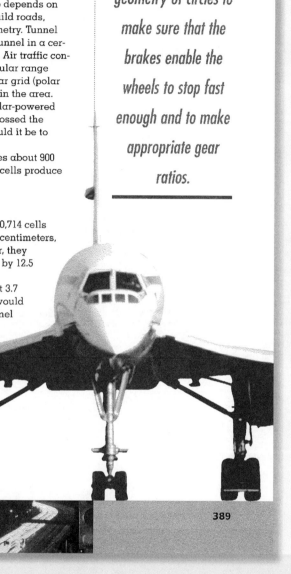

The Concorde is the fastest commercial aircraft, flying at an average speed of Mach 2.2.

Flash

The Concorde carries up to 100 passengers and 1300 pounds of cargo. It is 203 ft. 9 in. long, and the fuselage is 9 ft. 6 in. wide. The wingspan is 83 ft. 8 in., and the maximum take-off weight is 408,000 pounds. Its cruising speed is 1336 mph at an altitude of 55,000 feet. Its design includes many titanium parts to reduce heat. In January of 1976 it began scheduled passenger service and currently runs a daily roundtrip from London to New York (3 hr. and 50 min. flying time) and back. Special charters from London to Barbados are also available.

389

Inscribed Angles

Objectives

1. To identify and prove theorems relating inscribed angles to the measure of their intercepted arcs.
2. To state other relationships that involve inscribed angles.

Vocabulary
corollary

Assignment
- Intuitive: 1-16
- Standard: 1-24, 26-30
- Rigorous: 5-15 odd, 17-30

Flash
The baskets hang from the roof of the trading post. You can investigate students' reasoning by asking how many think the photo is upside down. If anyone does not think so, ask him to explain why. If no one gets the right explanation, ask for other possible explanations until someone does.

Resources
- *Activities Manual,* Math History Activity. Looks at the life and works of Ptolemy.
- *Test Packet,* Quiz 3, Chapter 9 covers Section 9.4.

Reading and Writing Mathematics
Scientific calculators have a button labeled "DRG," on which the letters stand for *degrees,* *radians,* and *grads.* The last (also called *gradients,* or *grades,* in some reference works) refers to the division of a circle into 400 parts. (Thus, the circle divides into 400 grads instead of 360 degrees, which are further subdivided into 100ths because of the greater convenience compared to 60 minutes and 60 seconds.)

Have the students convert 50° to grads.
$\frac{50°}{x} = \frac{360}{400} = \frac{9}{10}$; $9x = 500$; $x = 55.\overline{5}$ grads *(Note that the first two decimal places correspond to the subdivision for "minutes" and the next two decimals correspond to the "seconds.")*

You may also have them convert 380 grads, 91 minutes, and 8 seconds to the usual kind of degrees, minutes, and seconds.
$\frac{x°}{380.9108} = \frac{360}{400} = \frac{9}{10}$; $x = 342°\ 49'\ 11"$

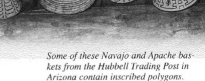

9.4 Inscribed Angles

Remember that an inscribed angle is an angle whose vertex is on a circle and whose sides lie on chords of the circle. In figure 9.18 $\angle ABC$ is an inscribed angle.

Some of these Navajo and Apache baskets from the Hubbell Trading Post in Arizona contain inscribed polygons.

Can you guess the relationship between the measure of an inscribed angle and the measure of its intercepted arc?

Figure 9.18

Theorem 9.13
The measure of an inscribed angle is equal to one-half the measure of its intercepted arc.

Given: $\odot K$ with inscribed $\angle ABC$ that intercepts $\overset{\frown}{AC}$
Prove: $m\angle ABC = \frac{1}{2}m\overset{\frown}{AC}$

To prove this theorem, you must consider three possible cases.

Case 1: The center K lies on $\angle ABC$.

Figure 9.19

Case 2: The center K lies in the interior of $\angle ABC$.

Figure 9.20

Presentation

Review central angles and inscribed angles. Draw two angles inscribed in the same arc but make the side of one pass through the center and make the vertex of the other very close to the arc itself. Ask students which angle has the greater measure (some will pick one, and some may realize that they have the same measure). Most students will be surprised when you tell them that the measures are always the same and that you can prove it.

Show students that there are three cases to Theorem 9.13. You can mention the Law of Cases, which is the applicable rule of logic. You may wish to give students examples of the Law of Cases. For instance, you may prove that something is true for all angles by proving it in four cases as follows: 1) for acute angles, 2) for right angles, 3) for obtuse angles, and 4) for straight angles. Ask students what cases they might use in proving that an equality is true for all real numbers (*three cases: positive numbers, zero, and negative numbers*).

Study through the first case of the proof of Theorem 9.13. Even though the second and third cases are left as exercises, it is good to anticipate that each of these will be proved by using auxiliary lines to change them back to case 1.

Read through Theorems 9.14-9.16. Then illustrate them on the chalkboard. Explain the term *corollary.* Students should be able to

Case 3: The center K lies in the exterior of $\angle ABC$.

Figure 9.21

The first case will be proved here, and the other two cases will be done as exercises. The proofs of the other two parts use this case as a reason.

STATEMENTS	REASONS
1. $\odot K$ with inscribed $\angle ABC$ that intercepts $\overarc{AC}$	1. Given
2. K lies on $\angle ABC$	2. Given for Case 1
3. Draw $\overleftrightarrow{KC}$	3. Auxiliary line
4. $\overline{KB} \cong \overline{KC}$	4. Radii of a circle are congruent
5. $\triangle KBC$ is an isosceles triangle	5. Definition of isosceles triangle
6. $\angle KBC \cong \angle BCK$	6. Isosceles Triangle Theorem
7. $m\angle KBC = m\angle BCK$	7. Definition of congruent angles
8. $m\angle KBC + m\angle BCK = m\angle CKA$	8. Exterior Angle Theorem
9. $m\angle CKA = m\overarc{AC}$	9. Definition of arc measure
10. $m\angle KBC + m\angle KBC = m\overarc{AC}$	10. Substitution (steps 7 and 9 into 8)
11. $2m\angle KBC = m\overarc{AC}$	11. Distributive property
12. $m\angle KBC = \frac{1}{2}m\overarc{AC}$	12. Multiplication property of equality

This theorem has some corollaries. A *corollary* is a theorem that follows immediately from some other theorem. The following corollaries are exercises.

> **Theorem 9.14**
> If two inscribed angles intercept congruent arcs, then the angles are congruent.

9.4 INSCRIBED ANGLES **391**

Given: In $\odot M$, $m\overarc{RT} = 80$, $m\overarc{SQ} = 64$

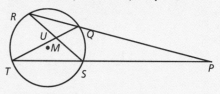

Find:
1. $m\angle QTS$ **32°**
2. $m\angle TQR$ **40°**
3. $m\angle TQP$ **140°**
4. $m\angle TPR$ **8°**

Given: In $\odot K$, $\overleftrightarrow{AB} \parallel \overleftrightarrow{DE}$ (tangent), $\overline{AC} \cong \overline{BC}$; $m\angle BAC = 56°$

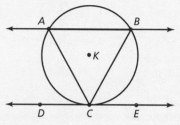

Find:
5. $m\overarc{AC}$ **112°**
6. $m\overarc{BC}$ **112°**
7. $m\angle ACB$ **68°**
8. $m\angle ABC$ **56°**
9. $m\overarc{AB}$ **136°**
10. *Given:* In $\odot Q$, $\overline{DB}$ is a diameter, $\overarc{AD} \cong \overarc{DC}$
    Prove: $\triangle ABQ \cong \triangle CBQ$

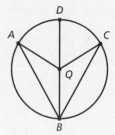

1. $\overarc{AD} \cong \overarc{DC}$; $\overline{BD}$ is a diameter	1. Given
2. $\angle AQD \cong \angle CQD$	2. Two minor arcs are congruent if and only if their central angles are congruent
3. $\angle AQD$ and $\angle AQB$ are supplementary; $\angle CQD$ and $\angle CQB$ are supplementary	3. Angles that form a linear pair are supplementary
4. $\angle AQB \cong \angle CQB$	4. Supplements of congruent angles are congruent
5. $\overline{AQ} \cong \overline{QC}$	5. All radii of a circle are congruent
6. $\overline{QB} \cong \overline{QB}$	6. Reflexive property of congruent segments
7. $\triangle AQB \cong \triangle CQB$	7. SAS

Tips

verbally explain in a sentence or two why these theorems are true based on Theorem 9.13. The simplicity of these proofs will show them what is meant by defining a *corollary* as an immediate consequence of an important theorem. If time allows, work some proofs in the exercise section or let students begin their homework.

Ex. 11. $m\angle 3 = \frac{1}{2}(68) = 34$ and $m\angle 1 = \frac{1}{2}(134) = 67$. Since the measures of the angles of $\triangle DXA$ must total 180, $m\angle DXA = 79$.

Ex. 16. Two of the angles of $\triangle MLY$ are inscribed in the given arcs and measure 49 and 43 degrees respectively. The third angle, $\angle MYL$, measures 88°. ∎

1. 30°   2. 80°
3. 50°   4. 65°
5. 28°   6. 94°
7. 305°   8. 218°
9. 35°   10. 280°
11. 79°   12. 222°
13. 60°   14. 196°
15. $m\angle MNO = 106°$, $m\angle MLO = 74°$
16. 88°
17.

1. ⊙K with inscribed ∠ABC	1. Given
2. K lies in the interior of ∠ABC	2. Given for Case 2
3. Draw diameter $\overline{BD}$	3. Auxiliary line
4. $m\angle ABD = \frac{1}{2}m\widehat{AD}$; $m\angle DBC = \frac{1}{2}m\widehat{DC}$	4. Proved in Case 1
5. $m\angle ABC = m\angle ABD + m\angle DBC$	5. Angle Addition Postulate
6. $m\widehat{AB} = \frac{1}{2}m\widehat{AD} + \frac{1}{2}m\widehat{DC}$	6. Substitution (step 4 into 5)
7. $m\angle ABC = \frac{1}{2}(m\widehat{AD} + m\widehat{DC})$	7. Distributive property
8. $m\widehat{AD} + m\widehat{DC} = m\widehat{AC}$	8. Arc Addition Postulate
9. $m\angle ABC = \frac{1}{2}m\widehat{AC}$	9. Substitution (step 8 into 7)

18.

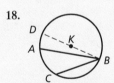

1. ⊙K with inscribed ∠ABC	1. Given
2. K lies in the exterior of ∠ABC	2. Given for Case 3
3. Draw diameter $\overline{BD}$	3. Auxiliary line
4. $m\angle DBC = \frac{1}{2}m\widehat{DC}$; $m\angle DBA = \frac{1}{2}m\widehat{DA}$	4. Proved in Case 1
5. $m\angle DBA + m\angle ABC = m\angle DBC$	5. Angle Addition Postulate
6. $m\angle ABC = m\angle DBC - m\angle DBA$	6. Addition property of equality
7. $m\angle ABC = \frac{1}{2}m\widehat{DC} - \frac{1}{2}m\widehat{DA}$	7. Substitution (step 4 into 6)
8. $m\angle ABC = \frac{1}{2}(m\widehat{DC} - m\widehat{DA})$	8. Distributive property
9. $m\widehat{DA} + m\widehat{AC} = m\widehat{DC}$	9. Arc Addition Postulate
10. $m\widehat{AC} = m\widehat{DC} - m\widehat{DA}$	10. Addition property of equality
11. $m\angle ABC = \frac{1}{2}m\widehat{AC}$	11. Substitution (step 10 into 8)

19.

1. ∠ABC and ∠PQR are inscribed angles and $\widehat{AC} \cong \widehat{PR}$	1. Given
2. $m\angle ABC = \frac{1}{2}m\widehat{AC}$; $m\angle PQR = \frac{1}{2}m\widehat{PR}$	2. Inscribed angle measures half of intercepted arc
3. $m\widehat{AC} = m\widehat{PR}$	3. Definition of congruent arcs
4. $m\angle ABC = \frac{1}{2}m\widehat{PR}$	4. Substitution (step 3 into 2)
5. $m\angle ABC = m\angle PQR$	5. Transitive property of equality
6. $\angle ABC \cong \angle PQR$	6. Definition of congruent angles
7. If two inscribed angles intercept congruent arcs, then the angles are congruent	7. Law of Deduction

---

Theorem 9.15
An angle inscribed in a semicircle is a right angle.

Theorem 9.16
The opposite angles of an inscribed quadrilateral are supplementary.

▶ A. Exercises

Using the diagram, find the indicated measures in exercises 1-10.

1. If $m\widehat{DC} = 60°$, find $m\angle 4$.
2. If $m\angle 1 = 40°$, find $m\widehat{AB}$.
3. If $m\angle 3 = 25°$, find $m\widehat{DC}$.
4. If $m\widehat{AB} = 130°$, find $m\angle 2$.
5. If $m\angle 3 = 28°$, find $m\angle 4$.
6. If $m\angle 3 = 47°$, find $m\widehat{DC}$.
7. If $m\widehat{DC} = 55°$, find $m\widehat{DBC}$.
8. If $m\widehat{AD} = 142°$, find $m\widehat{ACD}$.
9. If $m\widehat{ADB} = 290°$, find $m\angle 1$.
10. If $m\angle CBD = 40°$, find $m\widehat{CAD}$.

▶ B. Exercises

Use the diagram above for exercise 11.
11. If $m\widehat{DC} = 68°$ and $m\widehat{AB} = 134°$, find $m\angle DXA$.

Use the following figure for exercises 12-16.

12. If $m\widehat{LN} = 138°$, find $m\widehat{LMN}$.
13. If $m\widehat{MLO} = 240°$, find $m\angle MLO$.
14. If $m\angle LOM = 82°$, find $m\widehat{MNL}$.
15. If $m\widehat{MLO} = 212°$, find $m\angle MNO$ and $m\angle MLO$.
16. If $m\widehat{MN} = 98°$ and $m\widehat{LO} = 86°$, find $m\angle MYL$.

Prove the following theorems and statements.
17. Case 2 of Theorem 9.13
18. Case 3 of Theorem 9.13
19. Theorem 9.14
20. *Given:* ⊙Q; $\overrightarrow{IM}$ bisects ∠LIN
    Prove: $m\widehat{LM} = \frac{1}{2}m\widehat{LN}$

21. *Given:* $\odot R$; $m\angle TSU = \frac{1}{2}m\widehat{UV}$

    Prove: $\widehat{UV} \cong \widehat{TU}$

22. *Given:* $\odot F$; $\overleftrightarrow{GH} \parallel \overleftrightarrow{JI}$

    Prove: $\widehat{GJ} \cong \widehat{HI}$

23. Theorem 9.15
24. Theorem 9.16

▶ **C. Exercises**

25. *Prove:* If a trapezoid is inscribed in a circle, then it is isosceles.

■ Cumulative Review

Justify each statement with a reason.

    Given: $\triangle ABC$ is obtuse, and $\overleftrightarrow{CD} \perp \overline{AB}$ at D

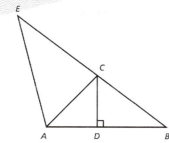

26. $\angle CDA$ and $\angle CDB$ are right angles
27. $BC > BD$
28. $m\angle ACE = m\angle B + m\angle CAD$
29. $AE + AB > BE$
30. $m\angle BAE + m\angle ABE + m\angle E = 180°$

20.

1. $\odot Q$; $\overrightarrow{IM}$ bisects $\angle LIN$	1. Given
2. $m\angle LIM = \frac{1}{2}m\angle LIN$	2. Angle Bisector Theorem
3. $m\angle LIM = \frac{1}{2}m\widehat{LM}$; $m\angle LIN = \frac{1}{2}m\widehat{LN}$	3. Inscribed angle measures half of intercepted arc
4. $\frac{1}{2}m\widehat{LM} = \frac{1}{2}(\frac{1}{2}m\widehat{LN})$	4. Substitution (step 3 into 2)
5. $m\widehat{LM} = \frac{1}{2}m\widehat{LN}$	5. Multiplication property of equality

21.

1. $\odot R$; $m\angle TSU = \frac{1}{2}m\widehat{UV}$	1. Given
2. $m\angle TSU = \frac{1}{2}m\widehat{TU}$	2. Inscribed angle measures half of intercepted arc
3. $\frac{1}{2}m\widehat{UV} = \frac{1}{2}\widehat{TU}$	3. Transitive property of equality
4. $m\widehat{UV} = m\widehat{TU}$	4. Multiplication property of equality
5. $\widehat{UV} \cong \widehat{TU}$	5. Definition of congruent arcs

22.

1. $\odot F$; $\overleftrightarrow{GH} \parallel \overleftrightarrow{JI}$	1. Given
2. $\angle HGI \cong \angle JIG$	2. Parallel Postulate
3. $m\angle HGI = m\angle JIG$	3. Definition of congruent angles
4. $m\angle HGI = \frac{1}{2}m\widehat{HI}$; $m\angle JIG = \frac{1}{2}m\widehat{GJ}$	4. Inscribed angle measures half of intercepted arc
5. $\frac{1}{2}m\widehat{HI} = \frac{1}{2}m\widehat{GJ}$	5. Substitution (step 4 into 3)
6. $m\widehat{HI} = m\widehat{GJ}$	6. Multiplication property of equality
7. $\widehat{HI} \cong \widehat{GJ}$	7. Definition of congruent arcs

---

23.

1. $\widehat{ABC}$ is a semicircle	1. Given
2. $m\widehat{ABC} = 180$	2. Definition of semicircle
3. $m\widehat{ABC} + m\widehat{ADC} = 360$	3. Arc Addition Postulate
4. $m\widehat{ADC} = 180$	4. Addition property of equality
5. $m\angle ABC = \frac{1}{2}m\widehat{ADC}$	5. Inscribed angle measures half of intercepted arc
6. $m\angle ABC = \frac{1}{2}(180) = 90$	6. Substitution (step 4 into 5)
7. $\angle ABC$ is a right angle	7. Definition of right angle

24.

1. $ABCD$ inscribed in $\odot L$	1. Given
2. $m\widehat{ABC} + m\widehat{ADC} = m\odot L$	2. Arc Addition Postulate
3. $m\odot L = 360$	3. Degree measure of a circle
4. $m\widehat{ABC} + m\widehat{ADC} = 360$	4. Transitive property of equality
5. $\frac{1}{2}m\widehat{ADC} + \frac{1}{2}m\widehat{ABC} = \frac{1}{2}(360) = 180$	5. Multiplication property of equality
6. $m\angle ABC = \frac{1}{2}m\widehat{ADC}$; $m\angle ADC = \frac{1}{2}m\widehat{ABC}$	6. Inscribed angle measures half of intercepted arc
7. $m\angle ABC + m\angle ADC = 180$	7. Substitution (step 6 into 5)
8. $\angle ABC$ and $\angle ADC$ are supplementary angles	8. Definition of supplementary angles

(continued) see Answer section

Lines and Circles

Objectives

1. Find the measures of angles formed by intersecting lines (tangents, secants, or both) based on the measures of the intercepted arcs.
2. Prove the relationships for such intersecting lines.

Assignment

- Intuitive: 1-15, 22-26
- Standard: 1-20, 22-26
- Rigorous: 1-21 odd, 22-26

Resources

- *Activities Manual,* Calculator Skills. Focuses on the use of a calculator to find angle measures between the lines studied in this section.
- *Test Packet,* Quiz 4, Chapter 9 covers Section 9.5.

Reading and Writing Mathematics

Have students build a set of definitions until they can explain the meaning of *parsec* using only terms they understand. Consider the terms used that they have not looked up and make a list of them as "undefined terms." Then write the definitions that they looked up in reverse order, building to parsec as the last one. They should also give a conversion to miles but should not use such a conversion as their definition. ***Answers will vary. However, their final term should be parsec. A parsec is a unit of measure for interstellar space equal to a distance having a heliocentric parallax of one second. They will need to define heliocentric (measured from the***

9.5 Lines and Circles

In figure 9.22 you can see several intersecting lines. A tangent and two secants intersect at *F*. In this section you will see special relationships involving the angles formed by specific intersecting lines.

The two cables carrying the ski gondolas form tangent segments to the circular gears at the top and bottom of the lift.

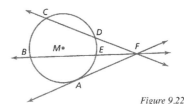

Figure 9.22

Theorem 9.17a

The measure of an angle formed by two secants that intersect in the exterior of a circle is one-half the difference of the measures of the intercepted arcs.

Given: $\odot O$ with secants $\overleftrightarrow{CA}$ and $\overleftrightarrow{EA}$
Prove: $m\angle 1 = \frac{1}{2}(m\widehat{CE} - m\widehat{BD})$

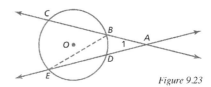

Figure 9.23

Presentation

Have the students study the first diagram and ask them to name tangent and secant lines. You may wish to continue this review and draw a similar diagram (on the board, overhead, or handout). Read Theorem 9.17a and go through the proof.

Discuss the remaining theorems and work through the example, which is similar to the exercises. The key to remembering the theorems is to synthesize the several parts into a single statement. Students will be asked to draw these conclusions in #1-3. You may want to do these orally to be sure they understand. It may help to lay out the six results as in the table (third column). The conclusions will be clear by noting where the italicized words match.

Students may need to review the various theorems on circles. The table below gives an overview of these relationships.

Chords-Arcs-Angles	Relationship (in congruent circles)
chords and arcs	congruent chords subtend congruent arcs and vice versa
central angles and arcs	minor arcs are congruent if the central angles are and vice versa
chords and central angles	chords are congruent if and only if the corresponding central angles are congruent

Lines-Arcs-Angles	Measure of Angle Formed
two secants	1. $\frac{1}{2}$ *difference* of arc measures if *exterior* 2. $\frac{1}{2}$ arc measure if on *curve* (inscribed angle) 3. $\frac{1}{2}$ *sum* of arc measures if *interior*
secant and tangent	1. $\frac{1}{2}$ *difference* of arc measures if *exterior* 2. $\frac{1}{2}$ arc measure if on *curve* (never interior)
two tangents	$\frac{1}{2}$ *difference* of arc measures (always *exterior*)

STATEMENTS	REASONS
1. $\odot O$ with secants $\overleftrightarrow{CA}$ and $\overleftrightarrow{EA}$	1. Given
2. Draw $\overleftrightarrow{BE}$	2. Auxiliary line
3. $m\angle CBE = m\angle BEA + m\angle 1$	3. Exterior Angle Theorem
4. $m\angle 1 = m\angle CBE - m\angle BEA$	4. Addition property of equality
5. $m\angle CBE = \frac{1}{2}m\widehat{CE};\ m\angle BEA = \frac{1}{2}m\widehat{BD}$	5. An inscribed angle measures half the measure of its intercepted arc
6. $m\angle 1 = \frac{1}{2}m\widehat{CE} - \frac{1}{2}m\widehat{BD}$	6. Substitution (step 5 into 4)
7. $m\angle 1 = \frac{1}{2}(m\widehat{CE} - m\widehat{BD})$	7. Distributive property

Two secants may intersect in the interior of a circle. If this happens, then the angle measure between the secants is not half the difference of the arc measures but half the sum of the arc measures.

> **Theorem 9.18**
> The measure of an angle formed by two secants that intersect in the interior of a circle is one-half the sum of the measures of the intercepted arcs.

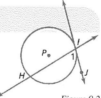

Figure 9.24

By Theorem 9.18 you know that the $m\angle 1 = \frac{1}{2}(m\widehat{AB} + m\widehat{DC})$. This theorem will be proved as an exercise.

The only other possibility for two secants is that they intersect on the circle itself. In this case, an inscribed angle is formed, which you have already studied in the previous section.

What happens to the measure of the angle if one of the lines is a tangent line?

> **Theorem 9.19**
> The measure of an angle formed by a tangent and secant that intersect at the point of tangency is one-half the measure of the intercepted arc:
> $m\angle HIJ = \frac{1}{2}m\widehat{HI}$.

We will prove this theorem in an exercise.

Figure 9.25

Tips

Ex. 9. Equation: $\frac{1}{2}(86 - x) = 36$

Ex. 13. Equation: $\frac{1}{2}[(360 - x) - x] = 116$

Ex. 14. Calculate $\frac{1}{2}(160 - 124)$

Ex. 23. This is a good review problem for students because it is not stated in the text and requires thinking. It is easy if the proof has been presented (Additional Problem 2 in Section 7.2) or discussed (Section 7.6 Presentation or Section 8.2, #20). Otherwise students must reason it out using congruent triangles. ■

---

sun's center), parallax, and interstellar at least. (Note that parsec abbreviates parallax of one second.) As a conversion, one parsec equals 206,265 times the radius of earth's orbit, or 3.26 light years, or 19.2 trillion miles.

Additional Problems

Find *x*.

1. **92°**

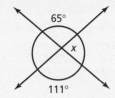

2. **122°**

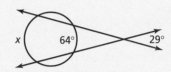

3. **9°**

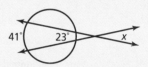

4. **244°**

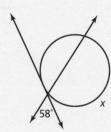

5. **102°**

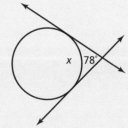

Challenge

Is there an upper bound for the measure of the angle between two secants? lower bound? **180°, 0°**

Answers

1. the angle formed measures half the difference of the measures of the intercepted arcs.
2. half the measure of the intercepted arc.
3. half the sum of the measures of the intercepted arcs.
4. Theorem 9.17a

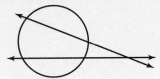

Theorem 9.17b

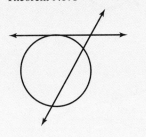

Theorem 9.17c

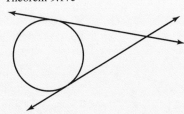

5. Theorem 9.19   Theorem 9.13

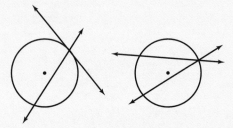

EXAMPLE Find the measure of $\angle ABC$ if $\overleftrightarrow{BC}$ is tangent to $\odot Q$ at B and $\overleftrightarrow{AB}$ is a secant. $m\widehat{AB} = 170$.

Answer $m\angle ABC = \frac{1}{2}m\widehat{AB}$

$m\angle ABC = \frac{1}{2}(170)$

$m\angle ABC = 85$

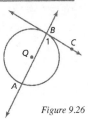

Figure 9.26

In the exercises you will see how to combine Theorems 9.17b and 9.17c with Theorem 9.17a.

Theorem 9.17b
The measure of an angle formed by a secant and a tangent that intersect in the exterior of a circle is one-half the difference of the measures of the intercepted arcs.

Theorem 9.17c
The measure of an angle formed by the intersection of two tangents is one-half the difference of the measures of the intercepted arcs.

The theorems that you have seen in this section will help you to compute angle measures.

▶ **A. Exercises**

1. Theorems 9.17a, 9.17b, and 9.17c are the three cases for a single theorem. Complete the theorem.

Theorem 9.17
If two lines intersect a circle and intersect each other in the exterior of the circle, then . . .

2. Complete the statement: If two lines that intersect a circle intersect each other at a point on the circle, then the angle formed measures . . .
3. Complete the statement: If two lines that intersect a circle intersect each other in the interior of the circle, then the angle formed measures . . .
4. Sketch the three cases of exercise 1. Label them.
5. Sketch the two cases for exercise 2. Label them (include theorem numbers).
6. Sketch the only case for exercise 3. Label it.

Find *x*.

7.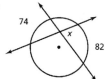

12.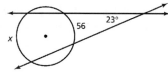

8.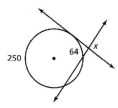

13.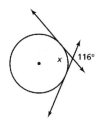

9.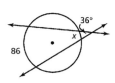

14.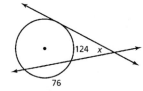

10.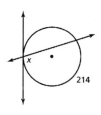

15.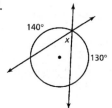

11.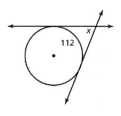

6. Theorem 9.18

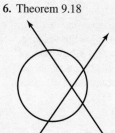

7. *x* = 78   12. *x* = 102
8. *x* = 93   13. *x* = 64
9. *x* = 14   14. *x* = 18
10. *x* = 107   15. *x* = 45
11. *x* = 68

16. Tangents do not intersect the interior of a circle; therefore, the cases in which one or both lines are tangents are eliminated.

17. Two tangents cannot have the same point of tangency. (Otherwise both tangents would be perpendicular to the same radius at the same point.)

18.

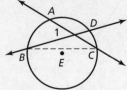

1. $\overleftrightarrow{AC}$ and $\overleftrightarrow{BD}$ are secants that intersect inside $\odot E$ and form $\angle 1$	1. Given
2. Draw $\overleftrightarrow{BC}$	2. Auxiliary line
3. $m\angle 1 = m\angle ACB + m\angle DBC$	3. Exterior Angle Theorem
4. $m\angle ACB = \frac{1}{2}m\widehat{AB}$; $m\angle DBC = \frac{1}{2}m\widehat{DC}$	4. Inscribed angles measure half the intercepted arcs
5. $m\angle 1 = \frac{1}{2}m\widehat{AB} + \frac{1}{2}m\widehat{DC}$	5. Substitution (step 4 into 3)
6. $m\angle 1 = \frac{1}{2}(m\widehat{AB} + m\widehat{DC})$	6. Distributive property

19.

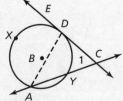

1. $\overleftrightarrow{DC}$ is a tangent and $\overleftrightarrow{AC}$ is a secant to $\odot B$	1. Given
2. Draw $\overleftrightarrow{AD}$	2. Auxiliary line
3. $\angle ADE = m\angle CAD + m\angle 1$	3. Exterior Angle Theorem
4. $m\angle ADE - m\angle CAD = m\angle 1$	4. Addition property of equality
5. $m\angle ADE = \frac{1}{2}m\widehat{AXD}$	5. Angle measure for secant and tangent at point of tangency
6. $m\angle CAD = \frac{1}{2}m\widehat{DY}$	6. Inscribed angle measures half of intercepted arc
7. $\frac{1}{2}m\widehat{AXD} - \frac{1}{2}m\widehat{DY} = m\angle 1$	7. Substitution (steps 5 and 6 into 4)
8. $\frac{1}{2}(m\widehat{AXD} - m\widehat{DY}) = m\angle 1$	8. Distributive property

▶ B. Exercises

16. Explain why there are no other cases in exercise 6.
17. Explain why there is no third case in exercise 5.

Prove the following theorems.
18. Theorem 9.18
19. Theorem 9.17b
20. Theorem 9.17c

▶ C. Exercises

21. Prove Theorem 9.19.

■ Cumulative Review

Use the quadrilateral shown for the following questions.

22. Name the type of quadrilateral.
23. How do the diagonals relate?

If the diagonals of the quadrilateral shown are 10 and 6 inches respectively, give the
24. perimeter.
25. area.
26. Name the type of polyhedron formed by using the quadrilateral shown as the base of a pyramid.

20.

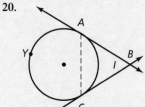

1. $\overleftrightarrow{AB}$ and $\overleftrightarrow{BC}$ are tangents	1. Given
2. Draw $\overline{CA}$	2. Auxiliary line
3. $m\angle DCA = m\angle BAC + m\angle 1$	3. Exterior Angle Theorem
4. $m\angle 1 = m\angle DCA - m\angle BAC$	4. Addition property of equality
5. $m\angle DCA = \frac{1}{2}m\widehat{CYA}$; $m\angle BAC = \frac{1}{2}m\widehat{CA}$	5. Angle measure for tangent and secant at point of tangency
6. $m\angle 1 = \frac{1}{2}m\widehat{CYA} - \frac{1}{2}m\widehat{CA}$	6. Substitution (step 5 into 4)
7. $m\angle 1 = \frac{1}{2}(m\widehat{CYA} - m\widehat{CA})$	7. Distributive property

(continued) see Answer Section

9.6 Sectors and Segments

The spokes of this antique fertilizer from the Badlands of South Dakota determine congruent sectors. The front wheel has 12 sectors; how many are on the back wheels?

To find the distance around a circle, you find the circumference of the circle, which is given by the following formula.

$$c = 2\pi r$$

But how can you find the length of an arc? You already know that the measure of the arc equals the degree measure of the corresponding central angle. But this is the degree measure of the arc and not the length of the arc. The next theorem gives a formula for finding the length of the arc. The Greek letter θ (theta) is often used as a variable for measures of arcs and angles.

Theorem 9.20

If the degree measure of an arc is θ and the circumference of the circle is c, then the length of the arc is l, given by $\frac{l}{c} = \frac{\theta}{360}$, or $l = \frac{c\theta}{360}$.

You can convert this formula to a more useful form by substituting $c = 2\pi r$ into the formula.

$$l = \frac{2\pi r\theta}{360}$$

$$l = \frac{\pi r\theta}{180}$$

We will now look at some special subsets of a circle and its interior.

Definitions

A **sector of a circle** is the region bounded by two radii and the intercepted arc.

A **segment of a circle** is the region bounded by a chord and its intercepted arc.

9.6 Sectors and Segments

Objectives

1. To derive and apply a formula for arc length.
2. To develop and apply formulas for the areas of sectors and segments.
3. To develop and apply a formula for the perimeter of a sector.

Vocabulary

sector of a circle
segment of a circle

Assignment

- Intuitive: no assignment necessary
- Standard: 1-24, 26-30
- Rigorous: 1-19 odd, 20-30

Resource

- *Activities Manual,* Practice

Flash

Answer: 14 sectors

Presentation

Emphasize the difference between arc measure and arc length. Arc measure is the degree measure of the central angle and is therefore proportional to the 360 degrees of arc contained in a circle. Arcs can have the same measure regardless of the radius of the circle. In contrast, arc length is a linear measure around a part of the circumference.

Theorem 9.20 shows how to find the arc length in a particular circle. Point out the use of θ in this theorem. The Greek letter θ (pronounced THAY tuh) is one of several used for angle and arc measures. (You may want to point out to students that they now know two of the 24 letters of the Greek alphabet; the other is π.) After studying Theorem 9.20, show the stu-

dents how to develop a formula for the arc length. They should easily understand the ratio used to develop this formula.

Common Student Error. Students learned in Section 9.3 that arcs of the same degree measure may not be congruent because they have different lengths. Now they may think that arcs with the same length are always congruent. Draw circles with radii of one inch and three inches. Calculate the arc length of a semicircle on the smaller circle (π *inches*). Now calculate the arc length of a 60° angle on the larger circle (π *inches*). Ask if they have the same arc length (*yes*) and whether they are congruent (*no*). Get students to explain why they are not congruent (*the arcs have different*

measures and do not satisfy the definition of congruent arcs; or the arcs have the same size but not same shape: one is a semicircle and the other is only one-sixth of a circle). Emphasize that arcs must have both the same arc length (size) and the same arc measure (shape) in order to be congruent.

Define and illustrate both a segment and a sector. Study through the procedure given for finding the area of a sector. Notice that this procedure also uses a ratio. As you go through the examples in this section, make sure that your students understand the procedures since they must use them to work the exercises.

It is important to show students that arc length and area of a sector are just fractional

Reading and Writing Mathematics

Have the students construct arcs of radius 1, 2, and 3 units, all with a central angle of 60°. Ask the following.

1. Find the arc length of each.

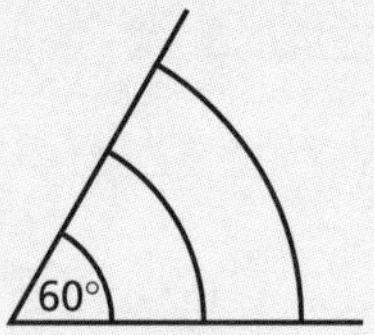

1.047, 2.094, 3.142

2. Are the arc lengths proportional to the radii? **yes**

3. Is the relationship a direct variation? If so, what is the constant of variation? **yes;** $\frac{\theta\pi}{180}$, **or 1.047**

Additional Problems

1. Find the area of a sector of 20° in a circle of radius 6. $2\pi \approx$ **6.28 sq. units**

2. Find the degree measure of the arc for a sector with an area of 96 in.² in a circle of radius 8 in. $\frac{540}{\pi} \approx$ **171.89°**

3. Find the radius of a circle containing a sector with an area of 50 m² and an arc of 24°. $\sqrt{\frac{750}{\pi}} \approx$ **15.45 m**

4. Find the perimeter of a sector with an arc of 20° in a circle of radius 6. $12 + \frac{2}{3}\pi \approx$ **14.09**

5. Find the area of a segment with an arc of 60° and a radius of 12 cm. $24\pi - 36\sqrt{3} \approx$ **13.04² cm**

The first diagram below shows a sector, and the second diagram shows a segment.

(a)

(b)

Figure 9.27

The area of a sector is to the area of the circle as the arc measure is to the degree measure of the circle.

> **Theorem 9.21**
>
> **The area of a sector is given by the proportion**
> $\frac{A}{A_c} = \frac{\theta}{360}$, **or** $A = A_c \frac{\theta}{360}$, **where** A **is the area of the sector,** A_c **is the area of the circle, and** θ **is the arc measure in degrees.**

By substituting the formula for the area of a circle, we obtain

$$A = \frac{\pi r^2 \theta}{360}.$$

To find the area of a segment, you need to use some common sense and some basic arithmetic operations.

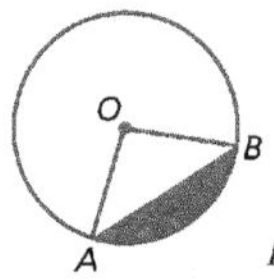

Figure 9.28

Find the area of the sector intercepting $\widehat{AB}$ and subtract the area of the triangle, $\triangle ABO$. An example will help you understand.

EXAMPLE 1   Find the area of the segment formed by $\overline{CD}$.

Answer   1. Find the area of the sector intercepting $\widehat{CD}$.

$$A = \frac{\pi r^2 \theta}{360}$$

$$= \frac{\pi 8^2 (60)}{360}$$

$$= \frac{64\pi}{6}$$

$$= \frac{32\pi}{3} \text{ square units}$$

Figure 9.29

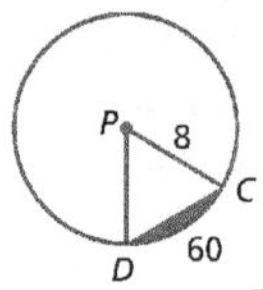

Continued ▶

---

parts of the circumference and area respectively. In these formulas, we measure the fractional part as the ratio of the central angle to 360°, using θ as the degree measure of the central angle.

$l = \text{fraction} \cdot \text{circumference}$

$l = \frac{\theta}{360}(2\pi r)$

$l = \frac{\pi r \theta}{180}$

$A = \text{fraction} \cdot \text{area}$

$A = \frac{\theta}{360}(\pi r^2)$

$A = \frac{\pi r^2 \theta}{360}$

Some of your students may find it easier to write and solve a proportion for each problem.

Do not discourage this, but encourage solving the proportion the fastest way (usually not by cross multiplying). For example, arc length is to the circle's circumference as the central angle is to 360. This results in the following proportion.

$$\frac{l}{2\pi r} = \frac{\theta}{360}$$

Students will easily understand this, and solving for l to obtain the previous formula is easy.

Motivational Idea. Some of your students in the rigorous track will enjoy looking at these ideas in another way. Look at the area of a sector—just as if it were a triangle with a curved base. We know that a triangle and a sector are different, but for small, narrow triangles

the difference is very small. The following illustrates this concept for the area of a sector and then is carried over to the area of a circle.

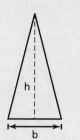

2. Find the area of the equilateral triangle, $\triangle PDC$. Recall $A = \frac{s^2\sqrt{3}}{4}$.

$$\text{Area } \triangle PDC = 8^2 \frac{\sqrt{3}}{4}$$

$$= \frac{64}{4}\sqrt{3}$$

$$= 16\sqrt{3} \text{ square units}$$

3. Subtract the area of the triangle from the area of the sector to find the area of the segment.

$$A_{\text{segment}} = A_{\text{sector}} - A_{\text{triangle}}$$

$$= \frac{32\pi}{3} - 16\sqrt{3} \approx 5.8 \text{ square units}$$

To find the perimeter of a sector, find the length of the arc and add the lengths of the two radii.

EXAMPLE 2   Find the perimeter of the sector intercepting $\overset{\frown}{XY}$.

Answer   1. Find the length of $\overset{\frown}{XY}$.

$$l = \frac{\pi r \theta}{180}$$

$$= \frac{\pi(12)(110)}{180}$$

$$= \frac{22\pi}{3}$$

$$\approx 23 \text{ units}$$

Figure 9.30

2. Add the two radii lengths to the arc length.

$$p = l + r + r$$

$$\approx 23 + 12 + 12$$

$$\approx 47 \text{ units}$$

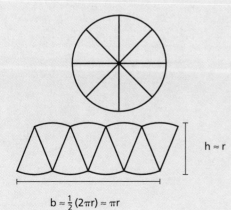

$$b \approx \frac{1}{2}(2\pi r) \approx \pi r$$

$$h \approx r$$

Again this method, though it seems very inaccurate, assumes that the figure of rearranged sectors is a parallelogram. This works best with extremely thin slices. These sectors would then be more nearly triangular. Investigations of the pattern as the number of sectors increases is a method commonly used in calculus.

Tips

Ex. 19. $A = 62,500\pi$ sq. ft.

Ex. 23. The simplest analysis is to use the area of a semicircle of $\odot K$ and the area of the segment of $\odot P$ determined by $\overline{AB}$. By the Pythagorean theorem, the diameter of $\odot K$ is $10\sqrt{2}$ and the radius is $5\sqrt{2}$. The area of the semicircle is 25π. For the 90° segment of $\odot P$, $A = 25\pi - 50$. Therefore, $A_{\text{shaded}} = 25\pi + (25\pi - 50) = 50\pi - 50$. If time permits, have students figure out the area of the unshaded portion of $\odot K$ (subtract shaded area from total area of smaller circle to get 50 sq. units). They will be surprised that the area is identical to the area of the right triangle $\triangle ABP$ (the fact that both equal $\frac{1}{2}r^2$ can be proved). ■

Answers

1. $\frac{10\pi}{3}$

2. $\frac{134\pi}{15}$

3. 6

4. 105

5. 2

6. $\frac{5\pi}{6}$

7. 10

8. $\frac{7\pi}{2}$

9. 300°

10. 5

▶ A. Exercises

Find the indicated measure in each diagram. The radius is *r*, the angle measure is θ, and the arc length is *l*.

1.

4.

2.

5.

3.

Copy and complete this table.

	Radius (units)	Central angle measure (degrees)	Arc length (units)
6.	3	50	
7.		16	$\frac{8\pi}{9}$
8.	7	90	
9.	7		$\frac{35\pi}{3}$
10.		220	$\frac{55\pi}{9}$

▶ B. Exercises

Copy and complete the table.

	Radius (units)	Arc measure (degrees)	Area of the sector	Perimeter of the sector
11.	2	55		
12.	12	80		
13.	4		$\frac{16\pi}{3}$	
14.		40	4π	$\frac{4\pi}{3} + 12$
15.	8		$\frac{128\pi}{3}$	$\frac{32\pi}{3} + 16$
16.		180	$\frac{\pi}{2}$	
17.	15	26		
18.	3		$\frac{9\pi}{8}$	

19. A farmer in the Great Plains irrigates a circular field with a radius of 500 ft. If he plants a 90° sector of that field with corn, how much area will he need to seed?

20. A 10-inch pizza is cut into 8 slices. How many square inches of topping does Janelle consume if she has just one slice?

Find the area of the shaded regions.

21.

22.

23.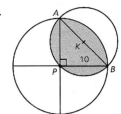

24. Develop a formula for the area of the sector of a circle with radius r and arc length l.

11.		$\frac{11\pi}{18}$	$\frac{11\pi}{18} + 4$
12.		32π	$\frac{16\pi}{3} + 24$
13.	120		$\frac{8\pi}{3} + 8$
14.	6		
15.	240		
16.	1		$\pi + 2$
17.		$\frac{65\pi}{4}$	$\frac{13\pi}{6} + 30$
18.	45		$\frac{3\pi}{4} + 6$

19. 196,350 sq. ft. (4.5 acres)

20. 9.8 sq. in.

21. $\frac{8\pi}{3} - 4\sqrt{3}$ sq. units

22. $9\pi - 18$ sq. units

23. $50\pi - 50$ sq. units

24. $A = \frac{lr}{2}$

25. $A = \frac{\pi r^2 d}{360} - a\sqrt{r^2 - a^2}$ or

$\quad\ A = \frac{lr}{2} - a\sqrt{r^2 - a^2}$

26. B [1.5]

27. A [9.5]

28. C [2.3]

29. E [2.2]

30. D [2.5]

▶ **C. Exercises**

25. Develop a formula for the area of a segment of a circle with radius r, chord length $2a$, and central angle d.

■ Cumulative Review

Match to each set the best description. Use each answer once.

26. $\overleftrightarrow{FG} \cap \overleftrightarrow{RS}$

27. $\overrightarrow{AB} \cap \odot A$ where B is on $\odot A$

28. $\overleftrightarrow{DH} \cap \overline{KL}$ where K and L are in opposite half-planes

29. $\overrightarrow{AB} \cap \overrightarrow{BA}$

30. $PQRS \cap \overline{MN}$ where M and N are in the interior of the convex polygon

A. at least one point

B. at most one point

C. exactly one point

D. less than one point

E. more than one point

9.7 Circle Constructions

Now you will see some constructions involving inscribed and circumscribed circles. You should remember the theorems from this chapter that justify them.

Construction 12

Circumscribed circle

Construct: A circle circumscribed about a given triangle

1. Draw any triangle, △ABC.
2. Construct the perpendicular bisector of two sides of the triangle and call their point of intersection D.
3. Measure the distance from D to one of the vertices and construct a circle with this radius and center D.

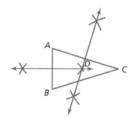 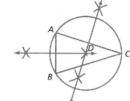

Figure 9.31

In the next example only the construction drawing is given. Look at the drawing and give the required steps for the construction.

The circular design of the Wheelie at Six Flags over Georgia tips passengers upside down.

Objectives

1. To construct the circumcenter, incenter, orthocenter, and centroid of a triangle.
2. To construct the circumscribed circle and inscribed circle of a triangle.
3. To construct regular polygons inscribed in circles.

Assignment
- Intuitive: no assignment necessary
- Standard: 1-15
- Rigorous: 1-25

Resources
- *Activities Manual*, Construction Skills: Inscribed and Circumscribed Constructions.
- *Test Packet*, Quiz 5, Chapter 9 covers Sections 9.6 and 9.7.

Reading and Writing Mathematics
Have the students research *radian* measure. ***Explanations will vary but should at least include 1) a radian is a unit of angle measure such that one radian corresponds to a central angle subtending an arc exactly one radius long, 2) 1 radian is therefore about 57.296 degrees, and 3) there are π radians in a semicircle (or 2π in a circle).***

Presentation

Students will need compasses and straightedges for this section. Remind them that constructions must be neat. Their pencils should be kept sharp—especially in their compass. They should not make their constructions too small because trying to make an arc with a small radius often results in errors. It would be good at this point to review the construction of angle bisectors and perpendicular bisectors. This section offers an inherent test for neatness. As students mark the vertices of a regular polygon on a circumscribed circle, the last arc mark should land precisely on the starting mark.

This section reviews some of the basic constructions that the students learned earlier and also presents some new ones, some of which

may be challenging even to your best students. Work through each of the constructions with your students, having students do them as you go through them in class. Allow time for working on the exercises in class (perhaps in pairs).

While students should be expected to know how to do most constructions, you may want to make an exception for construction 14 (regular pentagon). This is an interesting construction but is complicated and presented without proof. Since it is unproved, doing it on a test would be strictly a task of memorization. You can avoid this by listing the steps on the board or test (or permit them to bring an index card listing the steps). Another alternative is to count such quiz or test problems as extra credit.

The pentagon construction can lead to a fascinating study of 36° angles. Students can now construct angles measuring 6° (36 − 30), 9° (45 − 36), and 81° (36 + 45). This greatly expands the list of angle measures that they know how to construct. The pentagon is also related to Golden Ratios and golden rectangles (covered in Chapter 13).

Additional Problems

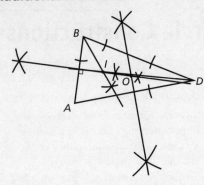

1. Construct the circumcenter, *O*, of △*ABD*.
2. Construct the incenter, *I*, of △*ABD*.
3. Given a circle *M* and an exterior point *P*, construct a pair of tangents to a circle from the exterior point.

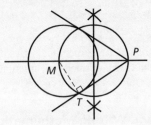

4. Construct a circle with given radius that is tangent to a given line.

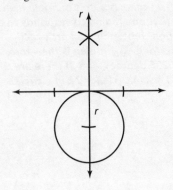

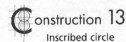onstruction 13

Inscribed circle

Construct: A circle inscribed in a given triangle

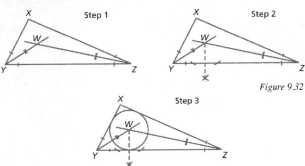

Figure 9.32

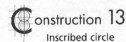onstruction 14

Regular pentagon

Figure 9.33

Construct: A regular pentagon

1. Draw a circle *M*. Draw a diameter of ⊙*M*, and construct its perpendicular bisector.
2. Bisect one of the radii. Point *X* is the midpoint.
3. Measure $\overline{XA}$ (midpoint of radius to the endpoint of another radius).
   Mark off the same length on the original diameter from the midpoint of the radius. Call this point *Y*.
4. Measure the length of $\overline{AY}$. Using this length, mark off consecutive arcs on the circle.
5. Connect consecutive marks with segments to form a regular pentagon.

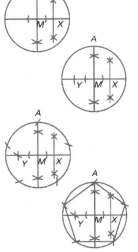

Tips

Ex. 8-11. Tell students they may do all four of these on one diagram if they clearly label each answer with the exercise number.

Ex. 18. Apply construction 15 to a regular pentagon. Construct a regular pentagon (construction 14), and then bisect any central angle to determine the arc midpoints. ∎

The next construction enables you to double the number of sides of a regular polygon. For instance you could use a regular decagon to construct a regular 20-sided polygon. Remember that an *n*-gon is a polygon with *n* sides.

 onstruction 15

Double the number of sides of a regular polygon

Given: A regular *n*-gon
Construct: A regular 2*n*-gon

1. Construct the perpendicular bisector of two sides.
2. The bisectors intersect at the center of the regular polygon.
3. Use the distance from the center to a vertex to construct the circumscribed circle.
4. Open your compass to measure the distance from the point where one perpendicular bisector intersects the circle to an adjacent vertex of the original polygon.
5. Use this distance on your compass to mark off equal arcs all the way around the circle (you should obtain all the original vertices and the arc midpoints between them).
6. Connect consecutive marks to form a regular 2*n*-gon.

▶ **A. Exercises**

Construct the following.
1. The circle circumscribed about △*PQR*

2. The circle inscribed in △*ABC*

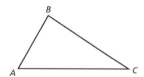

3. A regular pentagon
4. A regular hexagon from an equilateral triangle
5. A regular octagon (*Hint:* Construct a square first.)

1.
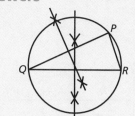

2.
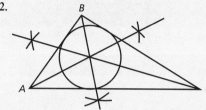

3.

4.

5.
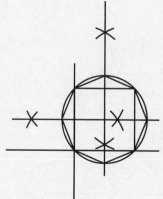

6. Circumcenter Theorem

7. Incenter Theorem

8-11.

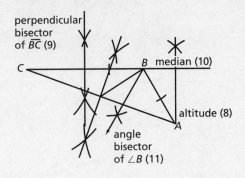

perpendicular
bisector
of $\overline{BC}$ (9)

B median (10)

altitude (8)

angle
bisector
of ∠B (11)

12.

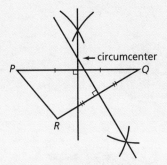

← circumcenter

13.

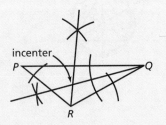

incenter

14.

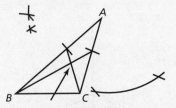

15.

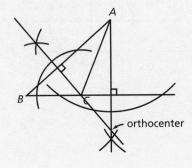

orthocenter

What theorem justifies

6. construction 12?

7. construction 13?

Use △ABC to construct the following.

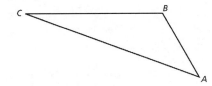

8. The altitude of △ABC through vertex A

9. The perpendicular bisector of $\overline{BC}$

10. The median of △ABC through vertex B

11. The angle bisector of ∠B

Use the two triangles for exercises 12-15.

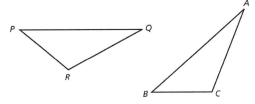

12. Construct the circumcenter of △PQR.

13. Construct the incenter of △PQR.

14. Construct the centroid of △ABC.

15. Construct the orthocenter of △ABC.

▶ **B. Exercises**

16. Construct a circle that passes through points P, Q, and R.

Q•   •R

P•

16.

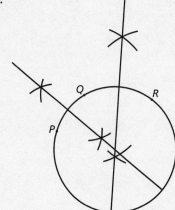

17. Inscribe a right triangle in ⊙A.

18. Construct a regular decagon.
19. What regular polygons can you construct so far (up to 25 sides)?

▶ C. Exercises

20. Construct a five-pointed star.

■ Cumulative Review

Construct the following and then justify your constructions.

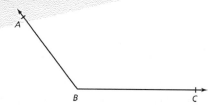

21. An angle congruent to ∠ABC
22. A line perpendicular to $\overleftrightarrow{AB}$ that passes through point C
23. A perpendicular bisector of $\overline{AB}$
24. A 45° angle
25. A 60° angle

17.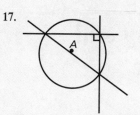

18.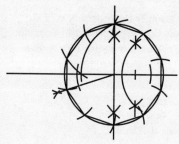

19. Answer with number of sides. 3, 4, 5, 6, 8, 10, 12, 16, 20, 24

20.

21. [4.6]

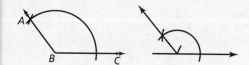

22. [5.7]

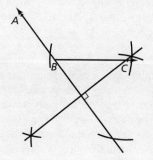

23. [3.6]

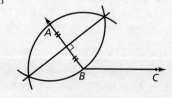

24. [5.7]

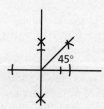

25. [5.7]

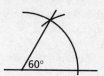

Geometry and Scripture

Objectives

1. To identify the occurrences of the words *circle* or *circular* in Scripture.
2. To calculate the value of π from a careful reading of Scripture.

Answers

1. carpenter
2. Isaiah 40:22
3. the earth
4. the sun
5. the sun's "orbit"
6. 10 cubits
7. 30 cubits

Higher Plane

II Chronicles 4:2-5

Geometry *and* Scripture

Do you recall constructing a circle with a compass? The Bible mentions the use of a compass for this purpose.

1. Read Isaiah 44:13. What occupation is mentioned as making use of compass constructions?
2. The word *circle* appears only once in the Bible. Find it.
3. In the verse above, what is described as circular?
4. Read Psalm 19. What do verses 4-6 describe?
5. What is described as (roughly) circular in these verses?

   The circle in 1 Kings 7:23-26 is the most important geometric figure for mathematical studies in the Bible.

6. Give the diameter of the circle.
7. Give the circumference of the circle.

> **HIGHER PLANE:** Can you find another passage in the Bible that describes the same circle?

Notice that the Jews measured circumference by stretching a line around the circle. Compare this with the discussion of circumference (p. 98). Notice also that since $\pi = \frac{c}{d}$, we can calculate that $\pi = \frac{30}{10} = 3$ from these verses.

Be careful, though! It does seem close to 3.14159, but some ancient civilizations already had better estimates of π. Egypt used

---

This is undoubtedly the most important Bible topic for math classes. The Bible has been criticized by secular and liberal scholars on the basis of the passages in this study, and students should find it exciting and have their faith strengthened to see a plain biblical answer to an objection raised by the skeptics.

You can raise the students' interest by quoting some Bible critics who base an argument on this passage. Tell them that they will discover the answer to the critics in this study. Two critics are cited below if you wish to quote (it will be more impressive if you obtain copies of one of the books so that they can see that you are reading from the primary source).

W. W. Rouse Ball, in *A Short Account of the History of Mathematics* (Dover Publications, 1960), calls the passage in I Kings 7:23 a mistake: "A small piece of evidence which tends to show that the Jews had not paid much attention to it [π] is to be found in the mistake made in their sacred books" (p. 6). It will be fun to show that it is Mr. Ball who is not "on the ball."

Petr Beckman, in *A History of* π (Golem Press, 1971), is equally critical: "The Book of Kings was edited by the ancient Jews as a religious work about 550 B.C., but its sources date back several centuries. At that time π was already known to a considerably better accuracy, but apparently not to the editors of the Bible" (p. 14). On the next page, he continues: "inaccuracy of the biblical value of π is . . . an amusing curiosity" since it is only a trivial example of "the confrontation between science and religion."

Beckman discusses the issue further on pages 75-76, but do not discuss those pages (if at all) until the students discover the answer through the study. In these pages Beckman quotes a second-century rabbi who points to the brim as the correct solution. However, both Beckman and the rabbi do the passage an injustice. Beckman ridicules the rabbinic explanation because I Kings says the brim is only one handbreadth wide, but he never bothers to calculate the value of π obtained by using that handbreadth and so fails to see its accuracy. The rabbi equates the ratio π to 3, and

$4 \cdot \left(\frac{8}{9}\right)^2$ or 3.16 and Babylon used $3\frac{1}{8}$ or 3.125. Because some civilizations had more accurate estimates, some modern critics have called this an error in the Bible.

God knows everything. He knows more than the Egyptians, the Babylonians, and the modern critics. Let's look more closely at what God said.

8. Reread the diameter measurement. It measures from where to where?

9. Reread the circumference measurement. What did it measure around?

10. Does the sea itself have the same diameter as the brim according to verse 26? What is the width of the brim?

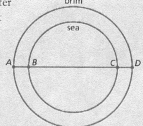

11. Use the conversions from Chapter 3 (p. 113) to give these measurements in inches: *AD*, *AB*, *CD*, *BC*, and the sea's circumference.

12. Using problem 11, what do you get for the value of π? Is it better or worse than the ancient values listed above?

This value of π is the only irrational number approximated by Bible measurements. The theme verse lays the basis for the real number system that includes both rational and irrational numbers.

Line upon Line

And He made a molten sea, ten cubits from the one brim to the other: it was round all about, and his height was five cubits: and a line of thirty cubits did compass it round about. ❧

I Kings 7:23

GEOMETRY AND SCRIPTURE **411**

---

8. brim to brim
9. the sea itself, not the brim
10. no; one handbreath
11. *AD* = 10 cubits = (10)(18) = 180 in.
   AB = *CD* = 1 handbreadth = 4 in.
   BC = *AD-AB-CD* = 180-4-4 = 172 in.
   C = 30 cubits = 30(18) = 540 in.
12. $\pi = \frac{540}{172} = 3.13953$; better

Tips

considers this more spiritual than using the "worldly" value of $3\frac{1}{7}$. By calling the value of 3 more spiritual, he makes ignorance of the order God made a spiritual virtue. Further, by discussing only the rational approximations of π, he fails to understand that the true ratio of circumference to diameter points beyond all rational numbers (integer ratios).

Higher Plane. The easiest way to find a parallel passage is to use a study Bible (one with parallel passages listed in the side or bottom margins). The parallel can also be found using a Bible handbook or concordance. ■

Review

Objective

To help students prepare for evaluation.

Vocabulary

See Appendix A.

Assignment

- Intuitive: 1-10, 15-21
- Standard: 1-27, 30
- Rigorous: 1-30

Resources

- *Activities Manual,* Cumulative Review
- *Activities Manual,* Terms and Symbols
- *Test Packet,* Chapter 9 Exam

Answers

1. *O*
2. $\overline{OQ}$ or $\overline{OC}$
3. $\overline{RB}, \overline{RP}, \overline{AB},$ or $\overline{PQ}$
4. $\overleftrightarrow{AB}$
5. $\overleftrightarrow{CD}$

6. 90
7. 6 units
8. $\angle QOC$
9. $\angle BRP$ or $\angle QPR$
10. 26 units

11.

1. $\odot P$; $\angle PDC$ is a right angle	1. Given
2. $\overline{DP} \perp \overline{AC}$	2. Definition of perpendicular
3. $\overline{DP}$ bisects $\overline{AC}$	3. Radius perpendicular to chord bisects the chord
4. *D* is the midpoint of $\overline{AC}$	4. Definition of segment bisector
5. $\overline{AD} = \overline{DC}$	5. Definition of midpoint
6. $\overline{AD} \cong \overline{DC}$	6. Definition of congruent segments
7. $\overline{BD} \cong \overline{BD}$	7. Reflexive property of congruent segments
8. $\angle ADB$ and $\angle CDB$ are right angles	8. Definition of perpendicular
9. $\triangle ADB$ and $\triangle CDB$ are right triangles	9. Definition of right triangle
10. $\triangle ADB \cong \triangle CDB$	10. LL
11. $\angle ABD \cong \angle CBD$	11. Definition of congruent triangles
12. $\overrightarrow{BP}$ bisects $\angle ABC$	12. Definition of angle bisector

12.

1. $\odot M$; $\overline{AB} \cong \overline{CD}$	1. Given
2. Draw $\overline{ML} \perp \overline{AB}$ and $\overline{MN} \perp \overline{CD}$	2. Auxiliary lines
3. $ML = MN$	3. Congruent chords are equidistant from center
4. $\overline{ML} \cong \overline{MN}$	4. Definition of congruent segments
5. $\angle MLB$ and $\angle MNC$ are right angles	5. Definition of perpendicular
6. $\triangle MLB$ and $\triangle MNC$ are right triangles	6. Definition of right triangle
7. $\overline{MB} \cong \overline{MC}$	7. Radii of a circle are congruent
8. $\triangle BLM \cong \triangle CNM$	8. HL
9. $\angle ABC \cong \angle BCD$	9. Definition of congruent triangles

---

Use the figure shown for exercises 1-10.

1. Name the center of the circle.
2. Name a radius.
3. Name a chord.
4. Name a secant.
5. Name a tangent.
6. Find $m\angle OCD$.
7. If $PQ = 12$ units, find XQ.
8. Name a central angle.
9. Name an inscribed angle.
10. If $OQ = 26$ units, find OC.

Prove the following statements.

11. *Given:* $\odot P$, $\angle PDC$ is a right angle
    Prove: $\overrightarrow{BP}$ bisects $\angle ABC$

12. *Given:* $\odot M$; $\overline{AB} \cong \overline{CD}$
    Prove: $\angle ABC \cong \angle BCD$

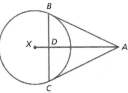

13. *Given:* $\overleftrightarrow{AB}$ and $\overleftrightarrow{AC}$ are tangent to $\odot X$;
    $\overrightarrow{AX}$ bisects $\angle BAC$
    Prove: $m\angle BDA = 90$

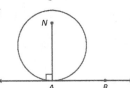

14. *Given:* $\overleftrightarrow{AB}$ is tangent to $\odot C$ at A. $\overrightarrow{AN} \perp \overleftrightarrow{AB}$
    Prove: $\overrightarrow{AN}$ contains center C

Motivational Idea. Write the vocabulary words on the chalkboard. Then have students go to the chalkboard and draw examples of the terms. Tell them to use colored chalk to indicate the specific part that they are illustrating. Discuss key formulas and theorems. Allow plenty of time for your students to work on the review exercises.

Use the diagram for exercises 15-16. Find the following measures if $m\widehat{MN} = 50$ and $m\widehat{PQ} = 30$.

15. $m\angle POQ$

16. $m\angle NOQ$

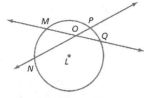

Use the figure for exercises 17-21. $\overline{HI}$ and $\overline{HJ}$ are tangent to $\odot A$.

17. If $HI = 18$ units, find HJ.

18. If $m\widehat{BC} = 50$, find $m\angle BAC$ and $m\angle BDC$.

19. Find $m\widehat{DJB}$. What special name does $\widehat{DJB}$ have?

20. Use the Arc Addition Postulate to express $m\widehat{JC} + m\widehat{CB}$.

21. If $m\angle ACD = 48$, find $m\widehat{CB}$.

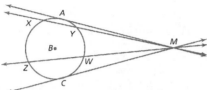

Use the figure for exercises 22-24. $\overleftrightarrow{AM}$ and $\overleftrightarrow{CM}$ are tangents to $\odot B$, and $\overleftrightarrow{XY}$ and $\overleftrightarrow{ZW}$ are secants of $\odot B$.

22. If $m\widehat{XZ} = 80$ and $m\widehat{WY} = 55$, find $m\angle WMY$.

23. If $m\angle AMZ = 30$ and $m\widehat{AW} = 70$, find $m\widehat{ZA}$.

24. If $m\widehat{CY} = 100$ and $m\widehat{CX} = 120$, find $m\angle CMX$.

Use the figure for exercises 25-27.

25. Find the length of $\widehat{AC}$.

26. Find the area of the sector intercepting $\widehat{AC}$.

27. Find the perimeter of the sector intercepting $\widehat{AC}$.

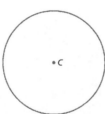

28. Construct a square circumscribed about $\odot C$.

29. Given two intersecting lines, first construct a circle tangent to both lines, then construct a pentagon inscribed in the circle.

30. Explain the mathematical significance of I Kings 7:23.

13.

1. $\overleftrightarrow{AB}$ and $\overleftrightarrow{AC}$ are tangent to $\odot X$; $\overrightarrow{AX}$ bisects $\angle BAC$	1. Given
2. $\angle BAD \cong \angle DAC$	2. Definition of angle bisector
3. $\overline{AB} \cong \overline{AC}$	3. Tangent segments from same point are congruent
4. $\overline{AD} \cong \overline{AD}$	4. Reflexive property of congruent segments
5. $\triangle BAD \cong \triangle CAD$	5. SAS
6. $\angle BDA \cong \angle CDA$	6. Definition of congruent triangles
7. $m\angle BDA = m\angle CDA$	7. Definition of congruent angles
8. $\angle BDA$ and $\angle CDA$ are supplements	8. Linear pairs are supplementary
9. $m\angle BDA + m\angle CDA = 180$	9. Definition of supplementary angles
10. $m\angle BDA + m\angle BDA = 180$	10. Substitution (step 7 into 9)
11. $2m\angle BDA = 180$	11. Distributive property
12. $m\angle BDA = 90$	12. Multiplication property of equality

14. *see Answer Section*

15. 40
16. 140
17. 18 units
18. 50; 25
19. 180; semicircle
20. $m\widehat{JB}$
21. 96
28.

22. 12.5
23. 130
24. 10
25. $\frac{2\pi}{3}$ units
26. 2π sq. units
27. $12 + \frac{2\pi}{3}$ units

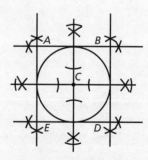

(continued) see Answer Section

Ex. 12. An alternative method avoids the auxiliary perpendicular lines.

1. $\overline{AB} \cong \overline{CD}$	1. Given
2. $\widehat{AB} \cong \widehat{CD}$	2. Congruent chords subtend congruent arcs
3. $m\widehat{AB} = m\widehat{CD}$	3. Definition of congruent arcs
4. $m\widehat{BAC} = 180 = m\widehat{CDB}$	4. Definition of semicircle
5. $m\widehat{AB} + m\widehat{CA} = m\widehat{BAC}$; $m\widehat{DB} + m\widehat{CD} = m\widehat{CDB}$	5. Arc Addition Postulate
6. $m\widehat{AB} + m\widehat{CA} = m\widehat{DB} + m\widehat{CD}$	6. Substitution (step 5 into 4)
7. $m\widehat{CA} = m\widehat{DB}$	7. Addition property of equality (steps 3, 6)
8. $\widehat{CA} \cong \widehat{DB}$	8. Definition of congruent arcs
9. $\angle ABC \cong \angle BCD$	9. Angles inscribed in congruent arcs are congruent

Ex. 14. This requires indirect proof. The diagram does not show the center because if it is drawn it would be on the perpendicular, but we cannot assume what has to be proved. This suggests that an indirect proof should be used here. ∎

Chapter 10

Space

Overview

This chapter introduces solid (3-dimensional) geometry. Just as the chapter on area (Chapter 8) built upon the theorems about plane figures in previous chapters, the chapter on volume (Chapter 11) will build upon the theorems about solids in this chapter. This chapter is therefore pivotal in the study of geometry.

Students first investigate perspective drawings and then proceed to prove parallel and perpendicular relationships. Next, they discover Euler's formula for polyhedra and study the special polyhedron called a parallelepiped. Many circle theorems (Chapter 9) are extended to spheres using great circles and then applied to the earth's latitude and longitude lines.

Presentation

Begin by having students identify some common surfaces and solids in our universe. They will name spheres (or oblate spheroids), which represent stars, planets, moons, and asteroids. They will also name spirals such as the galaxy, which opens the chapter. The first paragraph also reminds them of elliptical orbits and conical shadows (umbra and penumbra), which are most obvious during eclipses. You might ask if anyone knows about the orbits of comets (periodic comets like Halley's have very large ellipses, but others are on parabolic trajectories and never return).

Distances in space are so vast that miles and kilometers are not very useful. Ask students to define two common units of measurement in

space: light year (*distance light travels in one year*) and astronomical unit (*AU, average radius of the earth's orbit*). Many will know the first but few will know the second. Ask why two units developed (*AUs are appropriate for distances to planets in our solar system but become less and less useful as distances increase*). One AU is about 150,000,000 kilometers, or 93,000,000 miles. A third unit, the parsec, will not be used in this book (although the Reading and Writing Mathematics for Section 9.5 introduced it).

Astronomy requires methods for locating the heavenly bodies and for determining their distances. The system for locating heavenly bodies is much like latitude and longitude and

is described in the second paragraph. Determining distances to planets and stars is much harder since both the observer (on earth) and the object are moving. The method is similar to the method used in seeing.

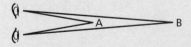

The base angles for the line of sight to an object at *B* are larger than those for the object at *A*. For two very distant objects, however, your eyes are too close together to distinguish the slight difference in the base angles. Distances to planets are found by measuring angles to the planet from different observatories. When the

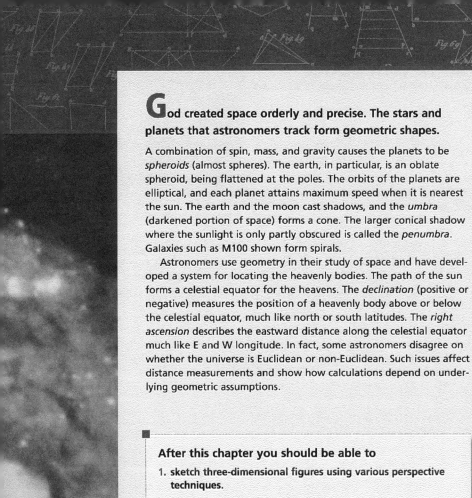

God created space orderly and precise. The stars and planets that astronomers track form geometric shapes.

A combination of spin, mass, and gravity causes the planets to be *spheroids* (almost spheres). The earth, in particular, is an oblate spheroid, being flattened at the poles. The orbits of the planets are elliptical, and each planet attains maximum speed when it is nearest the sun. The earth and the moon cast shadows, and the *umbra* (darkened portion of space) forms a cone. The larger conical shadow where the sunlight is only partly obscured is called the *penumbra*. Galaxies such as M100 shown form spirals.

Astronomers use geometry in their study of space and have developed a system for locating the heavenly bodies. The path of the sun forms a celestial equator for the heavens. The *declination* (positive or negative) measures the position of a heavenly body above or below the celestial equator, much like north or south latitudes. The *right ascension* describes the eastward distance along the celestial equator much like E and W longitude. In fact, some astronomers disagree on whether the universe is Euclidean or non-Euclidean. Such issues affect distance measurements and show how calculations depend on underlying geometric assumptions.

After this chapter you should be able to

1. sketch three-dimensional figures using various perspective techniques.

2. define and measure dihedral angles.

3. prove theorems involving perpendicular lines and planes in space.

4. prove theorems involving parallel lines and planes in space.

5. classify polyhedra and apply Euler's formula.

6. prove theorems involving spheres and apply the results to latitude and longitude.

7. contrast spherical geometry to Euclidean geometry.

415

Finally, the chapter concludes by giving an example of a non-Euclidean geometry. Spherical geometry is easily understood through the example of air routes between cities. Such routes follow great circles but are lines on a map.

Bulletin Board Idea

Check an encyclopedia for "stereographic projection." Make a bulletin board showing the projection of a point on a sphere to a point in a tangent plane, along a line determined by the North Pole and the point being projected.

Flash

Spiral galaxy M100 was photographed on the eve of 1994 by the Hubble Telescope across 2.5 minutes of arc. The telescope orbits 380 miles above the earth to avoid atmospheric disturbance. This enables it to obtain photos 10 times sharper than photos made from observatories on the ground. Launched in 1990, it is controlled from the Goddard Space Flight Center in Greenbelt, Maryland.

observatories are on opposite sides of the earth, astronomers obtain a longer baseline (one earth diameter) for improved measurements. This method of comparing two lines of sight is called *parallax*.

For stars, the earth's diameter is too small, so astronomers measure parallax using the diameter of the earth's orbit. In this variation, they can measure the base angles from opposite sides of the sun (such as at midsummer and midwinter).

For distances to remote galaxies even the baseline across the earth's orbit is too small. Instead, astronomers must make further assumptions about the nature of the universe. The issues involved are hinted at in the closing

sentences and will be introduced in the last section and in Geometry and Scripture.

Please Note. Check your schedule to determine whether you wish to omit 10.3-10.4 and/or 10.8. Even if you do cover these sections, you may wish to do so briefly, just reading through the material and assigning only a few problems. Consider both your time and the interest level of your students as you make your decision. ■

Objectives

1. To draw figures in perspective (one-point, two-point, and three-point).
2. To sketch three-dimensional figures such as cones, cylinders, and prisms.

Vocabulary

horizon
one-point perspective
perspective drawing

three-point perspective
two-point perspective
vanishing point

Assignment

• Intuitive: 1-17, 21-25
• Standard: 1-17, 21-25
• Rigorous: 1-25

Resource

• *Activities Manual,* Perspective in Brief. Gives additional experience with perspective drawing.

Reading and Writing Mathematics

Have students browse art books or magazines to find pictures painted with perspective. Have students make copies of what they find and locate the vanishing points. Finally, have them explain how they identified the type of perspective drawing.

Additional Problems

1. Draw a plane intersecting a square-based prism in a square.

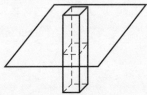

10.1 Perspective in Space

These identical Canadian fighter jets appear smaller in the background—an example of perspective.

Many times in geometry you will need to draw three-dimensional figures. To draw a good three-dimensional figure, you must understand the principle of perspective and must practice the skill. You have already seen many three-dimensional figures in this book, but can you draw them effectively? This section will give you some guidelines to follow for drawing them. Can you name the kinds of figures that are represented below?

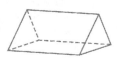

Figure 10.1

Notice that the dotted lines indicate lines that are unseen by the viewer. Many times you will need to visualize the intersection of two three-dimensional objects, so it will help if you can draw these dotted lines. Practice sketching a sphere by first drawing a circle as the outline of the sphere. Next draw an ellipse as in figure 10.1 with the nearest half solid and the farthest half dotted. This ellipse is like the equator of the earth viewed in perspective. For pyramids and cones, simply sketch the base, place a dot for the vertex, and connect the vertex to the base. For prisms and cylinders, draw both bases and connect them. Parallel lines are drawn parallel in these conceptual drawings.

In real life, however, parallel lines do not always look parallel. When you stand on railroad tracks and look into the distance, the two parallel rails appear to meet at the horizon. A drawing that captures this real-life appearance is a *perspective drawing.* Such drawings represent objects as they appear to the eye. Perspective drawing takes into account that an object will appear smaller in the distance than up close.

Figure 10.2

Presentation

Motivational Idea. Bring to class several examples of artwork or drawings having the three different types of perspective discussed in this section. Show them to the students and see if they observe any differences in them. Talk about perspective and how it influences drawings of three-dimensional figures.

Have the students look at the examples of one-, two-, and three-point perspective in figure 10.3. In three-point perspective all parallel lines meet at some vanishing point. However, in one-point perspective, only lines going into the distance meet at the vanishing point. Other pairs of lines (horizontal or vertical) are drawn parallel in one-point perspective (note the square front of the cube with opposite

sides parallel). In two-point perspective, two types of parallel lines meet at vanishing points and one type is drawn parallel. Ask students to identify which is which (*only vertical lines are drawn parallel*). This discussion will help to clarify the meaning of the last sentence in the paragraph below the figure.

Next, draw a cube such as the one shown above. Contrast the cube to the perspective drawings in figure 10.3. Point out that there are no vanishing points, but all parallel lines

are drawn parallel. On page 416, such diagrams are described as conceptual because they portray the concept rather than the appearance of parallel. The technical term for such drawings is *isometric,* and you may wish to introduce the term for contrast. Diagrams in math are always drawn as isometric to permit someone to tell at a glance whether a figure is a cube without having to find vanishing points or measure.

Motivational Idea. An art teacher or a professional artist would make a great guest speaker. Encourage the artist to bring samples of his works that employ perspective or to do some live sketches. He may also be able to explain how he knows which type of perspective will fit the mood or effect he wishes to

There are two main components of perspective drawings. One is the vanishing point(s) and the other is the horizon. The *horizon* is at the eye level of the observer, and the *vanishing point*, where parallel lines meet, is located on the horizon. There are three types of perspective drawings distinguished by the number of vanishing points: *one-point perspective, two-point perspective,* and *three-point perspective.* Each of these is shown in the following examples.

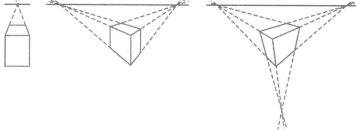

Figure 10.3

Notice that two vanishing points determine the horizon but can be in any position along the horizon. Notice also that in each dimension, parallel lines either meet at the vanishing point or appear parallel.

Both conceptual drawings and perspective drawings are tools for depicting spatial relationships. You will need to picture figures in space throughout this chapter, especially for proofs. You already know how to prove the following theorem for points *A, B, P,* and *Q* if they are coplanar. However, seeing that the proof works also for noncoplanar points requires perspective.

Theorem 10.1

If the endpoints of a segment are equidistant from two other points, then every point between the endpoints is also equidistant from the two other points.

Given: $\overline{AB}$ with points *P, Q*; *AP = AQ, BP = BQ,* and *A-X-B*
Prove: *XP = XQ*

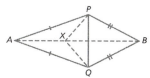

Figure 10.4

2. Draw the following figure in two-point perspective.

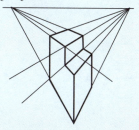

3. Draw the intersection of a plane with a right triangular prism if the plane cuts each base on the dotted line.

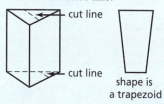

4. Find the intersection of a cone and a plane that passes through the axis of the cone. Could a plane intersect a cone in just one point? In just one segment? ***Yes, pass the plane through the vertex perpendicular to the axis; yes, pass the plane through the vertex and along the surface.***

shape of
intersection

---

create. Ask him also when he or other specialty artists may use isometric drawings.

Tell students that they will need to be able to sketch three-dimensional (isometric) figures such as those in figure 10.1, as well as a cube, such as you drew earlier, and a cylinder. Many students will already be able to do this, but have them try and check them.

One-on-one. If students have trouble sketching the figures, encourage them by pointing out that they will improve with practice. You can also guide them in two ways: tracing the text diagrams or stating principles for guidance such as those below.

Parallel planes—use two parallelograms, making the corresponding segments parallel.

Circular bases (cones or cylinders)—draw these as ellipses unless you are looking directly down on the circular base(s).

Cylinder—draw two identical ellipses (one directly above the other) to represent the bases. The upper part of the lower ellipse should be dotted (to represent the part hidden from view). Join the right and left sides of the ellipses with parallel segments.

Cone—draw an ellipse with the top half dotted (like the bottom base of the cylinder), and make a dot for the vertex above it. Join the vertex to the right and left ends of the ellipse with segments.

Cube—draw the square front face first; then draw another square overlapping it above and to

the right. The two segments that cross the original square should be dotted. Join corresponding vertices (the one to the vertex at the intersection of dotted lines should also be dotted).

Be sure to go through the proof of Theorem 10.1. It introduces proofs in space and shows the importance of using drawings to understand what needs to be proved.

5. Draw two parallel planes cut by a third plane perpendicular to them.

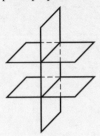

Answers

1.   **2.**

3.   **4.**

5.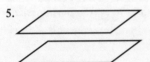

6.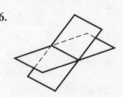

7.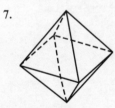

8.

9.

10.

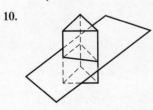

STATEMENTS	REASONS
1. $\overline{AB}$ with points P, Q; $AP = AQ$, $BP = BQ$, and A-X-B	**1.** Given
2. $\overline{AP} \cong \overline{AQ}$, $\overline{BP} \cong \overline{BQ}$	**2.** Definition of congruent segments
3. $\overline{AB} \cong \overline{AB}$, $\overline{AX} \cong \overline{AX}$	**3.** Reflexive property of congruent segments
4. $\triangle ABP \cong \triangle ABQ$	**4.** SSS
5. $\angle PAB \cong \angle QAB$	**5.** Definition of congruent triangles
6. Draw $\overline{XP}$ and $\overline{XQ}$	**6.** Line Postulate
7. $\triangle PAX \cong \triangle QAX$	**7.** SAS
8. $\overline{XP} \cong \overline{XQ}$	**8.** Definition of congruent triangles
9. $XP = XQ$	**9.** Definition of congruent segments

Work on your perspective sketches so that you will be ready for future three-dimensional proofs.

▶ A. Exercises

Draw each of the following figures on graph paper.
1. A sphere
2. A cone
3. A cylinder
4. A pentagonal prism
5. Two parallel planes
6. Two intersecting planes
7. An octahedron

Draw a picture of the intersection of the surface and the plane described.

8. A horizontal plane   **9.** A vertical plane   **10.** A horizontal plane

11. A plane can intersect a circular cylinder to form a circle or a rectangle. Draw a picture to show these different cases.

418 CHAPTER 10 SPACE

11. 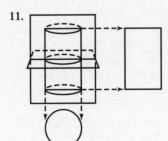   **12.**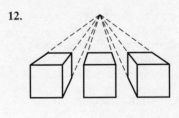

418 CHAPTER 10   SPACE

▶ B. Exercises

Make a sketch as directed in exercises 12-15.

12. Three cubes, all with different one-point perspectives
13. Two cubes, each with different two-point perspectives
14. A rectangular prism drawn from a three-point perspective
15. Segments representing a row of trees extending into the distance from a one-point perspective
16. Find a picture in a book or magazine that uses one-point perspective. Find the vanishing point.
17. Find a picture in a book or magazine that uses two-point or three-point perspective. Find all the vanishing points.

▶ C. Exercises

Each frame below represents an unfurnished room in perspective. Maintain the perspective (find vanishing points first!) and draw a couch along one wall and a window on the adjacent wall (include curtains if you wish). Try to draw the same room in all three perspectives.

18.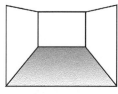

20.

19.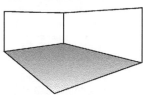

■ Cumulative Review

True/False

21. Two distinct lines can intersect at two distinct points.
22. Two parallel lines are contained in exactly one plane.
23. If $ST = \frac{1}{2}SV$, then T is the midpoint of $\overline{SV}$.
24. A line and a point not on that line are contained in exactly one half-plane.
25. Two intersecting lines are always coplanar.

Tips

Ex. 17. Find one vanishing point as in #16; then find parallel lines that meet at a different point (these will be perpendicular to lines that meet at the first vanishing point).

Ex. 18-20. Copy the forms on a copier before using them so that students do not write in their book. It will also help to enlarge them to four times their original size (200% setting used twice).

Ex. 23. T need not be on $\overleftrightarrow{SV}$.

Ex. 24. For a half-plane to contain a line, its edge must be parallel to the line. Infinitely many half-planes can meet the given conditions. ■

13.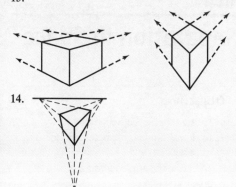

14.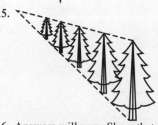

15.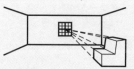

16. Answers will vary. Show that lines moving away from you meet at one point.
17. Answers will vary.
18. Answers will vary.

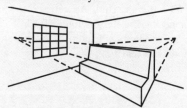

19. Answers will vary.

20.   Answers will vary.

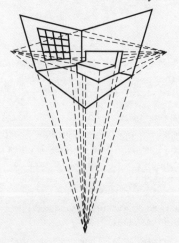

21. False [1.5]
22. True [1.6]
23. False [3.3]
24. False [1.6]
25. True [1.6]

Objectives

1. To state the Space Separation Postulate.
2. To define a dihedral angle and identify its parts.
3. To define the angle measure of a dihedral angle.

Vocabulary

closed surface
dihedral angle
edge of a dihedral angle
face of a dihedral angle
half-space
interior of a dihedral angle
measure of a dihedral angle
plane angle
solid

Assignment

- Intuitive: 1-10, 21-25
- Standard: 1-18, 21-25
- Rigorous: 1-25

Resources

- *Activities Manual,* Bible Activity: Atonement—The Restoration of Truth
- *Test Packet,* Quiz 1, Chapter 10 covers Sections 10.1 and 10.2.

10.2 Separation in Space

In Chapter 2 we saw that according to the Line Separation Postulate, a point separates a line into three disjoint sets. The three sets are the point and the two half-lines. We also saw that according to the Plane Separation Postulate, a line separates a plane into three disjoint sets: the line and two half-planes. Space can also be separated into three disjoint sets. What figure do you think would separate space into three disjoint sets? What do you think those sets would be called?

The surface of the water is a plane that divides space into three parts: the fish is underwater, the reflection lies on the surface, and the viewer lives in the air above water.

Postulate 10.1

Space Separation Postulate. **Every plane separates space into three disjoint sets: the plane and two half-spaces.**

In the figure, space is called S, and plane p divides S into two half-spaces: s_1 and s_2.

The plane is called the *face* of the half-space. So the face of half-space s_1 is plane p. Each half-space is convex because when you connect any two points of a half-space, the entire segment is contained in the half-space. If $A \in s_1$ and $B \in s_2$, what is true about $\overline{AB}$?

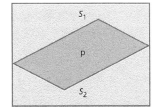

Figure 10.5

In a plane two intersecting lines form four angles as shown.

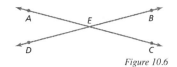

Figure 10.6

Exercise 26 on page 72 mentioned the Space Separation Postulate. Now explore this idea more thoroughly with your class. Show the students how the plane separates space into three disjoint sets. The Space Separation Postulate is analogous to the Line and Plane Separation Postulates.

Motivational Idea. There are a number of ways to visualize the concept of space separation: a wall that divides one room into two, a divider in a drawer, the glass wall of an aquarium, etc.

The subtle thing about these ideas is that none of the points in the dividing plane are in either half-space. This means that as you move

through a half-space toward the dividing plane you can never find the last point just before the plane.

Motivational Idea. Place one piece of cardboard through a slit in a second piece to show how the intersection of the two planes divides space into four parts.

Common Student Error. In defining a dihedral angle, it is not enough to say the union of the two half-planes. It is also necessary to include the line of intersection of the two planes.

Help students think of common objects that are examples of dihedral angles. The students need to be reminded when looking at visuals that the half-planes that form the angle are

infinite and that the interior of the dihedral angle is an infinite wedge in space.

The notation for a dihedral angle, $\angle L\text{-}PQ\text{-}M$, requires only a point in each face and two points on the edge. For this reason, a dihedral angle can be named correctly several ways. But the measurement of the dihedral angle requires that a plane angle be chosen so that its sides are perpendicular to the edge of the dihedral angle at the same point. When possible, it helps to use the plane angle points to name the dihedral angle. Notice that a straight dihedral angle forms a plane just as a straight angle in a plane forms a line.

What happens when two planes intersect in space? What is the intersection of two planes?

Two planes that intersect in space also form four angles. These angles are called *dihedral* angles. The notation is similar to other angles except that the vertex is replaced by two points on the edge. The four dihedral angles above are ∠P-MN-R, ∠R-MN-Q, ∠Q-MN-O, and ∠O-MN-P. ∠O-MN-R and ∠P-MN-Q are straight dihedral angles.

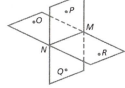

Figure 10.7

Definitions

A **dihedral angle** is the union of any line and two half-planes that have the line as a common edge.

The **edge of a dihedral angle** is the common edge of two half-planes that form a dihedral angle.

A **face of a dihedral angle** is the union of the edge of a dihedral angle and one of the half-planes that form the dihedral angle.

Dihedral angles abound in the world around us. For example, an open booklet forms a dihedral angle with the covers as faces and the spine as the edge. The walls in your classroom also form dihedral angles at the corners.

The *interior of a dihedral angle* can be described as an infinite wedge formed by the intersection of two half-spaces. Can you visualize the interior of a dihedral angle?

How do we measure dihedral ∠L-PQ-M?

∠LNM is a *plane angle* of the dihedral angle if $\overrightarrow{NM} \perp \overrightarrow{PQ}$ and $\overrightarrow{NL} \perp \overrightarrow{PQ}$. The *measure* of the dihedral angle is the measure of the plane angle. Thus if the plane angle is a right angle, the dihedral angle is a right dihedral angle. Dihedral angles are *congruent* if they have equal measures.

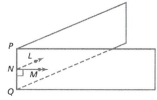

Figure 10.8

The closed surface of a polyhedron determines several dihedral angles but also determines a solid. Remember that a solid is the union of a closed surface and its interior.

Tips

One-on-one. Some students may grasp the idea better with a physical model. Bring a file folder to class and label it as shown in figure 10.8. By adding a point *A* on the folder several inches left of point *L*, students will clearly see that ∠MNL and ∠MNA do not have the same measure and that the latter is larger.

Students will use dihedral angles infrequently in this book. If you wish to give the topic greater emphasis, you can assign some proofs such as the Angle Addition Theorem for dihedral angles or prove that congruence of dihedral angles is an equivalence relation. If you do this, you may also want to use it as an opportunity to practice paragraph style proofs.

Ex. 9-16. You may wish to stress that the labels s_1 and s_2 refer to half-spaces (not edges or vertices). ∎

Reading and Writing Mathematics

Have your students contrast parallel and intersecting in all possible combinations of lines and planes. ***There are three possibilities for two parallel figures: parallel lines, parallel planes, and a line parallel to a plane. In these cases, the figures do not intersect. The contrasting figures that do intersect are intersecting lines, intersecting planes, and a line intersecting a plane respectively. The only cases that are coplanar involve lines (parallel or intersecting).***

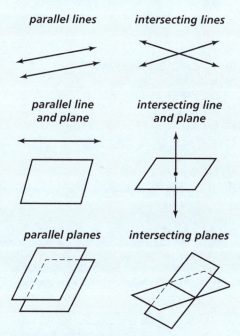

parallel lines   intersecting lines

parallel line and plane   intersecting line and plane

parallel planes   intersecting planes

Additional Problems

1. Name all the dihedral angles in the figure.

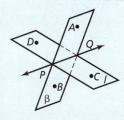

∠A-PQ-C, ∠A-PQ-B, ∠A-PQ-D,
∠B-PQ-C, ∠B-PQ-D, ∠D-PQ-C

Given the following diagram, where plane *p* divides space into two half-spaces s_1, s_2, $p \cap q = \overleftrightarrow{LM}$; $B \in \overleftrightarrow{LM}$. Find

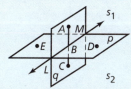

2. $q \cap s_1$. **half-plane ALM**
3. $\overleftrightarrow{AC} \cap s_1$. **$\overrightarrow{AB}$ without endpoint B**
4. $\overleftrightarrow{AC} \cap s_2$. **$\overset{\circ}{BC}$**
5. ∠D-LM-A $\cap s_2$. **∅**

Answers

1. ∠A-CD-E, ∠F-CD-E, ∠F-CD-A
2. ∠A-YZ-X, ∠X-YZ-E, ∠E-YZ-D
   ∠D-YZ-C, ∠C-YZ-B, ∠B-YZ-A
   ∠A-YZ-E, ∠A-YZ-D, ∠A-YZ-C
   ∠X-YZ-D, ∠X-YZ-C, ∠X-YZ-B
   ∠E-YZ-C, ∠E-YZ-B, ∠D-YZ-B
3. ∠P-LM-R, ∠R-LM-U, ∠U-NO-T,
   ∠T-NO-V, ∠V-NO-S, ∠S-NO-U,
   ∠U-LM-Q, ∠Q-LM-P, ∠U-NO-V,
   ∠P-LM-U, ∠Q-LM-R, ∠T-NO-S
4. a, b
5. $\overleftrightarrow{PQ}$
6. ∠MXL
7. right dihedral angle
8. $\overleftrightarrow{PQ}$
9. ∠X-LM-Y, excluding $\overleftrightarrow{LM}$
10. half-space s_1 and plane p
    (face of the half-space)
11. empty set
12. space
13. $s_1 \cup s_2$
14. s_2
15. empty set
16.

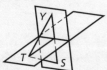

17. No, it divides space into 3 disjoint sets but
    it does not have finite size (its surface area
    is infinite).
18. four
19. a.

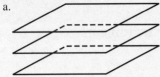

    b.

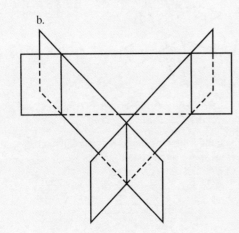

▶ A. Exercises

Use the proper notation to describe all the dihedral angles in exercises 1-3.

1.   2. 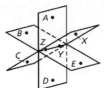   3.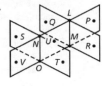

Use the figure for exercises 4-8.

4. Name the faces of the dihedral angle.
5. What is the edge of the dihedral angle?
6. Name a plane angle.
7. If $m\angle MXL = 90$, what is the dihedral angle called?
8. Find $a \cap b$.

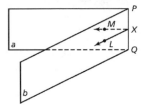

▶ B. Exercises

Use the figure shown for exercises 9-16.

9. Describe half-plane *XLM* ∪ half-plane *YLM*.
10. Describe $s_1 \cup p$.

Perform each set operation.

11. $s_1 \cap s_2$
12. $s_1 \cup s_2 \cup p$
13. p'
14. $(s_1 \cup p)'$
15. $(s_1 \cup s_2 \cup p)'$
16. Draw the plane determined by *S*, *T*, and *Y*.
17. Is a dihedral angle a closed surface? Explain.
18. How many parts do two intersecting planes separate space into?

▶ C. Exercises

19. How can three planes separate space into four parts? seven parts? (include diagrams)
20. Show two ways in which three planes can separate space into six parts.

20. a. 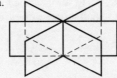   b.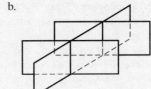

Tell whether these statements are true or false.
21. If $\angle LMN \cong \angle PQR$, then $m\angle LMN = m\angle PQR$.
22. If $\angle LMN \cong \angle PQR$, then $\angle LMN \cong \angle PRQ$.
23. Vertical angles are congruent.
24. Supplementary angles form a linear pair.
25. A transversal perpendicular to one line is perpendicular to the other.

10.3 Perpendiculars in Space

The roof of this covered bridge in Bucks County, Pennsylvania, illustrates a dihedral angle.

Proofs of theorems in space are very much like proofs in the plane. The theorems you have learned can be used in these proofs as long as each is applied in a single plane. Recall that perpendicular lines form right angles.

Definitions

Perpendicular planes are two planes that form right dihedral angles.

A **line perpendicular to a plane** is a line that intersects the plane and is perpendicular to every line in the plane that passes through the point of intersection.

A **perpendicular bisecting plane** of a segment is a plane that bisects a segment and is perpendicular to the line containing the segment.

---

21. True [4.2]
22. False [4.2]
23. True [4.4]
24. False [4.4]
25. False [6.4]

10.3

Perpendiculars in Space

Objectives
1. To define perpendicular figures in space.
2. To prove theorems involving perpendiculars in space.

Vocabulary
lines perpendicular to planes
perpendicular bisecting plane
perpendicular lines in space
perpendicular planes

Assignment
• Intuitive: no assignment necessary
• Standard: 1-16, 19-23
• Rigorous: 1-23

Presentation

Define "perpendicular planes" and "lines perpendicular to a plane."

Motivational Idea. It will be helpful to students who have trouble picturing lines and planes in space if you bring some dowel rods and poster board to illustrate. Put one dowel rod on the board to represent a line in the plane, and then hold a second dowel so that it touches the first rod at right angles but is not perpendicular to the plane. This will show students that a line can be perpendicular to a line in a plane without being perpendicular to the plane. However, if it is perpendicular to two lines in the plane, it will be perpendicular to the plane (thus illustrating Theorem 10.2).

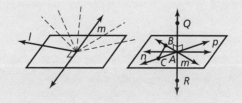

The plan for the proof of Theorem 10.2 is to get the line l perpendicular to all the lines of the plane determined by lines m and n, and hence by definition it will be perpendicular to the plane. The key step is to be able to use Theorem 10.1: If the endpoints of a segment are equidistant from two other points, then every point between the endpoints is also equidistant from

the two other points. This guarantees that l is perpendicular to any line in the plane through that point. By choosing a pair of points R and Q equidistant from the point of intersection A, the requirement of Theorem 10.1 can be met by a pair of points C and B on the given pair of lines m ($\overleftrightarrow{AB}$ in the proof) and n ($\overleftrightarrow{AC}$ in the proof).

The best way to ensure understanding and preparation for exercises is for students to go through textbook proofs and examples on their own without looking at the text. Theorems 10.2 and 10.3 provide models for proofs in space and are important results that can be used in later proofs. Encourage students to work through the proof of Theorem 10.3 on their own before reading the proof in the text. Then

Additional Problems

Answer each True/False question and draw a picture to illustrate your answer.

1. Two planes perpendicular to the same plane are parallel? *False*

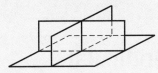

2. Two lines perpendicular to the same plane are parallel? *True*

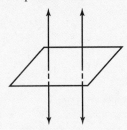

3. Two planes perpendicular to the same line are parallel? *True*

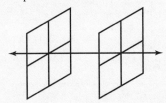

Study the following proofs to see how to do proofs in space.

Theorem 10.2

A line perpendicular to two intersecting lines in a plane is perpendicular to the plane containing them.

Given: Line *l* is perpendicular to lines *m* and *n* at *A*; plane *p* contains *m* and *n*

Prove: Line *l* is perpendicular to plane *p*

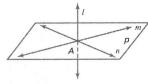

Figure 10.9

According to the definition of a line perpendicular to a plane, we must prove that *l* is perpendicular to every line in plane *p* that passes through *A*. Let $\overrightarrow{AK}$ be a representative line in plane *p*. Since *K* is interior to one of the four angles formed by lines *m* and *n*, find auxiliary points on *m* and *n* respectively so that *B-K-C*.

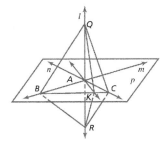

Figure 10.10

---

read through Theorems 10.4-10.7. The first three of these proofs are #16-18, while Theorem 10.7 is proved as #26 in the Chapter Review.

Ex. 2-5. Cover at least #2-4 in class or illustrate them with models if you plan to assign the proofs (#16-18). Students will better understand what they are trying to prove if they have the correct diagram in their mind. Also, if you label the diagrams as shown on the answers to #16-18, you will simplify the grading process because all students will be using the same letters.

Ex. 10-15 are theorems about space, which correspond to Theorems 4.1 through 4.6 about the plane. They can be proved by mimicking the original proofs or by using the original theorems and applying them to the plane angles of the dihedral angles.

Ex. 16-18. See tips on #2-5.

Ex. 22-23. Answers assign the right angle to an *A*. If a student considers SAS and ASA where the right angle is not one of the 3 given pairs, other answers are possible (HA or LA for #22, HA for #23). ■

STATEMENTS	REASONS
1. $l \perp m$ at A, $l \perp n$ at A	1. Given
2. Lines m and n determine a plane p	2. Two intersecting lines lie in the same plane
3. $Q \in l$; let R be on the opposite ray to $\overrightarrow{AQ}$ so that $AR = AQ$	3. Completeness Postulate
4. $\overleftrightarrow{AK}$ is another line in plane p; $B \in m$; $C \in n$; B-K-C	4. Auxiliary lines
5. m is the perpendicular bisector of $\overline{QR}$ in the plane of points Q, B, and R; n is the perpendicular bisector of $\overline{QR}$ in the plane of points Q, C, and R	5. Definition of perpendicular bisector
6. $BQ = BR$; $CQ = CR$	6. Points on a perpendicular bisector are equidistant from the endpoints
7. $QK = RK$	7. B and C are equidistant from Q and R, so point K between B and C is also (Theorem 10.1)
8. K is on the perpendicular bisector of $\overline{QR}$ (in the plane of points K, Q, and R)	8. Points equidistant from the endpoint lie on the perpendicular bisector
9. $\overleftrightarrow{AK} \perp l$ at point A	9. Definition of perpendicular bisector
10. $l \perp p$	10. Definition of line perpendicular to plane

Theorem 10.3

If a plane contains a line perpendicular to another plane, then the planes are perpendicular.

Given: $\overleftrightarrow{AB} \perp m$ at B, plane n contains $\overleftrightarrow{AB}$
Prove: $m \perp n$

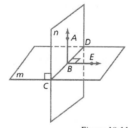

Figure 10.11

4. On one wall of a rectangular room is point A and on the opposite wall is point B. What points on the floor are equidistant from points A and B? Explain. *The perpendicular bisecting plane of $\overline{AB}$ contains all points equidistant from A and B. Therefore, the intersection of the floor and the perpendicular bisecting plane is the required set of points.*

Answers

1.

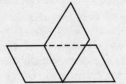

2.

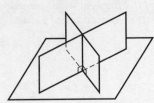

3.

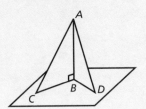

4.

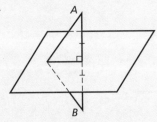

5.

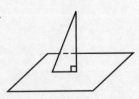

6. any two: $\angle A\text{-}BC\text{-}D$, $\angle A\text{-}BC\text{-}X$, $\angle X\text{-}BC\text{-}D$
7. $m\angle A\text{-}BC\text{-}X + m\angle X\text{-}BC\text{-}D = m\angle A\text{-}BC\text{-}D$
8. two dihedral angles the sum of whose measures is 180°
9. two dihedral angles the sum of whose measures is 90°
10. congruent (dihedral angles)
11. congruent (dihedral angles)
12. right dihedral angles
13. form a dihedral linear pair
14. supplementary (dihedral angles)
15. so is the other
16.

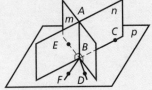

STATEMENTS	REASONS
1. $\overrightarrow{AB} \perp m$ at B	1. Given
2. $m \cap n = \overleftrightarrow{CD}$	2. Plane Intersection Postulate
3. $\overleftrightarrow{BE} \perp \overleftrightarrow{CD}$ at B	3. Auxiliary perpendicular
4. $\overrightarrow{AB} \perp \overleftrightarrow{BE}$ and $\overrightarrow{AB} \perp \overleftrightarrow{CD}$	4. Definition of line perpendicular to plane
5. $\angle ABE$ is right	5. Definition of perpendicular bisector
6. $\angle ABE$ is a plane angle	6. Definition of plane angle
7. $\angle A\text{-}CD\text{-}E$ is a right dihedral angle	7. Definition of dihedral angle measure
8. $m \perp n$	8. Definition of perpendicular planes

The following theorems are discussed in the exercises. (Proofs of the first three are exercises 16-18 and the fourth is in the chapter review.)

Theorem 10.4
If intersecting planes are each perpendicular to a third plane, then the line of intersection of the first two is perpendicular to the third plane.

Theorem 10.5
If $\overrightarrow{AB}$ is perpendicular to plane p at B, and $\overline{BC} \cong \overline{BD}$ in plane p, then $\overline{AC} \cong \overline{AD}$.

Theorem 10.6
Every point in the perpendicular bisecting plane of segment $\overline{AB}$ is equidistant from A and B.

Theorem 10.7
The perpendicular is the shortest segment from a point to a plane.

1. $m \perp p$, $n \perp p$, and m intersects n	1. Given	6. $m\angle ABD = 90$ $m\angle ABF = 90$	6. Transitive property of equality
2. $m \cap n = \overleftrightarrow{AB}$	2. Plane Intersection Postulate	7. $\angle ABD$ and $\angle ABF$ are right angles	7. Definition of right angle
3. $\angle A\text{-}BC\text{-}D$ and $\angle A\text{-}BE\text{-}F$ are right dihedral angles	3. Definition of perpendicular planes	8. $\overleftrightarrow{AB} \perp \overleftrightarrow{DB}$, $\overleftrightarrow{AB} \perp \overleftrightarrow{BF}$	8. Definition of perpendicular lines
4. $m\angle A\text{-}BC\text{-}D = 90$ $m\angle A\text{-}BE\text{-}F = 90$	4. Definition of right dihedral angles	9. $\overleftrightarrow{AB} \perp p$	9. Line perpendicular to two intersecting lines is perpendicular to the plane containing them
5. $m\angle A\text{-}BC\text{-}D =$ $m\angle ABD$; $m\angle A\text{-}BE\text{-}F =$ $m\angle ABF$	5. Definition of dihedral angle measure		

► A. Exercises

Make a sketch of the following.
1. A dihedral linear pair
2. Theorem 10.4
3. Theorem 10.5
4. Theorem 10.6
5. Theorem 10.7

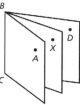

Use the diagram for exercises 6-7.
6. Name 2 dihedral angles.
7. State an Angle Addition Theorem for Dihedral Angles.

Explain or define each term below.
8. Supplementary dihedral angles
9. Complementary dihedral angles

► B. Exercises

Draw conclusions about dihedral angles (based on your knowledge of plane angles).
10. All right dihedral angles are . . .
11. Vertical dihedral angles are . . .
12. Supplementary dihedral angles that are congruent are . . .
13. Supplementary dihedral angles that are adjacent . . .
14. The dihedral angles in a dihedral linear pair are . . .
15. If one dihedral angle of a dihedral linear pair is a right angle, then . . .

► C. Exercises

Prove each theorem below.
16. Theorem 10.4
17. Theorem 10.5
18. Theorem 10.6

■ Cumulative Review

19. Name two postulates for proving triangles congruent.
20. Name two theorems for proving triangles congruent.
21. Name a fifth method for proving triangles congruent that works only for right triangles.
22. What is SAS called when applied to right triangles?
23. What is ASA called when applied to right triangles?

19. SAS, ASA [6.6]
20. SSS, SAA [6.7, 6.8]
21. HL (SSA) [7.1]
22. LL [7.1]
23. LA [7.1]

17.

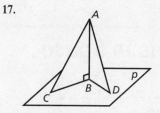

1. $\overleftrightarrow{AB} \perp p$ at B, $\overline{BC} \cong \overline{BD}$; $C, D \in p$	1. Given
2. $\overline{AB} \perp \overline{BC}$, $\overline{AB} \perp \overline{BD}$	2. Definition of line perpendicular to plane
3. $\angle ABC$ and $\angle ABD$ are right angles	3. Definition of perpendicular
4. $\angle ABC \cong \angle ABD$	4. All right angles congruent
5. $\overline{AB} \cong \overline{AB}$	5. Reflexive property of congruent segments
6. $\triangle ABC \cong \triangle ABD$	6. SAS (or LL)
7. $\overline{AC} \cong \overline{AD}$	7. Definition of congruent triangles
8. If $\overleftrightarrow{AB}$ is perpendicular to plane p at B, and $\overline{BC} \cong \overline{BD}$ in plane p, then $\overline{AC} \cong \overline{AD}$	8. Law of Deduction

18.

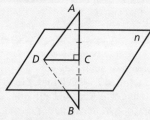

1. Perpendicular bisecting plane n of $\overline{AB}$ contains C and D, $C \in \overleftrightarrow{AB}$	1. Given
2. C is the midpoint of $\overline{AB}$ and $\overleftrightarrow{AB} \perp n$	2. Definition of perpendicular bisecting plane
3. $AC = BC$	3. Definition of midpoint
4. Draw $\overline{CD}$, $\overline{AD}$, and $\overline{BD}$	4. Line Postulate
5. $\overleftrightarrow{CD} \perp \overleftrightarrow{AB}$	5. Definition of line perpendicular to plane
6. $\angle ACD$ and $\angle BCD$ are right angles	6. Definition of perpendicular
7. $\angle ACD \cong \angle BCD$	7. All right angles congruent
8. $\overline{AC} \cong \overline{BC}$	8. Definition of congruent segments
9. $\overline{CD} \cong \overline{CD}$	9. Reflexive property of congruent segments
10. $\triangle ACD \cong \triangle BCD$	10. SAS (LL)
11. $\overline{AD} \cong \overline{BD}$	11. Definition of congruent triangles
12. $AD = BD$	12. Definition of congruent segments

Objectives

1. To define parallel figures in space.
2. To prove theorems about parallel figures in space.

Vocabulary

line parallel to a plane

Assignment

• Intuitive: no assignment necessary
• Standard: 1-15, 19-23
• Rigorous: 6-23

Resources

• Appendix K presents two proofs (Theorems 10.8 and 10.15) that are not in the text or exercises.
• *Activities Manual,* Proofs in Detail. Shows students how to prove that a figure exists or that it is unique.
• *Activities Manual,* Practice.
• *Test Packet,* Quiz 2, Chapter 10 covers Sections 10.3 and 10.4.

Flash

Satellites may orbit daily, orbit several times daily, or appear stationary over a point. Some are for communications, others for scientific data collection, and still others for military reasons. You may wish to point out the Space Shuttle docked on the satellite in the photo.

10.4   Parallels in Space

The study of parallels builds on the study of perpendiculars. You have studied perpendicular lines, perpendicular planes, and lines perpendicular to planes. Likewise, you must know when lines are parallel, planes are parallel, and lines are parallel to planes. Recall that parallel lines are two coplanar lines that do not intersect. Skew lines are not coplanar, which means that they are neither concurrent nor parallel.

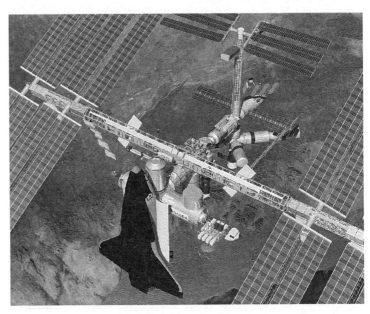

The solar panels of the International Space Station illustrate parallel planes. The station is one of 2,465 functional man-made satellites orbiting Earth.

This section is similar to the previous section. If you assign the proofs, you may want to discuss #1-6 in class or to illustrate each with poster board and dowels. The proof of Theorem 10.8 is trivial for coplanar lines, but it takes 14 steps to prove that they are coplanar. The proof is in Appendix K if you desire to present it (or to assign it as extra credit).

Motivational Idea. The spokes of two wheels on the same axle are all perpendicular to the axle. Yet it is easy to see that the spokes of one wheel are never parallel and the spokes of two different wheels do not have to be parallel. Certainly when the spokes of two different wheels are perpendicular to a plane

containing the axle, those spokes are parallel. This illustrates Theorem 10.8.

The proof of Theorem 10.9 is an indirect proof (using the Law of Contradiction). You can do it at the chalkboard or overhead projector and call on students to give successive steps. Step 5 will be the hardest for most students to grasp. Remind them that according to step 4, $\overleftrightarrow{AB}$ is the intersection of planes n and m (which contains $\overleftrightarrow{CD}$). According to step 2, $\overleftrightarrow{CD}$ (of plane m) intersects n at P. Since P is therefore part of the intersection of planes m and n, it must be on the line of intersection $\overleftrightarrow{AB}$.

The proofs of Theorems 10.10-10.15 are mostly exercises. See #16-18 for the first three

and #27-28 in the Chapter Review for Theorems 10.13-10.14. The proof of Theorem 10.15 is in Appendix K if you wish to cover it (or use it for extra credit).

Definitions

Parallel planes are two planes that do not intersect.

A line parallel to a plane is a line that does not intersect the plane.

Theorem 10.8

Two lines perpendicular to the same plane are parallel.

Given: Plane m containing points B and D,
$\overleftrightarrow{AB} \perp m$ and $\overleftrightarrow{CD} \perp m$
Prove: $\overleftrightarrow{AB} \parallel \overleftrightarrow{CD}$

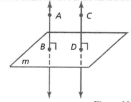

Figure 10.12

To prove that lines are parallel, we must prove two things: they must be coplanar and they must not intersect. You can see that $\overleftrightarrow{AB} \perp \overleftrightarrow{BD}$ and $\overleftrightarrow{CD} \perp \overleftrightarrow{BD}$, but lines perpendicular to the same line are not parallel unless they are also coplanar. This theorem is important because it enables you to prove lines parallel without first having to prove them coplanar.

Some exercises require indirect proofs. Study the proof of Theorem 10.9 to review this method, which assumes the theorem is false and finds a contradiction.

Theorem 10.9

If two lines are parallel, then any plane containing exactly one of the two lines is parallel to the other line.

Given: $\overleftrightarrow{AB} \parallel \overleftrightarrow{CD}$, plane n contains $\overleftrightarrow{AB}$
but not $\overleftrightarrow{CD}$
Prove: Plane n is parallel to $\overleftrightarrow{CD}$

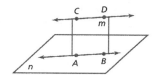

Figure 10.13

Reading and Writing Mathematics

Have each student write a paragraph in which he discusses the presence of the following in a physical example of his choice.
a) parallel planes
b) parallel lines
c) line parallel to a plane
d) skew lines ***Answers will vary.***

Additional Problems

1. Draw two lines l and m perpendicular to the same line but not parallel to each other. Name their relationship. ***skew lines***

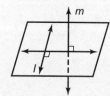

2. Given a line l and two planes p and q, suppose $l \parallel p$. If $l \perp q$, is $p \perp q$? ***yes***
3. Given a line l and two planes p and q, suppose $l \parallel p$. If $p \perp q$, is $l \perp q$? ***no***
4. Does the phrase skew planes make sense? Why? ***no; planes either intersect or are parallel***
5. State a theorem for planes similar to the Parallel Postulate for lines. Define necessary terms first. ***A transversal plane is a plane that intersects two other planes in different lines. Alternate interior dihedral angles are dihedral angles on opposite sides of the transversal plane and between the two intersected planes. Theorem: Two planes are parallel if and only if a transversal plane intersects them in congruent alternate interior dihedral angles.***

Tips

Ex. 1-6. Cover at least #1-3 in class or illustrate them with models if you plan to assign the proofs (#16-18) to help students understand what they are trying to prove. Also, if you label the diagrams as shown on the answers to #16-18, you will simplify the grading process because all students will be using the same letters.

Ex. 7-11. Having students think through these statements develops their thinking and their spatial abilities to visualize and gives practice with counterexamples.

Ex. 16-18. See tip on #1-6.

Ex. 19. False. It is interior to a rectangular face of the prism but not interior to the prism. ■

Answers

1.
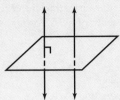

2.

3.
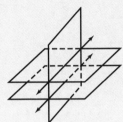

4.
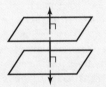

5.
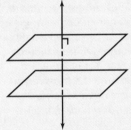

6.
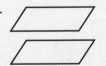

7.
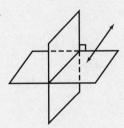

8.
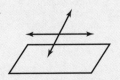

STATEMENTS	REASONS
1. $\overleftrightarrow{AB} \parallel \overleftrightarrow{CD}$, n contains $\overleftrightarrow{AB}$, n does not contain $\overleftrightarrow{CD}$	1. Given
2. n intersects $\overleftrightarrow{CD}$ at point P	2. Assumption
3. Let m be the plane containing $\overleftrightarrow{AB}$ and $\overleftrightarrow{CD}$	3. Definition of parallel lines (they are coplanar)
4. Planes m (containing $\overleftrightarrow{CD}$) and n intersect in exactly one line, $\overleftrightarrow{AB}$	4. Plane Intersection Postulate
5. $\overleftrightarrow{AB}$ intersects $\overleftrightarrow{CD}$ at point P	5. Two intersecting lines intersect in exactly one point (compare steps 2 and 4)
6. Plane n is parallel to $\overleftrightarrow{CD}$	6. Law of Contradiction (see steps 1 and 5)
7. If two lines are parallel and a plane contains exactly one of them, then the plane is parallel to the other line	7. Law of Deduction

Theorem 10.10
A plane perpendicular to one of two parallel lines is perpendicular to the other line also.

Theorem 10.11
Two lines parallel to the same line are parallel.

Theorem 10.12
A plane intersects two parallel planes in parallel lines.

Theorem 10.13
Two planes perpendicular to the same line are parallel.

Theorem 10.14
A line perpendicular to one of two parallel planes is perpendicular to the other also.

Theorem 10.15
Two parallel planes are everywhere equidistant.

430 CHAPTER 10 SPACE

9.
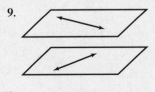

10.
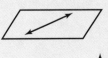

11.
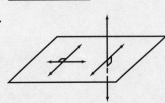

12.
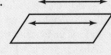

13.
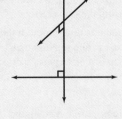

▶ A. Exercises

Make a sketch for each theorem below.
1. Theorem 10.10
2. Theorem 10.11
3. Theorem 10.12
4. Theorem 10.13
5. Theorem 10.14
6. Theorem 10.15

▶ B. Exercises

Disprove each of these false statements by sketching a counterexample.
7. Two planes parallel to the same line are parallel.
8. Two lines parallel to the same plane are parallel.
9. If two planes are parallel, then any line in the first plane is parallel to any line in the second.
10. If a line is parallel to a plane, then the line is parallel to every line in the plane.
11. Lines perpendicular to parallel lines are parallel.

Sketch each.
12. A plane containing exactly one of two parallel lines
13. A line perpendicular to both of two skew lines
14. A plane containing one of two skew lines and parallel to the other
15. A plane parallel to a line so that a point of the plane is farther from the line than the distance between the line and the plane

▶ C. Exercises

Prove the theorems.
16. Theorem 10.10 (*Hint:* Use proof by contradiction and the Historic Parallel Postulate.)
17. Theorem 10.11
18. Theorem 10.12

▮ Cumulative Review

Answer true or false. Refer to the prism shown.
19. Point *G* is interior to the prism.
20. △*DEF* is a base of the prism.
21. $\overline{CD}$ is an edge of the prism.
22. △*DEF* ≅ △*ABC*
23. If *Q* is between *G* and *H*, then *Q* is interior to the prism.

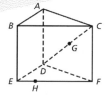

14.
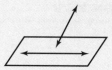

15.
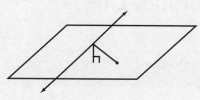

16.

1. $\overleftrightarrow{AB} \parallel \overleftrightarrow{CD}$, $\overleftrightarrow{AB} \perp p$	1. Given
2. Assume $\overleftrightarrow{CD}$ is not $\perp p$	2. Assumption
3. Draw $\overleftrightarrow{CE} \perp p$ at *E*	3. Auxiliary line
4. $\overleftrightarrow{AB} \parallel \overleftrightarrow{CE}$	4. Lines perpendicular to same plane are parallel
5. $\overleftrightarrow{AB}$ and $\overleftrightarrow{CD}$ determine plane *q* $\overleftrightarrow{AB}$ and $\overleftrightarrow{CE}$ determine plane *t*	5. Two parallel lines are contained in exactly one plane (Theorem 1.4)
6. *q* = *t*	6. Plane Postulate (points *A*, *B*, *C* determine exactly one plane)
7. $\overleftrightarrow{CE}$ and $\overleftrightarrow{CD}$ are both parallel to $\overleftrightarrow{AB}$ through *C* in plane *q*	7. See steps 1, 4, 5, 6
8. $\overleftrightarrow{CE} = \overleftrightarrow{CD}$	8. Historic Parallel Postulate
9. $\overleftrightarrow{CD} \perp P$	9. Law of Contradiction

17.
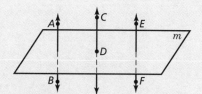

1. $\overleftrightarrow{AB} \parallel \overleftrightarrow{CD}$, $\overleftrightarrow{CD} \parallel \overleftrightarrow{EF}$	1. Given
2. Draw plane *m* perpendicular to $\overleftrightarrow{CD}$ at *D*	2. Auxiliary plane (Theorem 10.4)
3. $\overleftrightarrow{AB} \perp$ plane *m* $\overleftrightarrow{EF} \perp$ plane *m*	3. Plane perpendicular to one of two parallel lines is perpendicular to the other
4. $\overleftrightarrow{AB} \parallel \overleftrightarrow{EF}$	4. Lines perpendicular to same plane are parallel

18.
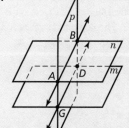

1. *m* ∥ *n*; plane *p* intersects both *n* and *m*	1. Given
2. *p* ∩ *n* = $\overleftrightarrow{AB}$, *p* ∩ *m* = $\overleftrightarrow{CD}$	2. Plane Intersection Postulate
3. $\overleftrightarrow{AB}$ lies entirely in *n*; $\overleftrightarrow{CD}$ lies entirely in *m*	3. Flat Plane Postulate
4. Assume $\overleftrightarrow{AB}$ intersects $\overleftrightarrow{CD}$ at some point *P*	4. Assumption
5. Planes *n* and *m* intersect at *P*	5. Definition of intersecting lines (*P* is on $\overleftrightarrow{AB}$ in *n* and on $\overleftrightarrow{CD}$ in *m*)
6. $\overleftrightarrow{AB} \parallel \overleftrightarrow{CD}$	6. Law of Contradiction (see steps 1, 5)

19. False [2.7]
20. True [2.6]
21. False [2.7]
22. True [2.6, 6.8]
23. True [2.7]

Analytic Geometry

Slopes of Parallel Lines

Objectives

1. To prove that parallel lines have equal slopes.
2. To find the equations of lines parallel to given lines.

Assignment

- Intuitive: 1-3
- Standard: 1-5
- Rigorous: 1-5

Additional Problems

Find the equation.

1. The line parallel to $y = \frac{1}{5}x - 7$ with y-intercept $(0, -2)$ $y = \frac{1}{5}x - 2$
2. The line parallel to $y = 3x + 1$ and containing $(2, -3)$ $y = 3x - 9$
3. The line parallel to $2x + 3y = 5$ and passing through $(-1, -4)$ $y = -\frac{2}{3}x - \frac{14}{3}$
4. The line passing through $(6, 2)$ and parallel to the line containing points $(1, 3)$ and $(4, -1)$ $y = -\frac{4}{3}x + 10$
5. The line parallel to $y = 5$ and containing the point $(2, 1)$ $y = 1$

Slopes of Parallel Lines

Do you remember what slope means? In Chapter 4 we defined slope as the ratio of vertical to horizontal change. Slope measures the angle that a line makes with the horizontal axis. The angle between the line and x-axis is the angle of inclination. The relationship between slope and angle of inclination can be used to prove that lines with the same slope are parallel.

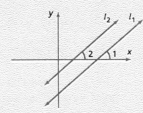

STATEMENTS	REASONS
1. $m_1 = m_2$	1. Given
2. $m\angle 1 = m\angle 2$	2. Same slopes define same angle of inclination
3. $\angle 1 \cong \angle 2$	3. Definition of congruent angles
4. $l_1 \parallel l_2$	4. Corresponding Angle Theorem
5. If the slopes of two lines are equal, then the lines are parallel	5. Law of Deduction

Presentation

This topic reviews slope in the context of parallel lines and provides further practice with analytic geometry. You may wish to look back to page 127, where slopes were first discussed.

The relation between parallel lines and slopes (#5) corresponds to a relation for perpendicular lines in Chapter 13. Most students will accept the fact that parallel lines have the same slope without proof; however, the proof of the theorem relating the slopes of perpendicular lines is harder and is frequently skipped. This topic should be used as preparation for that proof as well as review of the methods of finding equations of lines.

Tips

Ex. 5. The desired biconditional combines the two theorems described. One direction is proved on page 432. The converse is mentioned at the top of page 433 and proved in #4. ∎

You can also prove the converse that parallel lines have equal slopes. You can find equations of lines using this relationship together with point-slope form.

EXAMPLE Find the equation of the line through (2, 5) and parallel to $3x + y = 7$.

Answer 1. $3x + y = 7$ 1. Find the slope of the given line.
                $y = -3x + 7$ The slope of the parallel line is
                  $m = -3$ the same.

          2. $y - y_1 = m(x - x_1)$ 2. Use point-slope form to obtain
             $y - 5 = -3(x - 2)$ the desired equation.
             $y - 5 = -3x + 6$
               $y = -3x + 11$

▶ Exercises

1. Find the slope of a line parallel to $2x + 5y = 3$.

Find the equation of the line
2. parallel to $x - 3y = 9$ and having the y-intercept of (0, 4).
3. parallel to $2x - y = 4$ and passing through (−1, 3).
4. Prove that parallel lines have the same slope.
5. Combine the two theorems about parallel lines and slopes by writing a biconditional.

Answers
1. $-\frac{2}{5}$
2. $y = \frac{1}{3}x + 4$
3. $y = 2x + 5$
4.

1. $l_1 \parallel l_2$	1. Given
2. $\angle 1 \cong \angle 2$	2. Corresponding Angle Theorem
3. $m\angle 1 = m\angle 2$	3. Definition of congruent angles
4. $m_1 = m_2$	4. Definition of slope
5. If lines are parallel, then their slopes are equal	5. Law of Deduction

5. Lines are parallel if and only if their slopes are equal.

10.5   Polyhedra

Objectives

1. To classify hexahedra and define related terms.
2. To prove theorems for parallelepipeds.
3. To state and apply Euler's formula.

Vocabulary

cube
diagonal of a hexahedron
diagonal of a parallelepiped
opposite edges of a parallelepiped
opposite faces of a parallelepiped
parallelepiped

Assignment

• Intuitive: 1-11
• Standard: 1-19, 24-28
• Rigorous: 1-28 and Mind over Math

Flash

The lunar module carried *Apollo 16* astronauts John Young and Charles Duke to the moon. They landed at the Descartes site near Stone Mountain.

Do you remember the relationship between a polygon and its angles? Quadrilateral *ABCD* determines ∠*ABC*, but ∠*ABC* is not a subset of the quadrilateral. In the same way polyhedra determine dihedral angles.

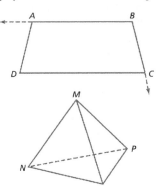

Figure 10.14

The top half of the lunar module Orion *from Apollo 16 forms a concave polyhedron.*

For instance, ∠*M-PQ-N* is a dihedral angle determined by the tetrahedron. ∠*M-PQ-N* is called an angle of the tetrahedron. Can you name other angles of this tetrahedron?

Another similarity between polygons and polyhedra is classification. In Chapter 2, you learned to classify by the number of sides or faces, respectively. Just as you further classified quadrilaterals, you can also further classify *hexahedra.*

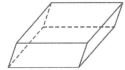 

Figure 10.15

Remember that a prism is *rectangular* if its bases are rectangles and that a cube is a right rectangular prism with all sides congruent.

Presentation

Euler's formula as well as the definition of parallelepiped should be taught to all students. Other theorems and all proofs in this section are optional.

Common Student Error. It is easy to confuse the two kinds of diagonals. In figure 10.16, students should see that $\overline{AD}$ is the only segment that contains points of the cube's interior that can be named from the diagram. The diagonals of faces of the cube (such as $\overline{AC}$ and $\overline{BD}$) lie on the surface (one face) of the cube. They are diagonals of square faces but not of the cube itself. Likewise, the vertical edges at *B* and *D* are opposite edges of the cube, but the vertical edges at *B* and *C* are only opposite edges of a square face of the cube.

Motivational Idea. Concrete models may help some students visualize the part of the figure hidden from view. A ream (500 sheets) of paper offers a practical representation of a parallelepiped. The neatly stacked pile forms a rectangular solid. By tilting or sliding the stack, you show a parallelepiped that is not rectangular. The advantage of the representation is that you can tilt the stack in two directions at once by letting it slide toward one corner. Be sure to show the tilt both in one direction and in two directions. In all three forms, the top and bottom sheets are parallel and congruent; this will show students that parallelepipeds are a special type of prism.

Common Student Error. Students may think that all parallelepipeds must be tilted. However, while parallelepipeds must have faces that are parallelograms, students must remember that rectangles, rhombi, and squares are all special types of parallelograms. Thus, cubes and rectangular prisms (right or oblique) are also parallelepipeds.

A box with the top and bottom removed (as in Section 8.2, One-on-one) forms the lateral surface of a rectangular prism. By pulling at opposite corners, the surface will tilt into a parallelepiped. This method is especially useful for illustrating faces, edges, and diagonals of a parallelepiped. You can also attach string for the diagonals to illustrate Theorems 10.17-10.18.

Definitions

A **parallelepiped** is a hexahedron in which all faces are parallelograms.

A **diagonal of a hexahedron** is any segment joining vertices that do not lie on the same face.

Opposite faces of a hexahedron are two faces with no common vertices.

Opposite edges of a hexahedron are two edges of opposite faces that are joined by a diagonal of the parallelepiped.

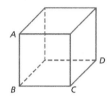

Figure 10.16

Be sure you do not confuse these concepts: $\overline{AB}$ is an edge of the cube; $\overline{AC}$ is a diagonal of the square face of the cube; $\overline{AD}$ is a diagonal of the cube. Similarly, do not confuse opposite edges of the cube with opposite edges of one face of the cube.

Here are some other theorems on parallelepipeds.

Theorem 10.16
Opposite edges of a parallelepiped are parallel and congruent.

Theorem 10.17
Diagonals of a parallelepiped bisect each other.

Theorem 10.18
Diagonals of a right rectangular prism are congruent.

Resources
• *Visual Packet,* Three-Dimensional Figures
• *Visual Packet,* Solids. Use the 5 Platonic Solids, parallelepiped, and 3 other polyhedra that are not prisms for checking Euler's formula. Point out the 2 truncated solids to help students understand the Mind over Math question (frustum is a truncated cone and cuboctohedron is a cube with all 8 corners truncated).
• *Activities Manual,* Construction Skills: Regular Polygons. Looks at the construction of several regular polygons.

Reading and Writing Mathematics
Have the students give written descriptions of five real-life objects that are polyhedra. *Answers will vary.*

Additional Problems
Complete the table for faces, vertices, sides of base, and edges of pyramids. Also check Euler's formula.

	Faces F	Vertices V	Sides of base S	Edges E	$V - E + F$
1.	6	6	5	10	$6 - 10 + 6 = 2$
2.	8	8	7	14	$8 - 14 + 8 = 2$
3.	10	10	9	18	$10 - 18 + 10 = 2$
4.	21	21	20	40	$21 - 40 + 21 = 2$
5.	$n + 1$	$n + 1$	n	$2n$	$(n + 1) - 2n + (n + 1) = 2$

Encourage the students to see patterns and relationships during your class discussion. For example, a right hexagonal prism consists of two hexagons in parallel planes with the corresponding vertices joined by segments. This means that each base has 6 edges while 6 more edges join the two hexagons for a total of 6 edges (base 1) + 6 edges (base 2) + 6 edges (connecting segments) = 18 edges. The pattern tells us to multiply the number of sides in the base by three to get the number of edges: $E = 3n$.

Similarly, the number of vertices turns out to be twice the number of sides in the base: $V = 2n$. Also, since each side of the base corresponds to a lateral face, the total number of faces is the number of sides of the base plus two: $F = n + 2$.

Have students use the relationships they discover to illustrate Euler's formula. You can do this for a particular type of prism (such as dodecagonal) or for a general n-gon. For the dodecagonal prism, have students calculate the vertices, edges, and faces:
$E = 3n = 3(12) = 36$, $V = 2n = 2(12) = 24$, and $F = n + 2 = 12 + 2 = 14$. This matches Euler's formula:
$V - E + F = 24 - 36 + 14 = 2$. In general, $V - E + F = 2n - 3n + (n + 2) = 2$. The last calculation proves that Euler's formula holds for any convex prism. A similar calculation for cones would obtain

$V - E + F = (n + 1) - 2n + (n + 1) = 2$.

Read the paragraph after Euler's formula. Ask students if they can find a polyhedron for which Euler's formula does not work. Of course, trying convex polyhedra is a waste of time since the formula works for all of them according to the theorem. One example of a polyhedron to which Euler's formula does not apply is shown on page 75. Notice that $V - E + F = 12 - 12 + 12 = 12$ rather than 2.

6. Make a Venn diagram for types of hexa-hedra. ***Do not expect students to show the set of rectangular prisms or the set of quadrilateral prisms. Discuss these when you discuss their diagrams. Also, see if any student can give an example of a hexahedron that is in neither the set of quadrilateral prisms nor the set of pentagonal pyramids. One possible example is obtained by gluing two congruent tetrahedra together base to base.***

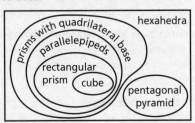

Challenge

Given: A cube labeled as shown with sides of length s

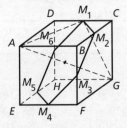

Use paragraph form to prove: The midpoint of edges $\overline{BC}$, $\overline{CD}$, $\overline{DH}$, $\overline{HE}$, $\overline{EF}$, and $\overline{FB}$ lie in the perpendicular bisecting plane of diagonal $\overline{AG}$.

We will show that each midpoint M is equidistant from the endpoints of $\overline{AG}$ and therefore on its perpendicular bisecting plane. For any of the six midpoints, $\overline{MG}$ is the hypotenuse of a right triangle having an edge of the cube as a leg and half an edge of the cube for the other leg. By the Pythagorean theorem, $GM^2 = (\frac{1}{2}s)^2 + s^2 = \frac{5}{4}s^2$. So, $GM = s\frac{\sqrt{5}}{2}$. Likewise, $AM = s\frac{\sqrt{5}}{2}$. Thus, GM = AM as desired.

One last theorem, called Euler's formula, applies not only to parallelepipeds but to all convex polyhedra. The following diagrams will help you discover this important formula for polyhedra. Which polyhedra are not regular?

(*a*)   (*b*)   (*c*)   (*d*)

Figure 10.17

Look again at diagram (*a*) in figure 10.17. How many vertices can you count? How many edges? How many faces?

> Let V = number of vertices
> E = number of edges
> F = number of faces
> Compute $V - E + F$

The table below summarizes this computation for all four diagrams in figure 10.17. Find the value for the last column in each case.

Diagram	V	E	F	$V - E + F$
(a)	4	6	4	2
(b)	8	12	6	
(c)	6	12	8	
(d)	12	30	20	

The Swiss mathematician Leonard Euler (OY–ler) was the first to discover the numerical relationship that you just discovered about a polyhedron. For any convex polyhedron the following equation is true.

> **Euler's Formula**
> $V - E + F = 2$ where V, E, and F represent the number of vertices, edges, and faces of a convex polyhedron respectively.

This formula works for some other polyhedra also, but it always works for convex polyhedra. Although the relationship can be proved, the proof involves concepts you have not yet studied.

Tips

Ex. 20-23. These proofs require theorems about parallel lines and planes from previous sections. Students may need a little guidance to get started. Several steps involve multiple applications of a theorem, but they must be the correct statements. ∎

You can *truncate* a solid by slicing off part of it. Begin with a regular polyhedron and slice off all the corners so that the faces of the truncated polyhedron are regular polygons. Can you describe two possible truncated cubes (give the number and types of faces)?

▶ A. Exercises

Tell whether the following statements are true or false.
1. The faces of a regular octahedron are equilateral triangles.
2. Euler's formula can be written $V + F = E + 2$.
3. A hexagonal prism is an octahedron.
4. A regular dodecahedron has hexagonal faces.
5. A regular tetrahedron is a pyramid.

For each decahedron below, determine the number of faces, edges, and vertices. Check Euler's formula for each.

6.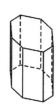

8.

10.

7.

9.

11.

▶ B. Exercises

Each exercise below refers to a prism having the given number of faces, vertices, edges, or sides of the base. Determine the missing numbers to complete the table below. Draw the prism when necessary; find some general relationships between these parts of the prism to complete exercise 18.

Mind over Math

See Appendix B.

Answers
1. True
2. True
3. True
4. False
5. True
6. 10 faces, 24 edges, 16 vertices (octagonal prism)
7. 10 faces, 20 edges, 12 vertices
8. 10 faces, 19 edges, 11 vertices
9. 10 faces, 18 edges, 10 vertices (nonagonal pyramid)
10. 10 faces, 15 edges, 7 vertices
11. 10 faces, 16 edges, 8 vertices

12. 5 faces, 3 sides
13. 5 sides, 15 edges
14. 6 faces, 12 edges
15. 9 faces, 14 vertices, 21 edges
16. 16 faces, 14 sides, 42 edges
17. 12 vertices, 6 sides, 18 edges
18. $n + 2$ faces, $2n$ vertices, $3n$ edges
19. The diagonals bisect each other and are congruent.

20.

1. A parallelepiped	1. Given
2. ABCD, EFGH, ABFE, CDHG, BCGF, and ADHE are parallelograms	2. Definition of parallelepiped
3. $\overleftrightarrow{AB} \parallel \overleftrightarrow{CD}$, $\overleftrightarrow{CD} \parallel \overleftrightarrow{GH}$, $\overleftrightarrow{GH} \parallel \overleftrightarrow{EF}$ $\overleftrightarrow{AD} \parallel \overleftrightarrow{BC}$, $\overleftrightarrow{BC} \parallel \overleftrightarrow{GF}$, $\overleftrightarrow{GF} \parallel \overleftrightarrow{HE}$ $\overleftrightarrow{AE} \parallel \overleftrightarrow{BF}$, $\overleftrightarrow{BF} \parallel \overleftrightarrow{CG}$, $\overleftrightarrow{CG} \parallel \overleftrightarrow{DH}$	3. Definition of parallelogram
4. $\overleftrightarrow{AB} \parallel \overleftrightarrow{GH}$, $\overleftrightarrow{CD} \parallel \overleftrightarrow{EF}$ $\overleftrightarrow{AD} \parallel \overleftrightarrow{GF}$, $\overleftrightarrow{BC} \parallel \overleftrightarrow{HE}$ $\overleftrightarrow{AE} \parallel \overleftrightarrow{CG}$, $\overleftrightarrow{BF} \parallel \overleftrightarrow{DH}$	4. Lines parallel to the same line are parallel

21.

1. A parallelepiped	1. Given
2. ABCD, EFGH, ABFE, CDHG, BCGF, and ADHE are parallelograms	2. Definition of parallelepiped
3. $\overline{AB} \cong \overline{CD}$, $\overline{CD} \cong \overline{GH}$, $\overline{GH} \cong \overline{EF}$, $\overline{AD} \cong \overline{BC}$, $\overline{BC} \cong \overline{GF}$, $\overline{GF} \cong \overline{HE}$, $\overline{AE} \cong \overline{BF}$, $\overline{BF} \cong \overline{CG}$, $\overline{CG} \cong \overline{DH}$	3. Opposite sides of a parallelogram are congruent
4. $\overline{AB} \cong \overline{GH}$, $\overline{CD} \cong \overline{EF}$, $\overline{AD} \cong \overline{GF}$, $\overline{BC} \cong \overline{HE}$, $\overline{AE} \cong \overline{CG}$, $\overline{BF} \cong \overline{DH}$	4. Transitive property of congruent segments

22. Each pair of opposite edges of the parallelepiped are parallel and congruent (#20-21). So AEGC, BFHD, ABGH, CDEF, BCHE, and ADGF are parallelograms (quadrilateral with congruent and parallel opposite sides). Therefore, $\overline{AG}$, $\overline{BH}$, $\overline{CE}$, and $\overline{DF}$ bisect each other (as diagonals of a parallelogram).

	F	V	n	E
	Faces	Vertices	Sides of the base	Edges
Example	14	24	12	36
12.		6		9
13.	7	10		
14.		8	4	
15.			7	
16.		28		
17.	8			
18.			n	

19. Based on this section, draw two conclusions about the diagonals of a cube.

Use the figure to prove the following theorems.

20. Opposite edges of a parallelepiped are parallel (part of Theorem 10.16).
21. Opposite edges of a parallelepiped are congruent (part of Theorem 10.16).

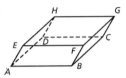

▶ **C. Exercises**

Prove each theorem. You may write a paragraph rather than a two-column proof.

22. Theorem 10.17
23. Theorem 10.18

■ **Cumulative Review**

Do not solve exercises 24-27 below, but write (in complete sentences) what you would do to solve them.

24. Find the area.

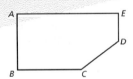

25. Prove that $\angle A \cong \angle B$.

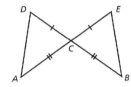

26. Find the distance between two numbers *a* and *b* on a number line.
27. True/False: Water contains helium or hydrogen.
28. When are the remote interior angles of a triangle complementary?

23. Since a rectangular prism is a parallelepiped (bases are rectangles and four lateral faces are also parallelograms), the diagonals bisect each other (#22). Since the rectangular prism is right, the parallelograms determined by opposite edges are rectangles. Since diagonals of a rectangle are congruent, the diagonals of the right rectangular prism are congruent.

24. Subdivide the pentagon into 3 triangles. Find the area of each triangle and add the areas together. [8.1]

25. Using the marked congruence and vertical angles, the triangles are congruent by SAS. By definition (of congruent triangles), the desired angles are congruent. [6.6]

26. Subtract *a* and *b*. The distance is the absolute value of this difference. [3.2]

27. Use the disjunction truth table to evaluate the statement $(F \wedge T = T)$. [5.3]

28. Remote interior angles are complementary when the exterior angle from which they are remote is a right angle. [7.3]

10.6 Spheres

In 1978, astronomers at the U.S. Naval Observatory near Flagstaff, Arizona, found Charon, the only moon of Pluto, with a 61-inch reflecting telescope. The hemispherical dome rotates on its cylindrical base to track the heavenly bodies.

Many of the concepts that you have learned about circles also apply to spheres. So if you understand the basic definitions and theorems of circles, you will understand how these same ideas apply to spheres. From this section you should see how a strong foundation will help you be better prepared for the future. The same principle applies to your spiritual life. If you build a strong Bible-based foundation while you are young, you will be better prepared for the adult life you have before you. In I Timothy 6:17-19 Paul admonishes Christians that they should trust "in the living God" (v. 17) and lay a "good foundation against the time to come" (v. 19).

Let us see how your knowledge of circles helps you in the study of spheres. Earlier in this book you saw the definition of *sphere*. A sphere is the set of points in space that are a given distance from a given point. A sphere is a surface or a shell. The given point is the center of the sphere, and the segment from the center to a point on the surface is the radius. In sphere S, O is the center, and $\overline{OA}$ is a radius.

Figure 10.18

A chord of a sphere is a segment with endpoints on the sphere. A diameter of a sphere is a chord containing the center, and a secant of a sphere is a line that contains a chord. A tangent is a line containing exactly one point of the sphere.

What results when a plane and a sphere intersect?

Objectives

1. To define terms related to a sphere: *tangent plane, secant plane,* and *great circles.*
2. To state and prove theorems about spheres.
3. To derive and apply a formula for arc length on a sphere.

Vocabulary

great circle
secant plane
tangent plane

Assignment

- Intuitive: 1-15, 21-25
- Standard: 1-17, 21-25
- Rigorous: 8-25

Resource

- *Test Packet,* Quiz 3, Chapter 10 covers Sections 10.5 and 10.6.

Flash

From Lowell Observatory, also at Flagstaff, Pluto was discovered in 1930. Observatories are closed surfaces (flat floor, cylindrical lateral surface, and hemispherical dome) having an interior and exterior.

Presentation

Motivational Idea. If possible, bring a physical model of a sphere and a plane that passes through the sphere so that students will be better able to visualize this concept. You can use a plastic or rubber ball for the sphere and a piece of cardboard for the plane. Cut a hole in the cardboard and set the ball in it to give the illusion that the plane passes through the ball. Discuss a tangent plane and illustrate it by placing the ball on a table. The table represents the tangent plane. Remind the students that it touches the sphere in one and only one point.

All students should learn the definitions and arc length formula in this section. You should also read the theorems and illustrate them. However, the proof of Theorem 10.19 is

difficult and optional. Students on the rigorous track should go through it, and students on the standard track should be told the plan stated below without going through it. Students on the intuitive track should skip it.

The plan of the proof of Theorem 10.19 requires two key things. First, the secant may or may not contain the center of the sphere. Thus, steps 1-5 delineate these two cases for the center of the circle. If the secant does contain the center, the proof is easy (step 4). The rest of the proof covers the second case. Taking any two arbitrary points A and B in the intersection of the sphere and secant plane, we must prove that their distances from the center are equal (and thus, all points of intersection are

equidistant from the center). Drop a perpendicular from the center of the sphere to the intersecting plane. The point of intersection (D) will be the center of the circle. Congruent triangles are used to get the equal distances for points A and B. This will help students see that many theorems involving spheres can be proved using theorems on circles.

Read through Theorems 10.20-10.24 and have students make sketches to illustrate them.

Discuss the idea of distance between two points along the surface of a sphere. Remind the students that the distance on a sphere involves a curved distance, not a straight distance. Illustrate this idea with a globe or the models used earlier. Students can think of the

Flash

Answer: the rings form an annulus. Notice that the planet's shadow obscures a portion of the rings. Also, point out the black dot in the southern hemisphere of the planet. Tell students that it is the shadow of one of the three moons shown. Ask them which moon it is and why (Rhea; the angle of the sun is known by the planet's shadow on the rings, so the shadows of the other two moons do not hit the planet). The Voyager project is managed for NASA by Jet Propulsion Labs in Pasadena, California.

Reading and Writing Mathematics

Have the students look up *projection* in an encyclopedia and answer the following question.

The surface of a sphere is said to be nondevelopable. What does this mean? **No substantial portion may be represented on a plane surface without some stretching and distortion.**

Additional Problems

Find the length of each arc with the given angle measure on a sphere with a radius of 3 m.

1. $m\widehat{AB} = 15°$ $\frac{\pi}{4}$ **m**
2. $m\widehat{AB} = 30°$ $\frac{\pi}{2}$ **m**
3. $m\widehat{AB} = 45°$ $\frac{3\pi}{4}$ **m**
4. If the radius of the earth is taken as 3950 miles and two cities are 9° apart, how far is a plane flight between the cities? **198π; approximately 620 miles**
5. What figure represents the intersection of two distinct spheres? **If they are tangent, a point; if they are disjoint, the empty set; otherwise a circle**

Voyager 2 viewed Saturn from a distance of only 13 million miles. The three icy moons below the planet are Tethys, Dione, and Rhea (left to right). Do you remember the name for the shape made by the rings?

Definitions

A **secant plane** to a sphere is a plane that intersects a sphere in more than one point.

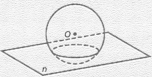

Figure 10.19

A **tangent plane** to a sphere is a plane that intersects a sphere in exactly one point. The point is called the **point of tangency**.

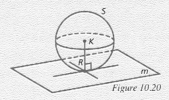

Figure 10.20

In the diagram above, sphere *S* with center *K* is tangent to plane *m* at point *R*.

distance between two points on a sphere as a fraction of the circumference of the great circle that includes the points.

Tips

Ex. 16-20. These proofs are optional and should be assigned only if you have worked through the proof of Theorem 10.19 and have had students draw diagrams for each theorem.

Ex. 20. This proof is especially difficult because Theorem 10.24 is a biconditional statement. Further, the second conditional requires an indirect proof. You can help students get started correctly by asking students to write the two conditionals in class (or even elicit the correct plan of attack on the second part). ∎

Theorem 10.19
The intersection of a sphere and a secant plane is a circle.

Given: Sphere S with center C and secant plane n
Prove: $n \cap S$ is a circle

Figure 10.21

STATEMENTS	REASONS
1. Sphere S with center C and secant plane n	1. Given
2. S intersects n in at least two points A and B	2. Definition of secant plane
3. $AC = BC$; $\overline{AC} \cong \overline{BC}$	3. Definitions of sphere, congruent segments
4. If C is in plane n, then A, B, and C are coplanar and A and B are equidistant from C, which is the center of a circle of radius AC	4. Definition of circle
5. If C is not in plane n, then there is a perpendicular $\overleftrightarrow{CD}$ to plane n at D	5. Exactly one line passes through a point perpendicular to a plane
6. $\overleftrightarrow{AD}$ and $\overleftrightarrow{BD}$ exist	6. Line Postulate
7. $\overleftrightarrow{CD} \perp \overleftrightarrow{AD}$, $\overleftrightarrow{CD} \perp \overleftrightarrow{BD}$	7. Definition of line perpendicular to a plane
8. $\angle ADC$ and $\angle BDC$ are right angles	8. Definition of perpendicular
9. $\triangle ACD$ and $\triangle BCD$ are right triangles	9. Definition of right triangle
10. $\overline{CD} \cong \overline{CD}$	10. Reflexive property of congruent segments
11. $\triangle ACD \cong \triangle BCD$	11. HL
12. $\overline{AD} \cong \overline{BD}$	12. Definition of congruent triangles
13. $AD = BD$	13. Definition of congruent segments
14. A and B (and every point of intersection) are on a circle centered at D with radius AD	14. Definition of circle

The intersection of the sphere with center O and plane m is a circle. If a plane passes through the center of the sphere, it intersects the sphere in what is called a great circle.

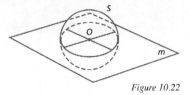

Figure 10.22

Definition

A **great circle** of a sphere is the intersection of the sphere and a secant plane that contains the center of the sphere.

The following theorems give important facts concerning spheres.

Theorem 10.20
Two points on a sphere that are not on the same diameter lie on exactly one great circle of the sphere.

Theorem 10.21
Two great circles of a sphere intersect at two points that are endpoints of a diameter of the sphere.

Theorem 10.22
All great circles of a sphere are congruent.

The next theorems are similar to theorems about circles and can be proved in a similar manner.

Theorem 10.23
A secant plane of a sphere is perpendicular to the line containing the center of the circle of intersection and the center of the sphere.

Theorem 10.24
A plane is tangent to a sphere if and only if it is perpendicular to the radius at the point of tangency.

When traveling on the surface of the earth, it is useful to find the shortest distance between two points on the surface of a sphere—for example, the distance between points A and B.

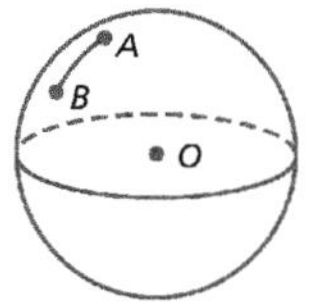

Figure 10.23

Notice that the distance could not be a straight segment because the sphere has curvature. To find the distance between A and B, you must find the length of the arc on the great circle that contains A and B. The symbol for the distance is $d\widehat{AB}$.

If $m\widehat{AB}$ is $3°$, the arc is $\frac{3}{360}$ of the circumference of the great circle. Use $c = 2\pi r$ with $r = 8$.

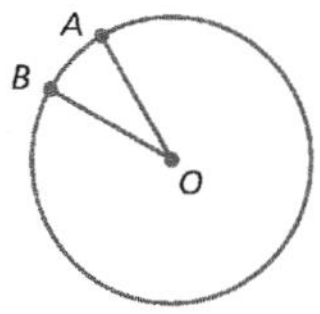

Figure 10.24

$$d\widehat{AB} = \frac{m\widehat{AB}}{360}(2\pi r)$$

$$d\widehat{AB} = \frac{3}{360}(2\pi \cdot 8)$$

$$= \frac{1}{120}(16\pi)$$

$$= \frac{2\pi}{15} \text{ or about } 0.4189 \text{ units}$$

So the distance from A to B is a little less than half a unit.

This method can be used to find the distance between two places on the earth. Although the earth is not a perfect sphere, it is so close to the shape of a sphere that the variations are usually insignificant.

Answers

1. ∅, a point, a circle

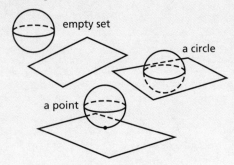

empty set

a circle

a point

2. They are tangent to the sphere.

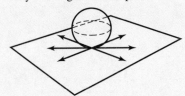

3.

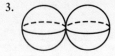

4. $\frac{16\pi}{9} \approx 5.6$ units

5. $\frac{7\pi}{9} \approx 2.4$ units

6. $\frac{18\pi}{5} \approx 11.3$ units

7. $\frac{14\pi}{45} \approx 1.0$ unit

8. $2\pi \approx 6.3$ units

9. $\frac{8\pi}{3} \approx 8.4$ units

10. $\frac{64\pi}{15} \approx 13.4$ units

11. $\frac{43\pi}{2} \approx 67.5$ units

12. $36\pi \approx 113$ units

13. $790\pi \approx 2480.6$ mi.

14. $\frac{395\pi}{18} \approx 68.9$ mi.

15. $\frac{37,525\pi}{18} \approx 6546.0$ mi.

16.

1. Sphere S with center C contains points A and B that are not on the same diameter	1. Given
2. A, B, and C are not collinear	2. Definition of collinear points
3. A, B, and C determine exactly one plane p	3. Plane Postulate
4. p ∩ S is a great circle	4. Definition of great circle

444 CHAPTER 10 SPACE

▶ A. Exercises

1. Draw three diagrams showing the three possible cases of the intersection of a sphere and a plane.
2. Draw a sphere and a plane tangent to the sphere. Draw three lines that are contained in the plane and that pass through the point of tangency. What is true about these lines?
3. Draw two spheres whose great circles are externally tangent circles.

For exercises 4-7, find $d\widehat{XY}$ if A is the center of a sphere, and ∠XAY has the indicated measure. The radius of the sphere is 4 units.

4. $m\angle XAY = 80$
5. $m\angle XAY = 35$
6. $m\angle XAY = 162$
7. $m\angle XAY = 14$

Find the distance between two points H and I on sphere J if ∠HJI and $\overline{IJ}$ have the indicated measures. Find to the nearest tenth.

8. $m\angle HJI = 30; IJ = 12$
9. $m\angle HJI = 160; IJ = 3$
10. $m\angle HJI = 48; IJ = 16$
11. $m\angle HJI = 90; IJ = 43$
12. $m\angle HJI = 270; IJ = 24$

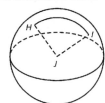

▶ B. Exercises

Consider the earth to be a sphere. If its diameter is 7900 miles, find the distance between two cities that are the given degree measures apart.

13. 36°
14. 1°
15. 95°

Prove each theorem.
16. Theorem 10.20
17. Theorem 10.21

17.

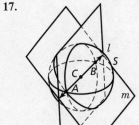

1. Sphere S with center C and two great circles	1. Given
2. Plane m and plane n contain C and the great circles respectively	2. Definition of great circle
3. m ∩ n is a line l	3. Plane Intersection Postulate
4. l contains a diameter $\overline{AB}$, with points A and B as the only points of the sphere	4. Definition of diameter (since C is in both planes)
5. l intersects each great circle at A and B	5. A line in a plane of a circle that intersects the interior of the circle intersects the circle at exactly two points
6. The intersection of the two great circles is {A, B}	6. Definition of intersection

▶ C. Exercises

Prove each theorem.
18. Theorem 10.22
19. Theorem 10.23
20. Theorem 10.24

▪ Cumulative Review

Find each area.

21.

22.

23.

24.

25.

21. 7 [8.2]
22. 2√77 [8.3]
23. 20 [8.2]
24. 32 [8.2]
25. $\frac{9\sqrt{3}}{2}$ [8.3]

18.

1. Sphere *S* with center *C* and radius *r*; for any two great circles, let *A* be a point on one and *B* be on the other	1. Given
2. *C* is the center of each great circle, and *A* and *B* are on sphere *S*	2. Definition of great circle
3. *AC* = *BC* = *r*	3. Definition of sphere
4. $\overline{AC} \cong \overline{BC}$	4. Definition of congruent segments
5. The great circles are congruent	5. Definition of congruent circles

19. Theorem 10.23

1. Sphere *S* with center *C* and secant plane *m*	1. Given
2. *S* intersects *m* in ⊙*P*	2. Sphere and secant intersect in circle
3. *l* is any line through *P* in *m*	3. Auxiliary line
4. $l = \overleftrightarrow{AB}$ where $\overline{AB}$ is a diameter of ⊙*P*	4. Definition of diameter
5. $\overline{AP} \cong \overline{BP}$	5. Radii of a circle are congruent
6. $\overline{AC} \cong \overline{BC}$	6. Radii of a sphere are congruent
7. $\overline{CP} \cong \overline{CP}$	7. Reflexive property of congruent segments
8. △*ACP* ≅ △*BCP*	8. SSS
9. ∠*CPA* ≅ ∠*CPB*	9. Definition of congruent triangles
10. ∠*CPA* and ∠*CPB* are supplementary	10. Linear pairs are supplementary
11. $\overline{PC} \perp \overline{AB}$	11. Congruent supplements
12. $\overline{PC} \perp m$	12. Definition of line perpendicular to plane (step 3)

(continued) see Answer section

Riemann

Objectives

1. To appreciate the immense contributions Riemann made to the field of mathematical physics.
2. To appreciate Riemann's Christian example of persevering in the face of great obstacles.
3. To recognize Riemann as a great mathematician and discoverer of non-Euclidean geometry.

Geometry Through History

GEORG FRIEDRICH BERNHARD RIEMANN

Georg Bernhard Riemann was born on September 17, 1826, in the village of Breselenz, in Hanover, Germany. His father was a Lutheran pastor. The Lutheran congregation in the small village could not sufficiently support the pastor and his six children, and the Riemann family barely survived. The children were undernourished, and their mother, Charlotte Ebell, died before her children had grown to maturity.

Through the struggle for survival, the Riemann family grew to be a close family, and Bernhard had a very happy childhood. He, however, was a timid boy and remained extremely shy throughout his life. He was often homesick when he was away from his family and made frequent trips home.

Bernhard received his first educational instruction from his father. He loved to learn, and his earliest interest was in history. He began studying arithmetic at the age of six, at which time his mathematical genius became apparent. Bernhard enjoyed solving every problem he could find, and he often made up difficult problems for his brothers and sisters. They found the problems impossible to solve. By the time Bernhard was ten, his father found it necessary to delegate further mathematical instruction to a professional tutor. He began advanced study in arithmetic and geometry but soon surpassed his teacher. His formal education began at fourteen when he entered the Gymnasium at Hanover. Two years later he transferred to the Gymnasium at Lüneburg.

Presentation

After the students have read this biographical sketch of Georg Riemann, use questions like the following to stimulate discussion. Having students express in writing, or verbally, the ideas they formulate helps clarify their thinking. Therefore, questioning helps them understand what they believe.

1. If Riemann's father had a lifelong wish that his son study theology, why do you suppose the father changed his mind?
2. To what principle of authority do you see Georg Riemann being submissive?
3. In what ways do you see Riemann's life illustrating the adage "Life is not fair"?
4. From the context of the article, what do you think a "gymnasium" was?

5. What clue in the article tells us what Riemann thought most important in his life?

The last paragraph is especially important. At the end, it identifies Riemann's great talent. However, many students will not be able to explain what it means to "unify physical and mathematical thoughts" in their own words. The example of Copernicus may help. He understood the mathematics of circles and ellipses and other figures very well, and he also had observed the physical universe very closely (positions of planets and other bodies). By comparing observations with mathematics of various possible shapes for orbits, he made a new theory of elliptical orbits with the sun at the center. The theory unified (brought together)

the physical observations and mathematics. While Riemann's contributions were not in astronomy, he had this same capacity to solve major issues in physics and other fields through scientific observation and abstract mathematics.

The most important aspect of the last paragraph, however, is the phrase "non-Euclidean geometry." These systems of geometry conflict sharply with things that students take for granted as facts. Two geometric systems that are non-Euclidean are called Riemannian and Lobachevskian. Each is named after its discoverer. At this point, simply mention that these geometries were probably the most important mathematical discovery of the twentieth century and that Riemann is therefore one of

Riemann's father wanted him to study theology, so at the age of nineteen Reimann entered the University of Göttingen to study theology but continued studying mathematics privately. He could not escape his delight in the subject and soon asked his father's permission to leave preparation for the ministry to study mathematics. His father agreed, and Riemann joyously entered the University of Berlin to study math. Throughout his life Riemann remained a faithful Christian.

Riemann finished his doctorate at Göttingen in 1851. Even the greatest mathematician of his day praised his dissertation on the "Foundation for a General Theory of Functions of a Complex Variable." His dissertation showed his ability in pure mathematics but also his interests in applied mathematics. Combining his abilities in pure math and physical science, he excelled in mathematical physics. Investigations in mathematical physics occupied him until he became an assistant professor at the University of Göttingen in 1857 and a full professor in 1859. The professorship improved his financial state, and he married Elise Koch at the age of thirty-six.

Soon after his marriage Riemann became ill and never really recovered. He died of tuberculosis on July 20, 1866. Engraved on his tombstone were the words from Romans 8:28: "All things work together for good to them that love the Lord."

Riemann's major mathematical contributions include his study of functions of both real and complex variables. He also introduced Riemannian geometry—a type of non-Euclidean geometry—in his *Habilitationsshrift*. This essay (and his first lecture as a lecturer in 1854) revolutionized both geometry and physics. Probably his greatest gift was his ability to unify physical and mathematical thoughts connected with some large problem.

He loved to learn, and his earliest interest was in history.

the great mathematicians of all time. These comments will build interest for Section 10.8, which probes the important geometry named after this great man. ∎

Latitude and Longitude

10.7 **Latitude and Longitude**

Objectives

1. To define latitude and longitude as a means of global positioning on the earth.
2. To identify cities and countries given their latitude and longitude, and vice versa.
3. To relate great circle, opposite points, and points of intersection on a sphere to global positioning via latitude and longitude.

Vocabulary

Eastern Hemisphere	Northern Hemisphere
equator	prime meridian
international date line	Southern Hemisphere
latitude	Western Hemisphere
longitude	

Assignment

- Intuitive: 1-20, 27-31
- Standard: 1-25, 27-31
- Rigorous: 1-19 odd, 21-31

Flash

Answer: North Africa (Sahara), Arabian Peninsula between Red Sea and Persian Gulf, Spain at the west end of the Mediterranean Sea, and portions of central Asia

---

The earth is nearly spherical. The diameter of the earth from the North Pole to the South Pole is 7885 miles, while the diameter at the equator is about 7912 miles. This 27-mile difference is almost nothing compared to the size of the earth. Since we can consider the earth a sphere, the definitions and theorems that you learned about spheres can apply to the earth.

What parts of the Eastern Hemisphere do you recognize on this satellite photo?

Two important great circles are marked on every globe. The first great circle to consider is the equator. The plane that cuts off the equator passes through the center of the earth and is perpendicular to the diameter that passes through the North and South Poles. The equator divides the earth into two hemispheres called the Northern and Southern Hemispheres. Planes that are parallel to the plane of the equator cut off smaller circles that appear to be parallel to the equator on the globe. These lines are called *latitudinal lines*. These lines help locate cities and other points of interest on the earth in a north-south direction and on most globes are marked off in 10-degree divisions from the equator.

A great circle that passes through Greenwich, England, is also an important reference circle. The semicircle that goes from the North Pole to the South Pole and passes through Greenwich, England, is called the *prime meridian*. The other semicircle of this great circle is called the *International Date Line*.

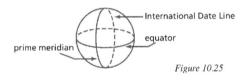

Figure 10.25

Presentation

This lesson shows a relationship between math and geography. Read the first paragraph together. Then find the (average) diameter of the earth from the maximum and minimum diameters stated (7898.5, or about 7899 miles). Next, calculate the average radius of the earth (3949 or 3950 miles, depending on the diameter used, but 3950 is easier to work with and remember). Use the radius to find the average circumference (24,856.3 miles) and the surface area (196,066,797.5 sq. miles). These calculations will provide review of basic formulas concerning spheres.

Motivational Idea. Bring as many globes to class as you can. Many students will enjoy working with them, and they are helpful in

explaining latitude and longitude. Explain where the important circles on the globe are located. Refer to the globes throughout the discussion of the lesson, including the examples. Then write down at least ten places and their locations, and let the students practice using latitude and longitude to find these locations. Depending on the number of globes, students may need to work in groups.

One-on-one. Sometimes students have trouble differentiating the actual earth from the imaginary sphere on which we place our lines of latitude and longitude. Some may even think there are lines drawn on the earth. Remind them that if that were the case, most of the lines would be on water, since most of the earth is water.

Motivational Idea. The development of a modern Global Positioning System (GPS) through the use of satellites has far surpassed previous methods for accuracy of locations on the surface of the earth. Anyone can buy a GPS and use it to establish his location and maintain a path or direction of travel. Besides identifying your location, the GPS can do many other things. One operation it performs is to give the direction and distance to travel between two locations (with latitude and longitude). Some students may be interested in doing some research on other GPS capabilities.

Locations that are opposite endpoints of a diameter of the earth are called antipodal points (or *antipodes*). The two most famous antipodes

The great circle containing the prime meridian and International Date Line divides the earth into two hemispheres called the Eastern and Western Hemispheres. Great circles that pass through the North and South Poles are called *longitudinal lines*.

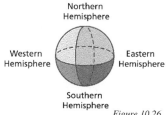

Figure 10.26

These longitudinal and latitudinal lines form a grid by which places can be located. The means of locating places seems complicated at first but is much like wrapping graph paper around the earth. A place is located according to degree and direction. Latitude is the degree measure of the arc from the equator to a particular location. The degree of latitude is always measured north or south and lies between 0° and 90°. Point *s* is located at 60° north latitude.

Longitude is measured according to degree measure east or west from the prime meridian. This measure ranges from 0° to 180°. Point *x* is located at 110° east longitude. With these longitudinal and latitudinal lines, the location of any place on the earth can be specified.

Figure 10.27

EXAMPLE 1 What city is located at 30° north latitude, 90° west longitude?

Answer   1. Start at the intersection of the equator and the prime meridian.
2. Move to 30° north.
3. Move to 90° west along the 30° north latitudinal line.
4. New Orleans is located at the intersection of 30° north latitude and 90° west longitude.

Many times the place you are interested in will not fall directly on an intersection of a longitudinal and a latitudinal line. When this happens, simply estimate the distance between the longitudinal or latitudinal lines.

Resources
- Any world atlas and/or a globe.
- *Activities Manual,* Calculator Skills. Focuses on the use of the calculator with longitudes and latitudes and finding arc distances.

Reading and Writing Mathematics

Have the students look up *projection* in an encyclopedia and explain some desirable properties when projecting from a sphere onto a plane to make a map. **Ideally, the map would correctly represent shapes (similarity preserved); permit accurate calculation of areas (area preserved); obtain accurate distances from the scale (distance or congruence preserved); represent great circles as straight lines; be easy to produce and use.**

Additional Problems

Identify each location and give the approximate latitude and longitude.

1. The highest mountain in the world, Mt. Everest, Nepal **28° N, 87° E**
2. The tallest waterfall in the world, Angel Falls, Venezuela **6° N, 62° W**
3. The most violent volcanic eruption in modern history, Krakatau, Indonesia **6° S, 105° E**
4. Find the great circle distance in miles between Los Angeles (118.24° W, 34.05° N) and Rio de Janeiro (43.22° W, 22.90° S). Use the equatorial radius of 3963 miles.

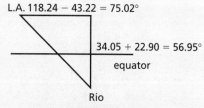

$x = \sqrt{(75.02)^2 + (56.95)^2}$
$x = 94.19°$ (change x to arc length)
$d = \frac{94.19}{360}[2\pi(3963)]$
$d = 6514.71$ miles

---

are the North and South Poles; however, every location on the earth has an antipode. Exercise 24 investigates the antipode of Honolulu.

You can help students understand antipodal points by imagining that your classroom is spherical. Stand in the center of the room and hold a pointer (or yardstick) to roughly represent the diameter. Hold the diameter in the middle with two fingers and orient it vertically to point to the "poles" of the room. Have a student move one end to produce a corresponding but opposite movement on the other end. Moving one end right moves the other left, and so on. The two ends always point 180° apart, and any point in the Northern Hemisphere has

its opposite in the Southern Hemisphere. The same is true with the Eastern and Western Hemispheres.

If you wish to apply the conceptual idea above, you can mark a prime meridian on the wall, and estimate a location such as 105° W, 32° N. Students will note that the antipode is at 75° E and 32° S. This will show them how to find antipode coordinates (75 is the supplement of 105). Since the application will also make #23-25 very easy, some teachers may want to postpone the application until they go over the homework.

We can also make some fairly accurate estimates of distances between two locations

by using a spherical right triangle. The difference in their longitudes becomes one leg and the difference between latitudes becomes the other leg. Applying the Pythagorean theorem lets us calculate the hypotenuse and the great circle path between locations.

Using spherical geometry, these numbers should be 91.2° and 6307 miles. The accuracy of this method (using Pythagorean theorem) improves for locations that are fairly close.

5. Find the great circle distance between *P* (100° W, 30° N) and *Q* (60° W, 12°N) **approximately 3034 miles**

Answers
1. Philadelphia, Pennsylvania
2. Hawaiian Islands
3. Cape Town, South Africa
4. Singapore
5. Paris, France
6. Rio de Janeiro, Brazil
7. Monterrey, Mexico
8. Fiji Islands
9. Alexandria, Egypt
10. Tahiti
11. 13° north, 122° east
12. 56° north, 36° east
13. 42° north, 14° east
14. 34° north, 35° east
15. 72° south, 70° west
16. 40° north, 4° west
17. 22° north, 117° east
18. 16° south, 47° west
19. 33° north, 8° west
20. 1° south, 38° east
21. North and South Poles
22. 0°, 0° (Atlantic just south of Ghana, Africa)
    0°, 180° (Pacific just west of Baker Island)
23. 21° S, 158° W, Avarua, Rarotonga in the Cook Islands
24. 21° S, 22° E, Tsau, Botswana
25. 21° N, 22° E, Libya
26. Arctic Circle 66 $\frac{1}{2}$° N; tropic of Cancer 23 $\frac{1}{2}$° N; tropic of Capricorn 23 $\frac{1}{2}$° S; Antarctic Circle 66 $\frac{1}{2}$° S. The earth is tilted on its axis with respect to the sun at 23 $\frac{1}{2}$°. Therefore, the tropic of Cancer and tropic of Capricorn are the northernmost and southernmost latitudes reached by perpendicular rays from the overhead sun. The Arctic and Antarctic Circles (degree measures are complements of the tropics) mark the farthest distance from the poles with 24-hour light or darkness.
27. 196 million sq. mi. [8.8]
28. congruent radii [6.3]
29. SAS [7.6]
30. same length [6.1]
31. congruent edges [10.5]

EXAMPLE 2   Give the location of Sydney, Australia.

Answer   1. Find Sydney, Australia.
2. Move down along the longitudinal line to Sydney, counting the degrees from the equator. Sydney is located between 30° and 40° (about 34°) south.
3. Locate the prime meridian and count the degrees east along the equator until you are even with Sydney, Australia just beyond 150° (151° east).
4. Sydney, Australia, is located at 34° south, 151° east.

▶ A. Exercises

Find the city, state, or country at each location. Use globes or atlases.
1. 41° north, 76° west
2. 20° north, 160° west
3. 34° south, 18° east
4. 1° north, 104° east
5. 48° north, 3° east
6. 23° south, 43° west
7. 25° north, 100° west
8. 18° south, 178° east
9. 31° north, 30° east
10. 18° south, 150° west

Find the latitude and longitude of each place indicated below.
11. Manila, Philippines
12. Moscow, Russia
13. Rome, Italy
14. Beirut, Lebanon
15. Alexander Island, Antarctica
16. Madrid, Spain
17. Hong Kong
18. Brasília, Brazil
19. Casablanca, Morocco
20. Nairobi, Kenya

▶ B. Exercises

Give the location described by the following.
21. Every pair of longitudinal lines intersect at what points?
22. The great circles containing the prime meridian and the equator intersect at what points?

For the following give the latitude, longitude, name of country, and city.
23. Find the location in the Southern Hemisphere corresponding to Honolulu, Hawaii.
24. Find the location opposite Honolulu on a diameter of the earth.
25. Find the location in the Northern Hemisphere on the other side of the world from Honolulu.

▶ C. Exercises

The Arctic Circle, tropic of Cancer, tropic of Capricorn, and Antarctic Circle divide the earth into five latitudinal zones.

450   CHAPTER 10   SPACE

Tips

Ex. 1-26. A world atlas or a globe will be needed. Having both available is wise.

Ex. 23-25. Honolulu (and every other location) has three "opposite points." For #23, use the same longitude and change only latitude from north to south, i.e., go below the equator to the opposite hemisphere. For #25, go 180° around the world on the same latitude. (This is what is meant when people on the Great Plains of the U.S. and Canada say that Siberia is on the "opposite" side of the world.) In #24, the true opposite (across a diameter) is found. Students will enjoy finding the three opposites for their hometown, but at least one opposite will probably be in an ocean. ∎

26. Give the latitude of each of the four lines and explain the significance of the numbers.

Cumulative Review

27. The average radius of the earth is 3953 miles. Find the surface area to the nearest million square miles.

Give a condition for the congruence of each pair of figures.

28. two circles
29. two parallelograms
30. two segments
31. two cubes

10.8 Spherical Geometry

Euclidean geometry results from valid reasoning based on the postulates so far presented. If you replace some of the postulates, you obtain other systems, called *non-Euclidean geometries*. One of these systems is *Riemannian geometry*, named after its developer Bernhard Riemann.

A farm on the flat plains of Iowa has a rectangle boundary. What shape does it have on the sphere of the earth?

Riemannian geometry is also called spherical geometry because you can use a sphere to represent it. Think about the earth. To go in a straight line from Memphis Tennessee, to Dacca, Bangladesh, you would have to dig a tunnel along the chord of the sphere. An airline pilot considers the shortest distance to be an arc of the great circle of the sphere. In this context it is useful to use great circles as the "lines" of our system and the places on the surface of the earth as points. Thus, the surface of the earth is used to represent the "plane." This system has properties different from Euclidean geometry.

Figure 10.28

10.8

Spherical Geometry

Objectives

1. To identify the concepts of spherical geometry as an example of a non-Euclidean geometry.
2. To stress the importance of Scripture as the only absolute source of truth.

Vocabulary

non-Euclidean geometry
Riemannian geometry
spherical geometry

Assignment

- Intuitive: no assignment necessary
- Standard: no assignment necessary
- Rigorous 1-18

Resources

- Appendix H on Parallel Postulates. Non-Euclidean postulates are at the end.
- *Activities Manual,* Math History Activity on Lobachevsky. Introduces the students to men who developed hyperbolic geometry.
- *Activities Manual,* Hyperbolic Geometry in Principle. Further develops concepts of this non-Euclidean geometry.
- *Test Packet,* Quiz 4, Chapter 10 covers Sections 10.7 and 10.8.

Reading and Writing Mathematics

Have the students look up *projection* in an encyclopedia and name three kinds of "perspective" projections and describe them.

Presentation

This lesson should be thought provoking and interesting to the students as long as you use it mostly for discussion purposes and do not expect detailed knowledge of it.

Non-Euclidean geometries are distinguished from Euclidean geometry by their particular assumptions for a parallel postulate. The postulates answer this question: through a given point not on a given line, how many parallels exist? Each type is named after its discoverer.

Euclidean—exactly 1 parallel
Lobachevskian (hyperbolic)—at least 2 parallels
Riemannian (spherical)—0 parallels

Notice the alternate names for two of these. From the postulate that two parallels exist, it can be proved that there are infinitely many parallels.

Thus, there are only three cases, and a summary is available in Appendix H. Further, each case has several significant consequences. For instance, the sum of the measures of the angles of a triangle depends on the postulate system.

Euclidean—angle sum = 180°
Lobachevskian—angle sum < 180°
Riemannian—angle sum > 180°

Motivational Idea. As you begin the discussion of spherical geometry, bring out a globe or other large sphere. You should illustrate all of the terms given here on the large model.

Common Student Error. Students often confuse terms in spherical geometry because it is so different. It will help them to remember

the way things look on earth. The "plane" in this case is the surface of a sphere. The "lines" are great circles, and the "segments" are minor arcs of the great circles. This is strange, but it makes sense. Farms on the plains look flat, but we know that the earth is round and that the apparently plane surface is actually part of the sphere. Likewise, walking in a straight line will circle the globe on a great circle. If you stress that "lines" are great circles, students should be able to sketch lines in exercises.

Discuss the concepts of distance and triangles to build familiarity with the system. The distance between two points in spherical geometry is the length of the great circle arc joining them (geodesic). On a sphere of radius *r*, the

Plane—the earth is projected onto a flat plane
Conic—the earth is projected onto a cone whose base intersects the earth and whose lateral surface is tangent to the earth
Cylindrical—the earth is projected onto a cylinder that is tangent to the earth at the equator

Additional Problems

Use spherical geometry concepts to answer the following.

1. Draw a quadrilateral on the surface of a sphere.

2. Give an upper bound (limit) for the area of a quadrilateral. *surface area of a hemisphere* $= \frac{1}{2}(4\pi r^2) = 2\pi r^2$

3. Draw a Lambert quadrilateral (a quadrilateral with three right angles).

4. Can you draw a rectangle? Explain. *No. The fourth angle is always obtuse.*

5. Use a globe to explain why you can do #3 but not #4. *Think of l as an equator; find meridians at A and B. These meridians p and q are perpendicular to l, but not to m (or any other great circle—study a globe).*

Answers

1. 90°
2. equator, longitudes
3. The circle at 45° N latitude is not a great circle, so it is not a line in the system.

Since all great circles intersect, there is no such thing as parallel lines in spherical geometry. For instance, no line (great circle) passes through New Orleans (a given point) parallel to the equator (a given line). In the exercises you will also see that the sum of the measures of the angles of a triangle is never 180° in spherical geometry.

Some scientists believe that space is Riemannian. This is what is meant by "curved space." Just as one can travel around the world without perceiving the curve of the earth's surface, Riemannian scientists conceive that if you could travel through space far enough you could reach your starting point.

How can a Christian explain these contradictory systems? Does truth depend on viewpoint or usefulness? No! Both systems display valid reasoning—but which has true premises? God knows, but as humans we do not. This is an important lesson. Man cannot arrive at truth on his own—not even in math. We cannot know whether apparent parallel lines intersect. We do know that the only source of absolute truth is the Bible. God's Word provides a sure foundation because God wrote it.

These systems also reflect honesty and Christian faith. Each type of geometry clearly states its postulates without double talk; the facts are open to scrutiny. God, likewise, reveals Himself in His Word, which we should study closely. We trust postulate systems as they are used by engineers to build bridges. This faith is reasonable and practical. In the same way, we trust God for salvation. It makes sense to trust God-given math principles in building bridges; but do not put faith in human accomplishment. We must have faith in Jesus Christ: "That your faith should not stand in the wisdom of men, but in the power of God" (I Cor. 2:5).

▶ A. Exercises

1. Imagine walking south along a longitudinal line from the North Pole and turning east at the equator. What angle did you turn?

2. Which of the following are "lines" in spherical geometry: the equator, tropic of Cancer, latitudinal circles, longitudinal circles, prime meridian, tropic of Capricorn, Arctic Circle?

3. Minneapolis is at 45° N latitude. The circle of latitude at 45° N is parallel to the equator. Why do we say that there are no parallels in the model of Riemannian geometry?

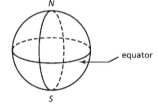

maximum distance is the length of a semicircle, i.e., πr. A triangle is the union of three segments (geodesic arcs) joining three vertices (points). Be careful not to identify a triangle on which two of the points are antipodal (opposite ends of a diameter), because all three points will lie on some line and there will not be a triangle.

Motivational Idea. Use a map and a globe to teach this lesson. Take a world map and find Memphis and Dacca. Have a student connect the cities with a straight line. Ask students if it is a straight line. Now find the cities on a globe. Show that the shortest route between them goes over the North Pole. Measure the distance with a string and compare it with that of the route marked on the map. (Find several

places that the map line goes through to identify the same route on the globe. Measure this route with another string to compare.) Point out that the shortest distance would actually be a tunnel through the earth, but for air flight purposes, traveling in a straight line means the shortest distance on the surface of the earth.

These illustrations will not only teach students the limitations of flat maps but also explain why "line" refers to a great circle of the earth. Once you have established this usage of line you can demonstrate that this spherical geometry has no parallel lines.

The table summarizes how the concepts of Riemannian geometry relate to the spherical model. A second table summarizes some of the properties that contrast to Euclidean geometry.

Concept	Spherical Model
line	great circle
plane	surface of sphere
segment	arc of great circle
triangle	three arcs

Concept	Euclidean	Riemannian
parallels	1	none
sum of angle measures of triangle	180°	more than 180°
sum of angle measures of quadrilateral	360°	more than 360°

▶ B. Exercises

Use the system of spherical geometry to check these incidence statements.

4. Does the "plane" of the earth contain at least three noncollinear points?
5. Does every "line" contain at least two points?
6. Are every pair of points on a "line"?
7. Do two intersecting "lines" intersect in exactly one point?
8. Do every pair of points determine exactly one "line"?
9. How does the sum of the measures of the angles in △PST compare to 180°? Explain.
10. Sketch a triangle with three right angles (an equilateral right triangle).

▶ C. Exercises

Answer the questions using Riemannian geometry.

11. Why are trapezoids and parallelograms impossible?
12. If ABCD is a quadrilateral with three right angles, what kind of angle is the fourth angle?
13. How does the measure of an exterior angle of a triangle compare to the sum of the measures of the remote interior angles?

▊ Cumulative Review

14. A regular heptagon and a regular octagon are inscribed in congruent circles. Which polygonal region has more area?
15. Is the following argument valid? Sound? What type of argument is it?
    All lizards are reptiles.
    All salamanders are lizards.
    Therefore, all salamanders are reptiles.
16. Sketch and label the altitude, perpendicular bisector, angle bisector, and median to a side in a triangle. They must be different lines and intersect the same side.
17. Draw an illustration for the Angle Addition Postulate and explain it. One angle must be 47°.
18. What definition acts as a Segment Addition Postulate?

10.8 SPHERICAL GEOMETRY **453**

Tips

Several other Euclidean theorems also fail because of the change in the parallel postulate. If you want students to explore more, ask whether two lines perpendicular to the same line are parallel (*no*) or whether congruent alternate interior angles guarantee parallelism (*no*).

Ex. 2. As defined here and in most geography books, the prime meridian is the 0° longitude and not the 180° longitude. Thus, it is only half of a great circle (although less technical sources may not make the distinction).

Ex. 4-9. These show which incidence postulates fail in spherical geometry.

Ex. 13. This is easy to see in △PST at top of page. The exterior angle is 90°, but the remote interior angles total 180°.

Ex. 15. The second premise is a false premise since salamanders are amphibians (like frogs) rather than reptiles (which include lizards, snakes, turtles). ▪

4.
   yes

5.
   yes

6.
   yes

7.
   no, two points

8.
   not if they are antipodes (ends of a diameter), otherwise, yes

9. more (180° even without ∠P)

10.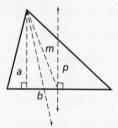

11. no parallels exist
12. obtuse
13. less than
14. octagon [8.5]
15. valid, unsound deductive argument by transitivity [5.6]

16.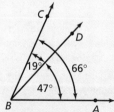

    p = perpendicular bisector [7.2]
    m = median
    b = angle bisector
    a = altitude

17.

    m∠ABC = m∠ABD + m∠CBD
    (since 66° = 47° + 19°) [4.2]
18. betweenness [3.2]

10.8 SPHERICAL GEOMETRY **453**

Geometry and Scripture

Objectives

1. To identify arguments for and against the universe being finite.
2. To identify arguments for and against the universe having a Euclidean or non-Euclidean structure.

Answers

1. False
2. True

Higher Plane

Isaiah 1:18; Luke 5:21

3. Job 22:5; Ps. 147:5; Nah. 3:9. No.
4. Great circles on the sphere. Yes (twice)

Geometry and Scripture

how big is the universe? Is it Euclidean? Let's look for a Bible answer to each of these two difficult but important questions.

Finite or Infinite?

Some Christians and most of the secular world think the universe is infinite. However, proof would require either infinite travel or omniscience. Other Christians insist that only God is infinite. It may be true that nothing else is infinite, but this cannot be proved from the Bible. Just as man reflects some of God's qualities because he is made in God's image, space may reflect His infinitude. Thus, neither view can be proved.

Evaluate each statement as true or false.

1. Only God can reason.   2. Only God can forgive sin.

> **HIGHER PLANE:** Support your answers to questions 1 and 2 with Scripture.

3. List all Bible references to "infinite." Do any refer to physical things?

The lack of physical examples is the best evidence for a finite universe. This inductive evidence is strong but by no means conclusive. At present many theologians think the universe is finite on this basis.

Euclidean or Non-Euclidean?

You have probably always thought that the universe is Euclidean, but have you ever analyzed your reasons for thinking so?

4. Euclidean geometry teaches that parallel lines never meet. However, we cannot identify parallel lines in our universe. Space may model spherical geometry. What are lines on the earth? Do they always meet?

Presentation

Like the Scripture study on dimensions, this study has great potential for arousing interest by addressing controversial issues. The goal is to help students be open to views other than their own without dogmatism in areas in which Scripture is silent.

You will need to spend extra effort presenting views that are unfamiliar to students. On the finite/infinite issue, most students will find the finite view unfamiliar since it is ignored by secular media and educators. If students find it difficult to conceive that the world is finite, remind them that people once thought that the world was flat and could not imagine a round world. From our view of the earth, we can easily

imagine a finite surface with no end. Perhaps space is similar.

The issue over which geometry applies in the universe is even tougher. In a region as small as the earth, the differences in distances predicted by the systems are so small that they cannot be detected. Thus, the issue arises primarily in the field of astronomy. The traditional view of a Euclidean universe is the most familiar, but it has been abandoned by modern thinkers in favor of Einstein's views of relativity, which employ Riemannian geometry. Here is a case in which the modern view is unfamiliar because it involves difficult mathematics that few people know. While Einstein's view is

popular, it cannot be proved absolutely, and Christians are still divided over the strength of the evidence. You may need to spend time justifying the modern view (since it is unfamiliar) and then also presenting its weaknesses (since secular writers rarely acknowledge them).

5. In Euclidean geometry, every triangle's angle measures total 180°. In practice, when we measure three angles and add them up, our measurements always include a margin of error. Suppose the total comes to 179.96° ± 0.05°. Could the true value be less than or greater than 180°? Which would be true spherical geometry?

6. Some argue that only Euclidean geometry has had practical application in physical science; however, scientists have used non-Euclidean geometry in studying the retina of the eye. Moreover, usefulness is not conclusive evidence. Give an ancient view of the earth that was practical for navigation and for predicting seasons but was incorrect.

7. The best evidence for the Euclidean view is in the description of quadrilaterals. What key term in Exodus 27:1 could not exist in non-Euclidean geometry?

This Bible reference to foursquare constitutes weighty evidence but is inconclusive. Sometimes the Bible records events the way they appear to man (using the language of appearance). Match each passage below to the phrase describing the human perspective in the verse.

8. Genesis 32:31   A. sun sets
9. Psalm 113:3   B. sun rises
10. Ecclesiastes 9:11   C. both setting and rising of the sun
11. Luke 4:40   D. four corners of the earth
12. Revelation 7:1   E. chance

There is no conclusive evidence that references to foursquare in Exodus 27:1 and elsewhere are using the language of appearance. Such references therefore provide strong evidence for a Euclidean universe.

> ### Line upon Line
>
> AND THOU SHALT make an altar of shittim wood, five cubits long, and five cubits broad; the altar shall be foursquare: and the height thereof shall be three cubits. 🐛
>
> EXODUS 27:1

GEOMETRY AND SCRIPTURE **455**

---

5. $179.91 \leq \text{total} \leq 180.01$; yes, greater than 180°
6. Flat earth view or the geocentric view (review that arguments from utility are only probable [inductive], not certain [deductive])
7. "foursquare"
8. B
9. C
10. E
11. A
12. D

Tips

Ex. 8-12. The "language of appearance" is a phrase describing the way things appear to man as opposed to the way God knows them to be. Remind students that the sun doesn't really set (the earth turns) even though it looks that way to observers. This is not an error in the Bible or in daily speech. It is simply a figure of speech appropriately based on the human perspective. Students will better understand the purpose of these exercises if you remind them about the way we use the term *sunset* first. ∎

GEOMETRY AND SCRIPTURE **455**

Objectives

To help students prepare for evaluation.

Vocabulary

See Appendix A.

Assignment

• Intuitive: 1-21, 30
• Standard: 1-25, 30
• Rigorous: 1-30

Resources

• *Activities Manual,* Cumulative Review
• *Activities Manual,* Terms and Symbols
• *Test Packet,* Chapter 10 Exam

Answers

1. True
2. False
3. True
4. True
5. False
6.

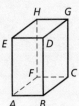

7. 12; ∠A-BC-D is one of the possible answers
8.

9.

10.

11.

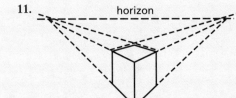
horizon

True/False

1. A dihedral angle separates space into three disjoint sets.
2. Two lines parallel to the same plane are parallel.
3. All cubes are parallelepipeds.
4. All great circles of a sphere are congruent.
5. The faces of a parallelepiped are rectangular regions.

6. Sketch a rectangular prism.
7. How many dihedral angles are determined by your rectangular prism? Name one.
8. Draw a sphere with a tangent plane. Label a radius.

Sketch each figure:

9. two great circles of a sphere that are not perpendicular.
10. a cube in one-point perspective.
11. a cube in two-point perspective.
12. a parallelepiped.

13. How many vertices, edges, and faces does a parallelepiped have?
14. If a convex polyhedron could have forty-three faces and one hundred edges, how many vertices would it have?
15. Find the distance between two points, *A* and *B*, on sphere *C* if $m\angle ACB = 40$ and $AC = 8$ units. Find to the nearest tenth.
16. Show how two planes can separate space into five disjoint sets (including the planes themselves).
17. Show how two planes can separate space into nine disjoint sets (including half-planes and a line).
18. Diagram the possibilities for separating space with three planes. Label each with the number of disjoint sets.
19. Find the city located at 12° south, 78° west.
20. Give the longitude and latitude of Athens, Greece.
21. Give the longitude and latitude for the place that is at the opposite end of a diameter from Athens.
22. If a city is at *x*° west longitude and *y*° north latitude, what will the latitude and longitude be at the other end of a diameter of the earth?

Use Riemannian geometry for exercises 23 and 24.

23. Explain the points, lines, and planes in the system.
24. Sketch triangles with one, two, and three right angles.

12.

13. 8 vertices, 12 edges, 6 faces
14. $V - E + F = 2$; $V - 100 + 43 = 2$;
    $V = 59$
15. $\frac{16\pi}{9} \approx 5.6$ units

16.

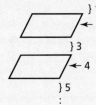
} 1
← 2
} 3
← 4
} 5

Prove

25. The radius perpendicular to a chord of a sphere S with center C bisects the chord.
26. Theorem 10.7
27. Theorem 10.13
28. Theorem 10.14

29. *Given:* Planes m, n, and p intersect in lines $\overleftrightarrow{AB}$, $\overleftrightarrow{CD}$, and $\overleftrightarrow{EF}$ as shown; $\overleftrightarrow{AB} \parallel \overleftrightarrow{CD}$
    Prove: $\overleftrightarrow{EF} \parallel \overleftrightarrow{AB}$ and $\overleftrightarrow{EF} \parallel \overleftrightarrow{CD}$

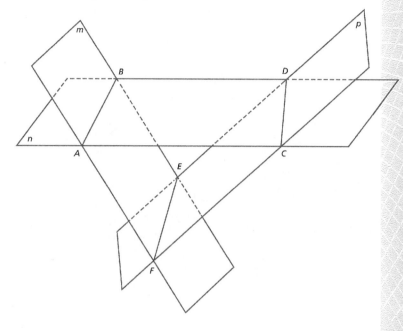

30. Explain the mathematical significance of Exodus 27:1.

17.

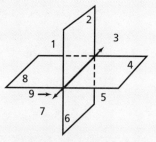

18. **a.** 7 disjoint sets (3 planes, 4 parts of space)

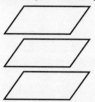

  b. 15 disjoint sets (2 lines, 7 parts of planes, 6 parts of space)

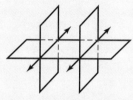

  c. 13 disjoint sets (1 line, 6 half-planes, 6 parts of space)

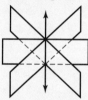

  d. 27 disjoint sets (1 point, 6 half-lines, 12 quarter-planes, 8 quarter-spaces)

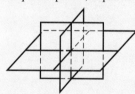

  e. 19 disjoint sets (3 parallel lines, 6 half-planes, 3 strips of planes, 7 parts of space)

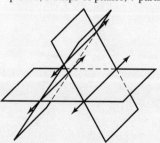

19. Lima, Peru
20. 38° N, 24° E
21. 38° S, 156° W
22. $y°$ south, $(180° - x°)$ east
23. The plane is the surface of the sphere.
    The points are the points of the sphere.
    The lines are the great circles.
    (continued) see Answer section

Presentation

Motivational Idea. Have the students use the vocabulary list for a game of geometry Pictionary. Separate them into groups of four or five and give a student in each group a list of five terms from the vocabulary list that can be drawn either in symbol form or by pictures. Give each student 90 seconds to draw as many of the terms on his list as possible and get his team to give the correct term from the drawings. After 90 seconds, have the students count the number they guessed correctly and then begin another round by giving another list to the next student.

Tips

Ex. 2. False. Consider two parallel planes, one of which contains two intersecting lines. Both lines are parallel to the other plane.

Ex. 5. False. The faces are parallelograms and need not be rectangles. Besides a right rectangular prism, there can be 2 rectangular and 4 nonrectangular parallelogram faces (oblique prism with rectangular base), or 4 rectangular and 2 nonrectangular parallelogram faces (right prism with parallelogram base), or 6 nonrectangular parallelogram faces (oblique prism with parallelogram base). ∎

11 Volume

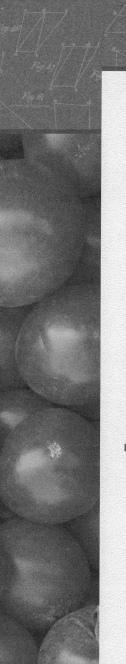

Volume

Tomatoes are one of America's favorite fruits. You may not think of them as fruits, but they are, and they are grown from Oregon to sunny Florida.

Who could enjoy spaghetti or pizza without tomato sauce? We eat cherry tomatoes in salads, diced tomatoes in tacos, tomato chunks in shish kabobs, and tomato wedges in stuffed tomatoes; we even drink tomato juice. Many people like tomatoes on hamburgers, and BLT might be one of America's most delicious abbreviations. Yes, this spherical culinary delight is one of the nation's best-loved fruits.

Did you ever consider the geometric problems involved in producing tomato-related products? For example, tomato cartons seek to minimize wasted space, which is not easy with round fruits. Volume measurements are also important in the manufacture of tomato juice. What volume of tomato concentrate is needed to fill a cylindrical can of tomato juice? In this chapter you will calculate the volume of such spheres and cylinders.

Christians should also bear fruit. Like natural fruits, the fruit of the Spirit takes time to mature. John 15 tells some of the things that produce mature fruit when we live as branches of the True Vine. Abiding, purging, depending on God, answered prayer, and steadfast love are all necessary for producing more fruit in our hearts. As the tomato grower who watches over his plants, God is interested in the quality and quantity of our fruit. Remember that fruit is not meant to beautify the plant but to nourish others.

After this chapter you should be able to

1. define volume.
2. state the volume postulates and compare them to the area postulates.
3. state and apply Cavalieri's principle.
4. prove various formulas for volume.
5. state and apply formulas for volumes of prisms, cylinders, pyramids, cones, spheres, and regular polyhedra.
6. explain the construction of some 3-dimensional figures.
7. recognize three classical constructions that are impossible.

459

Overview

Volume is an essential topic useful to students in all tracks and the chapter develops much like Chapter 8 on area. First the concept of volume and the postulates are presented; then formulas for finding the volumes of geometric solids are derived. Several of these derivations depend on Cavalieri's principle. The chapter concludes with a discussion of constructions in space.

Bulletin Board Idea

Show the solids emphasized in this chapter with their dimensions labeled and their volume formulas. The board should include the cube, prism, cylinder, pyramid, cone, regular polyhedron, and sphere. Title the board *Volume.* (An alternative is to use the posters on volume from the Visual Packet.)

Presentation

Introduce the topic of volume by showing its importance even for packaging plants. Use the discussion of tomatoes for this purpose. When discussing the last paragraph on the fruit of the Spirit, you may wish to turn to Galatians 5:22-23.

Next, give students an overview of the chapter's six sections. The chapter begins with a section on the meaning of volume just as Chapter 8 (area) began with a section on the meaning of area. Following sections prove volume formulas for basic figures from the postulates just as most of Chapter 8 proved area formulas from the area postulates. ∎

11.1

Meaning of Volume

11.1 Meaning of Volume

Objectives

1. To state the volume postulates.
2. To apply the Volume Addition Postulate to solids.
3. To prove volume formulas and apply them to various solids.

Vocabulary

Congruent Solids Postulate
cubic unit
volume
Volume Addition Postulate
Volume of a Cube Postulate
Volume Postulate

Assignment

- Intuitive: 1-17, 21-25
- Standard: 1-19, 21-25
- Rigorous: 5-25

Resources

- Appendix L summarizes the postulates in the book. It is good for review and for giving students a way to classify the postulates.
- *Activities Manual*, Bible Activity: Hell—The Rejection of Truth.

Remember that solid objects consist of both a surface and its interior. In Chapter 8 you learned to compute the surface area of solids. Now you will learn to calculate the volume of the interior of solids. The *volume* of a three-dimensional figure is the number of cubic units needed to fill up the interior. A *cubic unit* is a cube whose side measures one unit—a cubic centimeter, a cubic foot, a cubic yard, a cubic meter, or any cubic unit. Cubic units are different from the square units used for surface area. Keep in mind that volume is the number of these cubes that fill up the solid.

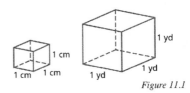

Figure 11.1

> **Definition**
>
> The **volume** of a solid is the number of cubic units needed to fill up the interior completely.

Just as cubic units fill up a three-dimensional object, the love of God should fill up a Christian. Ephesians 3:17-19 says that the Christian can know the love of Christ and that he "might be filled with all the fulness of God." If you are a Christian, you should be demonstrating the love of God to all those around you.

The following postulates form the basis for the study of volume. Compare the volume postulates to the corresponding postulates for area (8.1, 8.2, 8.3, 8.4).

> **Postulate 11.1**
> *Volume Postulate.* Every solid has a volume given by a positive real number.

Motivational Idea. Display a rectangular solid with one end cut out (such as a shoe box without a lid). Ask a student to define the volume of the prism. Guide them to see that *volume* means the number of unit cubes needed to fill the prism. Emphasize the filling aspect and contrast it to the covering idea for surface area.

Motivational Idea. Ask students whether a gallon of water or a cubic foot of water is larger (*cubic foot*). Then ask the number of gallons in a cubic foot (7.5). Few students will be able to answer either question. Display a cubic foot (made by cutting twelve strips of cardboard each a foot long and taping them together to form a cube) to convince students of these answers. Then place two yardsticks on the floor

at right angles and hold a third vertical (perpendicular to the others). Use the cubic foot model to show that the cubic yard determined by the three yardsticks contains 27 cubic feet.

Common Student Error. Some students will think that water is not measured in cubic feet. Correct them by saying that the rate of water flowing through a dam to generate power is usually reported in cubic feet per second (cfs). You can show them such measurements in an almanac. Other examples include flow over major waterfalls and waterflow readings used by whitewater rafters. Another example is the usage of cc's (cubic centimeters) for measuring medicine for shots.

Discuss the four volume postulates. These postulates are intuitively simple and correspond to the four area postulates. They may question the need for Postulate 11.1. This postulate assures us that the concept of volume is meaningful (every solid has a volume and the volume is a positive real number) just as the Ruler Postulate and Area Postulate are for distance and area respectively.

One-on-one. The volume postulate requires volumes to be positive. Some students will think that there is a smallest possible volume (1 cubic unit). Remind them that fractional volumes (one-half, one-tenth, one-thousandth) approach a volume of zero. However, zero is not a volume because the figure would be a

Postulate 11.2
Congruent Solids Postulate. Congruent solids have the same volume.

Postulate 11.3
Volume of Cube Postulate. The volume of a cube is the cube of the length of one edge: $V = e^3$.

Postulate 11.4
Volume Addition Postulate. If the interiors of two solids do not intersect, then the volume of their union is the sum of the volumes.

This puzzle called Rubik's cube contains 27 cubic units of volume.

Finding the volume of simple three-dimensional figures is very easy. Look at figure 11.2 and see how many cubic units are contained in the figure.

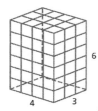

Figure 11.2

In this three-dimensional figure you can count the seventy-two cubes. The area of the base is twelve square units. There are six layers in this figure, each containing twelve cubes. Notice that six layers of twelve make a total of seventy-two cubes. Since the interiors of these cubes do not intersect, the Volume Addition Postulate allows us to add them together for a total of seventy-two cubic units.

The volume of a rectangular prism is found by using the Volume Addition Postulate.

Theorem 11.1
The *volume of a rectangular prism* is the product of its length, width, and height: $V = lwH$.

Reading and Writing Mathematics
Have the students explain in writing how to solve the following problem; then solve it.

The volume and surface area of a cube are numerically equal. How big is the cube? *Set the formulas for volume of a cube and surface area of a cube equal; solve for e.*
$e^3 = 6e^2$;
$e^3 - 6e^2 = 0$; $e^2(e - 6) = 0$;
$e^2 = 0$ or $e - 6 = 0$; $e = 0$ or $e = 6$
The edge of a cube cannot be 0; therefore, e = 6 is the only correct answer.

Additional Problems
Find the volume of the following right rectangular prisms.

1. 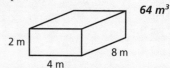 **64 m³**
2 m, 4 m, 8 m

2. 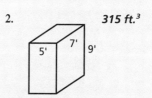 **315 ft.³**
5', 7', 9'

3. 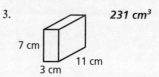 **231 cm³**
7 cm, 3 cm, 11 cm

4. How much concrete (yd.³) will be needed for a two-lane road that is 30 ft. wide and 21 miles long? Assume the concrete road is 1 ft. thick. **123,200 yd.³; note: this is 12,320 truckloads and would cost more than $6 million**

plane figure with no height and therefore would cease to be a solid.

Postulate 11.4 assures us that volume is additive just like area and linear values. Solids that intersect each other (overlap) require an adjustment (subtracting the common volume, which was counted twice).

Review the formula for the volume of a rectangular solid (from elementary school). Since most of the other volume formulas are built on this foundation, make sure that the students understand it.

One-on-one. Depending on the level of your students, you may want to use some models to illustrate how the area of each layer times the number of layers gives the volume of the solid.

This makes the connection between the actual solid and the formula. Remind them that the product of the three dimensions can apply only to right rectangular prisms. The height dimension (altitude) counts the number of layers. This is more obvious in oblique prisms (next section), where the height differs from the length of the side.

Go over the example in this section, making sure that the students understand how to use the Volume Addition Postulate.

Tips

Ex. 9-12. First, use the Pythagorean theorem to find any needed length, width, or height dimensions. Then calculate the volume. These exercises stress the difference between diagonals of prisms and rectangles.

Ex. 9. Since $s^2 + s^2 = 10^2$, $s = 5\sqrt{2}$ and $V = s^3 = 125\sqrt{8} = 250\sqrt{2}$.

Ex. 10. Using the tip for #9, the square of the diagonal of the base is 25^2, therefore $s^2 + 2s^2 = 6^2$, $s = 2\sqrt{3}$ and $V = s^3 = 8\sqrt{27} = 24\sqrt{3}$.

Ex. 11. Since $w = 4$ and $h = \sqrt{39}$, $V = lwh = 12\sqrt{39}$.

Ex. 12. Since $w = \sqrt{33}$ and $h = \sqrt{15}$, $V = lwh = 4\sqrt{445} = 12\sqrt{55}$.

5. Find the volume of the following solid.
730 units³

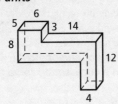

Answers

1. 64 cu. units
2. 81 cu. units
3. 70 cu. units
4. 13,824 cu. in.
5. x^3 cu. units
6. 416 cu. ft.
7. 1200 boxes
8. 1440 cu. ft.

EXAMPLE   Find the volume of the figure.

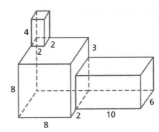

Figure 11.3

Answer   Volume of the central cube $= e^3 = 8^3 = 512$
Volume of the tower $= lwH = 2 \cdot 2 \cdot 4 = 16$
Volume of the rectangular solid $= lwH = 10 \cdot 6 \cdot 5 = 300$

According to the Volume Addition Postulate, add to obtain the total volume.
$V = 512 + 16 + 300 = 828$ cubic units

▶ **A. Exercises**

Find the volume of each solid.

1.

2.

3.

4. A cube edge measures 24 inches
5. A cube with edge x
6. A rectangular prism with a base area of 26 square feet and a height of 16 feet
7. If your bedroom were fifteen feet long by ten feet wide by eight feet high, how many cubic-foot boxes would fit into the room?
8. The Williamses rented a truck for their move that is 24 feet long by 7.5 feet wide. If items can be stored to a height of eight feet, how much can they move per load?

Ex. 13-14. Use the Volume Addition Postulate in any of several ways.

Ex. 13. Towers are $3 \times 3 \times 7 = 63$ and low middle is $3 \times 3 \times (7 - 4) = 27$.
$V = 63 + 63 + 27 = 153$.

Ex. 14. Back tower is $2 \times 3 \times 7 = 42$.
$V = 42 + (3^3) + (5 \cdot 2 \cdot 3) = 99$.

Ex. 15. Generalize #10. Solve $s^2 + 2s^2 = x^2$ for s. Thus, $s = \frac{x\sqrt{3}}{3}$ and $V = s^3 = \frac{x^3\sqrt{3}}{9}$.

Ex. 16. This requires methods from Algebra 1. Substitute into the formula for the volume of a prism to obtain the equation
$(w + 9)w(26) = 3536$.
Thus, $w^2 + 9w - 136 = 0$.

Factoring, $(w - 8)(w + 17) = 0$.
Thus, $w = 8$ and $l = w + 9 = 17$.

Ex. 17. Volume (cm³) times density (grams per cm³) $= (12 \cdot 18 \cdot 10)13.6 = 29,376$ grams.

Ex. 19. Generalize #9. ■

▶ B. Exercises

Find the volume of each solid.

9.
cube

11.

13.

10.
cube

12.

14.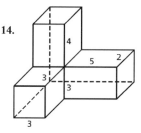

15. Find the volume of a cube with diagonal x.

16. A right rectangular prism has a volume of 3536 cubic feet, and the length of the base of the prism is 9 feet longer than its width. The height of the prism is 26 feet. What are the dimensions of the base of the prism?

17. How many grams of mercury must be poured into a rectangular container with dimensions 12 cm by 18 cm by 10 cm in order to fill it? The density of mercury is $13.6 \frac{g}{cm^3}$.

18. Find the volume of the figure and identify any volume postulates and theorems that you use.

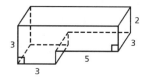

▶ C. Exercises

Prove each volume formula.

19. The volume of a cube having a face with a diagonal x units long is
$V = x^3 \frac{\sqrt{2}}{4}$.

20. Prove your formula from exercise 15.

---

9. $250\sqrt{2}$
10. $24\sqrt{3}$
11. $12\sqrt{39}$
12. $12\sqrt{55}$
13. 153
14. 99
15. $x^3 \frac{\sqrt{3}}{9}$
16. 8 ft. by 17 ft.
17. 29,376 g
18. Volume Postulate; by the Volume of Cube Postulate $V_{cube} = 3^3 = 27$
By the Volume of Rectangular Prism Theorem $V_{prism} = 5 \cdot 3 \cdot 2 = 30$
By the Volume Addition Postulate $V_{solid} = V_{cube} + V_{prism} = 27 + 30 = 57$ cu. units

19.

1. x is the length of a diagonal of a face of a cube	1. Given
2. Each face of the cube is a square with side s	2. Definition of cube
3. $s^2 + s^2 = x^2$	3. Pythagorean theorem
4. $2s^2 = x^2$	4. Distributive property
5. $s^2 = \frac{x^2}{2}$	5. Multiplication property of equality
6. $s = \frac{x}{\sqrt{2}}$	6. Take square root on both sides
7. $V = s^3$	7. Volume of Cube Postulate
8. $V = \left(\frac{x}{\sqrt{2}}\right)^3 = \frac{x^3}{2\sqrt{2}} = \frac{x^3\sqrt{2}}{4}$	8. Substitution (step 6 into 7)

20.

1. Cube of diagonal x	1. Given
2. All edges have same length s	2. Definition of cube
3. Diagonal of face $= \sqrt{s^2 + s^2}$	3. Pythagorean theorem
4. $s^2 + (\sqrt{s^2 + s^2})^2 = x^2$	4. Pythagorean theorem
5. $s^2 + s^2 + s^2 = x^2$	5. Simplify
6. $3s^2 = x^2$	6. Distributive property
7. $s^2 = \frac{x^2}{3}$	7. Multiplication property of equality
8. $s = \frac{x}{\sqrt{3}}$	8. Take square root of both sides
9. $V = s^3$	9. Volume of Cube Postulate
10. $V = \left(\frac{x}{\sqrt{3}}\right)^3 = \frac{x^3}{3\sqrt{3}} = \frac{x^3\sqrt{3}}{9}$	10. Substitution

21. Area Postulate and Congruent Regions Postulate [8.1]
22. Area of Square Postulate [8.1]
23. $A = 6A_{\text{triangle}} = 6s^2 \dfrac{\sqrt{3}}{4} = 6 \cdot 16^2 \dfrac{\sqrt{3}}{4}$

$= 384\sqrt{3} = 665.1$ [8.4]
24. $A = \dfrac{9\pi}{2} + 36 + 3\sqrt{55}$ [8.5]
25. $S = 2lw + 2lH + 2wH$ [8.6]

11.2

Prisms

Objectives

1. To state Cavalieri's principle and use it to prove theorems.
2. To derive a formula for the volume of a prism.
3. To find volumes of prisms using the formula.

Vocabulary

Cavalieri's principle
cross section
oblique prism

Flash

You may wish to give the students the dimensions and have them calculate the volumes of the boxes. The 15-oz. Corn Pops box is 257 cu. in. ($12 \frac{1}{16} \times 7 \frac{3}{4} \times 2 \frac{3}{4}$). The 14-oz. Cheerios box contains 197 cu. in. ($10 \frac{3}{4} \times 7\frac{1}{2} \times 2 \frac{7}{16}$). The 10.5-oz. popcorn box contains 77 cu. in. ($6\frac{1}{4} \times 4\frac{1}{2} \times 2\frac{3}{4}$). The 9.5-oz. Fudge Rounds box contains 79 cu. in. ($11 \frac{1}{16} \times 3 \frac{1}{4} \times 2 \frac{3}{16}$). Notice that the Fudge Rounds box weighs the least, but the popcorn occupies the least space.

Reread the explanation of the first three *area* postulates, then explain the following.
21. Which postulates guarantee that areas exist and are meaningful?
22. Which postulate provides a first method for finding an area without counting squares?
23. Find the area of a regular hexagon with a 16-in. side.
24. Find the area of the figure in the diagram.

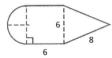

25. Find the surface area of the rectangular prism with dimensions *l*, *w*, and *H*.

11.2 Prisms

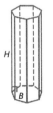
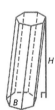

You can already find the volumes of rectangular prisms. In order to develop formulas for the volumes of other prisms,

Food packaging includes boxes of various volumes.

you need to understand the idea of a cross section. A *section* is the intersection of a three-dimensional figure and a plane that passes through the figure. A *cross section* is a section that is perpendiular to the altitude.

Look at the two three-dimensional figures in figure 11.4.

Figure 11.4

Presentation

The major goal of this section is to help students understand Cavalieri's principle. Have your students study the diagram at the beginning of this section; then define an oblique prism and compare it to a right prism. Afterwards, show the development of the volume formula by using Cavalieri's principle.

Motivational Idea. An effective way to show the volume equivalence between a right prism and an oblique prism is with a stack of 3" × 5" cards. Square up the stack and find its volume using the formula for a right prism. Tilt the stack into an oblique prism. Since you have not removed any cards from the stack, the volume has not changed and the prism must have the same volume as the right prism.

Common Student Error. While the same formula applies to both right and oblique prisms, students may use the length of the slanted side rather than the vertical distance. Draw a prism showing both measurements and ask students to find the volume. Any that choose the wrong measurement need the One-on-one below.

One-on-one. Show students that the slanted side is the hypotenuse of a right triangle having the altitude of the prism as a leg. Therefore, the slanted side is longer than the leg (Longest Side Inequality). Go back over Cavalieri's principle to show them that the altitude is the quantity needed, so the slanted side is incorrect because it is too long.

The figure on the left is a right prism, while the figure on the right is called an oblique prism. An *oblique prism* is a prism whose slant height is not perpendicular to the base. The bases of these figures are congruent regular heptagons (seven sides) of area *B*. Every cross section of both figures (*a*) and (*b*) is a regular heptagon with area equal to *B*. Since the heights (*H*) are the same and corresponding cross sections have equal areas, the next postulate guarantees that the volumes are equal.

Postulate 11.5
Cavalieri's Principle. **For any two solids, if all planes parallel to a fixed plane form sections having equal areas, then the solids have the same volume.**

Bonaventura Cavalieri, an Italian mathematician, came up with the idea behind this principle. The development of this principle was a steppingstone to the development of integral calculus.

Another helpful theorem in determining the volume of a prism is given below. You will prove a special case of this theorem in the exercises. Notice how it is used in the proof of the volume formula.

Theorem 11.2
A cross section of a prism is congruent to the base of the prism.

Theorem 11.3
The *volume of a prism* is the product of the height and the area of the base: *V* = *BH*.

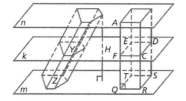

Figure 11.5

Assignment
- Intuitive: 1-16, 21-25
- Standard: 1-19, 21-25
- Rigorous: 1-13 odd, 15-25

Resources
- *Activities Manual,* Math History Activity on Cavalieri.
- *Test Packet,* Quiz 1, Chapter 11 covers Sections 11.1 and 11.2.

Additional Problems
Find the volume of each prism.

1.
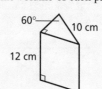

$150\sqrt{3}$ *cm³*

2.
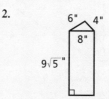

$135\sqrt{3}$ *in.³ (requires Heron's formula)*

3.
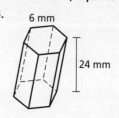

$1296\sqrt{3}$ *mm³*

Tips

The overall plan for the proof of Theorem 11.3 is to generate a right prism of volume equal to the given prism and apply Cavalieri's principle. This then justifies the use of the formula *V* = *BH* for both right and oblique prisms.

Ex. 15. Recall the formula for the area of a rhombus, $A = \frac{1}{2} d_1 d_2$.

Ex. 17. Since the heights and bases correspond, the volume of the hexagonal prism must be the same (468) as the triangular prism by Cavalieri's principle. To find the heights (which are equal), use *V* = *BH*, or 468 = 52*H*, or *H* = 9 cm.

Ex. 20. Step 10 uses the Polygon Triangulation idea (see Presentation for 6.3). ∎

4. Find the capacity in gallons of a drainage ditch with a trapezoidal cross section that is $\frac{1}{2}$ mile long. The water can flow 18 inches deep and the cross section at that depth has bases 3 ft. and 5 ft. Assume 1 ft.³ of water contains 7.5 gallons. **6 ft.² cross section • 2640 ft. length = 15,840 ft.³; then multiply by 7.5 gal. per cubic foot to obtain 118,800 gallons; this ditch would hold the runoff from a 3-inch rainfall on a 1.5-acre parking lot**

5. Find the volume of Fiberglass needed to construct the insulated heating duct shown here. **9120 in.³, or 5.28 ft.³**

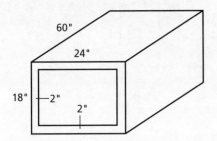

STATEMENTS	REASONS
1. Prism with height H, volume V, and base Z having area B	1. Given
2. The bases lie in parallel planes m and n	2. Definition of prism
3. Square $QRST$ exists in plane m with side length $\sqrt{B}$; draw a perpendicular to m at Q, which intersects plane n at a point A; draw other perpendiculars from each vertex of $QRST$ to form a square prism; take any plane k forming cross sections Y of prism P and $CDEF$ of the square prism	3. Auxiliary lines and plane
4. $RS = QR = \sqrt{B}$	4. Definition of square
5. Area $QRST = s^2 = (\sqrt{B})^2 = B$	5. Area of Square Postulate
6. Area Z = Area $QRST$	6. Transitive property of equality
7. $QA = H$	7. Parallel planes are everywhere equidistant
8. $V_{\text{square prism}} = lwH = \sqrt{B}\,\sqrt{B}H = BH$	8. Volume of rectangular prism
9. $Y \cong Z$; $CDEF \cong QRST$	9. Cross section congruent to base of prism
10. Area Y = Area Z; Area $CDEF$ = Area $QRST$	10. Congruent Regions Postulate
11. Area Y = Area $CDEF$ (so corresponding cross sections have equal areas)	11. Substitution (step 10 into 6)
12. $V = V_{\text{square prism}}$	12. Cavalieri's principle
13. $V = BH$	13. Substitution (step 8 into 12)

EXAMPLE   Find the volume of the following regular prism.

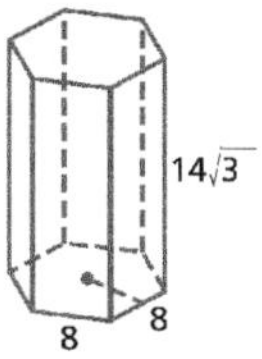

14√3

8   8

Answer   1. Find the apothem of the base. Recall that a regular hexagon divides into 6 equilateral triangles.

$4^2 + a^2 = 8^2$

$a^2 = 64 - 16 = 48$

$a = 4\sqrt{3}$

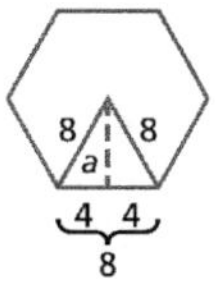

2. Find the area of the base.

$B = \frac{1}{2}ap$

$B = \frac{1}{2}(4\sqrt{3})(48)$

$B = 96\sqrt{3}$ square units

8   8
a
4   4
8

Figure 11.6

3. Find the volume.

$V = BH$

$V = (96\sqrt{3})(14\sqrt{3})$

$V = 4032$ cubic units

So 4032 cubes would fill this regular hexagonal prism.

▶ A. Exercises

Find the volume of each prism.

1.

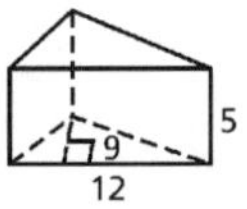

3
3
3
18

3.

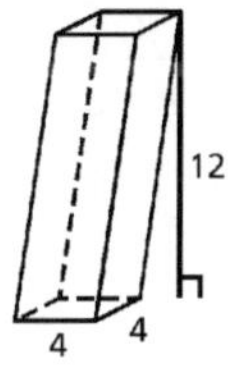

12
4   4

2.

5
9
12

4.

23
7   7
7
4.8

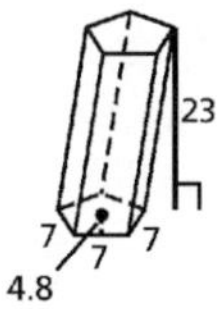

Answers

1. $81\frac{\sqrt{3}}{2}$ cu. units
2. 270 cu. units
3. 192 cu. units
4. 1932 cu. units

5. 216 cu. units
6. 4884 cu. units
7. 14,924 cu. units
8. $416\sqrt{3}$ cu. units
9. 480 cu. units
10. 3248 cu. units
11. 2288 cu. units
12. 36,924 cu. units
13. 576 cu. units
14. 285 cu. units

5.

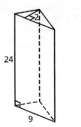

24

21

9

10.

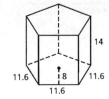

14

11.6   8   11.6

11.6

6.

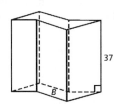

37

B

B = 132 square inches

11.

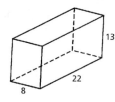

13

8   22

7.

41

10.4

10   10

10   10

12.

34

18.1   15

15   15   15

8.

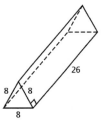

26

8   8

8

13.

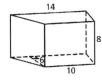

14

8

6

10

9.

10

8   12

14.

19

B

B = 15 square units

▶ B. Exercises

15. The bases of a prism are rhombi that have diagonals measuring 16 feet and 24 feet. The height of the prism is 3 feet. What is the volume of the prism?

16. A concrete water trough is a rectangular prism. The trough measures 24 by 48 by 96 inches. How many gallons of water will fill the trough if 1 gallon fills 231 cubic inches?

17. If the areas of the bases of a triangular prism and a hexagonal prism are both 52 square centimeters, the heights of both are the same, and the volume of the triangular prism is 468 cubic centimeters, what is the height of each prism and the volume of the hexagonal prism?

18. Consider a square cake pan as a rectangular prism having an 8-by-8-inch base and a height of 2 inches. If 114 cubic inches of batter are poured into the pan, how many cubic inches does the cake need to expand during baking to fill the pan?

19. Find simple formulas for the volume of square prisms and triangular prisms.

▶ C. Exercises

20. Supply reasons to prove Theorem 11.2. A cross section of a prism is congruent to the base.

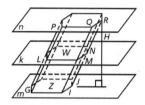

STATEMENTS	REASONS
1. Prism has height H and a base Z with area B; cross section W in plane k with $k \parallel m$	1.
2. The bases of the prism in planes m and n are congruent; $m \parallel n$; each pair of lateral edges are parallel: $\overleftrightarrow{GP} \parallel \overleftrightarrow{IQ}$, $\overleftrightarrow{GP} \parallel \overleftrightarrow{JR}$, $\overleftrightarrow{IQ} \parallel \overleftrightarrow{JR}$, etc.	2.
3. $k \parallel n$	3.

Continued ▶

continued

15. 576 cu. ft.
16. 478.75 gal.
17. $H = 9$ cm; $V = 468$ cm^3
18. 14 cu. in.
19. $V = s^2H$, $V = \frac{1}{2}bhH$
20.
   1. Given
   2. Definition of prism
   3. Plane parallel to one of two parallel planes is parallel to the other

4. Two parallel lines are contained in one and only one plane (or definition of parallel)
5. Plane Intersection Postulate
6. A plane intersects parallel planes in parallel lines
7. Definition of parallelogram (steps 2, 6)
8. Opposite sides of parallelogram are congruent
9. SSS
10. If corresponding triangular subdivisions are congruent, the polygons are congruent

21. $P = 4s$ [3.4]
22. $A = s^2$ [8.1]
23. $S = 6s^2$ [8.8]
24. $V = e^3$ [11.1]
25. $S = 2\pi rH + 2\pi r^2$ [8.6]

4. Each pair of lateral edges determines a plane	4.
5. k intersects each plane in a line (planes determined by pairs of lateral edges)	5.
6. The sides of W are parallel to corresponding sides of Z: $\overline{LM} \parallel \overline{GI}$, $\overline{MN} \parallel \overline{IJ}$, etc. ($Z$ and W have same number of sides). The diagonals of W are parallel to corresponding diagonals of Z: $\overleftrightarrow{LN} \parallel \overleftrightarrow{GJ}$, etc.	6.
7. Each pair of sides or diagonals of Z and W determine a parallelogram: $LMIG$, $MNJI$, $LNJG$, etc.	7.
8. Corresponding sides and diagonals of Z and W are congruent: $\overline{LM} \cong \overline{GI}$, $\overline{MN} \cong \overline{IJ}$, $\overline{LN} \cong \overline{GJ}$	8.
9. Each triangular subdivision of W is congruent to a corresponding triangular subdivision of Z: $\triangle LMN \cong \triangle GIJ$, etc.	9.
10. $Z \cong W$	10.

◼ Cumulative Review

State a formula for each.
21. Perimeter of a square
22. Area of a square
23. Surface area of a cube
24. Volume of a cube
25. Surface area of a circular cylinder

11.3 Cylinders

Look at the following diagrams of a prism and a cylinder.

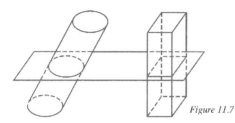

Figure 11.7

If the bases of the prism and the cylinder have area *B* and the heights of both of them are the same, what does Cavalieri's principle tell you about the volumes of these three-dimensional figures? Since the areas of the cross sections in every plane parallel to the bases of the figures are the same and the heights are the same, then the volumes are the same. This suggests that the formula for the volume of a cylinder is

$$V = BH,$$

where *B* is the area of the circular base, and *H* is the height of the cylinder.

The proof of this formula uses the fact that cross sections parallel to the base are congruent to the base.

Cylindrical silos on a farm in central Wisconsin

> **Theorem 11.4**
> The *volume of a cylinder* is the product of the area of the base and the height: $V = BH$. In particular, for a circular cylinder $V = \pi r^2 H$.

Theorem 11.4 can be proved just like Theorem 11.3 in the previous section. Do you see how to get the alternate formula $V = \pi r^2 H$?

Cylindrical oil tanks at a refinery

> ## Objectives
> 1. To derive the formula for the volume of a cylinder.
> 2. To apply the formula to specific cylinders.

Assignment
- Intuitive: 1-15, 21-25
- Standard: 1-19, 21-25
- Rigorous: 1-15 odd, 16-25, and Mind over Math

Resources
- *Visual Packet,* Volume Formulas. This poster covers cubes, prisms, and cylinders.
- *Test Packet,* Quiz 2, Chapter 11 covers Section 11.3.

Reading and Writing Mathematics
Which cylinder has the largest volume? Explain your answer.
  a) Let radius equal height.
  b) Let radius equal twice the height.
  c) Let the height equal twice the radius.
First, find the volume of each in terms of the radius. If r = H, then V = πr³. If r = 2H, then H = $\frac{r}{2}$ and V = $\frac{1}{2}$ πr³. If H = 2r, then V = 2πr³. Next, compare the volumes. All have πr³ as a factor, so compare the coefficients and observe that 2 is the largest (others are 1, $\frac{1}{2}$). Thus, cylinder (c) results in the largest volume.

Additional Problems
Find the volume of each cylinder. Assume the bases are circular.

1.
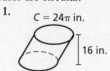
C = 24π in.

16 in.

2304π in.³ ≈ 7238 in.³

2.
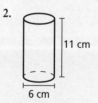
11 cm

6 cm

99π cm³ ≈ 311 cm³

3.
4 cm

2 mm

800π mm³ ≈ 2513 mm³ or 0.8π cm³ ≈ 2.5 cm³

Presentation

Motivational Idea. If possible, bring in or make a prism and a cylinder that have approximately the same base area and the same height. Find the volume of the prism by methods discussed in the last section. Fill the prism with water or sand, and then pour the water or sand into the cylinder. The contents of the prism should fill the cylinder.

Motivational Idea. A roll of coins can illustrate the equality between the volumes of right and oblique circular cylinders. As in the last section, square up the stack to form the right circular cylinder and then tilt them (perhaps with a pencil) into an oblique cylinder. Remind students that the vertical distances between the bases is the height (same for both

cylinders, even though the slant height of the oblique one increased). Emphasize that since no coins were removed, the volumes are the same.

The plan for the proof of Theorem 11.4 is to make an auxiliary prism (since we already know how to find its volume) to which Cavalieri's principle applies. Students should see in figure 11.7 that the height of the prism should be the same as that of the cylinder, and the square base will need to have the same area as that of the circle (#19).

4. What is the height of a 5 gallon cylindrical container if its diameter is 12 inches? (1 cubic foot is 7.5 gallons) **10.2 inches**

5.

8"

1"

$\frac{1}{4}$" diameter

A designer needs to know the weight of an aluminum part in the shape of a regular prism with a hexagonal base. It is one inch across the base and 8 inches long as shown in the diagram. A $\frac{1}{4}$-inch diameter hole is drilled through it lengthwise. Assume that the density of aluminum is 168.5 lbs. per ft.³.   **V = 3√3 − $\frac{\pi}{8}$ ≈ 4.80 in.³; approximately 0.47 lb., or 7.5 oz.**

6.

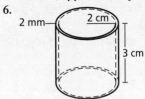

2 mm—

2 cm

3 cm

What volume of stainless steel is needed to make the napkin ring shown in the diagram? Assume the figure is right and circular. **2.52π cm³, or ≈ 7.9 cm³**

Answers

1. 441π cu. units
2. 92π cu. units
3. 240π cu. units
4. 384π cu. units
5. 2299π cu. units
6. 2304π cu. units
7. 1500π cu. ft.
8. 50 ft.

EXAMPLE   Find the number of cubic inches of sand needed to fill the following cylinder.

12

5

Figure 11.8

Answer   Use the formula to find the volume.
$$V = \pi r^2 H$$
$$V = \pi(5)^2(12)$$
$$V = 300\pi$$
$$V \approx 942 \text{ cu. in. of sand}$$

▶ A. Exercises

Find the volume of each cylinder.

1.

9

3.

15

4

5.

19

11

2.

23

2

4.

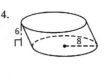

6

8

6.

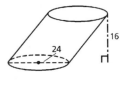

16

24

7. A cylindrical gas tank has a lateral surface area of 300π square feet and is 15 feet high. How many cubic feet of gas will the tank hold?

8. A cylindrical water tower has a volume of 20,000π cubic feet. What is the height if the radius is 20 feet?

Tips

Ex. 7. Since 300π is the *lateral* surface area L, and H = 15, solve L = cH to obtain c = 20π. Next, use c = 2πr to obtain r = 10. Now, find $V = \pi r^2 H = \pi 10^2 \cdot 15 = 1500\pi$ ≈ 4712 cu. ft.

Ex. 8. $V = \pi r^2 H$, so 20,000π = π20²H = 400πH. H = 50 ft.

Ex. 11. First find r = 43 from the circumference. This is a good review of the difference between surface area and volume.

Ex. 13. From the diameter, r = 1. Melting changes the shape but not the volume.

Ex. 14. Find the volume in cubic feet (87,028.4) and then multiply by 7.5 gallons per cubic foot.

Ex. 15. Most errors will stem from the mixed units. Change the 4" thickness to one-third of a foot. Total the areas of the patio (80 sq. ft.) and walk (9 + 72 + 9 = 90 sq. ft.) for 170 sq. ft.; then multiply by the thickness. Remember 1 cu. yd. = 27 cu. ft.

Ex. 16. You can refer students to the photo on page 68. The given diameter results in a radius of 26 feet.

Ex. 19. Set the area of the circle equal to the area of the square: $s^2 = \pi r^2$. Take the square root of both sides to obtain $s = r\sqrt{\pi}$. ∎

9. A cylinder is lodged inside a square prism similar to the figure shown. How many cubic inches are within the prism but outside the cylinder?

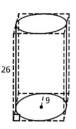

26

9

10. A cube is placed inside a right circular cylinder. How many cubic feet of water will fill the cylinder that has the cube in it?

$12\sqrt{2}$

24

▶ B. Exercises

11. The circumference of a cylinder is 86π meters, and the height is 63 meters. Find the surface area and volume of the cylinder.

12. The circumference of a cylinder is 24π inches, and its volume is 4896π cubic inches. What is the height of the cylinder?

13. A cylindrical piece of iron has a diameter of 2 inches and a length of 16 inches. If it is melted down and poured into a rectangular mold that has a 1-by-3-inch base, what will be the length of the rectangular piece of iron?

14. How many gallons of water will fill a circular cylinder that has a radius of 27 feet and a height of 38 feet? (1 cubic foot of water is 7.5 gallons.)

15. How many cubic yards of concrete are needed to pour the patio and sidewalk if the thickness is to be four inches?

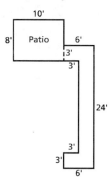

10'

8' Patio 6'

3'

3'

24'

3'

3'

6'

9. $8424 - 2106\pi \approx 1808$ cu. in.
10. $6912\pi - 13{,}824$ or approximately 7890.7 cu. ft.
11. $S = 9116\pi$ m^2; $V = 116{,}487\pi$ m^3
12. 34 in.
13. 16.8 in.
14. 652,713 gal.
15. $\frac{1}{3}(170) \approx 56.7$ cu. ft., or 2.1 cu. yds.

16. $V = \pi(26)^2 (183) = 123{,}708\pi \approx$
388,640 cu. ft.

17. 15,708 cu. ft.

18.

1. A circular cylinder with radius r and height H	1. Given
2. Base is a circle of radius r	2. Definition of circular cylinder
3. Area of base: $B = \pi r^2$	3. Area of circle
4. Volume: $V = BH$	4. Volume of cylinder
5. $V = \pi r^2 H$	5. Substitution (step 3 into 4)

19. $r\sqrt{\pi}$

20.

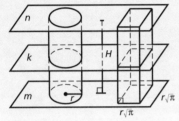

1. A circular cylinder with radius r and height H	1. Given
2. Area of base $B = \pi r^2$	2. Area of circle
3. Rectangular prism with height H and square base of side length $r\sqrt{\pi}$	3. Auxiliary lines
4. Area of square base $A = s^2 = (r\sqrt{\pi})^2 = \pi r^2$	4. Area of Square Postulate
5. Plane k contains a circular cross section of the cylinder congruent to the base	5. Cross section of cylinder is congruent to the base
6. Plane k forms a square cross section of the rectangular prism congruent to its base	6. Cross section of rectangular prism is congruent to base
7. The areas of the cross sections are equal to the areas of the bases	7. Congruent Regions Postulate
8. The areas of the cross section are equal	8. Transitive Property of Equality
9. $V_{\text{cylinder}} = V_{\text{prism}}$	9. Cavalieri's principle
10. $V_{\text{prism}} = BH$	10. Volume of prism
11. $V_{\text{cylinder}} = BH$	11. Substitution (step 10 into 9)

16. The Leaning Tower of Pisa is about 183 ft. high, but the centers of the bases deviate horizontally by at least 14 ft. The tower is roughly 52 feet in diameter. Since the tower is a right circular cylinder that has begun to lean, approximate the volume of the Leaning Tower of Pisa.

17. Find the volume of a silo that is 50 feet high and 20 feet in diameter.

18. Use $V = BH$ to show that $V = \pi r^2 H$ for a circular cylinder.

▶ C. Exercises

19. What must the length of one side of a square be that has the same area as a circle of radius r?

20. Prove Theorem 11.4 that $V = BH$ for a cylinder. (*Hint*: Mimic proof of Theorem 11.3.)

■ Cumulative Review

Identify the horizontal cross section for each of the following figures.

21. circular cylinder
22. parallelepiped
23. tetrahedron
24. circular cone
25. sphere

What happens to the volume of each figure?
1. The radius of a cylinder is tripled (without changing the height).
2. The lengths of the edges of a cube are doubled.
3. The area of the faces of a cube are doubled.
4. The diagonals of a cube are multiplied by a factor of 5.

21. circle [11.2]
22. parallelogram [10.5]
23. triangle [11.2]
24. circle [2.7]
25. circle [10.6]

Mind over Math

See Appendix B.

11.4 Pyramids and Cones

The Pyramid at the Louvre in Paris

If cross sections of the pyramid and cone have equal areas, and the height of each three-dimensional figure is H, then according to Cavalieri's principle, the volumes of the two figures must be the same. If we can develop a formula for the volume of one of these figures, then the other formula will follow easily.

First we will develop the formula for the volume of a pyramid. Look at the triangular prism shown in figure 11.10.

If the area of the base of this prism is B, and the height of the prism is H, then $V = BH$. Now the volume of the prism is equal to the total volume of three pyramids as shown in figure 11.11.

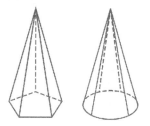

Figure 11.9

Figure 11.10

Objectives

1. To justify the formula for the volume of a pyramid.
2. To derive the formula for the volume of a cone.
3. To apply the volume formulas for cones and pyramids.

Assignment
- Intuitive; 1-9, 19-22
- Standard: 1-17, 19-23
- Rigorous: 1-23

Resources
- *Visual Packet,* Other Volumes. Focus on the part of the poster that covers cones.
- *Activities Manual,* Volume in Brief. Looks at models of pyramids and prisms and the relationship of their volumes.
- *Test Packet,* Quiz 3, Chapter 11 covers Section 11.4.

Flash

The architect I. M. Pei emigrated to the U.S. from China in 1935. He taught at Harvard during the mid-1940s and has designed buildings in Denver, Boston, Philadelphia, and New York. His design of the modern glass pyramid as a new entrance to the Louvre was quite controversial.

Presentation

Compare the pyramid and the cone in figure 11.9. Review Cavalieri's principle with your students. Discuss the fact that if a formula for the volume of a pyramid can be found, then that formula can be used to find a formula for the volume of a cone.

Motivational Idea. Bring in a prism and a pyramid that have the same base area and the same height. Use plastic ones or make cardboard ones. Fill the pyramid with water (sand, gravel, salt, or similar substance). Pour the contents of the pyramid into the prism. After repeating this a second and third time, the prism should be full. (Or fill the pyramid three times from a full prism.)

You can discuss the plan of the proof in class or just go through the entire proof (#16). Either way, begin with figure 11.10 and ask for its volume ($V = BH$ *from previous prism formula*). Next, point out that figure 11.11 shows the same prism three times (note labels). In each case a different part of the prism is occupied by a pyramid, but all three pyramids have the same volume. Thus, the volume of a pyramid is one-third the volume of a prism, or $V = \frac{1}{3} BH$.

While the proof above is easy, many students will not understand that the three pyramids have the same volume. The paragraph below figure 11.11 explains the easier part—that pyramid (a) with base $\triangle EFG$ and height EH and pyramid (c) with base $\triangle HIJ$ and height GJ have the

same volume (top and bottom bases of a prism are congruent). The hard part (in the second paragraph) is that pyramid (a) with base $\triangle EFH$ and pyramid (b) with base $\triangle HIF$ have the same volume. Figure 11.12 shows the prism turned on its side (note labels) to show both pyramids sitting on their bases with common height (altitude from G to $\overline{EF}$). You will need to consider $\triangle EFH$ as the base of pyramid (a) and note that the bases are congruent halves of rectangle $EFIH$ on which the prism now rests.

Motivational Idea. The explanation above will be easier with a clay or cardboard model. Using modeling clay, make the prism and with a sharp knife cut the figure into the pyramids of figure 11.11. With construction paper, make

Reading and Writing Mathematics

A cone and a square pyramid have the same volume and the same height. Have the students explain how to find the ratio of the side of the base in the pyramid to the radius of the base of the cone. Then have them find it.

> **Set the volume formulas equal and solve for $\frac{s}{r}$.**
>
> $\frac{1}{3}s^2H = \frac{1}{3}\pi r^2 H;\ s^2 = \pi r^2;\ s = r\sqrt{\pi};$
>
> $\frac{s}{r} = \sqrt{\pi} \approx 1.772$

Additional Problems

Find the volume of each figure.

1.

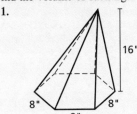

$512\sqrt{3}$ in.$^3 \approx 886.8$ in.^{3}

2.

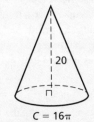

$C = 16\pi$

$\frac{1280\pi}{3}$ units$^3 \approx 1340.4$ units^3

3.

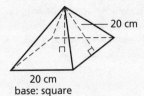

20 cm

20 cm
base: square

$\frac{4000\sqrt{3}}{3}$ cm$^3 \approx 2309.4$ cm^3

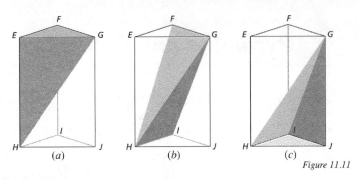

(a)　　　(b)　　　(c)

Figure 11.11

Pyramids (*a*) and (*c*) have the same volume. The areas of the bases in pyramids (*a*) and (*c*) are the same since the bases of a prism are congruent. Pyramids (*a*) and (*c*) also have the same height since they share the height of the prism. By Cavalieri's principle, pyramids (*a*) and (*c*) have the same volume.

To show that pyramids (*a*) and (*b*) have the same volume, turn the prism on its side as shown.

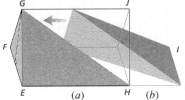

(a)　　(b)

Figure 11.12

Notice that the pyramids have the same height. Also △*EFH* of pyramid (*a*) and △*HIF* of pyramid (*b*) form the bases of the pyramids. These bases have the same area since they are each half of the original back left face of the prism. Since the pyramids also have the same height (to point *G*), they must have the same volume. Thus, you can see that the prism is divided into three pyramids with the same volume. So the volume of each pyramid must equal one-third of the volume of the prism. This proves the formula for the volume of a pyramid.

> **Theorem 11.5**
>
> The *volume of a pyramid* is one-third the product of the height and the area of the base: $V = \frac{1}{3}BH$.

As noted earlier, Cavalieri's principle proves that the same formula works for cones. In the case of a circular cone, substitute for *B* using the area of the circular base.

the pyramids to fit inside the prism snugly. Show the prism all together when discussing figure 11.10; then take it apart to illustrate figure 11.11. Turn the models base to base to show that the bases are congruent. For heights, turn (a) upside down to match (c), then turn (a) and (b) on their sides as in figure 11.12.

Discuss the volume of a cone. You may want to return to the first paragraph of this presentation. Now that the formula for the pyramid is known, the cone with the same height and base area will also satisfy $V = \frac{1}{3}BH$. You can discuss the formal proof by doing #17 in class. It is also possible to demonstrate this using models if you prefer (with a cone and cylinder of equal radius and height, three

cones should fill the cylinder or the cylinder can fill the cone three times).

Go through the example of applying the volume formula. If time allows, work exercises as a class activity or let students begin their homework.

Tips

Ex. 8. Substitute volume and height into $V = \frac{1}{3}BH$, and solve to obtain $B = 144\pi$. Since $B = \pi r^2$, find $r = 12$. Thus, the diameter is 24.

Ex. 11. For a cube with $V = s^3 = 729$, $s = 9$. Find V using a cone with $H = 9$ and $r = 4.5$.

Ex. 12. This is easy if you remember that the cone has one-third the volume of the cylinder: $3(324\pi) = 972\pi$ cubic feet and $r = 9\sqrt{3}$ feet.

Ex. 13-14. The frustum of a pyramid or a cone is the part remaining after the top is sliced off. Find the volume of the top (cut off) part and subtract it from the volume of the entire figure.

Theorem 11.6

The *volume of a cone* is one-third the product of its height and base area: $V = \frac{1}{3}\pi r^2 H$.

EXAMPLE Find the volume of the cone.

Figure 11.13

Answer $V = \frac{1}{3}BH$

$V = \frac{1}{3}\pi r^2 H$

$V = \frac{1}{3}\pi(4^2)(7)$

$V = \frac{112}{3}\pi$

$V \approx 117.3$ cu. units

▶ **A. Exercises**

Find the volume of each figure.

1.   **3.**   **5.**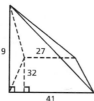

2.   **4.**   **6.**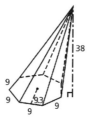

7. The base of a pyramid is a rhombus with diagonals equal to 24 inches and 29 inches. The height of the pyramid is 35 inches. What is the volume of this pyramid?

---

4. A piece of tin in the shape of a semicircle of radius 8 inches is rolled into a cone. Find the volume. $\frac{64\pi\sqrt{3}}{3}$ *in.³* $\approx$ *116.1 in.³*

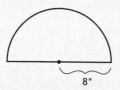

5. Find the volume of the frustum of the cone shown in the diagram.
$\frac{1}{3}\pi r_1{}^2(H) + \frac{1}{3}\pi h(r_1{}^2 - r_2{}^2)$

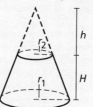

6. The volume of a square Egyptian pyramid is 98,304 m³ and its height is 72 m. What are the dimensions of the base?
64 m by 64 m

Answers

1. 672 cu. units
2. 1428 cu. units
3. $3371\frac{2}{3}\pi$ cu. units
4. 1581.1 cu. units
5. 3264 cu. units
6. 3710.7 cu. units
7. 4060 cu. in.

Ex. 18. Several methods are possible. Here is one: the apothem is $a = \frac{\sqrt{3}}{6} s = 2\sqrt{3}$ (Theorem 8.12). The slant height of the pyramid is the height of a triangular face, $h = 3a = 6\sqrt{3}$ (Theorem 8.11). By the Pythagorean theorem, $h^2 = H^2 + a^2$, and $H = \sqrt{96} = 4\sqrt{6}$. Use the cone height H and cone radius a (apothem is radius of inscribed circle) to find $V = 16\pi\sqrt{6}$.

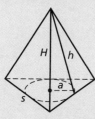

Ex. 19. It is false if the three vertices determine three diagonals of faces as shown in the diagram. Point out that $\triangle ABC$ is equilateral since all of its sides are diagonals of square faces. Thus, all three angles are sixty degrees and none are right. ∎

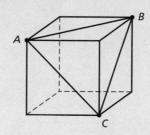

8. 24 ft.

9. 2700 cm^3

10. $\frac{87,505}{3} - \frac{15,895}{3\pi} \approx 12,523.1$ cu. in.
(12,531.6 cu. in. using $\pi \approx 3.14$)

11. $H = 9$ in.; $r = 4.5$ in.; $V = 60.75\pi$
≈ 190.76 cu. in. using $\pi \approx 3.14$

12. $V = 972\pi$ cu. ft.; $r = 9\sqrt{3}$ ft.

13. $V = \frac{1}{3} \cdot 27 \cdot 18 - \frac{1}{3} \cdot 3 \cdot 6 = 156$ cm^3

14. $V = \frac{1}{3}\pi \cdot 8^2 \cdot 12 - \frac{1}{3}\pi \cdot 2^2 \cdot 6 = 248\pi$
≈ 779.1 cu. units

8. The volume of a circular cone is 1728π cubic feet. If the height is 36 feet, what is the diameter of the base of the cone?

9. Find the volume of a pyramid that has a square base with a side measuring 18 centimeters and an altitude (height) measuring 25 centimeters.

▶ B. Exercises

10. A circular cone is placed inside a rectangular pyramid. The pyramid has a 37-by-43-inch base and a height of 55 inches. The diameter of the cone is 34 inches, and the vertices of both the pyramid and the cone are the same. What is the volume outside the cone but inside the pyramid?

11. A cone sits point down in a cube. The base of the cone is inscribed in the base of the cube. If the cube has a volume of 729 cubic inches, what is the height, radius, and volume of the cone?

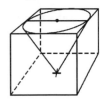

12. A cylinder encloses a cone. The cylinder and cone have the same base area. If the volume of the cone is 324π cubic feet and both have a height of 4 feet, what is the volume and radius of the cylinder?

13. The area of $\triangle FED$ is 27 square centimeters. The area of $\triangle ABC$ is 3 square centimeters. Find the volume of the three-dimensional figure *ABCDEF*.

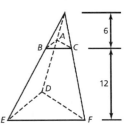

14. Find the volume of the frustum (shaded area) of the cone.

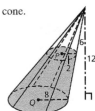

15. The Cheops Pyramid in Egypt is almost a perfect right pyramid. It has a height of 481 feet and a square base with a side measuring 250 feet. What is the volume of this pyramid? What is the surface area of the part exposed to view?

16. Prove Theorem 11.5 by supplying the reasons.

STATEMENTS	REASONS
1. $V_{prism} = V_a + V_b + V_c$ (as in figure 11.11)	1.
2. $V_a = V_b = V_c$ or simply V	2.
3. $V_{prism} = V + V + V$	3.
4. $V_{prism} = 3V$	4.
5. $V_{prism} = BH$	5.
6. $3V = BH$	6.
7. $V = \frac{1}{3}BH$	7.

17. Prove Theorem 11.6.

▶ **C. Exercises**

18. If a regular tetrahedron has an edge 12 units long, find the volume of the inscribed circular cone.

■ **Cumulative Review**

19. Any three vertices of a cube determine a right triangle. Is this a true statement?

Find the volume of each.

20. A cube with a 7-meter edge
21. A prism with a height of 4 feet and an 8-by-12-foot rectangular base
22. A cylinder with a height of 9 inches and an oval base of 72 sq. in.
23. If K is a cube, then its vertices can be inscribed in a sphere S. What rule of logic would be needed to prove this conditional statement?

15. $V = 10,020,833$ cu. ft.; $L \approx 248,488.4$ sq. ft.

16.
1. Volume Addition Postulate
2. Cavalieri's principle
3. Substitution (step 2 into 1)
4. Distributive property
5. Volume of prism
6. Transitive property of equality
7. Multiplication property of equality

17.

1. Circular cone of radius r and height H	1. Given
2. Area of base $B = \pi r^2$	2. Area of circle
3. $V = \frac{1}{3}BH$	3. Volume of prism (#16)
4. $V = \frac{1}{3}\pi r^2 H$	4. Substitution

18. $V = 16\pi\sqrt{6} \approx 123$ cu. units
19. False [10.5]
20. 343 cu. m [11.1]
21. 384 cu. ft. [11.2]
22. 648 cu. in. [11.3]
23. Law of Deduction [5.6]

Analytic Geometry

Conic Sections

Objectives

1. To define a conical surface and related terms.
2. To illustrate the conic sections.
3. To classify equations of conic sections by graphing.

Vocabulary

axis of a conical surface
conical surface
conic section
element of a conical surface
equation of a parabola
generating curve

Assignment

• Intuitive: 1-5
• Standard: 1-5
• Rigorous: 1-5

Resource

Visual Packet, Solids. Shows a hyperboloid, a solid with curves that are hyperbolas, one of the conic sections. Note also the similarity to a nuclear power plant (p. 166).

Additional Problems

Graph the following equations.

1. $y = \frac{1}{2}x^2$

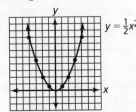

2. $y = x^2$

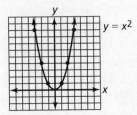

3. $y = -3x^2$

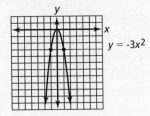

Conic Sections

Given a circle and a point *V* not in the plane of the circle, the union of all lines that connect the point *V* to a point of the circle forms a *conical surface*. The connecting lines are the *elements* of the conical surface and the point *V* is the vertex. The circle is the *generating curve* and the line joining *V* to the center of the curve is its *axis*. If the axis is perpendicular to the plane of the curve, it is a right conical surface such as the one shown.

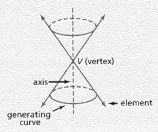

You have already learned to graph three of the figures below. These figures are called *conic sections* because they are cross sections of a conical surface.

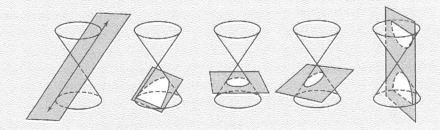

In Chapter 2 you graphed some parabolas. The top or bottom point of a parabola is the *vertex* of the parabola. When the vertex is at the origin, the parabola is in standard position. The equation of a parabola in standard position is $y = ax^2$. You will discover what the sign of the coefficient *a* tells you in the exercises.

Presentation

Motivational Idea. You can illustrate a conical surface by holding a thin wooden dowel in the middle with one hand while rotating an end of it with the other hand. The path of the dowel sweeps out a conical surface. Remind your students that a conical surface extends without bound in both directions just like a line does. Models are also available that show conic sections cut from a conical surface.

Explain that conic sections are found by taking sections of a right circular conical surface. See if your students can identify any cases other than those that are shown (for example, a point or a pair of intersecting lines). These ideas will expand on three-dimensional geometry.

Give the names of each conic section shown on the bottom of page 480. From left to right, they are a line, a parabola, a circle, an ellipse, and a hyperbola. See if students can identify the criteria that the plane section must meet for each conic section to be formed. (Section must contain the vertex to obtain a point, a line, or two intersecting lines; if the section does not contain the vertex, there are four possibilities: parallel to an element for a parabola, parallel to the base for a circle, intersecting both nappes for a hyperbola, otherwise an ellipse.)

Students have worked with lines and circles frequently, and parabolas should be familiar from graphing. See the Flash for a

▶ Exercises

Identify each conic section and graph it.
1. $x^2 + y^2 = 36$
2. $y = -2x + 5$
3. $y = 2x^2$
4. $y = -2x^2$
5. What does the sign of the coefficient a tell you in $y = ax^2$?
   (*Hint:* Compare exercises 3 and 4.)

The Very Large Array near Socorro, New Mexico, opened in 1980. Its 27 radio telescopes linked electronically make it the most powerful radio interferometer in the world. The radio telescopes use parabolas to collect and focus radio waves.

solid that contains a parabolic surface. Hyperbolas are perhaps least familiar, but the Solids poster (Visual Packet) shows a solid built on this figure, much like the nuclear power plant pictured in the text (see p. 166).

So far, equations for three conic sections have been identified and studied:

line: $y = mx + b$
circle: $x^2 + y^2 = r^2$
parabola: $y = ax^2$

By relating the geometric curves to equations, students will anticipate that ellipses and hyperbolas also have equations that they will encounter in future courses.

Tips

Ex. 5. The coefficient a in $y = ax^2$ tells you two things. The sign tells you whether the parabola opens up (positive) or down (negative) and the number part tells you how wide the parabola is. Students discover the sign property in this exercise. If you want them to see the other property, use the Additional Problems (the larger the number, the narrower the parabola). ∎

4. $y = 5x^2$

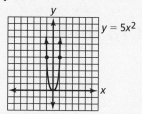

5. In the equation $y = ax^2$, what happens as $|a|$ becomes larger? **As $|a|$ gets larger, the graph of the parabola gets narrower.**

Flash

To see the parabola, tilt the radio telescope straight up and pass a plane vertically through the center of the dish. The plane section is a parabola. A surface with parabolic sections is called a paraboloid. In optical telescopes, the lens is a paraboloid designed to collect light waves rather than sound waves.

Answers

1. circle

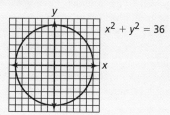

2. line

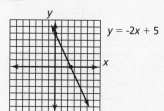

3. parabola

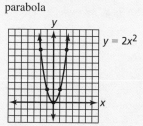

4. parabola

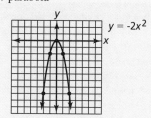

5. If $a > 0$, the parabola opens up.
   If $a < 0$, the parabola opens down.

Polyhedra and Spheres

Objectives

1. To prove the formula for the volume of a sphere.
2. To find volumes using appropriate formulas.

Vocabulary

annulus   concentric circles

Assignment

• Intuitive: 1-12, 24-28
• Standard: 1-21, 24-28
• Rigorous: 1-11 odd, 12-28

Resources

• *Visual Packet,* Other Volumes. Focus on the part of the poster that covers spheres.
• *Visual Packet,* Polyhedra. The various types of polyhedra on this poster help to illustrate Euler's formula.
• *Activities Manual,* Sphere Portions in Detail. Looks at the volumes of specific parts of spheres.
• *Activities Manual,* Calculator Skills. Provides further volume calculations.
• *Activities Manual,* Planar Projections in Principal.

Flash

The Peachoid, completed in June 1981, draws attention to the fact that South Carolina leads the nation in peach production (more than the Peach State). Artist Peter Freudenburg used fifty gallons of paint to make the Peachoid look like locally grown peaches.

11.5 Polyhedra and Spheres

The goal of this section is to develop the formula for finding the volume of a sphere. We will use Cavalieri's principle to find this formula. Notice how many previously learned principles you need to develop this formula. Figure 11.14 shows a right circular cylinder that has two right circular cones inside it.

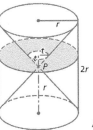

The Peachoid at Gaffney, South Carolina, has a volume of over 60,000 gallons. It modifies a typical spherical water tower by adding a 12-foot stem, a nipple at the bottom, a cleft of steel paneling, and a 60-foot leaf that weighs seven tons.

Figure 11.14

If a plane passes through this figure parallel to the base, then the intersection forms concentric circles. *Concentric circles* are circles that have the same center but radii of different lengths. The region bounded by concentric circles is called an *annulus.* Suppose the plane cuts through the figure at a distance *t* from the vertex *P.* If you look at this cross section from the top, it forms an annular region. This region is shaded in figure 11.15.

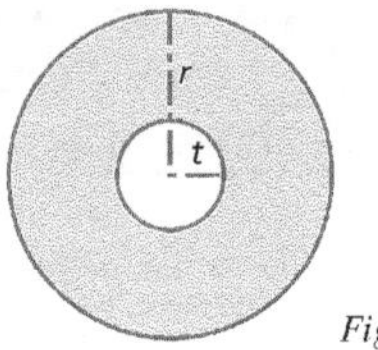

Figure 11.15

How can you find the area of the annulus? Simply subtract the area of the smaller circle from the area of the larger circle.

$$A_{annulus} = A_{lg.\ circle} - A_{sm.\ circle}$$
$$A_{annulus} = \pi r^2 - \pi t^2$$

Presentation

Be sure to go through the derivation of the formula for the volume of a sphere. This is a beautiful proof because it uses Cavalieri's principle to prove an unexpected relationship that enables the formula to be derived. The fact that the volume between a cylinder and two cones is the same as the volume of a sphere is amazing. Since the development of the formula for the volume of a sphere as given in the text involves several steps, make sure that you help the students understand the presentation and study each diagram carefully.

   Point out how the sections change as they are cut at different places. As the section through the sphere goes from the middle, where it is a great circle region, toward one of the poles, it

becomes a smaller and smaller circular region until it ends as a point (no area at the top or bottom of the sphere). Meanwhile the section through the cylinder/cone is a circular region in the middle, but the portion between the cylinder and the cones becomes an increasingly narrower annulus (ring) until at the top or bottom it is a circle (curve with no area). Even though the cross sections are different figures, they have the same area at each level.

   Go through the example in this section. Although some students may not fully grasp the proof, they should all benefit from it, recognizing that the formula does have a proof and stretching their own thinking skills. They will be better able to apply the formula to exercises.

   Finally, discuss the volume formulas for polyhedra at the end of the section. Explain that just as regular polygons can be inscribed in circles, so regular polyhedra can be inscribed in spheres. Ask students to name the regular polyhedra. (If they do not remember, remind them that Plato showed that there are only five.) The formulas are in the table. Two of the formulas are proved in the exercises, but the last two proofs are beyond the scope of this book. Point out using the table that the volume of a tetrahedron is one-fourth the volume of a regular octahedron with the same edge length.

Common Student Error. Students often write the formula for the volume of a cube as $V = s^3$. However, "side" applies to squares.

Now turn your attention to a sphere. In figure 11.16 you see a sphere of radius r with a secant plane passing through it at a distance of t units from the center. The secant plane intersects the sphere to form $\odot C$ with radius x.

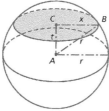

Figure 11.16

Since $\triangle ABC$ is a right triangle, the Pythagorean theorem applies to it:

$$t^2 + x^2 = r^2$$

Solving for x^2,

$$x^2 = r^2 - t^2$$

Since the area of this section is a circle, its area is found by

$$A_{section} = \pi x^2$$

Substituting for x^2 above,

$$A_{section} = \pi(r^2 - t^2)$$
$$A_{section} = \pi r^2 - \pi t^2$$

Are you surprised? The area of this circular region is the same as the area of the annulus! The heights of both figures are the same $2r$ (diameter of sphere and height of cylinder). Also, the sections are at the same distance t from the centers. Do you see what postulate applies?

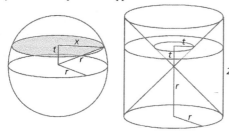

Figure 11.17

Since every horizontal plane cuts the figures into regions of equal areas, Cavalieri's principle applies. Therefore, the volume, V, of the sphere is equal to the volume of the solid between the cones and the cylinder.

Reading and Writing Mathematics

Derive a formula for the volume contained between a regular octahedron and its circumscribed sphere. Then calculate the volume between them for a sphere with a radius of 12 cm.

Use $e = r\sqrt{2}$; see answer to #23.

$$V = V_{sphere} - V_{reg.\ octahedron} =$$
$$\frac{4}{3}\pi r^3 - \frac{4}{3}r^3 = \frac{4}{3}r^3(\pi - 1)$$
For $r = 12$, $v = \frac{4}{3}(12)^3(\pi - 1) =$
$$2304(\pi - 1) \approx 4934\ cm^3$$

Additional Problems

Find the volume of each figure.

1. A sphere with radius 6 cm
   $288\pi\ cm^3 \approx 905\ cm^3$
2. A sphere with circumference 36 in.
   $\frac{7776}{\pi^2}\ in.^3 \approx 788\ in.^3$
3. A sphere with diameter 0.006 mm
   $3.6 \times 10^{-8}\pi\ mm^3 \approx 1.13 \times 10^{-7}\ mm^3$
4. A sphere with surface area 512 ft.^{2}
   $4096\frac{\sqrt{2\pi}}{3\pi}\ ft.^3 \approx 1089.38\ ft.^3$
5. An octahedron with edge 12 yd.
   $576\sqrt{2}\ yd.^3 \approx 814.6\ yd.^3$
6. Icosahedron with edge 12 in.
   $2160 + 720\sqrt{5}\ in.^3 \approx 3769.97\ in.^3$

Tips

Cubes have faces and edges, so the term *side* is ambiguous at best. The volume formula should be written using the length of the edge: $V = e^3$.

Ex. 6, 12. Find the radius first by finding half of the diameter.

Ex. 9, 11. Find the radius first from the circumference.

Ex. 13. First, solve the volume formula to obtain $r = 3$. Then compute the circumference of 6π inches.

Ex. 14. Find the volume of the outer sphere (2.5 cm radius) and subtract that of the inner sphere (2.25 cm radius).

Ex. 19-20. Use the Volume Addition Postulate. ■

$$V = V_{cylinder} - V_{two\ cones}$$

$$V = \pi r^2(2r) - 2\left(\frac{1}{3}\pi r^2\right)(r)$$

$$V = 2\pi r^3 - \frac{2}{3}\pi r^3$$

$$V = \frac{6}{3}\pi r^3 - \frac{2}{3}\pi r^3$$

$$V = \frac{4}{3}\pi r^3$$

That proves the next theorem.

Theorem 11.7
The *volume of a sphere* is four-thirds π times the cube of the radius: $V = \frac{4}{3}\pi r^3$.

EXAMPLE Find the volume of a sphere with a diameter of 10 inches.

Answer Substitute length of the radius into the formula.

$$V = \frac{4}{3}\pi r^3$$

$$V = \frac{4}{3}\pi(5^3)$$

$$V \approx 166.67\pi \text{ cubic inches}$$

10

Figure 11.18

A regular polyhedron can be inscribed in a sphere. Therefore, the center of the regular polyhedron is equidistant from the vertices; this distance is the radius of the sphere and is also called the radius of the polyhedron. These facts are useful in proving the volume formulas below. In each formula, e is the length of an edge.

Regular Polyhedron	Volume
tetrahedron	$V = \frac{\sqrt{2}}{12}e^3$
cube	$V = e^3$
octahedron	$V = \frac{\sqrt{2}}{3}e^3$
dodecahedron	$V = (\frac{15 + 7\sqrt{5}}{3})e^3$
icosahedron	$V = (\frac{15 + 5\sqrt{5}}{12})e^3$

The formula for the volume of a cube is a postulate you know already. The formulas for the volumes of a dodecahedron and an icosahedron are extremely difficult to prove. The proofs of the other two formulas are exercises.

▶ A. Exercises

Give the volume of the sphere or regular polyhedron.

1. sphere with a radius of 18 feet
2. sphere with a radius of $\frac{1}{4}$ meter
3. hexahedron with an edge of 3 yd.
4. tetrahedron with an edge of 5 cm
5. octahedron with an edge of $\sqrt{2}$ units
6. sphere with a diameter of $8\sqrt{3}$ inches
7. dodecahedron with an edge of 3 mm
8. tetrahedron with an edge of 2 units
9. sphere that has a great circle with a circumference of 32π centimeters
10. icosahedron with an edge of 6 m
11. A volleyball has a circumference of 27 inches. How many cubic inches of air are needed to inflate the ball?
12. A factory needs to produce ball bearings with 6-cm diameters. How many cubic centimeters of metal are needed to make 3000 ball bearings?

▶ B. Exercises

13. A spherical balloon has 36π cubic inches of air in it. What is the circumference of the balloon?
14. A racquetball is a hollow ball made of rubber. How much rubber is needed to make each ball if the inside hollow sphere has a radius of 2.25 centimeters and the ball has a diameter of 5 centimeters?
15. The volume of a sphere is $16,222.67\pi$ cubic millimeters. What is the radius of the sphere?
16. The circumference of the earth is approximately 40,000 kilometers. If you consider the earth to be a sphere, what is the volume of the earth?
17. A spherical water tower has a diameter of 75 feet. How many gallons of water will it hold? (1 gallon = 0.13398 cubic feet)
18. A ball whose diameter is 8 inches is placed in a cube whose edge measures 8 inches. How many cubic inches of sand will fill the box containing the ball?

Answers
1. $7776\pi \approx 24{,}429$ cu. ft.
2. $\frac{1}{48}\pi$ m³ ≈ 0.065 cu. m
3. 27 cu. yd.
4. $125\frac{\sqrt{2}}{12} \approx 14.7$ cm³
5. $\frac{4}{3} \approx 1.3$ cu. units
6. $256\sqrt{3}\pi$ cu. in. ≈ 1393 cu. in.
7. $135 + 63\sqrt{5} < 275.9$ mm³
8. $2\frac{\sqrt{2}}{3} \approx 0.94$ cu. units
9. $\frac{16{,}384}{3}\pi$ cm³ $\approx 17{,}157$ cm³
10. $270 + 90\sqrt{5} \approx 471.2$ m³
11. 106π cu. in. ≈ 333 cu. in.
12. $108{,}000\pi$ cm³ $\approx 339{,}292$ cm³
13. 6π in. ≈ 18.8 in.
14. 5.64π cm³ ≈ 17.7cm³
15. 23 mm
16. $1{,}080{,}759{,}300{,}000$ km³
17. $1{,}648{,}703$ (or $1{,}647{,}867.2$ gal. using $\pi \approx 3.14$)
18. 243.9 (or 244.05 cu. in. using $\pi \approx 3.14$)

19. 170.67π cu. in. ≈ 536.17 cu. in.

20. 48π cm³ ≈ 150.8 cm³

21. $818,833.3\pi \approx 2,572,440.7$ cu. ft.

22. $h = QB = \dfrac{\sqrt{3}}{2}e$

$a = \dfrac{1}{3}QB = \dfrac{\sqrt{3}}{6}e$

$r = h - a = \dfrac{2}{3}QB = \dfrac{2}{3}\left(\dfrac{\sqrt{3}}{2}e\right) = \dfrac{\sqrt{3}}{3}e$

$H^2 = e^2 - r^2 = e^2 - \left(\dfrac{\sqrt{3}}{3}e\right)^2 = \dfrac{2}{3}e^2$

$H = \sqrt{\dfrac{2}{3}}e = \dfrac{\sqrt{2}}{\sqrt{3}}e$

$V = \dfrac{1}{3}BH$

$V = \dfrac{1}{3}\left(e^2\dfrac{\sqrt{3}}{4}\right)\left(\dfrac{\sqrt{2}}{\sqrt{3}}e\right)$

$V = \dfrac{\sqrt{2}}{12}e^3$

19. A metal part is made in the shape of a cylinder with a hemisphere (half of a sphere) on top. Find the volume of the part.

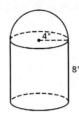

20. An ice-cream cone looks like the following diagram. Approximately how many cubic centimeters of ice cream are used to fill an ice-cream cone like this one?

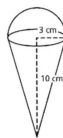

21. Find the number of cubic feet of hot gas needed to fill a spherical balloon that has a radius of 85 feet.

▶ **C. Exercises**

22. Use the regular tetrahedron shown to derive the formula for its volume in terms of its edge length *e*. (*Hint:* Use formulas for the apothem and altitude of the equilateral triangle [base] to show that the tetrahedron has altitude $H = \dfrac{\sqrt{2}}{\sqrt{3}}e$.)

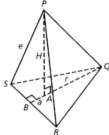

23. Use the regular octahedron shown to derive the formula for its volume in terms of its edge length e. Remember that the vertices are equidistant from the center. (*Hint:* Find *XY* in terms of *e* first and consider relation of center to each vertex.)

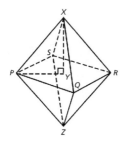

Cumulative Review

Identify each term defined below.

24. A line in the plane of a circle that intersects the circle in exactly one point
25. A triangle with no congruent sides
26. A line that intersects two parallel lines
27. A region of a circle bounded by a chord and the intercepted arc
28. A portion of a sphere determined by intersecting great circles

23. $XY^2 + PY^2 = e^2$
$r^2 + r^2 = e^2$
$2r^2 = e^2$
$\sqrt{2}r = e$
$r = \dfrac{e}{\sqrt{2}}$
$H = r = \dfrac{\sqrt{2}}{2}e$

$V = 2\left(\dfrac{1}{3}BH\right)$
$V = 2\left(\dfrac{1}{3} \cdot e^2 \cdot \dfrac{\sqrt{2}}{2}e\right)$
$V = \dfrac{\sqrt{2}}{3}e^3$

24. tangent [9.2]
25. scalene triangle [4.5]
26. transversal [6.4]
27. segment [9.6]
28. lune [8.8]

Geometry Around Us

Geometry and Engineering

Objectives

1. To gain an appreciation for the extensive use of geometry in engineering science.
2. To identify some specific concepts from geometry used by engineers.

GEOMETRY AND ENGINEERING

We all enjoy the benefits of technology as we ride in air-conditioned cars, use electric appliances, and listen to recorded music. The people who design all our fascinating gadgets are called engineers. Almost every type of engineer uses geometry in making the drawings of the parts he designs.

Mechanical engineers accomplish little without geometry. They design bearings and cams to make engines and machines. Some mechanical engineers design piping systems to convey liquids, such as water and oil. Pipes are just cylinders connected at turns by elbows and tees. The diameter of a pipe determines its carrying capacity (volume per unit of time). The formula $Q = Av$ says that the capacity (Q) equals the cross-sectional area (A) times the velocity (v). If the engineer wants a pipe to carry 500 gallons per minute at a velocity of 5 feet per second, what must the diameter of his pipe be? Did you get about 6.4 inches?

Circular pools of a water treatment plant

Presentation

The calculation requested in the text concerning the size of pipe needed to carry 500 gallons per minute (gpm) at 5 ft./sec. follows. Use the formula that relates capacity (Q) to the product of the area of a cross section of a pipe (A) and the velocity of the fluid (v). First, change 500 gallons per minute to cubic feet per second:

$$\frac{500 \text{ gal.}}{\text{min.}} \cdot \frac{1 \text{ ft.}^3}{7.5 \text{ gal.}} \cdot \frac{1 \text{ min.}}{60 \text{ sec.}} = \frac{1.11 \text{ ft.}^3}{\text{sec.}}$$

$$Q = Av$$
$$\frac{1.11 \text{ ft.}^3}{\text{sec.}} = A \cdot \frac{5 \text{ ft.}}{\text{sec.}}$$
$$A = 0.222 \text{ square feet}$$
$$\pi r^2 = 0.222$$
$$r = 0.266 \text{ ft.} \approx 3.19 \text{ in.}$$
$$d = 6.4 \text{ in.}$$

Sanitary and mechanical engineers who do these calculations on a regular basis have books, tables, charts, and graphs to get the information quickly and accurately. Engineers have always been problem solvers and decision makers, but the amount of time spent doing calculations has been reduced by specialized calculators and computer software. For example, earthwork calculations that in the past would have taken 3 weeks are now done in 3 hours. This is not only a significant savings in cost to the customer but the product is superior and more readily adjusted via computer-assisted drafting (CAD).

For further discussion of geometric concepts in engineering, consult the following table.

Engineering Field	Geometry Concept	Engineering Application
mechanical	circles, tangents, spheres, cylinders	wheels, pulleys, fillets, shafts, bearings, pipes
structural	prisms, cylinders, triangles, circles, tangents	beams, columns, footings, trusses, arches

Sanitation engineers provide us with two vital utilities—distribution of water and treatment of wastewater. When the sanitation engineer designs water-treatment plants and wastewater-treatment plants, he sizes and lays out tanks, circular clarifiers, and earthen dikes; he then connects these with various pipes and channels. He incorporates circles, cylinders, trapezoids, and prisms into his designs. Just like the mechanical engineer, the sanitation engineer must know and understand the volume-capacity relationships of all his tanks, basins, and pipes.

Structural engineers design dams, bridges, and buildings that are safe and functional. They must know which shapes best resist bending or breaking. They have to lay out curves and tangents so that forces are distributed properly. The engineers must calculate the volumes of the steel girders in order to plan a foundation that will support the weight of the building and its contents (volume × density = mass, from which weight can be found). Have you ever wondered why dams are shaped the way they are—curved toward the lake and with a long sweeping curve down the face of the dam? The structural engineer must balance the cost of concrete and the mass of concrete needed to hold back the water. The curved shape provides the needed strength but saves millions of dollars by reducing the amount of concrete needed.

All these engineers must read blueprints and other scale drawings. Engineers and architects draw their diagrams to scale, for example 1 inch to represent 10 feet or $\frac{1}{4}$ inch to represent 1 foot. Thus blueprints convey the engineer's design in a compact geometric form. The men who read these plans and direct the construction of the buildings must be knowledgeable about the geometric principles related to dimensions, diagonals, tangents to circles, and many other measurements. If they did not understand these concepts, builders would erect a poorly constructed building.

Almost every type of engineer uses geometry in making the drawings of the parts he designs.

A construction worker high on the skeleton of a skyscraper

civil	trapezoidal prisms, triangles, segments, Heron's formula	earthwork impoundments, property surveys, area of property
sanitation	cylinders, prisms, circles, tangents, volume, surface area	tanks, conduits, pumps and piping, capacities, distribution rates

Motivational Idea. You may want to ask an engineer to come to the class to talk about the use of mathematics in his work. ■

11.6 Constructions

Objectives

1. To identify when a figure in space can be constructed.
2. To construct congruent subdivisions of a segment.
3. To construct a regular hexagon from a circle.
4. To identify the three impossible constructions that intrigued the ancient Greeks.

Assignment
- Intuitive: no assignment necessary
- Standard: 1-10, 17-20
- Rigorous: 1-21

Resources
- *Activities Manual,* Construction Skills. Discusses more advanced constructions and looks at the impossible constructions in further detail.
- *Test Packet,* Quiz 4, Chapter 11 covers Sections 11.5 and 11.6.

Reading and Writing Mathematics
The construction of a cube of volume twice that of a given cube of edge *e* is impossible. Explain why by showing what would be needed algebraically.

If the volume is doubled, $V_{new} = 2V$. The new edge E must satisfy $E^3 = 2e^3$. Thus, $E = e\sqrt[3]{2}$. Constructing the edge of the cube would require constructing a length equal to the cube root of the given segment length.

Can you construct three-dimensional figures? An architect can build a structure from blueprints that give accurate specifications for each dimension. Likewise, solids are considered constructed if each dimension can be constructed. For example, a sphere is said to be constructed if the radius can be constructed. A right cylinder is considered constructed if its base region and its height can be constructed.

For this reason segment lengths and polygons are important for constructing surfaces and solids.

The cross sections of these basalt columns form hexagons at Giant's Causeway in Northern Ireland.

Construction 16

Segment division

Given: $\overline{AB}$
Construct: Five congruent segments with lengths that total $\overline{AB}$

1. Draw a ray from *A*, forming an acute angle.
2. Place the point of the compass at *A* and, without changing the compass measure, mark off five equal segments on the ray. Label the points *F, G, H, I, J*.
3. Draw $\overline{BJ}$.
4. Draw lines parallel to $\overleftrightarrow{BJ}$ through *F, G, H,* and *I*. You can do this by constructing congruent corresponding angles at each point. Copy $\angle AJB$ at vertices *F, G, H,* and *I*.

These parallel lines cut $\overline{AB}$ into five equal segments.

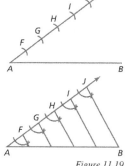

Figure 11.19

Here is a quick way to construct a regular hexagon.

Constructing a three-dimensional figure means that the defining dimensions can be constructed. For example, to construct a sphere, one must know the center and be able to construct a radius of the proper length. The center and radius determine the sphere, but to actually make the sphere would require a physical model like a ball that goes beyond the idea of constructions.

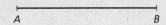

A   B

As a second example, ask students how to construct a right prism with a regular hexagonal base and a height that is one-fifth the length of $\overline{AB}$. They should be able to say that the prism

is constructed if the regular hexagon, $\frac{1}{5}$ AB, and a right angle (to make the right prism) can be constructed. Tell students that constructions 16 and 17 will enable them to construct the right prism.

Guide the students through constructions 16 and 17. Construction 17 should be easy for all students, but construction 16 may confuse some. Remind students that $\overline{AB}$ is to be divided into five equal parts and that $\overleftrightarrow{AF}$ is an auxiliary line.

Common Student Error. Students may be confused by construction 16 because they make an angle and use segments of no particular size. They may stop in the middle of the construction, not knowing what angle to form between the auxiliary line and the original or how long

$\overline{AF}$ should be. Stress that any acute angle and any length for $\overline{AF}$ will suffice. Have the students copy $\overline{AB}$ from figure 11.19 and repeat the segment division process using a larger or smaller angle for $\angle BAF$ and using a longer $\overline{AF}$. When they obtain the same points of division, they will see that these sizes really do not matter.

The proof of construction 16 requires the Parallel Projection Theorem. Since this theorem involves similar triangles, it must be postponed until Chapter 13. You will find the proof in the *Activities Manual* (Practice for Chapter 13, #15 and #16). The proof of construction 17 is outlined in the paragraph after the construction.

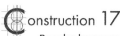onstruction 17

Regular hexagon

Construct: A regular hexagon
1. Draw a circle.
2. Using the radius of the circle, mark off six consecutive arcs.
3. Connect the arc intersections with segments to form a regular hexagon.

Figure 11.20

The construction works because of the theorem on central angles (Theorem 8.9). What kind of triangles do the central angles determine? This proves that the radius is the same length as the sides of the hexagon.

You should recognize that some constructions are impossible. In ancient Greece there were three famous unsolved construction problems. In modern times they have all been proved impossible as constructions though you could do any of them as drawings with rulers and protractors.

Impossible Construction 1

Squaring the circle

Given: A circle
Construct: A square that has the same area as the circle

Figure 11.21

Impossible Construction 2

Doubling a cube

Given: A cube with edge x
Construct: A length y that if used as the edge of a cube would form a cube whose volume would be twice the volume of the original cube

Figure 11.22

Additional Problems

What must be done to construct each solid?
1. A regular icosohedron having a face perimeter equal to a certain distance *AB*

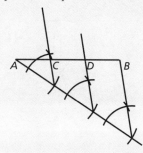

Trisect $\overline{AB}$ and construct an equilateral triangle with sides congruent to the trisection.

2. A right pyramid with a height equal to the diameter of its regular hexagonal base having perimeter equal to a certain distance *AB* **Divide $\overline{AB}$ into six congruent parts. Construct a circle with this radius and an inscribed regular hexagon. Also, construct a segment congruent to a diagonal of the hexagon for the height of the pyramid.**

Construct each of the following.
3. Trisect $\overline{AB}$.
4. A regular hexagon inscribed in a circle of diameter *AB*

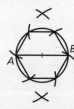

5. Discuss impossibility in mathematics. When you prove that $\sqrt{2}$ is irrational, what do you have to prove impossible? What type of proof is often useful in such proofs? **To prove $\sqrt{2}$ irrational, you prove that $\sqrt{2}$ could never be written as a ratio of integers in lowest terms. (It is impossible to express it as a rational number.) Impossibility in math is not just unlikely. You can use an indirect proof. Assume possibility and prove a contradiction.**

Finally, discuss the three problems of ancient Greece. Explain that the Greeks struggled for centuries to answer these questions. The problems even puzzled modern mathematicians until each was proved impossible. Remind students that *impossible* means that someone has figured out and deductively proved that no one will ever be able to construct them. Further information on these impossible constructions (including history and justifications of their impossibility) can be found in the *Activities Manual* (Construction activity).

You may want to mention some other areas in which two dimensions are used to represent three: paintings in art, holograms projected with lasers, and computer-generated objects such as images of automobiles (so that the viewer can turn the picture to see all sides of the proposed design). ■

Answers

1. base region and altitude

2.

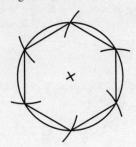

3.

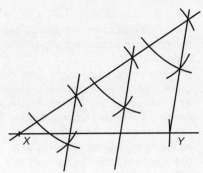

4.

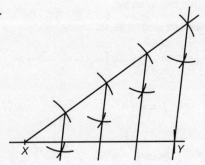

5. *see Answer section*

Impossible Construction 3

Trisecting an angle

Given: ∠XYZ

Construct: $\overrightarrow{YV}$ and $\overrightarrow{YW}$ such that
∠XYV ≅ ∠VYW ≅ ∠WYZ

Figure 11.23

▶ A. Exercises

1. To construct a right prism or cone, what must you be able to construct?
2. Construct a regular hexagon.
3. Construct a segment that is one-third of the length of $\overline{XY}$.

4. Divide $\overline{XY}$ into four congruent segments.
5. Divide $\overline{XY}$ into six congruent segments.

Use $\overline{AB}$ (where $AB = p$) for each construction.

6. Construct a triangle that has an angle measuring 30°, a side congruent to $\overline{AB}$, and another side measuring $\frac{1}{4}p$.
7. Construct a right triangle with a leg congruent to $\overline{AB}$ and the other leg with a measure that is one-third the length of $\overline{AB}$.
8. Construct an equilateral triangle having perimeter p.
9. Construct a square with perimeter p.
10. Construct a regular hexagon with perimeter $2p$.

▶ B. Exercises

Construct each.
11. A regular dodecagon
12. A regular hexagon having an inscribed circle

6.

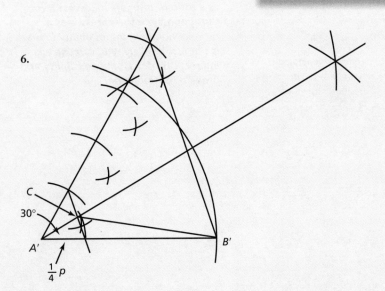

7.

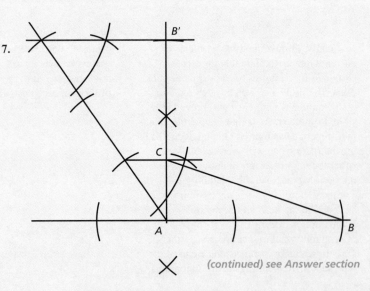

(continued) see Answer section

13. The inscribed and circumscribed circle for the square

14. The inscribed and circumscribed squares for ⊙*P*

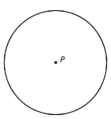

15. Bisector of $\overset{\frown}{AB}$

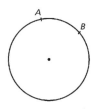

▶ C. Exercises

16. Explain how you solved exercise 15.

■ Cumulative Review

Copy the figure onto your paper for each construction below. Construct a line through the given point with the given characteristic.

17. point *A* and perpendicular to $\overset{\leftrightarrow}{EA}$

18. point *B* and perpendicular to $\overset{\leftrightarrow}{EC}$

19. point *A* and parallel to $\overset{\leftrightarrow}{EB}$

20. point *D* and parallel to $\overset{\leftrightarrow}{EC}$

21. midpoint of $\overline{ED}$ and perpendicular to $\overset{\leftrightarrow}{ED}$

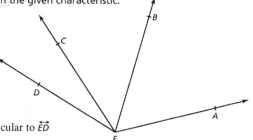

13.

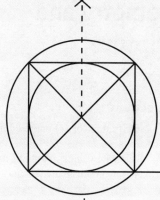

14.

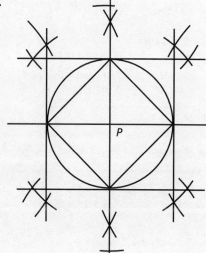

15.

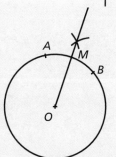

16. Draw chord $\overline{AB}$ and construct the perpendicular bisector of $\overline{AB}$ (or the line perpendicular to $\overline{AB}$ that passes through the center of the circle). This perpendicular line bisects the arc.

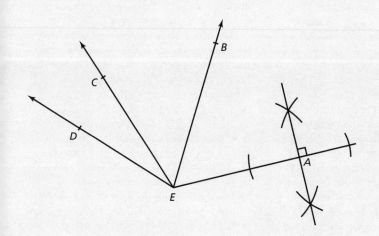

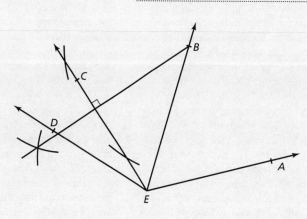

(continued) see Answer section

Geometry and Scripture

Objectives

1. To identify units of volume used in Scripture.
2. To identify how units of volume are broken down into smaller subunits.

Answers
1. 1728
2. 915.84 cu. in.

Higher Plane
I Kings 7:26, 38; II Chron. 2:10; 4:5; Ezra 7:22; Isaiah 5:10; Ezek. 45:10-14
3. the same
4. 10

Recall from your study of area that converting five square feet to square inches is harder than simply multiplying by twelve. Instead, multiply by 144 square inches per square foot. Volume requires even larger conversion factors.

1. How many cubic inches per cubic foot?
2. If we pump helium into a vacuum tube that holds 0.53 cubic feet of gas, how many cubic inches of helium are in the chamber?

The Hebrews used different units for measuring dry goods and fluids, in the same way that we use bushels for corn but gallons for milk. A container just big enough to hold 7.5 gallons of milk would contain one *bath* of milk, according to the Hebrew system.

> **HIGHER PLANE:** Find all the verses that refer to the fluid measurement known as a bath in the Bible.

Read Ezekiel 45:11. In this verse, God set standards of measure for His people.

3. According to God's command, what was the relationship between the size of an ephah and the size of a bath? (An *ephah* was used for measuring dry goods such as corn.)
4. A *homer* could be used for either dry or fluid measure. How many ephahs are in a homer?

Presentation

This study focuses on volume measurements in the Bible. The most important measures are the bath and the ephah. Emphasize these. The bath applied to fluid measures and the ephah to dry measures, but they held the same amount. The largest container in the photo is a bath (or ephah). Since it holds 7.5 gallons, it holds about one cubic foot of volume. These were the basic units of measure from which the others derived.

The other key measure is the seah (smaller round vessel in photo). The seah was the most common household unit and held one-third of an ephah. The word *measure* in the verses for #8-9 refers to the seah as explained in the paragraph below #6. Students may have trouble recognizing the word *measure* (which sounds

general) as specifying an exact amount. You can mention that the Greeks used the same quantity (but they called it a *saton* rather than a seah), and this word occurs in Matthew 13:33 and Luke 13:21, where it is also translated "measure" (KJV).

Of the less important units, the homer and omer are easily confused. The homer (not pictured) contained ten ephahs and was the amount that a donkey could carry. The Greeks used the term *kor* for this amount (as in Luke 16:7). The omer (bottom right of photo) was one-tenth of an ephah. Students also work with the cab and the hin in this study, both of which are shown. While the hin looks large, notice that it is quite shallow. After the students read

that it is one-sixth of a bath, they can see that it is only half the quantity of the seah shown.

You may wish to mention two other units not named in the study. The *handful* was the smallest unit of dry measure in the Hebrew system and is found in Leviticus 2:2 and 5:12. It contained the amount a person can hold in the cupped palm of his hand. The *log* (Lev. 14:10, 12, 15, 21, 24) was the smallest unit of fluid measure and contained one-twelfth of a hin. The log, the hin, and the bath measured fluids, while the handful, cab, omer, ephah, seah, and homer measured dry goods.

Finally, the study does not address the Greek system for volumes at all. The main Greek unit is the *sextarius* (about a pint), which occurs in

The bath and the ephah were the basic units of volume. The homer was used for very large volumes. Four other units helped the Hebrews to measure small volumes.

5. How many *omers* are in an ephah according to Exodus 16:36?

6. Use the conversions above to determine the number of omers in a homer.

The ancient measuring vessels shown are (clockwise from largest) one bath, one seah, one omer, one cab, and one hin. Compare each to the gallon of milk.

Bible Lands Collection, Bob Jones University

The *seah* was the common household unit of dry measure and is usually translated into English as *measure*. A seah is one-third of an ephah. A *cab* is one-sixth of a seah. In fluid measure, a *hin* is one-sixth of a bath.

Remember that a bath (and an ephah) hold about 7.5 gallons. Convert the following Bible measurements to modern units.

7. Numbers 28:14

8. Ruth 2:17

9. I Samuel 25:18

10. II Kings 6:25

11. Which of the four verses above shows that the priests needed to use volume measurements in order to obey God's command concerning sacrifices?

God expected all His people to be honest in their business transactions. No skimping was allowed. This command was explicitly applied to volumes in Ezekiel 45:10.

12. Which units of volume were used to express this warning from God?

> ## Line upon Line
>
> YE SHALL HAVE just balances, and a just ephah, and a just bath.
>
> EZEKIEL 45:10

5. 10
6. 100
7. about 0.6, 0.4, and 0.3 gal.
8. 7.5 gal.
9. 12.5 gal.
10. 0.1 gal. (less than a pint)
11. Num. 28:14
12. bath, ephah

Mark 7:8. The *choenix* (Rev. 6:6) is two sextarii (dry), the *metretes* (firkin, John 2:6) held 72 sextarii (liquid), and the *modius* (bushel, Matt. 5:15; Mark 4:21; Luke 11:33) held 16 sextarii (dry). The latter was the common household unit for the Greeks.

Dishonest merchants had an ephah vessel that was a bit small (but not so small as to be noticed by the buyer). When they sold an ephah of barley, they took full payment but measured out an amount with the vessel that was not a full ephah. The Line upon Line verse (Ezek. 45:10) commands people to report volumes honestly and fairly. Dishonest business is denounced. ■

Objective

To help students prepare for evaluation.

Vocabulary
See Appendix A.

Assignment
• Intuitive: 1-21, 30
• Standard: 1-27, 30
• Rigorous: 1-30

Resources
• *Visual Packet,* Solids. Shows a torus (relates to #23-27).
• *Activities Manual,* Cumulative Review
• *Activities Manual,* Terms and Symbols
• *Activities Manual,* Practice
• *Test Packet,* Chapter 11 Exam; Third-Quarter Quiz, Analytic Geometry: Third-Quarter Exam

Answers
1. $261\frac{1}{3}\pi$ cu. units $\approx$ 821 cu. units
2. 738 cu. in.
3. 130.2 cu. units
4. 150π cu. units $\approx$ 471.2 cu. units
5. 972π cu. units $\approx$ 3053.6 cu. units
6. $2208\sqrt{3}$ cu. units $\approx$ 3824.4 cu. units
7. 729 cu. units
8. $\frac{125\sqrt{2}}{3}$ cu. units $\approx$ 59 cu. units
9. $\frac{9\sqrt{2}}{4} \approx 3.2$ cu. units
10. $9 \cdot 8 + \frac{1}{3} \cdot 3 \cdot 8 \cdot 4 = 72 + 32 = $ 104 cu. units

Chapter 11 Review

Find the volume of each geometric solid.

1.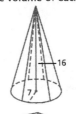
16
7

2.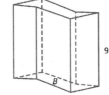
9
B
B = 82 square inches

3.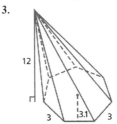
12
3   3.1   3
3

4.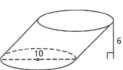
10
6

5.
18

6.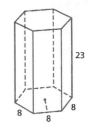
23
8   8
8

7.
9
9
9
9

8.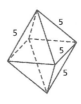
5
5
5
5

9.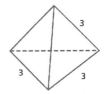
3
3   3

10.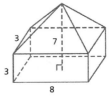
3   7
3
8

Presentation

Motivational Idea. Hand out a worksheet with the formulas from this chapter. (You can use the theorems list in the Appendix.) Then give the students fifteen minutes to explain why each formula works. Any formula a student is unable to explain requires review.

Tips

Ex. 17. Find $e = 2$ first.

Ex. 18. Find $e = 5$ first.

Ex. 19. Find $e = 5.8$ first.

Ex. 24. These refer to the diagram, which provides diameters for both circles. The area of the dotted circle is $\pi \cdot 1^2$. Then multiply by the circumference of the doughnut, 3π.

Ex. 25. Multiply the circumference of the dotted circle $(\pi \cdot 1)$ by the circumference of the doughnut, 3π. Some students may answer 14.8 cu. units, thinking that only the top half of the doughnut is frosted.

Ex. 26. Imagine a rubber doughnut that you could slit and stand into a cylinder. The volume would be $V = BH$, where the area of the base of the circular cross section is πr^2 and the height is the circumference at the center of the doughnut, or $2\pi a$. Thus, $V = (\pi r^2)(2\pi a) = 2\pi^2 a r^2$.

Ex. 27. Forming a cylinder from the doughnut as in #26, the surface area of the doughnut is given the lateral surface area of the cylinder. Thus, $S = cH$, where c is the circumference of the circular cross section $2\pi r$ and the height is as in #26. Thus, $S = (2\pi r)(2\pi a) = 4\pi^2 a r.$ ∎

In the following exercises H = height, V = volume, l = slant height, r = radius length, s = side length for base, e = edge length, d = diameter length, a = apothem, and S = surface area. Draw pictures and find the following.

11. Volume of a square prism with $s = 8$ and $H = 22$
12. Volume of an equilateral triangular pyramid with $s = 34$, $H = 38$
13. Volume of a right circular cone with $r = 6$, $H = 10$
14. Volume of a sphere with $r = 14$
15. Volume of a regular tetrahedron with $e = 6$ mm
16. Volume of a regular dodecahedron with a face having a perimeter of 10 m
17. Volume of a regular octahedron with $S = 50\sqrt{3}$ cu. units
18. Volume of a regular icosahedron with $S = 20\sqrt{3}$ sq. ft.
19. Surface area of a dodecahedron with $V = 1{,}993.6$ and $a = 4$
20. Volume of a hemisphere with $d = 12$ in.
21. Give the meaning of *volume*.
22. State Cavalieri's principle in your own words.

Exercises 23-27 involve tori. A *torus* is a surface shaped like a doughnut.

23. Imagine a rubber hose 10 inches long with an inside radius of one inch. Attach the ends to form a torus. Find the volume.
24. How much dough is there in the doughnut shown if it is one inch thick?
25. How much frosting is needed to cover the doughnut?

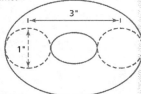

Use a torus with radius r through the dough and radius a across the hole.

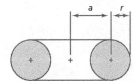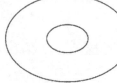

26. Give a formula for the volume of the torus.
27. Give a formula for the surface area of the torus.

Prove the following formulas for a cube with edge e inscribed in a sphere of radius r.

28. $r = \dfrac{\sqrt{3}}{2}e$

29. $V = \dfrac{8\sqrt{3}}{9}r^2$

30. Explain the mathematical significance of Ezekiel 45:10.

11. $V = 1408$ cu. units
12. $V = \dfrac{10{,}982}{3}\sqrt{3}$ cu. units ≈ 6340.5 cu. units
13. $V = 120\pi$ cu. units ≈ 377 cu. units
14. $V = \dfrac{10{,}976}{3}\pi$ cu. units $\approx 11{,}494$ cu. units
15. $V = 18\sqrt{2}$ cu. units ≈ 25.5 cu. units
16. $40 + \dfrac{56\sqrt{5}}{3} \approx 81.7$ m³
17. $\dfrac{125\sqrt{2}}{3}$ cu. units ≈ 58.9 cu. units
18. $\dfrac{30 + 10\sqrt{5}}{3} \approx 17.5$ ft.³

19. $S = 696$ sq. units
20. $144\pi \approx 452.4$ cu. in.
21. The number of cubic units needed to fill a solid
22. If two solids have the same height and if corresponding cross sections have the same area, then the solids have the same volume.
23. $10\pi \approx 31.4$ cu. in.
24. $0.75\pi^2 \approx 7.4$ cu. in.
25. $3\pi^2 \approx 29.6$ sq. in.
26. $V = (2\pi a)(\pi r^2) = 2\pi^2 a r^2$
27. $S = (2\pi a)(2\pi r) = 4\pi^2 a r$
28.

1. Cube	1. Given
2. If x = length of diagonal of a face and d = length of a diagonal of the cube (diameter of sphere), $e^2 + e^2 = x^2$ $e^2 + x^2 = d^2$	2. Pythagorean theorem
3. $e^2 + (e^2 + e^2) = d^2$	3. Substitution (see step 2)
4. $3e^2 = d^2$	4. Distributive property
5. $\sqrt{3}e = d$	5. Take square roots on both sides
6. $d = 2r$	6. Definition of diameter
7. $\sqrt{3}e = 2r$	7. Substitution
8. $r = \dfrac{\sqrt{3}e}{2}$	8. Multiplication property of equality

29.

1. Cube	1. Given
2. $r = \dfrac{\sqrt{3}}{2}e$	2. Exercise 28
3. $e = \dfrac{2}{\sqrt{3}}r$	3. Multiplication property of equality
4. $V = e^3$	4. Volume of Cube Postulate
5. $V = \left(\dfrac{2}{\sqrt{3}}r\right)^3 = \dfrac{8}{3\sqrt{3}}r^3 = \dfrac{8\sqrt{3}}{9}r^3$	5. Substitution (step 3 into 4)

30. This verse refers to ephahs and baths, ancient units of volume, while giving God's command to use fair measurements when doing business.

12 Transformations and Symmetry

Transformations and Symmetry

The butterfly is perhaps the loveliest insect in the world. Brilliant hues of yellow, blue, orange, purple, red, and green flutter like bright flags over many summer meadows.

How can a creature that begins life as a homely little caterpillar become such a gorgeous creature? Only God in His wisdom could design it that way.

Few of God's creatures can rival the peacock for loveliness. After finding one feather in 1913, naturalists searched the African plains until 1936 just to find a peacock. Lovers of brilliant hues can understand why those scientists persisted in their search.

The butterfly and the peacock have something more than beautiful colors in common. They are examples of geometric symmetry. The left wing of the butterfly is the mirror image of the right wing. Each peacock feather divides down the center into two perfectly symmetrical halves. Such symmetry contributes to their beauty.

In a similar way we should be a mirror image of God. God made us in His own image (Gen. 1:26), and He wants Christians to reflect that image by imitating His character and actions. Second Corinthians 3:18 tells us that when we look at God's glory in much the same way that we look in a mirror we can be changed from imperfection to perfection.

After this chapter you should be able to

1. identify transformations.
2. perform reflections, rotations, translations, and dilations of given figures.
3. classify transformations as isometries, dilations, or neither.
4. classify isometries as reflections, rotations, translations, or compositions of them.
5. state properties preserved by isometries or dilations.
6. apply isometries to light and to rolling objects.
7. define and identify types of symmetry.
8. define similar figures.

499

Overview

Transformational geometry may be new to you, but it is not difficult if you understand the basic principles taught in this chapter. Many geometric ideas can be explained and visualized in terms of transformational geometry. This chapter defines isometry and applies related properties. It also introduces some transformations called dilations, which do not preserve distance. These provide a contrast and help prepare students for the next chapter. Finally, it discusses symmetry in terms of transformations.

Bulletin Board Idea

Show two dilations, one an enlargement and the other a reduction. Use original figures of the same color or material to set them off as the originals. Draw lines of dilation with numerical values shown on them. Put the scale factor used on the enlargement and on the reduction. Title the board *Dilation*.

Presentation

Reflections are a central theme of this chapter. Mirrors or lakes that reflect mountains (p. 501) are familiar to every student. Mathematical reflections make this concept precise and technical. Combinations of reflections are used to obtain some other types of transformations, and the properties of all of these are studied. Reflections are also useful for identifying symmetrical figures such as the butterfly. ■

12.1 Transformations

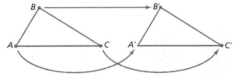

These zebras display their symmetric stripes at a water hole in Kenya.

Objectives

1. To define and illustrate geometric transformations.
2. To define and perform reflections.

Vocabulary

image
line of reflection
mapping
orientation
preimage
reflection
transformation

Assignment

• Intuitive: 1-10, 18-22
• Standard: 1-15, 18-22
• Rigorous: 5-22

Resources

• *Visual Packet*, Similar, Congruent, Symmetrical
• *Activities Manual*, Bible Activity: The Church—the Steward of Truth

Reading and Writing Mathematics

Have the students draw *x* and *y* axes and place a circle with center at the origin. The circle is to be mapped into a single 90° arc in quadrant I. Ask the students to find what lines of reflection would be used to send each of the other three arcs into the arc in quadrant I. *Quadrant IV points would need to be reflected through the x-axis, quadrant II points through the y-axis, and quadrant III points through the line y = −x.*

In general usage, a transformation is a major change in the form, appearance, or nature of something. In Acts 9 Saul converted to Christianity (vv. 3-18). This conversion changed his very nature from one of hatefulness (vv. 1-2) to one serving Christ (vv. 20-22). Men marveled at the striking transformation that took place in Paul's life after he accepted Jesus Christ as his personal Savior. Every person who comes to know Christ as his personal Savior will experience this same transformation of soul and spirit. Second Corinthians 5:17 says, "Therefore if any man be in Christ, he is a new creature: old things are passed away; behold, all things are become new." Have you been transformed by the shed blood of Jesus Christ?

In mathematics the term *transformation* describes a change in the appearance of points in a plane. It is therefore a correspondence between point locations before and after the change. The geometric figure before a transformation is called the *preimage*. The resulting geometric figure after the transformation is called the *image*.

In figure 12.1 the points of △*ABC* are matched with the points of △*A′B′C′*. △*ABC* is the preimage, △*A′B′C′* is the image, and the correspondence between them is the *transformation*.

Figure 12.1

Definition

> A **transformation** is a one-to-one function from the plane onto the plane.

A transformation can be thought of as a movement of figures. We will study various kinds of transformations in this chapter. Some movements, such as stretching, change the size and shape of a figure, whereas other transformations, such as rotating, do not.

Even if you have never studied transformational geometry, you will find this concrete material fun to teach. It builds key concepts and provides an additional problem-solving tool. The primary hurdle at the start of the chapter is the definition of a transformation.

Define *transformation* as in the text and display several examples for the class. Talk about the preimage and image of a transformation. Images of transformations are represented by *A′* and *A″*, which are read "*A* prime" and "*A* double prime" respectively.

The comments above will suffice for most students. Some teachers will want to go into detail about the two key terms in the definition:

one-to-one correspondence and *function.* The next two paragraphs review these terms.

Review from Algebra 1 the concept of a *function,* a correspondence that associates every element of set *A* with exactly one element of set *B*. Set *A* is called the domain, and set *B* is called the range. The correspondence results in a set of ordered pairs, each consisting of one domain element and one range element. A function, then, is a set of ordered pairs of which no two have the same first element. This last idea guarantees exactly one range value for each domain value. A transformation is a function having the plane as its domain and range. The term can be used in general of any such functions, but this book focuses on those that are one-to-one.

Students learned the term *one-to-one correspondence* on page 4. A transformation is a one-to-one correspondence from the plane to the plane. That is, every point corresponds to some point and no two points correspond to the same point.

All of this will make better sense as students learn specific transformations. Several types are discussed in the chapter but the most basic one is the reflection. Use one or more of the following three motivational ideas to introduce reflections.

Motivational Idea. Have each student bring a small hand-held mirror to class. You can illustrate many of these ideas with it.

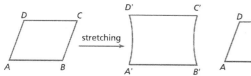

Figure 12.2

The transformation called a reflection is similar to a mirror image. A reflection in a line *l*, is shown in figure 12.3. Line *l* is called the *line of reflection*, or the *mirror*.

In this reflection, $X \rightarrow X'$ (*X* is mapped to X'), $Y \rightarrow Y'$, and $Z \rightarrow Z'$. If the vertices of the preimage are named in counterclockwise order, $\triangle XYZ$, then the image has clockwise order $\triangle X'Y'Z'$. This order of vertices is called *orientation*. Reversing the orientation is a characteristic of a reflection. Trace figure 12.3 onto your paper and connect each image vertex with its preimage vertex. Measure the distance from the line of reflection to *X* and to *X'*. Do this for each pair of vertices. Also measure the angle formed by each segment and *l*. The discoveries you have just made will help you understand the definition of *reflection*.

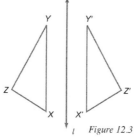

Figure 12.3

Definition

A **reflection** in a line, *l*, is a transformation that maps each point *A* of a plane onto the point *A'* such that the following conditions are met.

1. If *A* is on *l*, then $A = A'$.
2. If *A* is not on *l*, then *l* is the perpendicular bisector of $\overline{AA'}$.

It is easy to find the reflection of any given polygon in a given line.

Wonder Lake captures the reflection of Mt. McKinley at Denali National Park, Alaska.

Additional Problems

Find the image of the segment reflected in the given line.

1.

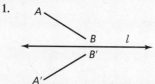

2.

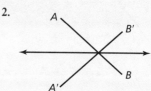

3.

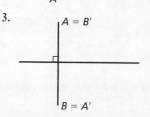

Draw the line of reflection that maps preimage *ABC* to image *A'B'C'*.

4.

5.

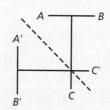

Motivational Idea. Use congruent posterboard triangles and an overhead projector. Draw the lines of reflection on acetate sheets and place the triangles on the projector field to show all of the isometries.

Motivational Idea. Paper folding also makes a clear illustration of reflections. The paper should be thin enough to see through when held up to the light. Waxed paper works extremely well. Draw a right triangle with unequal legs on the paper, then fold the paper in half, and hold it to the light to mark the vertices of the image. Unfold the paper, mark the vertices of the image through the paper, and complete the triangle. By marking the crease in

the paper, you have a triangle, the line of reflection, and the image.

Discuss the fact that the triangles appear congruent even after the reflection. Have the students fold the paper again and draw the reflection image in this new line of reflection. Point out that the triangles are again congruent. Students will prove this in #16-17. Ask the students what aspect of the figure changes from the folding process (*reflection reverses orientation*). Show how the orientation of the figure changes direction.

Define *reflection* and discuss the example with the students. Note the word *draw* in the example and review the difference between drawings, sketches, and constructions. Students

will need to use tools throughout this chapter to make accurate drawings.

A final point to emphasize is that it is not just the figure that is reflected. The entire plane is reflected. Remember that a transformation is a correspondence of every point of the plane to its image. Thus, we may draw a representative triangle to "see" what happens, but every point on each side of the line reflects to some point on the other side. This is also why we say that the line of reflection is *fixed* since the points on the line are the only points of the plane that do not move in the reflection. ∎

6.

$A = C'$
$B = B'$ $C = A'$

Answers

1.

$E \bullet$ $\overset{C \bullet}{\underset{D \bullet}{}}$
$\quad\quad B \bullet$ $\overset{D' \bullet}{\underset{\bullet B'}{}} \bullet C'$
$A \bullet$
$\quad\quad\quad l$
$\quad\quad\quad \bullet A'$ $\bullet E'$

2.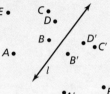

$P \bullet\ m$
$\quad\quad\quad P'$
$Q \bullet$
$\quad\quad\quad Q'$

3.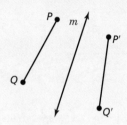

k

4.

l

5.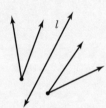

p

6.

n

7. It moves closer to the line.
8. 1 in.
9. 45°
10. yes

EXAMPLE   Reflect △*LMN* in line *k*.

Answer   1. Draw a line from each vertex perpendicular to *k*.
2. On each perpendicular line find a point on the other side of *k* that is the same distance from *k* as the corresponding vertex.
3. Connect these points.

Figure 12.4

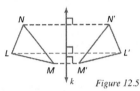

Figure 12.5

An image point for every point of △*LMN* can be found on △*L'M'N'*. Choose any point on △*LMN* and find its image point on △*L'M'N'*. What is true about the orientation of the triangles?

▶ A. Exercises

Copy each figure below onto your paper and reflect the preimage across the given line.

1.

$E \bullet$ $\overset{C \bullet}{\underset{D \bullet}{}}$
$\quad\quad B \bullet$
$A \bullet$
$\quad\quad\quad l$

3.

k

5.

p

2.

$P \bullet\ m$
$Q \bullet$

4.

l

6.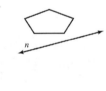

n

7. Draw a point and a line of reflection. As the point moves closer to the line, what happens to its image?

8. Draw a one-inch segment and a line of reflection. Reflect the segment in the line. Now measure the segment. How long is it?

9. Draw a 45° angle and a line of reflection. Reflect the angle in the line. What is the measure of the reflected angle?

10. Draw a line segment, $\overline{AC}$, with point B between A and C. Draw a line of reflection and reflect $\overline{AC}$ in the line. Is the reflection of B between the reflections of A and C?

▶ **B. Exercises**

Trace the following figures onto your paper and draw in the lines of reflection. Remember to consider the definition of reflection when doing these problems.

11.

13.

12.
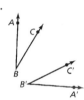

14.
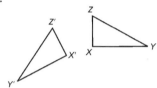

15. Explain how you can find the line of reflection if you are given the preimage and the image of a geometric figure.

▶ **C. Exercises**

16. *Given:* $\overline{A'B'}$ is a reflection of $\overline{AB}$ in l
    Prove: $\overline{AB} \cong \overline{A'B'}$

17. *Given:* A', B', and C' are reflections of A, B, and C in line l respectively; $\triangle ABC, \triangle A'B'C'$
    Prove: $\triangle ABC \cong \triangle A'B'C'$ and $\angle ABC \cong \angle A'B'C'$

11.
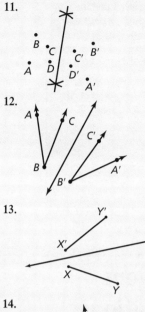

12.

13.

14.

15. Connect the preimage and the image points; their perpendicular bisector will be the line of reflection.

16.

1. $\overline{A'B'}$ reflects $\overline{AB}$ in l	1. Given
2. l is the perpendicular bisector of $\overline{AA'}$ at Q and $\overline{BB'}$ at P	2. Definition of reflection
3. Q is the midpoint of $\overline{AA'}$; P is the midpoint of $\overline{BB'}$	3. Definition of segment bisector
4. $AQ = A'Q$ $BP = B'P$	4. Definition of midpoint
5. $\overline{AQ} \cong \overline{A'Q}$; $\overline{BP} \cong \overline{B'P}$	5. Definition of congruent segments

17.

1. A', B', and C' are images of A, B, and C under a reflection in l; $\triangle ABC, \triangle A'B'C'$	1. Given
2. $\overline{AB} \cong \overline{A'B'}$, $\overline{BC} \cong \overline{B'C'}$, $\overline{AC} \cong \overline{A'C'}$	2. Exercise 16
3. $\triangle ABC \cong \triangle A'B'C'$	3. SSS
4. $\angle ABC \cong \angle A'B'C'$	4. Definition of congruent triangles

6. $\angle AQP, \angle A'QP$; $\angle BPQ, \angle B'PQ$ are right angles	6. Definition of perpendicular
7. $\overline{PQ} \cong \overline{PQ}$	7. Reflexive property of congruent segments
8. Draw $\overline{AP}$ and $\overline{A'P}$	8. Auxiliary lines
9. $\triangle AQP, \triangle A'QP$ are right triangles	9. Definition of right triangle
10. $\triangle AQP \cong \triangle A'QP$	10. LL
11. $\angle APQ \cong \angle A'PQ$; $\overline{AP} \cong \overline{A'P}$	11. Definition of congruent triangles
12. $\angle BPQ \cong \angle B'PQ$	12. All right angles are congruent
13. $\angle BPA \cong \angle B'PA'$	13. Adjacent Angle Portion Theorem
14. $\triangle BPA \cong \triangle B'PA'$	14. SAS
15. $\overline{AB} \cong \overline{A'B'}$	15. Definition of congruent triangles

18. regular tetrahedron, cube, regular
octahedron, regular dodecahedron,
regular icosahedron [8.8]

	Surface Area	Volume
19.	$4\pi r^2$ [8.8]	$\frac{4}{3}\pi r^3$ [11.5]
20.	$2\pi rH + 2\pi r^2$ [8.6]	$\pi r^2 H$ [11.3]
21.	$\pi rl + \pi r^2$ [8.7]	$\frac{1}{3}\pi r^2 H$ [11.4]
22.	$nsH + ans$ [8.6]	$\frac{1}{2}ansH$ [11.2]

12.2

Translations and Rotations

Objectives

1. To define and perform translations and rotations.
2. To illustrate translations and rotations as compositions of reflections.
3. To define the identity transformation.

Vocabulary

angle of rotation
center of rotation
composition
identity transformation
magnitude of rotation
rotation
translation

Assignment

• Intuitive: 1-14, 21-25
• Standard: 1-18, 21-25
• Rigorous: 5-25 and Mind over Math

18. Name the Platonic solids.

Give the surface area and volume formulas for each figure.

	Figure	Surface Area	Volume
19.	Sphere		
20.	Cylinder		
21.	Cone		
22.	Prism with regular n-gon as a base		

12.2 Translations and Rotations

The word *translated* is similar in origin to the word *transfer,* which means "to carry across." A translation in geometry has a similar meaning. *Translate* means "to slide into a different position." Figure 12.6 shows a geometric translation.

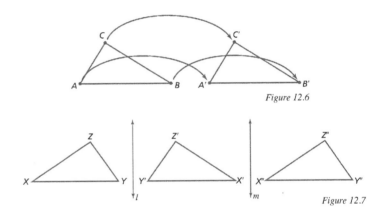

Figure 12.6

Figure 12.7

504 CHAPTER 12 TRANSFORMATIONS AND SYMMETRY

Presentation

Tell the students to think of a translation as a sliding movement of the plane.

Motivational Idea. To illustrate this concept, cut out a triangular piece of cardboard and trace it on the chalkboard; then slide it along the board to illustrate a translation.

Perform the exercise described in this section to show that a translation is the composition of two reflections. Have the students decide if the image of a triangle is congruent to the preimage.

Motivational Idea. You can explain some of the uses of transformations. 1) Euclid used the method of superposition to justify some of his congruence theorems. He never justified that

he could move things in the plane, but the material in this chapter shows that he could have. 2) Fractal geometry. 3) Computer applications such as virtual reality systems, computer animation, computer aided design (CAD), and computer simulation. 4) Vectors, defined by a length and direction, can be used to define translations.

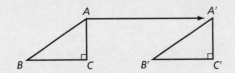

Common Student Error. Some students will be confused by the notation for function composition. Suppose R and T are two transformations. We write $R \circ T$ and this means $R(T(A))$. Remind students to start with the inside parentheses. Starting with point A, find its image under T and then the image of that point under R. Stress that $R \circ T$ means the same and that we perform the second transformation first. Students will remember this if they always convert to parentheses.

Define *rotation* as a composition of two reflections in lines that intersect. Do several rotations in which the angle between the intersecting lines is 45°, 90°, or 30°. Ask the students if the two transformations studied in this section

A translation can be defined in terms of reflections. $\triangle XYZ$ is reflected in line l to form $\triangle X'Y'Z'$, which is then again reflected in line m to obtain $\triangle X''Y''Z''$. Now compare $\triangle XYZ$ with $\triangle X''Y''Z''$. Since you can slide the first onto the second, a translation has occurred. Because a translation involves two reflections, the orientation of the triangle is not changed. The first reflection reverses the orientation, but the second reflection changes it back.

Any time you perform two or more transformations on a geometric figure, you are performing a *composition* of transformations. In figure 12.7 if the first reflection is called R, it is described by $R(\triangle XYZ) = \triangle X'Y'Z'$. The second reflection is called T such that $T(\triangle X'Y'Z') = \triangle X''Y''Z''$. The translation T composed with R is denoted $T \circ R$ or $T(R(\triangle XYZ))$. With this understanding of the composition of transformations, we can now define translation.

Definition

A **translation** is a transformation formed by the composition of two reflections in which the lines of reflection are parallel lines.

The third type of transformation that we will study in this chapter is a rotation. A rotation is also a composition of reflections.

Definition

A **rotation** is a transformation formed by the composition of two reflections in which the lines of reflection intersect.

Figure 12.8 shows an example of a rotation. The image of $\triangle HIJ$ is $\triangle H''I''J''$ by a composition of two reflections. Trace $\triangle HIJ$ onto a piece of paper and then turn the paper, keeping point X fixed. The triangle will rotate to coincide with $\triangle H''I''J''$.

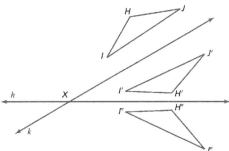

Figure 12.8

- *Activities Manual,* Math History Activity. Focuses on the life and works of Girard Desargues.
- *Test Packet,* Quiz 1, Chapter 12 covers Sections 12.1 and 12.2.

Reading and Writing Mathematics
Have the students consider the following three-dimensional transformations and describe how they think the image would be transformed.
1. Through a single plane *A looking-glass reflection*
2. Through parallel planes *A translation*
3. Through intersecting planes *A rotation about the line of intersection, a reflection in the line of intersection if the planes are perpendicular*

Additional Problems
Find the image of each figure under a composite transformation where l_1 is the first mirror and l_2 is the second mirror, etc.
1. *translation*

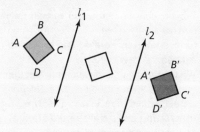

2. *counterclockwise rotation*

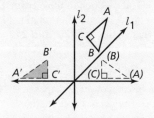

keep their orientation after the transformation. (*yes*) Discuss the identity transformation and ask the students to give an example.

When a figure such as a triangle is given along with its image, and the lines of reflection are needed, the solution is not obvious unless the transformation is a single reflection. We must find one line at a time by looking at just one vertex (B in the diagram below) and its image, B', and by finding the perpendicular bisector of the segment joining them. After the line is reflected through the first mirror, another line is found using a second vertex (A) and its image A' but not moving the first one. This means the second mirror will have to go through the first vertex (B'). The center of the rotation

shown is the point of intersection of the mirrors.

Have the students measure the actual amount of rotation by extending two corresponding sides until they meet; for example, $\overline{BC}$ and $\overline{B'C'}$ (as shown), and measuring the acute angle between them. Then have them measure the acute angle between the mirrors to verify the fact that the angle of rotation will be twice the angle between the mirrors.

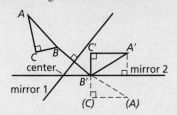

Ex. 21. To the nearest thousandth, the numbers are 3.143, 3.140, 3.162, 3.175, 3.138, 3.142 respectively. ∎

3. the rotation is a half-turn because the mirrors are perpendicular, making the angle of rotation 2 times 90 = 180

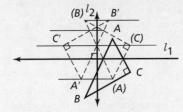

4. The result is a reflection followed by a translation. This is sometimes called a glide.

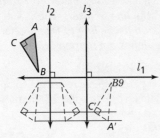

5. What happens to a rotation when the same mirrors are used but the reflections are performed in reverse order? **The direction of rotation is reversed.**

6. What happens to a translation when the same mirrors are used but the reflections are performed in reverse order? **The translation goes the same distance but in the opposite direction.**

7. If an equilateral triangle is rotated about its centroid (intersection of the medians), it will line up with itself after rotating through what angles? **at 120° and 240°**

Flash

Note that nine of each of three shapes of kites are formed (large ones point to the cars, narrow ones lie between larger ones, and the smallest ones lie between the narrow ones and reach the center). Each large kite spans four cars, making a total of 36. Note also the concentric circles (three, red).

Mind over Math

See Appendix B.

The ferris wheel at Cedar Point, Ohio, rotates ten degrees between cars while loading passengers. Notice also the overlapping red radii and silver kite shapes in the design.

The *center of the rotation* in figure 12.8 is the point X, the intersection of the two mirrors. The angle that the rotation takes to move to the new position is called the *magnitude* of the rotation. So if $m\angle HXH''$ is 95°, the magnitude of the rotation is 95°. The direction of the rotation is also important. When talking about the magnitude of a rotation, always indicate whether the rotation is clockwise or counterclockwise.

An interesting fact about rotations is that the magnitude is twice the measure of the acute or right angle between the lines of reflection. A 95° rotation would require a 47.5° angle between the lines of reflection. In summary, a rotation can be described by its center, the magnitude of rotation, and the direction of the rotation.

An *identity transformation* is a transformation that maps each point of a geometric figure onto itself. For example, if two 180° rotations have the same center, their composition will map every figure onto itself, thus producing an identity transformation.

> **MIND OVER MATH**
>
> Consider the set of all transformations. Which properties does the operation of composition have?
>
> 1. Commutative 3. Identity
> 2. Associative 4. Inverse

▶ A. Exercises

Trace the following diagrams onto your paper. Reflect the geometric figures in *l* and then in *m* to obtain a composite transformation. Name the types of transformations.

1.

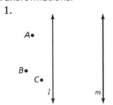

2.

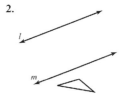

Answers

1.

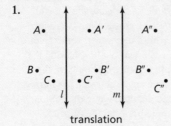

translation

2.

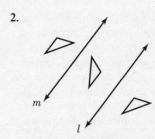

translation

3.

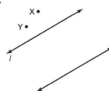

6.

4.

7.

5.

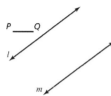

8.

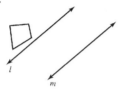

▶ **B. Exercises**

Translate and rotate each figure below. Indicate whether the size or shape of the geometric figure was changed. Show all your work.

9.

11.

10.

12.

13. If the magnitude of a rotation is 80°, what is the measure of the acute angle between the lines of reflection?

14. If the angle between the lines of reflection is 27°, what is the magnitude of the rotation?

12.2 TRANSLATIONS AND ROTATIONS **507**

3.

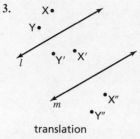

translation

4.

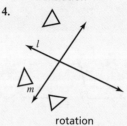

rotation

5.

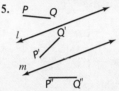

translation

6.

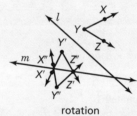

rotation

7.

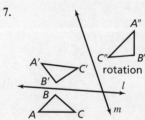

rotation

8.

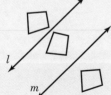

translation

9.

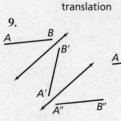

translation   rotation

10.

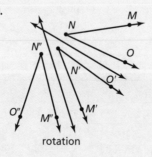

rotation

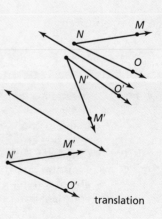

translation

12.2 TRANSLATIONS AND ROTATIONS **507**

11.

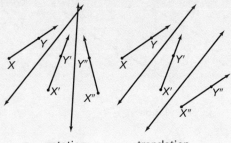

rotation   translation

12.

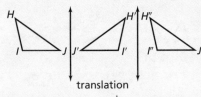

translation

Size and shape
are not changed.

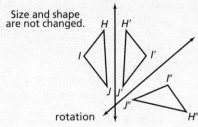

rotation

13. 40°
14. 54°
15. identity transformation
16. translation
17. rotation; P, 80°
18. no, not commutative
19. Remember that rotations and translations
    are the composition of two reflections $R \circ T$

1. Reflections $R(AB) = A'B'$ and $T(A'B') = A''B''$	1. Given
2. $\overline{AB} \cong \overline{A'B'}$, $\overline{A'B'} \cong \overline{A''B''}$	2. Preimage and image segments of a reflection are congruent
3. $\overline{AB} \cong \overline{A''B''}$	3. Transitive property of congruent segments

20.

1. Reflections $R(\triangle ABC) = \triangle A'B'C'$, $T(\triangle A'B'C') = \triangle A''B''C''$	1. Given
2. $\triangle ABC \cong \triangle A'B'C'$, $\triangle A'B'C' \cong \triangle A''B''C''$	2. The preimage and image triangles of a reflection are congruent
3. $\triangle ABC \cong \triangle A''B''C''$	3. Transitive property of congruent triangles

15. Draw an acute triangle and rotate it 70° clockwise about point O. Then rotate the image 70° counterclockwise about point O. What is the composition of these rotations called?
16. Repeat exercise 15, using two different centers. What is this composition called?
17. If l and m intersect at point P to form a 40° angle, then what is the composite of the reflections in l and m? Give the center and magnitude of this transformation.
18. If R is the reflection in l, and T is the reflection in m, does $R \circ T = T \circ R$? (Is the composition commutative?) *Hint:* Answer the question by finding $R(T(X))$ and $T(R(X))$.

▶ **C. Exercises**

Use the exercises in the previous section to show that rotations and translations share the following two properties.
19. If $\overline{A''B''}$ is a translation or rotation of $\overline{AB}$, then $\overline{AB} \cong \overline{A''B''}$.
    Given: $R(\overline{AB}) = \overline{A'B'}$ and $T(\overline{A'B'}) = \overline{A''B''}$
    Prove: $\overline{AB} \cong \overline{A''B''}$
20. If $\triangle A''B''C''$ is a rotation or translation of $\triangle ABC$, then $\triangle ABC \cong \triangle A''B''C''$.

■ **Cumulative Review**

21. Decide which numbers are greater than others and put them in increasing order (*Hint:* decimals). $\frac{22}{7}$, 3.14, $\sqrt{10}$, $\sqrt[3]{32}$, $(1.1)^{12}$, π
22. Graph the set on the number line: $\{-2, -\frac{3}{2}, \sqrt{2}, \pi, 4.1\}$

Give the area and perimeter of each figure.

	Figure	Perimeter	Area
23.	Circle		
24.	Rectangle		
25.	Regular polygon		

21. $(1.1)^{12}$, 3.14, π, $\frac{22}{7}$, $\sqrt{10}$, $\sqrt[3]{32}$ [3.1]
22. [3.1]

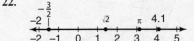

	Perimeter	Area
23.	$2\pi r$ [3.4]	πr^2 [8.5]
24.	$2l + 2w$ [3.4]	bh [8.1]
25.	ns [3.4]	$\frac{1}{2} ap$ (or $\frac{1}{2}ans$) [8.4]

Analytic Geometry

Translating Conic Sections

Plot $y = 2x^2$ and $y = 2(x - 1)^2$. You should see that the graphs are the same size and shape. The movement of the first graph one unit *to the right* illustrates another application of transformations.

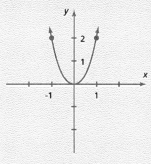

$y = 2x^2$
standard position

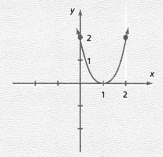

$y = 2(x - 1)^2$
translated position

Do you see that replacing x with $x - h$ translates the graph h units horizontally? Similarly, to translate the graph k units vertically, replace y with $y - k$.

	Circle	Parabola
standard position	$x^2 + y^2 = r^2$	$y = ax^2$
translated position	$(x - h)^2 + (y - k)^2 = r^2$ with center (h, k)	$y - k = a(x - h)^2$ or: $y = a(x - h)^2 + k$ with vertex (h, k)

Analytic Geometry

Translating Conic Sections

Objectives

1. To identify the general form of translated equations or conics.
2. To graph translated conics from their equations.
3. To write the equations of conics whose translated graphs are shown.

Assignment
- Intuitive: 1-5
- Standard: 1-5
- Rigorous: 1-5

Additional Problems
Graph each of the following equations.

1. $x^2 + (y - 1)^2 = 1$

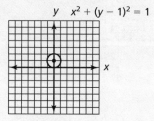

$y \quad x^2 + (y - 1)^2 = 1$

2. $y = (x - 2)^2 - 3$

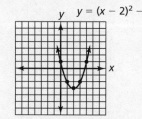

$y \quad y = (x - 2)^2 - 3$

Presentation

Translations provide an opportunity to demonstrate the close relationship between algebra and geometry. The first example shows how to interpret translated equations.

Common Student Error. Students often ignore the subtractions in the expressions $x - h$ and $y - k$ in the translated equations. It is easy to take the minus as part of the constant, forgetting that the subtractions are part of the format. For example, in $x - 4$, the minus is part of the standard form, so $h = 4$. For $x + 7$, we must express the sum as a subtraction: $x - (-7)$. Now we can see that $h = -7$.

Review the standard form of the equations for circles and parabolas as given in the table on page 509. Recall that in standard position,

the circle has its center at the origin (p. 372) and the parabola has its vertex at the origin (pp. 480-81). The point (h, k) shows the coordinates to which the center or the vertex moves under a translation. You can view the entire plane as shifting, but for most students it will be easier to think of shifting the figure.

If you have time, you can also mention another application of translations. Students should remember graphing lines using the slope and intercept (p. 196). The y-intercept is a vertical translation (and the slope can be viewed as a rotation).

Tips

Ex. 1. This exercise is easier than #5 because less work is necessary. However, some students will need to be told to view y^2 as $(y - 0)^2$ to identify that $k = 0$.

Ex. 3. Like #1, except that $h = 0$. ∎

3. $(x + 4)^2 - y = 3$

$(x + 4)^2 - y = 3$

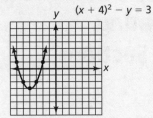

4. $(x - 4)^2 + (y + 1)^2 = 9$

$(x - 4)^2 + (y + 1)^2 = 9$

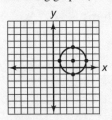

5. Write the equation that describes the following graph. $(x - 3)^2 + (y - 1)^2 = 4$

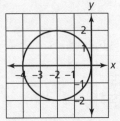

Answers

1.

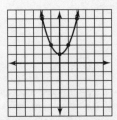

2.

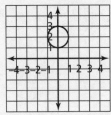

3.

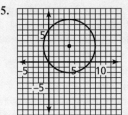

EXAMPLES Graph $(x - 2)^2 + (y + 1)^2 = 9$ and $y = 2(x - 1)^2 - 3$
Find (h, k)

Answers $(2, -1)$ $(1, -3)$
                 $r = 3$ Opens up $2 > 0$

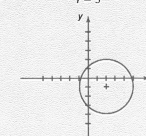   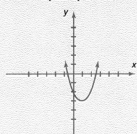

▶ **Exercises**

Graph.
1. $(x + 2)^2 + y^2 = 4$
2. $y = x^2 + 1$
3. $x^2 + (y - 2)^2 = 1$
4. $y = 2(x + 1)^2 + 4$
5. $(x - 4)^2 + (y - 3)^2 = 25$

4.

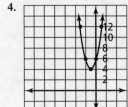

5.

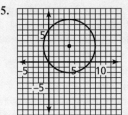

12.3 Dilations

When was the last time you went to the eye doctor? Did he put drops into your eyes that caused them to dilate? Dilating the eyes makes the pupils bigger so that the doctor can study them more easily. This enlargement is one type of mathematical dilation. After a few hours the eye drops wear off and the pupils contract to their normal size. Such a contraction represents the other type of mathematical dilation.

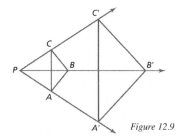

Figure 12.9

Figure 12.9 shows a dilation with center P. Notice that △ABC and △A'B'C' are not congruent.

Definition

A **dilation** is a transformation that expands or contracts the points of the plane in relation to a fixed point, *P*.

Find the ratio of *PA'* to *PA*. Do the same with *PB'* to *PB*, and with *PC'* to *PC*. You should get the same number each time. This constant positive ratio is called the *scale factor* of the dilation and is represented as *k*. Always calculate *k* as a ratio of image to preimage lengths.

So, for any dilation the image of *P* is *P* (the fixed point) and for any other point *R*, the image *R'* is on $\overrightarrow{PR}$ so that $PR' = k(PR)$.

In figure 12.9 the scale factor is greater than 1 and the size of the triangle is expanded. The result of a dilation depends on the scale factor.

12.3
Dilations

Objectives

1. To define and illustrate dilation transformations.
2. To define similar figures.

Vocabulary

dilation
enlargement (expansion)
fixed point (center) of a dilation
reduction (contraction)
scale factor of a dilation
similar figures

Assignment

- Intuitive: 1-18
- Standard: 1-24, 26-30
- Rigorous: 1-21 odd, 22-30

Resources

- *Visual Packet,* Similar, Congruent, Symmetrical. Focus on the top row of the poster about similar figures.
- *Activities Manual,* Topological Transformations in Principle. Looks at the different transformations related to topology.

Additional Problems

1. Find the image of point *Q* for the given dilation.
   Q' must lie on $\overrightarrow{PQ}$ and $\overline{AQ} \parallel \overline{A'Q'}$

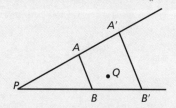

Presentation

Discuss the information concerning dilations as related to the dilating of the eye for an eye exam. Some students will have experienced this procedure.

Motivational Idea. This would be a good time to ask an ophthalmologist to come to class to discuss the use of mathematics in his profession. There is much geometry involved in the study of the eye and light.

Instruct the students to study the diagram at the beginning of this section. Discuss the material below the diagram; then state and explain the definition of *dilation* (also called *dilatation,* though this term is rarely used).

Motivational Idea. Show a diagram on an overhead transparency and then show it on the overhead projector. Point out how the overhead projector (like film and slide projectors) enlarges the diagram. Ask whether the diagram and the projected image are congruent (*no*). See if students can explain why (*the projected image is much larger*). Discuss the three possible results of a dilation transformation based on the scale factor, i.e., enlargement if *k* > 1, reduction if *k* < 1, and no change if *k* = 1.

Point out that although the figures are not congruent, they do have the same shape. When figures have the same shape but not necessarily the same size, they are called *similar*. Similar figures are the topic of Chapter 13.

Tips

Ex. 22. This one shows students that angle measures do not change under a dilation. This property of dilations foreshadows Section 12.4.

Ex. 23. This is another property of dilations.

Ex. 25. The scale factor of the given contraction is $0.8 = \frac{8}{10} = \frac{4}{5}$. The inverse of this contraction must expand in reciprocal ratio $\frac{5}{4} = 1.25$. ∎

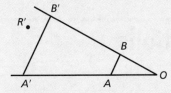

2. Find the preimage of the point R' for the given dilation. ***Draw $\overline{OR'}$ and $\overline{A'R'}$; then find R by making $\overline{AR}$ parallel to $\overline{A'R'}$.***

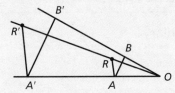

If O is the fixed point of a dilation with scale factor k, find the value of k for the given segments and their images.

3. $OA = 5$ units, $OA' = 25$ units $k = 5$

4. $OB = 3.5$ units, $OB' = 14$ units $k = 4$

5. $OC = 256$ units, $OC' = 32$ units $k = \frac{1}{8}$

The irregular tesselation by M. C. Escher entitled Circle Limit 3 *shows fish shapes successively reduced toward the circular border.*

If $k > 1$, then the dilation is an *enlargement* (or expansion) of the figure.

If $k = 1$, then the dilation does not change the size of the figure; it is the identity transformation.

If $0 < k < 1$, then the dilation results in a *reduction* (or contraction) of the figure.

Values of $k < 0$ can be studied in college.

EXAMPLE Classify the dilation by its scale factor.

Answer Measure the corresponding sides of △XYZ and △X'Y'Z'. Determine the scale factor of this dilation by finding the ratio $k = X'Y'/XY$. Since $0 < k < 1$, the dilation is a reduction, and the image of △XYZ is a smaller triangle, △X'Y'Z'.

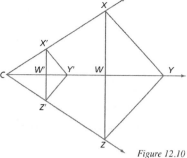

Figure 12.10

Answers
1. ≈ 2.6
2. $1\frac{1}{2}$
3. 45
4. 20 units
5. 8
6. $\frac{12}{5}$ units
7. 82
8. 15

Measure the angles of △XYZ in figure 12.10 and compare these angle measurements to the corresponding angle measures of △X'Y'Z'. You should find that corresponding angles have the same measure. This means that the triangles have the same shape even though they are not the same size.

When two geometric figures have the same shape but not necessarily the same size, the figures are called *similar figures*. A dilation always results in a similar figure. So in figure 12.10 △XYZ and △X'Y'Z' are similar, designated △XYZ ~ △X'Y'Z'. You will study similar figures in the next chapter.

► A. Exercises

For each diagram determine the scale factor that would take the figure to its image under a dilation with center O.

1.
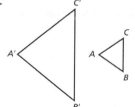

2.
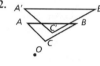

In a dilation, X is the center and A is mapped onto A'; B onto B'; and C onto C'. Find the indicated measure if the scale factor is 5.

3. $AX = 9$ units; find $A'X$
4. $AB = 4$ units; find $A'B'$
5. $XC' = 40$ units; find XC

6. $A'C' = 12$ units; find AC
7. $m\angle ABC = 82$; find $m\angle A'B'C'$
8. $m\angle B'C'A' = 15$; find $m\angle BCA$

9. 3, enlargement (or expansion)
10. $\frac{1}{4}$, reduction (or contraction)
11. 1, identity transformation
12. 2, enlargement (or expansion)
13. $\frac{y}{x}$
14. $\frac{2}{5}$
15. 1.67
16.

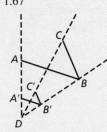

17. *see Answer section*

18. *see Answer section*

19.

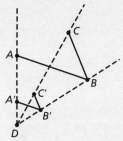

20.

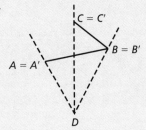

21.

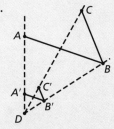

Under a certain dilation with center *P*, *L* is mapped onto *L'*, *K* is mapped onto *K'*, *M* is mapped onto *M'*, and *N* is mapped onto *N'*. Find the scale factor for each pair of measurements and classify the type of dilation.

9. *PL* = 10 units; *PL'* = 30 units   11. *M'N'* = 8 units; *MN* = 8 units
10. *PN* = 20 units; *PN'* = 5 units   12. *M'N'* = 14 units; *MN* = 7 units

▶ B. Exercises

Give the scale factor for the dilation that maps *KM* to *K'M'*.
13. *KM* = *x* units; *K'M'* = *y* units

For each diagram determine the scale factor that would take the figure to its image under a dilation with center *O*.

14.

15.

Trace the following figure onto your paper; then using *D* as center, find the image of the given points with the given scale factors.

16. $k = \frac{1}{2}$
17. $k = 3$
18. $k = 2$
19. $k = \frac{1}{3}$
20. $k = 1$
21. $k = \frac{1}{4}$
22. Measure $\angle ABC$ in the figure and then measure $\angle A'B'C'$ in exercises 16-20. What do you observe?
23. If *X-B-Y* in exercise 14, what can you say about *B'*?
24. Draw $\overleftrightarrow{AB}$ and a point *P* not on the line. Perform a dilation with fixed point *P* and a scale factor of 2. What kind of figure results? Do these figures have any special relation?

▶ C. Exercises

25. A contraction has a scale factor of 0.8. What dilation will return the image to its original size? What is the composition of these two dilations?

22. same measures
23. *X'-B'-Y'*
24. A line results; they are parallel.
25. expansion with same fixed point and scale factor 1.25; identity transformation

26. Prove that two parallel lines are everywhere equidistant.
27. Would exercise 26 be a theorem in Riemannian geometry? Why?

True/False
28. Parallel planes are everywhere equidistant.
29. Skew lines are everywhere equidistant.
30. A plane and a line parallel to the plane are everywhere equidistant.

12.4 Invariance Under Transformations

Invariance means "not varied," or "constant." Invariance in a Christian's spiritual life is important. The main goal of a Christian is to become more Christlike. God is constant and unchanging. James 1:17 states that there is no variableness with God. You need to be constant in obeying biblical truths and displaying godly traits. Consistency and dependability are characteristics that everyone needs to develop fully. Learn to be spiritually constant and true.

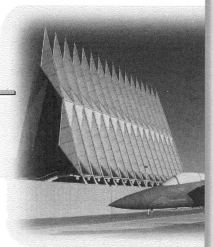

The design of the Air Force Academy chapel in Colorado Springs, Colorado, involves a repeated translation from the front to the back of the building.

Some transformations have invariant qualities. If the preimage and image of a given transformation always share a certain characteristic, the transformation *preserves* that characteristic.

You should remember that reflections, rotations, and translations all preserve distance because the image is always exactly the same size as the preimage.

Definition

An **isometry** is a transformation that preserves distance.

---

26. [7.6]

1. $\overleftrightarrow{AB} \parallel l$; $\overleftrightarrow{AC} \perp \overleftrightarrow{AB}$, where $\overleftrightarrow{AC}$ intersects l at C; and $\overleftrightarrow{BD} \perp \overleftrightarrow{AB}$, where $\overleftrightarrow{BD}$ intersects l at D	1. Given
2. $\overleftrightarrow{AC} \parallel \overleftrightarrow{BD}$	2. Lines perpendicular to the same line are parallel
3. $ABDC$ is a parallelogram	3. Definition of parallelogram
4. $\overline{AC} \cong \overline{BD}$	4. Opposite sides of a parallelogram are congruent
5. $AC = BD$	5. Definition of congruent segments [7.6]

27. No, there are no parallels. [10.8]
28. True [10.4]
29. False [10.4]
30. True [10.4]

12.4

Invariance Under Transformations

Objectives

1. To identify and prove properties of transformations.
2. To define isometry.

Presentation

Discuss the spiritual principle that opens this section. Stress the importance of consistency in the lives of your students.

Ask which types of transformations always result in images that are congruent to the preimage. (*reflections, translations, and rotations*) Explain that when a transformation has the property that every image is always congruent to its preimage, it is called an *isometry* (meaning equal measure). Ask students to give an example of an isometry other than the three types named above (*a reflection followed by a rotation, or any other composition*). Then point out the list of isometries on page 516.

Tell students that a given transformation, *T*, is an isometry. If a segment is 2 units long, how long is its image? (*2 units*) Repeat the exchange for a segment of 7 units. Ask them how they know (*isometry means that images must have equal measures to the preimage*). In other words, every isometry preserves distance. Whenever preimages and images must have the same property, the transformation is said to *preserve* that property. Isometries are a type of transformation that preserves distance.

Common Student Error. Some students confuse which distances must be equal when distance is preserved. For points *P* and *Q* with images *P'* and *Q'* respectively under an isometry, $PQ = P'Q'$. However, $PP' = QQ'$ is generally false. The key idea to convey is that however far apart a pair of points are, they will be the same distance apart after the transformation.

Motivational Idea. Have students illustrate each of the six properties of isometry.

Discuss Theorem 12.1 with the class. The students may ask why Theorem 12.1 refers to at most three reflections when we know that translation and rotation involve only two reflections. Remind them that all compositions of reflections are isometries. Thus, the composition of a translation and a reflection (called a *glide*) requires three reflections. Show examples of the composition of three or fewer reflections.

Remind students that reflections reverse the orientation of a figure (if the vertices of a triangle are labeled clockwise in the preimage the

Vocabulary

invariance   preserve
isometry

Assignment

- Intuitive: no assignment necessary
- Standard: 1-14, 21-26
- Rigorous: 1-26

Resources

- *Visual Packet,* Similar, Congruent, Symmetrical. Use the poster to compare similar and congruent figures.
- *Activities Manual,* Construction Skills. Looks at a method to construct a regular 15-gon and a regular 30-gon.
- *Test Packet,* Quiz 2, Chapter 12 covers Sections 12.3 and 12.4.

Reading and Writing Mathematics

Given that ⊙*O* rests in space above and entirely out of plane *k*. Ask the students to write a description of all possible figures that could result if the circle is projected directly downward into the plane.   ***A circle if the plane of the circle is parallel to plane k, a segment equal in length to the diameter of circle O if the plane of the circle is perpendicular to plane k, an ellipse if the plane of the circle intersects plane k at any other angle. (Students may not be familiar with the term ellipse. They may use oval or elongated circle.)***

Additional Problems

1. When does the composition of two rotations result in a rotation?   ***when the rotations have the same center***

2. Is orientation preserved by isometries? Explain.   ***No, reflections are isometries that reverse orientation.***

3. Name something else that may not be preserved by isometries.   ***direction of figure, location***

The word *isometry* has a Greek origin. *Isos* means "equal," and *metron* means "measure." So the basic meaning of *isometry* is "equal measure." You have studied the following isometries.

Isometries

Reflection

Translation

Rotation

Identity transformation

Composite of isometries

Six invariant properties are listed below. Remember that each of these invariant properties is left unchanged by the isometries that you have studied.

Properties of Isometries

1. *Distance is preserved.* This property is guaranteed by the definition. Example: If $AB = 3$, then after a rotation $A'B' = 3$.

2. *Collinearity of points is preserved.* Example: If A, B, and C are collinear, then A', B', and C' are collinear after a reflection.

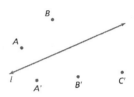

Figure 12.11

3. *Betweenness of points is preserved.* Example: If X-Y-Z, then after a translation X'-Y'-Z'.

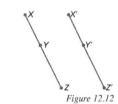

Figure 12.12

4. *Angle measure is preserved.* Example: If $\triangle ABC$ is reflected across line l, then $m\angle ABC = m\angle A'B'C'$.

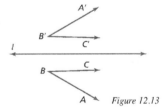

Figure 12.13

---

image vertices will run counterclockwise). Orientation is important because it is an example of a property that isometries do not preserve. We can classify isometries based on orientation. Translations and rotations preserve orientation (*same*), while reflections and glides reverse orientation (*opposite*). Ask students the orientation after an even number of reflections (*same*) and then after an odd number (*opposite*).

Ask for an example of a transformation that does not preserve distance (*dilation*). Dilations generally do not preserve distance and are therefore not isometries. Discuss and illustrate the properties of dilation. Mention that a homothety is a composition of a translation

and a dilation. Ask whether it preserves distance (*no*) or angle measure (*yes*). Allow students time to begin their assignment.

Ex. 6. Students who recognize the letter *A* will quickly see that this is a reflection. Some who see only one figure may reason that the figure has been mapped onto itself and give the identity transformation as an answer. This alternate answer is acceptable.

Ex. 19. Although the two lines of reflection may vary, the angle between them and the point of intersection should be identical to that in the key. ■

5. *Parallelism is preserved.* Example: If $\overleftrightarrow{A'B'} \parallel \overleftrightarrow{C'D'}$ and the lines are rotated around a point, then $\overleftrightarrow{A'B'} \parallel \overleftrightarrow{C'D'}$.

6. *Triangle congruence is preserved.* Example: If $\triangle XYZ$ is translated, then $\triangle XYZ \cong \triangle X'Y'Z'$.

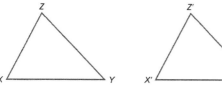

Figure 12.14

Since collinearity, betweenness, and distance are preserved, it follows that subsets of lines are preserved. In other words, the image of a ray is always a ray, and the image of a segment is always a segment, and so on.

An interesting theorem about isometries is given here without a proof.

Theorem 12.1
Isometry Theorem. **Every isometry can be expressed as a composition of at most three reflections.**

Dilations do not preserve distance and so are not isometries. Since dilations preserve angle measure, they preserve shape but may not preserve size. A transformation that preserves shape is a similarity while a transformation that preserves both size and shape is an isometry.

Properties of Dilation
1. A dilation preserves collinearity of points.
2. A dilation preserves betweenness of points.
3. A dilation preserves angle measure.
4. A dilation preserves parallel lines.

Of course similarities and isometries are not the only types of transformations. It is possible to have a transformation with none of these invariant properties. For example, the transformation that doubles the distance from a given line l is neither an isometry nor a dilation because it does not preserve angle measure.

For each transformation T, which of the six properties are preserved by T? Is T an isometry?

4. T translates all points of one half-plane two units right and all points of the other half-plane two units left. ***no property preserved, not an isometry***

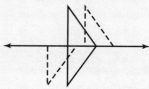

5. T doubles the distance of each point from the line. ***preserves collinearity, betweenness, and parallelism only, not an isometry (does not preserve distance, angle measure, or triangle congruence)***

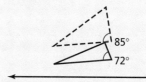

Answers

1. translation, isometry
2. rotation, isometry
3. dilation (reduction), not an isometry
4. reflection, isometry
5. identity transformation, isometry
6. reflection
7. rotation
8. translation
9. translation

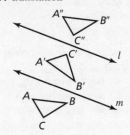

10. rotation

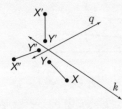

11. a subset of a line because collinearity is preserved
12. an angle since angle measure is preserved by similarities
13. parallel lines since parallelism is preserved by isometries
14. distance, triangle congruence
15. 180° rotation around C

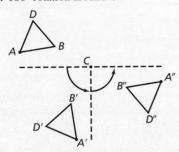

16.

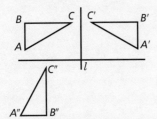

17. enlarge from point P by a scale factor of 3

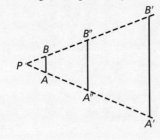

18. Find the perpendicular bisector of $\overline{CC'}$, reflect △ABC across l_1 to obtain the intermediate stage △A'B'C'. Construct the perpendicular bisector $\overline{B'B''}$ to obtain l_2. The bisectors intersect at the center.

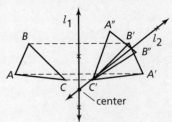

► A. Exercises

Name the type of transformation illustrated by each pair of figures. Which are isometries?

1.

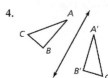

2.

3.

4.

5.

Name the type of transformation illustrated in each figure below.

6.   7. A   8. B B

Trace the following onto your paper and then find the image and identify the type of isometry.

9. Reflect △ABC in m; then reflect it in l.   10. Reflect $\overline{XY}$ in q; then reflect it in k.

► B. Exercises

If each figure below is transformed as indicated, what must the image be and why?

11. A subset of a line by an isometry
12. An angle by a reduction
13. Parallel lines by a reflection
14. Which two properties are invariant for isometries but not for similarities?

Draw the following transformations and, if possible, give the following composite transformations in simpler form.

15. Point *A* rotated 90° around *C* and then rotated another 90° around *C*

16. △*ABC* reflected in *l* and then rotated 90° clockwise around *B*

17. $\overline{AB}$ enlarged from point *P* by a scale factor of 6 and then contracted from point *P* by a scale factor of $\frac{1}{2}$

•*P*

18. Find the center of rotation.

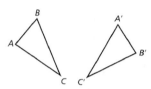

▶ C. Exercises

19. Use Theorem 12.1 to prove that every isometry preserves angle measure (property 4).
20. Prove that every isometry preserves triangle congruence. (*Hint:* Just prove △*ABC* ≅ △*A‴B‴C‴*.)

Cumulative Review

Name a *theorem* that could be used to show that two *segments* are congruent if the segments are related to the figure indicated.

21. quadrilateral
22. triangle
23. circle
24. perpendiculars
25. lines
26. space

19.

1. An isometry *I* and ∠*A*	1. Given
2. *I* = *T* ∘ *S* ∘ *R*	2. Isometry Theorem
3. ∠*A* ≅ ∠*A*′, where *R*(∠*A*) = ∠*A*′; ∠*A*′ ≅ ∠*A*″, where *S*(∠*A*′) = ∠*A*″; ∠*A*″ ≅ ∠*A*‴, where *T*(∠*A*″) = ∠*A*‴	3. Exercise 17, Section 12.1
4. ∠*A* ≅ ∠*A*‴	4. Transitive property of congruent angles
5. *m*∠*A* = *m*∠*A*‴	5. Definition of congruent angles

20.

1. Isometry *I*	1. Given
2. *I* = *T* ∘ *S* ∘ *R*	2. Isometry Theorem
3. △*ABC* ≅ △*A*′*B*′*C*′ where *R*(△*ABC*) = △*A*′*B*′*C*′; △*A*′*B*′*C*′ ≅ △*A*″*B*″*C*″ where *S*(△*A*′*B*′*C*′) = △*A*″*B*″*C*″; △*A*″*B*″*C*″ ≅ △*A*‴*B*‴*C*‴ where *T*(△*A*″*B*″*C*″) = △*A*‴*B*‴*C*‴	3. Exercise 17, Section 12.1
4. △*ABC* ≅ △*A*‴*B*‴*C*‴	4. Transitive property of congruent triangles

21. opposite sides of parallelogram or diagonals of a rectangle [7.6]
22. Isosceles Triangle Theorem: A triangle is an equiangular triangle if and only if it is equilateral. [6.7]
23. radii, chords equidistant from center, or chords subtended by congruent arcs [9.1]
24. Points on the perpendicular bisector of a segment are equidistant from the endpoints or points on the perpendicular bisecting plane are equidistant from the endpoints. [7.2]
25. bisections of congruent segments [6.1]
26. Altitudes between parallel planes are congruent or opposite edges of parallelepiped are congruent or radii of a sphere are congruent. [10.4]

David Hilbert

Geometry Through History

Objectives

1. To appreciate the contribution Hilbert made to the foundations of geometry.
2. To gain insight into the time and effort necessary for success in mathematics.

DAVID HILBERT

Resources

- Appendix H for Hilbert's parallel postulate.
- Introduction to *Teacher's Edition* for information on his philosophy of formalism.

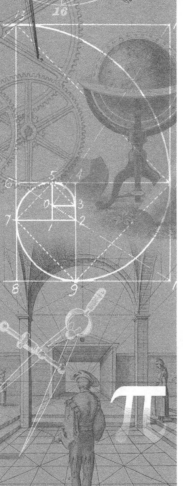

On January 23, 1862, David Hilbert was born to Maria and Otto Hilbert in Königsberg, East Prussia, which is now a part of Russia. Königsberg was close to the Baltic Sea, and David became familiar with boats and the life of a fisherman. His mother was his first teacher, and she introduced him to the constellations and to prime numbers. His father was a very strict judge who strongly believed in living a proper life. He tried to instill virtues such as punctuality, thrift, and discipline into his young son.

At the age of eight, David started his formal education at the Vorschule of the royal Friedrichskolleg. The Hilbert family became close friends with a Jewish family named the Minkowskis. Their children, who were about David's age, were good mathematicians, and they influenced David in this area. David did not do exceptionally well in most subjects, because he had great trouble memorizing material, but mathematics appealed to him because it was easy for him. In 1879 he transferred to Wilhelm Gymnasium, a school that placed much emphasis on the subject. David did excellent work in mathematics there.

In 1880 Hilbert entered the University of Königsberg, where he concentrated on mathematics. He and his friend Herman Minkowski studied there together and shared a deep love for mathematics. On February 7, 1885, Hilbert received his doctor of philosophy degree, and by 1893 he had attained a full professorship at the university. While at Königsberg, Hilbert married Käthe Jerosch. In 1895 the Hilberts moved to the University of Göttingen, where he had a long teaching and research career.

Presentation

Have your students read the biographical sketch of David Hilbert. His most relevant contribution to this course is his correction of Euclid. For a statement of his parallel postulate, see Appendix H.

Use questions such as the following to stimulate interest and discussion. Sometimes it helps to have students write a few thoughts about each question before the discussion starts. Some students need time to do their own thinking before being influenced by others.

1. Why do you think Hilbert had trouble with other subjects and not mathematics?
2. What effect did Hilbert's father have on Hilbert's career in mathematics?

3. What importance did the eight years between Hilbert's doctorate and his receiving a full professorship play in his receiving that appointment?
4. Do you think Hilbert's work on geometry was as important as Euclid's?
5. Why do you think Hilbert was more interested in consistency than in truth?

Hilbert's philosophy is called formalism and is critiqued in Chapter 12 of the *Activities Manual*. Although Hilbert made many valuable contributions to mathematics, his philosophy was not one of them. ∎

David Hilbert studied number theory and was the first to show that if a geometric contradiction existed, then the corresponding arithmetic of real numbers must also contain contradictions. He also believed in establishing a definite step-by-step procedure for solving problems. In fact, in 1899 his book *Grundlagen der Geometrie* (*Foundations of Geometry*) provided the first systematic treatment of geometry that corrected Euclid's flaws. To him we owe the use of undefined terms (point, line, and plane) as well as the need for more postulates. He used twenty-one postulates, including the axioms of continuity. He also restated the Parallel Postulate in a form similar to the Historic Parallel Postulate.

In Paris in 1900 he gave a lecture to an international math convention in which he challenged mathematicians with twenty-three unsolved problems. Some of these are still unsolved and his challenge has stimulated much of the research of this century.

Hilbert also studied an infinite dimensional geometry called Hilbert Space. In the space, the square of the infinitely many coordinates must have a finite sum. Transformations of many kinds can be studied in Hilbert Space.

Hilbert developed a philosophy of mathematics that abandoned any considerations about the truth of mathematics and was concerned only about the consistency of the mathematical system. He studied proof theory in relation to his philosophy but was never able to establish the truth of the philosophy. Hilbert's philosophy was dangerous because it threw out truth at the beginning. Nothing can be built without certain true building blocks. Therefore, one must be sure that his knowledge is built on a true foundation.

In 1942 Hilbert fell and broke his arm. As a result of complications from the fall, he died on February 4, 1943.

He also believed in establishing a definite step-by-step procedure for solving problems.

Applications
of Isometries

12.5 Applications
of Isometries

Objectives

To apply isometries to the solutions of specific problems of a practical nature.

Assignment
- Intuitive: 1-12, 16-17
- Standard: 1-19, 21-25
- Rigorous: 6-25

Resources
- *Activities Manual,* Isometries in Detail. Takes a closer look at isometries and proofs involving them.
- *Test Packet,* Quiz 3, Chapter 12 covers Sections 12.5 and 12.6.

Reading and Writing Mathematics

Give the students a double nappe cone with *P* as the vertex point and with axis *k*. Ask them to write a description of how you would pass a plane through the figure to generate an intersection that is a) a circle, b) a parabola.
a) perpendicular to the axis, b) parallel to an element in the surface of the cone

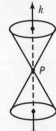

You may often ask (and justifiably so), "When will I ever use this?" You are probably asking that question now about transformations and isometries. One pure mathematical reason for studying isometries is to give a new light to the idea of congruence. But besides the pure mathematical applications of isometries, there are also some practical applications.

The Belle of Louisville is the oldest of the six remaining sternwheel-style steamboats in the U.S. Its sixteen paddle blades (called bucket planks) are isometric and rotate around the hub, and each blade consists of five panels that are side by side (translated) and are also isometric.

EXAMPLE 1   A beam will be sent from satellite *A* to satellite *B* by being sent to the earth and reflected by a booster station to satellite *B*. The satellite engineers are trying to place the booster station in the spot where the total distance that the beam travels will be the shortest. If the booster station must be located somewhere along line *h*, what is the best location?

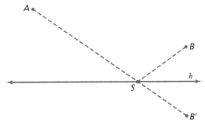

Figure 12.15

Answer   1. To find the appropriate location of the booster station, *S*, first reflect *B* in *h* to find *B'*.
2. Connect *A* and *B'*.
3. The point where $\overline{AB'}$ intersects *h* is the appropriate location for the booster station.

Presentation

Motivational Idea. If possible, set up a couple of holes of miniature golf that require bank shots. You will need to bring putters and golf balls. Have each student putt a couple of times and record his scores.

Ask students if they think geometry can help their game. Discuss examples 1 and 2, which apply isometries in their solutions. Example 1 will require careful preparation to remember the steps. In example 2, point out that the hole is reflected first across the last line of ricochet. Also, observe that some walls (such as side 1) need to be extended in order to draw the reflections.

Explain that the principles of reflection apply in miniature golf, billiards, and even bowling.

Lenses for everything from cameras to telescopes also involve reflections. Emphasize that light (or ball without spin) always bounces off something at the same angle that it arrived. More technically, the angle of incidence is equal to the angle of reflection. Students have studied this in physical science, but review will help. Emphasize the fact and have students write it in their notes.

Let them play another round of your mini-golf and suggest that they try to beat their previous score using the principles of reflection. Not all will beat their score because such skill requires practice, but those who never aimed when putting will show marked improvement. The activity should be fun and will emphasize the relevance of geometry to the skill.

Tips

Ex. 23. All the points on the mirror line are fixed. ∎

You should be asking, "How do I know that $\overline{AS}$ to $\overline{SB}$ represents the shortest path?" Suppose we said some other point on h, called T, was the correct answer.

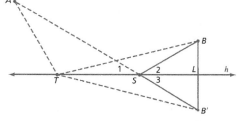

If our assumption is true, then $AT + TB < AS + SB$. If we can prove this statement false, S would be the correct position for the booster station. Since reflections preserve distance, $\overline{SB}$ and its reflection $\overline{SB'}$, must be congruent. Likewise, $\overline{TB}$ must be congruent to $\overline{TB'}$. So $AS + SB = AS + SB'$, and $AT + TB = AT + TB'$. Now consider $\triangle ATB'$. Do you remember what the Triangle Inequality states? From this theorem we can conclude that $AT + TB' > AB'$. Because of betweenness of points, $AS + SB' = AB'$. By substitution $AT + TB' > AS + SB'$. Also by substitution $AT + TB > AS + SB$. This contradicts the preliminary assumption, so T cannot be the correct location. Therefore, S must be the correct position for the booster station.

One more example is given before you do some problems on your own.

EXAMPLE 2   Figure 12.17 shows a miniature golf green. Notice that it would be impossible to putt a ball directly from the tee (T) to the hole (H). What spots should you aim for on sides 1 and 2 so that you will make a hole in one?

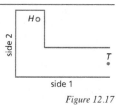

Figure 12.17

Answer
1. Reflect H in side 2.
2. Reflect H' in side 1.
3. Connect H'' and T; the point of intersection of this segment and side 1 is the point you need to aim for on side 1.
4. Connect the point of intersection found in step 3 and H' to find the intersection with side 2.

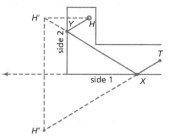

Additional Problems

1. Draw the shot on the miniature golf hole that would produce a hole in one by hitting exactly 2 parallel sides.

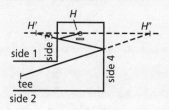

2. Draw the shot that would produce a hole in one by hitting exactly 2 adjacent sides.

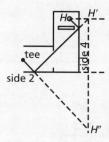

3. Two towns on opposite sides of a river are to be joined by a road that takes the shortest path; the new bridge across the river must be perpendicular to the shorelines. Write a plan for finding the location of the bridge and draw a diagram showing its location. ***Plan: We know the shortest path would be a straight line but the bridge being perpendicular to the shorelines causes a problem. Let A and B represent the towns. Temporarily eliminate the river by translating B a distance equal to the width of the river and in the direction perpendicular to the river. Call this point B′. At P make the bridge perpendicular across to Q. Then head straight to B. See diagram.***

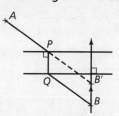

Answers

1.

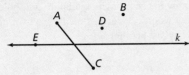

2. Shortest distance between two points is a line.

3.

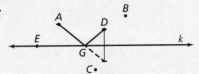

4. $AE + ED \cong AG + GD$

5.

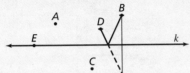

6.

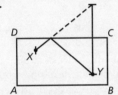

7.

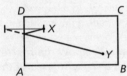

8.

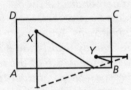

9.

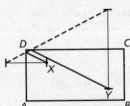

10.

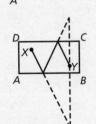

11.

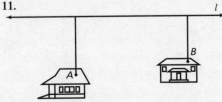

▶ A. Exercises

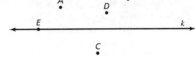

Trace the diagram onto your paper and then follow the steps in exercises 1-5.

1. Find the point on k that marks the shortest distance from A to C.
2. Explain why E is not the answer to exercise 1.
3. Find the point G on k that marks the shortest distance from A to k to D.
4. Compare $AG + GD$ to $AE + ED$.
5. Find the point on k that marks the shortest distance from D to k to B.

An electron moves from point X to Y by bouncing off the sides of a four-sided enclosure. Find the path it will follow if it bounces off the given side(s).

6. $\overline{DC}$
7. $\overline{AD}$
8. $\overline{AB}$ and then $\overline{BC}$
9. $\overline{AD}$ and then $\overline{DC}$
10. $\overline{AB}$ and then $\overline{DC}$

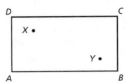

▶ B. Exercises

The telephone company wants to connect two houses to the main line in the least expensive way. To reduce expenses, they want to use the least amount of wire possible. The drawing below illustrates the problem.

11. Find the places on the phone line, l, where the two houses should be connected.

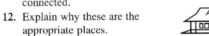

12. Explain why these are the appropriate places.
13. What theorem was used to prove that the method of reflection provides the point on a line with the shortest distance to two points?
14. Name three types of transformations that preserve distance.
15. What is a transformation called that preserves distance?

Here is the first hole on a miniature golf course. Find the appropriate place to aim your putt for a hole in one under the following conditions.

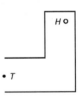

16. By hitting one side
17. By hitting two sides
18. By hitting three sides
19. By hitting four sides

12. Perpendicular distance is the shortest distance from a point (house) to a line.
13. Triangle Inequality
14. reflection, rotation, translation
15. isometry
16. impossible

17.

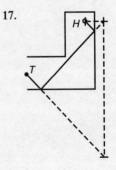

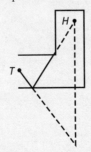

20. Putt from the tee to the hole by hitting all five sides.

Cumulative Review

21. What is the fixed point of a rotation called?
22. How many fixed points does a translation have?
23. How many fixed points does a reflection have?
24. If T is a transformation that is a dilation and X is the fixed point, what is $T(X)$?
25. If an isometry has three noncollinear fixed points, what can you conclude?

12.6 Symmetry

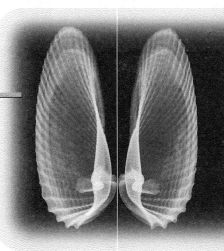

If you reflect the left side of the seashell across line l, it coincides with the right side. The line drawn in the photograph of the shell is called the *axis of symmetry*, and the figure is said to be symmetric.

Seashells display line symmetry.

Definition

A figure has **line symmetry** when each half of the figure is the image of the other half under some reflection in a line.

In figure 12.18 three symmetric geometric figures are shown. Can you find an axis of symmetry for each figure?

Figure 12.18

12.6 SYMMETRY **525**

12.6

Symmetry

Objectives

To define and illustrate the three types of plane symmetry—line, rotational, and point.

Vocabulary

axis of symmetry	point symmetry
line symmetry	rotational symmetry

Assignment

- Intuitive: 1-17, 21-25, and Symmetry activity (*Activities Manual*)
- Standard: 1-19, 21-25, and Symmetry activity (*Activities Manual*)
- Rigorous: 1-25 and Calculator activity (*Activities Manual*)

Resources

- *Visual Packet,* Similar, Congruent, Symmetrical. Use the third row of the poster to summarize symmetry.
- *Activities Manual,* Symmetry in Brief. Helps students gain a better understanding of symmetry by creating various designs.
- *Activities Manual,* Calculator Skills. Looks at methods of using a calculator and symmetry ideas to find areas.

....

20.

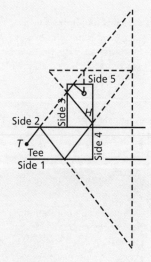

21. center [12.4]
22. none [12.2]
23. infinitely many [12.4]
24. X [12.2]
25. It's the identity. [12.4]

18.

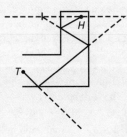

19.

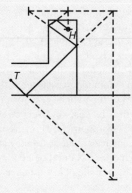

Reading and Writing Mathematics

As a continuation of the Reading and Writing Math in 12.5, have the students give a written description of how a plane would have to pass through the double nappe cone previously described to produce the so-called degenerate conics, that is a) a point, b) a single line, and c) two intersecting lines. *a) through point P perpendicular to the axis, b) passing through P and lying on and tangent to an element in the surface of the cone, c) containing the axis of the cone in its entirety*

Flash

The main stem of the mimosa is the line of symmetry with leaflets matched in pairs. You may wish to point out that each leaflet is also symmetric.

Additional Problems

What kinds of symmetry does each figure have?
1. A regular polygon   **point, line, and rotational symmetry**
2. A cross   **line symmetry**

3. Do isometries preserve symmetry? Explain. **Yes, they preserve congruence so they preserve shape as well as size.**

Answers

1. one axis (horizontal)

2. four axes (diagonals of octagon shown)

3. no axes
4. two axes (vertical and horizontal)

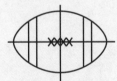

5. one axis (vertical)

6. five axes (connect each point of star through the center)

Another form of symmetry is called *rotational symmetry.*

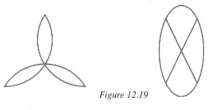

Definition

A figure has **rotational symmetry** when the image of the figure coincides with the figure after a rotation. The magnitude of the rotation must be less than 360°.

The left diagram in figure 12.19 has rotational symmetry. Trace it onto your paper and place the traced figure on top of the figure in the book. By keeping the center fixed, rotate the figure until it again coincides with the figure in the book. Since you rotated your paper 120°, the figure has a rotational symmetry of 120°.

Figure 12.19

Rotational symmetry of 180° is also called *point symmetry.* The right diagram in figure 12.14 provides an example of point symmetry. Notice that you can "reflect" each point of the figure through the center of the rotation to obtain another point of the figure.

The stem is the axis of symmetry for this mimosa.

▶ A. Exercises

How many axes of symmetry does each figure have?

1.
3.
5.

2.
4.
6.

Presentation

The photographs in this section illustrate line symmetry. Ask your students to name some other objects that are symmetrical. During this discussion, give the definition of *line symmetry.* While most living things display some kind of symmetry, it is never perfect. The two sides of the butterfly or flower are not exact mirror images; however, we see them as nearly symmetrical. Humans are right-left symmetrical, but again they are close but not perfect. Natural objects such as crystals and man-made objects such as buildings and vehicles have nearly perfect symmetry. However, careful measurements reveal invisible margins of error.

Do the exercises involving figure 12.18, in which the students must find the line of symmetry. Point out that each of these figures has a different number of lines of symmetry. The triangle has one—the altitude through *C*. The circle has infinitely many—one through each diameter. The rectangle has two—the perpendicular bisectors of *XW* and *XU*.

Motivational Idea. A small hand-held mirror is helpful in finding lines of symmetry. Test the suspected line of symmetry by standing the mirror on the line. If the reflected half looks the same as the original, it is a line of symmetry. You may want to bring photos of faces (front views from yearbooks or magazines) for practice.

7.

8.

▶ B. Exercises

9. Which figures in exercises 1-8 have rotational symmetry?
10. List the angle of rotation for each rotational symmetry of exercise 9.
11. Which figures in exercises 1-8 have point symmetry?

Draw each figure listed in exercises 12-17 and then draw all lines of symmetry. Identify any figures with rotational symmetry.

12. A square
13. A parallelogram
14. A regular pentagon
15. A concave hexagon
16. An isosceles triangle
17. A circle with one diameter
18. Can a figure have point symmetry without having rotational symmetry? Why?
19. A figure has 90° rotational symmetry. Will it also have point symmetry?

▶ C. Exercises

20. Classify the capital letters of the alphabet according to the number of axes of line symmetry. Identify *any* rotational symmetry.

▪ Cumulative Review

Let U = the set of integers.
$A = \{x \mid -3 \leq x < 2 \text{ and } x \text{ is an integer}\}$
$B = \{1, 2, 4, 8, 16, \ldots\}$
$C = \{5^0, -\sqrt{9}\}$
$D = \{x \mid x \text{ is a prime number}\}$

21. Write set C in simpler form; then write the correct subset relation for C.
22. Express sets A and D in list form.
23. Express set B in set-builder notation.
24. Find $B \cap D$ and $A \cap D$.
25. Find $A \cup C$ and $B \cup C$.

---

7. no axes
8. one axis (vertical)

9. #2, 4, 6, 7
10. #2-45, 90, 135, 180, 225, 270, 315
    #4-180, #6-72, 144, 216, 288, #7-180
11. #2, 4, 7
12. rotational symmetry

13.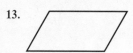

14. rotational symmetry

15.

16. no rotational symmetry

17.

18. No, point symmetry is 180° rotational symmetry.
19. Yes, because it will also have 180° symmetry.
20. no symmetry: *F, G, J, L, P, Q, R*
    one axis that is horizontal: *B, C, D, E, K*
    one axis that is vertical: *A, M, T, U, V, W, Y*
    two axes (horizontal and vertical) *H, I, X*
    infinitely many axes: *O*
    rotational symmetry: *N, O, S, Z*
21. $\{1, -3\}, C \subseteq A$ [1.1]
22. $A = \{-3, -2, -1, 0, 1\}$
    $D = \{2, 3, 5, 7, 11, \ldots\}$ [1.1]
23. $B = \{x \mid x \text{ is a power of 2}\}$ or $B = \{x \mid x = 2n, \text{ where } n \text{ is a whole number}\}$ [1.1]
24. $\{2\}, \varnothing$ [1.2]
25. $A \cup C = \{-3, -2, -1, 0, 1\} = A$,
    $B \cup C = \{-3, 1, 2, 4, 8, 16, \ldots\}$ [1.2]

Define rotational and point symmetry as in the text and see if your students can give examples of each of these types of symmetry. The following questions focus on the three different kinds of symmetry.

1. Does 90° rotational symmetry imply point symmetry? **yes**
2. Does point symmetry imply 90° rotational symmetry? **no**
3. Do two perpendicular mirrors of line symmetry imply point symmetry? **yes**
4. Does point symmetry imply two perpendicular mirrors of line symmetry? **no**
5. Does line symmetry imply point symmetry? **no**
6. Does rotational symmetry imply point symmetry? **no**
7. Does point symmetry imply rotational symmetry? **yes**

Tips

Ex. 15. While most concave hexagons have no symmetry, it is possible to draw some that have all types (such as a bow-tie shape).

Ex. 16. If the isosceles triangle is equilateral, it also has rotational symmetry.

Ex. 20. Assume basic forms of capital letters. These are not intended to be tricky. ▪

Geometry and Scripture

1. To identify how the term *transformation* is used in Scripture.
2. To identify instances of transformations in Scripture to help students understand the root of the mathematical term.
3. To compare and contrast the term *translation* as used in Scripture and in mathematics.

Answers

1. Renew the mind.
2. the Bible
3. Holy Ghost
4. day by day
5. Jesus was transfigured: His form changed, so the disciples could see His glory.
6. to be like His glorious body
7. Satan and the demons changing form to pose as saints

Geometry *and* Scripture

Remember how God transformed Paul into a man of God? The word *transformed* comes from the idea of a change (*trans*) in form. No Christian is perfect, so all must desire God to change or transform them. God changes both our mind and our body.

1. How does Romans 12:2 tell us to be transformed?
2. Colossians 3:10 says that our new nature in Christ is "renewed in knowledge" of our Creator. Where do we get this knowledge?
3. Who gives us this knowledge and transforms us according to Titus 3:5?
4. How often should we seek this knowledge and let Him transform us (II Cor. 4:16)?
5. Matthew 17:2 and Mark 9:2-3 related a change in form of our Lord Jesus. What happened?
6. Into what does Christ transform our bodies according to Philippians 3:20-21?
7. What kind of transformation is discussed in II Corinthians 11:13-15?

Presentation

Of course, the transformations and translations in the Bible are not used in their technical mathematical sense. However, the mathematical term was chosen for its descriptive power. A study of the root words should help students better grasp the mathematical concept.

The Line upon Line verse describes the translation of Enoch as an analogy to mathematical translation. The verse also reminds us of the example Enoch set in pleasing God. His fellowship with God was so close that God took him directly to heaven. You may wish to read Genesis 5:21-24 for the background to the verse in Hebrews. ■

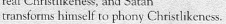

You have just studied three kinds of transformations. God transforms minds to real Christ-likeness, he transforms bodies to real Christlikeness, and Satan transforms himself to phony Christlikeness. This can help you understand transformations in math. Such transformations also represent changes in the position or form of figures.

8. Name three kinds of transformations in math in which the size and shape do not change but the position changes. What is the general term for this?

9. Name two kinds of transformations in which the size changes but not the shape. What is the general term for this?

Did you notice that a translation in math is a transformation that changes the position of the figure? In the Bible, "translation" also emphasizes a change of position.

10. Read Hebrews 11:5. What happened to Enoch?

HIGHER PLANE: Find the Old Testament reference to the translation of Enoch. Was it before or after the Flood?

Hebrews 11:5 refers to Enoch's translation three times. This "translation" clearly conveys the "change in position" idea. The term is used two other times, but in those passages the "change in position" is used more figuratively to describe a change.

11. What change in "position" have Christians already experienced according to Colossians 1:13?

12. The other reference to translation in Scripture is in II Samuel 3:10. Describe the change in this passage.

> ### Line upon Line
> By faith Enoch was translated that he should not see death; and was not found, because God had translated him: for before his translation he had this testimony, that he pleased God. ❧
>
> HEBREWS 11:5

8. reflections, translations, rotations; isometry
9. enlargement, reduction; *dilation* (the term for the transformations), or *similarity* (the term for the pair of figures)
10. God translated him to heaven.

Higher Plane
Genesis 5:24, before the Flood

11. They become part of Christ's kingdom at salvation.
12. Saul's kingdom transferred to David

Chapter 12

Review

Objective
To help students prepare for evaluation.

Vocabulary
See Appendix A.

Assignment
• Intuitive: 1-4, 11-25, 30
• Standard: 1-30
• Rigorous: 1-30

Resources
• *Activities Manual,* Cumulative Review
• *Activities Manual,* Terms and Symbols
• *Activities Manual,* Practice
• *Test Packet,* Chapter 12 Exam

Answers

1.
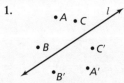

2.
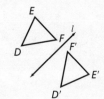

3.
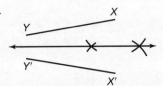

4.
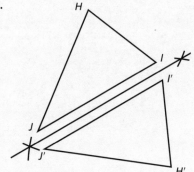

5. rotation
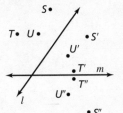

6. translation
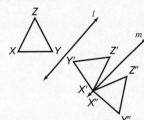

Chapter 12 Review

Trace the figures below and find the reflections in line *l*.

1.
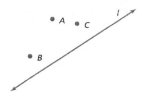

2.
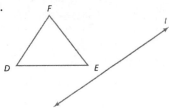

Find the line of reflection for each of these transformations.

3.
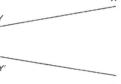

4.
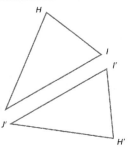

Trace the following figures and then find the composite of two reflections for each exercise. Tell whether the transformations performed result in a reflection, translation, or rotation.

5.
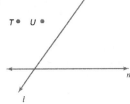

6.
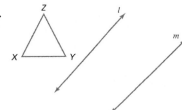

Presentation

Motivational Idea. Separate the students into groups of three or four students. Have each group create a test for this chapter. Each test must include at least two questions from each section and one proof at the end. Groups can exchange tests and work them as a group. You may prefer to make copies of these tests so that the students can take them home and work on them as review and bring them back the next day to be graded by the group that originated the test. When students make up tests, they review and anticipate questions and topics that will be on the test that you give. ■

7.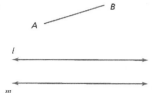

8.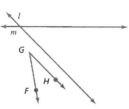

9. If the angle of rotation is 76°, what is the measure of the acute angle between the intersecting lines?

10. Find the correct isometry for the pair of congruent triangles shown.

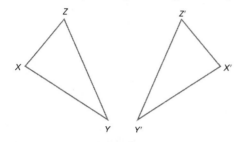

11. An underground cable is to be installed to connect two houses to the main telephone line that runs along the curb of the street. If both lines are to be connected at the same point and the least amount of cable possible is to be used, where should the cable be connected to the main line? The figure below shows the location of the houses and the main line.

7. translation

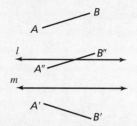

8. rotation

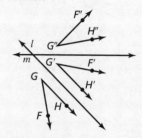

9. 38°

10.

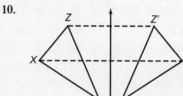

reflection

11.

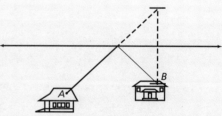

12. window
13. house
14. face
15. pinwheel
16. 120°
17. window
18. 12
19. 17
20.

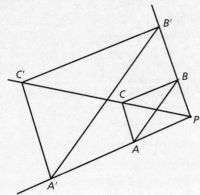

21. similar
22. congruent
23. neither
24. similar

Consider the four figures below.

12. Which has both line symmetry and rotational symmetry?
13. Which has neither line symmetry nor rotational symmetry?
14. Which has line symmetry only?
15. Which has rotational symmetry only?
16. Give the magnitude of the rotational symmetry for exercise 15.
17. Which has point symmetry?

Given a scale factor of $k = 3$, answer exercises 18-20.
18. If $MN = 4$, find $M'N'$.
19. If $P'Q' = 51$, find PQ.
20. Using $\triangle ABC$ and point P as shown, find $\triangle A'B'C'$.

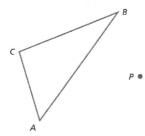

Identify $\triangle ABC$ and its image as being congruent, similar, or neither.
21. Contraction toward a point P
22. Translation composed with a reflection
23. Transformation that triples the distance of points from a given line
24. Rotation around a point P composed with a dilation with center P

Answer the following questions.

25. How would you locate the axis of symmetry for an isosceles right triangle?
26. Find the composition of a 125° clockwise rotation about point P and a 235° clockwise rotation about P.
27. What is the key characteristic preserved by an isometry?

Assume that dilations preserve angle measure to complete the following proofs.

28. *Given:* $\overrightarrow{OX}$ bisects $\angle ABC$; a dilation with center O and scale factor k maps A onto D, B onto E, and C onto F

Prove: $\overrightarrow{OE}$ bisects $\angle DEF$

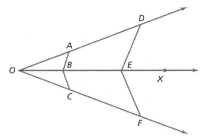

29. *Given:* $\overline{KI} \perp \overline{HJ}$; a dilation with scale factor k and center O maps H onto H', I onto I', J onto J', K onto K'

Prove: $\overline{K'I'} \perp \overline{H'J'}$

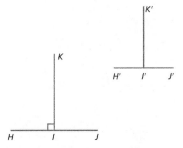

30. Explain the mathematical significance of Hebrews 11:5.

25. Draw the perpendicular from the vertex to the hypotenuse.
26. identify transformation
27. distance
28.

1. $\overrightarrow{OX}$ bisects $\angle ABC$; a dilation with center O and scale factor k maps A onto D, B onto E, and C onto F	1. Given
2. $m\angle ABE = m\angle DEX$; $m\angle CBE = m\angle FEX$	2. Dilations preserve angle measure
3. $\angle ABE \cong \angle DEX$; $\angle CBE \cong \angle FEX$	3. Definition of congruent angles
4. $\angle ABE \cong \angle CBE$	4. Definition of angle bisector
5. $\angle DEX \cong \angle FEX$	5. Substitution (step 3 into 4)
6. $\overrightarrow{OE}$ bisects $\angle DEF$	6. Definition of angle bisector

29.

1. $\overline{KI} \perp \overline{HJ}$; a dilation with scale factor k and center O maps H onto H', I onto I', J onto J', and K onto K'	1. Given
2. $\angle KIJ$ is a right angle	2. Definition of perpendicular
3. $m\angle KIJ = 90°$	3. Definition of right angle
4. $m\angle KIJ = m\angle K'I'J'$	4. Dilations preserve angle measure
5. $m\angle K'I'J' = 90°$	5. Substitution (step 3 into 4)
6. $\angle K'I'J'$ is a right angle	6. Definition of right angle
7. $\overline{K'I'} \perp \overline{H'J'}$	7. Definition of perpendicular

30. "God had translated him [Enoch]" directly to heaven. This translation involved a change of position and provides a physical example of a mathematical translation in which a figure is moved a fixed distance. The verse uses Enoch's translation by faith to teach us the importance of pleasing God by believing and obeying Him: "before his translation he had this testimony, that he pleased God."

Chapter 13
Similarity

13 Similarity

Overview

This chapter opens by defining similar polygons and applies the property of proportionality of sides. AA similarity is introduced as a postulate, followed by SSS and SAS similarity theorems. The altitude to the hypotenuse divides a right triangle into two triangles similar to the original. This leads into geometric means and proportionality theorems. Similar triangles are used to solve word problems. Theorems concerning the intersection of chords and of secants intersecting exterior to a circle and the segment lengths related to them are proved and applied. The chapter concludes with a study of the Golden Ratio.

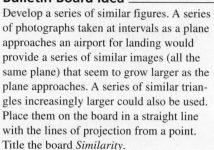

What do a submarine, a poet named Oliver Wendell Holmes, the ocean floor, and geometry all have in common?

The chambered nautilus, of course! Did you know that the first nuclear submarine was named the U.S.S. *Nautilus*? Holmes wrote a famous poem on the subject: "The Chambered Nautilus." And the ocean floor is the home of the lovely shellfish named the nautilus.

But what about geometry? Well, the nautilus is one of nature's geometric masterpieces. As the nautilus grows and builds new chambers, its size increases, but its shape remains the same. Thus some geometry teachers use the nautilus to illustrate proportion and ratio. The spiral shape of the nautilus also demonstrates the geometric concept of the golden rectangle and the golden spiral. The ancient Greeks thought that this geometric shape enhanced the beauty of an object. The nautilus also illustrates two other geometric ideas—rotation and dilation.

Not just the nautilus but all God's creation shows His wonderful design. You might feel inferior, but Psalm 139 says that you are "fearfully and wonderfully made." God's work is "marvellous." God did more, however, than just design your body. He died on the cross to pay the penalty for your sin. Have you trusted Christ as Savior? If so, God has forgiven you, adopted you as His child, and provided an eternal home in heaven.

After this chapter you should be able to

1. define similar polygons.

2. solve proportion problems.

3. state and apply similarity criteria.

4. define and find geometric means.

5. prove and apply theorems on proportions.

6. solve word problems using similar triangles.

7. prove and apply theorems on lengths of segments determined by secants or tangents of circles.

8. define and recognize applications of the Golden Ratio.

535

Bulletin Board Idea

Develop a series of similar figures. A series of photographs taken at intervals as a plane approaches an airport for landing would provide a series of similar images (all the same plane) that seem to grow larger as the plane approaches. A series of similar triangles increasingly larger could also be used. Place them on the board in a straight line with the lines of projection from a point. Title the board *Similarity*.

Presentation

The chambers in the nautilus shell all have the same shape but are increasingly larger in size. Thus, they are similar but not congruent. This concept of similarity was defined in Chapter 12 and will be developed more thoroughly in this chapter.

If you did not cover Chapter 12, you may wish to give students a brief overview of that material by using the activity on transformations (see Resources for 13.1). ∎

Similar Figures

Objectives

1. To define similar polygons.
2. To apply proportions to problems involving similar figures.

Vocabulary

cross multiplication
proportion
ratio
similar polygons

Assignment

- Intuitive: 1-15
- Standard: 1-16, 21-25, and art activity
- Rigorous: 1-13 odd, 15-25

Resources

- Appendix M on Leonardo da Vinci
- *Visual Packet,* Similar, Congruent, Symmetrical. Focus on the row for similar figures.
- *Activities Manual,* Transformations in Brief. This is intended as a quick summary for classes that did not cover Chapter 12.
- *Activities Manual,* Paper Folding in Principle

13.1 Similar Figures

Recall that two figures are similar if they have the same shape but not necessarily the same size. A more formal definition is given here.

The scale model of Jerusalem showing the city at the time of Christ is a favorite tourist stop in Israel.

Definition

Similar polygons are polygons having corresponding angles that are congruent and corresponding sides that are proportional. If $\triangle ABC$ and $\triangle DEF$ are similar, the proper notation is $\triangle ABC \sim \triangle DEF$.

Do you remember what a proportion is? A ratio is the comparison of two numbers, usually integers, using division. If a and b are integers and $b \neq 0$, then $\frac{a}{b}$ is their ratio. $\frac{1}{4}$ and $\frac{9}{1}$ are examples of ratios. A proportion is an equation with two equal ratios. For example, $\frac{1}{2} = \frac{3}{6}$ is a proportion.

Presentation

Talk about model airplanes and how they are exact replicas of the real planes they represent. You can also have students turn back to the photo on page 281 and locate a model (scale model of the Eiffel Tower in the corner of the room).

Define similar polygons and stress that the notation $\triangle ABC \sim \triangle DEF$ means that corresponding angles are congruent and corresponding sides are proportional. In other words, $\angle A \cong \angle D$, $\angle B \cong \angle E$, $\angle C \cong \angle F$, and $\frac{AB}{DE} = \frac{BC}{EF} = \frac{CA}{FD}$. Be sure to read the proportion as "AB is to DE as BC is to EF as CA is to FD" to stress the equality of ratios.

Common Student Error. Identifying corresponding parts becomes more difficult when the figures are not oriented the same way. In triangles, the key is that corresponding sides will be opposite congruent angles.

Common Student Error. Some students will set up incorrect proportions even after identifying the corresponding parts because they do not keep the ratios in the same order.

Since proportions play a key role throughout this chapter, you may want to use the extended discussion below of correct alternatives for a proportion. Answers are shown only one way since there are too many correct alternatives to list. Recognizing valid alternatives is essential to grading student homework.

Many students may set up their proportion differently from the printed answer and still get the correct answer. Many will not understand how both proportions can be correct. If you cover the following material on proportions, it will show the students which alternative proportions are correct and why.

Proportion: $\frac{a}{b} = \frac{c}{d}$

Alternation: $\frac{a}{c} = \frac{b}{d}$

Inversion: $\frac{b}{a} = \frac{d}{c}$

Both: $\frac{c}{a} = \frac{d}{b}$

You need not present the names of the variations, but if you do name them, you will have a tool for discussing them. The term *inversion* is easy to remember since you simply invert both sides of the equation.

The fact that all four proportions mean the same follows easily from the multiplication

You may remember a process called cross multiplication, which helps you check or solve proportion problems.

If $\frac{1}{2} = \frac{3}{6}$

then $1(6) = 2(3)$.

After cross multiplying, you get the same answer on each side; thus the ratios are equal, and the equation is a proportion. You can solve certain first-degree equations by using cross multiplication.

EXAMPLE   Solve $\frac{x}{5} = \frac{9}{15}$.

Answer $\frac{x}{5} = \frac{9}{15}$

$15x = 45$

$x = 3$

So $\frac{3}{5}$ and $\frac{9}{15}$ are equivalent ratios.

The lengths of the sides of similar figures are proportional. Look at figure 13.1.

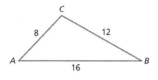

Figure 13.1

Look at the ratios of the corresponding sides:

$\frac{A'B'}{AB}$, $\frac{B'C'}{BC}$, and $\frac{A'C'}{AC}$

What number do you get in each case? Thus if $\triangle ABC \sim \triangle A'B'C'$,

$\frac{A'B'}{AB} = \frac{B'C'}{BC} = \frac{A'C'}{AC}$

If the corresponding angles of two polygons are congruent and the sides are proportional, then you know that the two figures are similar.

In the dilations that you studied earlier, the scale factor of the dilation equals the common ratio of the corresponding sides. It may help to do the cumulative review questions on dilations first.

Have students explain why alternation and inversion obtain the same answer as the original proportion.

Students may attack this at least two ways. The proof is best, but an example will at least show that the student understands.

$$\begin{matrix} \text{1st} & & & \text{3rd} \\ & \frac{a}{b} & = \frac{c}{d} & \\ \text{2nd} & & & \text{4th} \end{matrix}$$

Proof: For the proportion $\frac{a}{b} = \frac{c}{d}$, by alternation $\frac{a}{c} = \frac{b}{d}$. By inversion, $\frac{b}{a} = \frac{d}{c}$. No matter which one you use, cross multiplying obtains $ad = bc$. Since they all result in this equation, solving for the same variable must result in the same expression for all three forms.

Example: Given the proportion $\frac{7}{8} = \frac{x}{9}$, by alternating terms, $\frac{7}{x} = \frac{8}{9}$. By inverting the terms, $\frac{8}{7} = \frac{9}{x}$. In every case, solving the proportion obtains $x = 7.875$.

Additional Problems

Set up proportions for the following dilations and solve for the missing term.

1. $AB = 5$, $A'B' = 75$, $CD = 3$. Find $C'D'$. $\frac{75}{5} = \frac{C'D'}{3}$, **$C'D' = 45$**.

2. $A'B' = 20$, $CD = 12$, $C'D' = 8$. Find AB. $\frac{20}{AB} = \frac{8}{12}$, **$AB = 30$**

3. For #1 and #2 give the scale factor and classify the dilation. **1) $k = 15$, enlargement; 2) $k = \frac{2}{3}$, reduction**

4. If the pairs of figures are similar, find the unknown values.

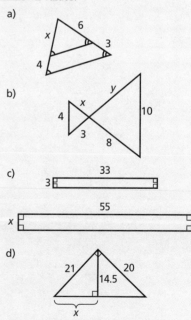

a) $x = 8$; b) $x = 3.2$, $y = 7.5$; c) $x = 5$; d) $x \approx 15.2$

Tips

property of equality. Multiply both sides by the product of the denominators (also called clearing fractions or cross multiplying). In all four cases, this results in the same equation, namely $ad = bc$. Show the examples below.

Alternation: If $\frac{3}{4} = \frac{6}{8}$, then $\frac{3}{6} = \frac{4}{8}$

Inversion: If $\frac{3}{4} = \frac{6}{8}$, then $\frac{4}{3} = \frac{8}{6}$

Motivational Idea. The ratios based on figure 13.1 are all equal. Students should see that each ratio is equal to the scale factor of the dilation. This is made explicit in the last paragraph. Have students write some other proportions using alternation and inversion. For instance, ask what $\frac{AC}{BC}$ is proportional to. $\left(\frac{A'C'}{B'C'}\right)$ or $\frac{BC}{B'C'}\left(\frac{AC}{A'C'}\text{ or }\frac{AB}{A'B'}\right)$

Ex. 18. This exercise will be used to complete the proof of Theorem 13.3 in the next section.

Ex. 20. This is the proof of Theorem 13.10 in Section 13.4. The key is to get the ratios of corresponding sides equal to the same constant k. ∎

Answers

1. 50
2. 12
3. 7
4. 11
5. $\frac{1}{4}$
6. 10
7. $\frac{1}{4}$
8. $\frac{2}{3}$
9. $m = 16$ units, $n = 12$ units
10. $x = 8$ units
    $y = 6$ units
    $z = 4$ units
11. $x = 4\frac{1}{2}$ units; $y = 7\frac{1}{2}$ units
12. $x = 3$ units; $y = 6$ units

▶ A. Exercises

Solve each proportion.

1. $\frac{x}{100} = \frac{1}{2}$ 4. $\frac{5}{y} = \frac{55}{121}$

2. $\frac{2}{3} = \frac{y}{18}$ 5. $\frac{1}{8} = \frac{x}{2}$

3. $\frac{6}{x} = \frac{54}{63}$ 6. $\frac{9}{5} = \frac{18}{y}$

Find the ratio of the lengths in the right figure (image) to those in the left figure (preimage) for each pair of similar figures.

7.

8.

Given that the figures are similar in each problem, find the length of the indicated sides.

9.
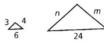

11.
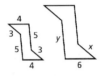

10.
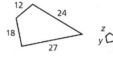

12.

13. If $\triangle LPQ \sim \triangle RST$, what angles are congruent, and what sides are proportional?

14. Is every square similar to every other square? Why or why not?

15. Are congruent triangles also similar?

16. What is the common ratio or scale factor in exercise 15?

17. *Prove:* If two triangles are congruent, then they are also similar.

18. *Prove:* Similarity of triangles is reflexive.

19. If $\triangle ABC \sim \triangle XYZ$, find the perimeter of $\triangle ABC$ and $\triangle XYZ$. Are the perimeters of the triangles in any particular ratio?

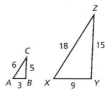

▶ C. Exercises

20. *Prove:* The ratio of the perimeters of two similar triangles is equal to the ratio of the lengths of any pair of corresponding sides.

▮ Cumulative Review

21. Find the center of the dilation.

22. Give the scale factor.

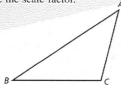

23. If the image of a dilation is congruent to the preimage, then what is the scale factor?

24. Classify three types of dilations based on scale factors.

25. Find $\triangle A'B'C'$, if P is the center of a dilation with scale factor $\frac{4}{3}$.

---

13. $\angle L \cong \angle R$; $\angle P \cong \angle S$; $\angle Q \cong \angle T$; $\frac{RS}{LP} = \frac{ST}{PQ} = \frac{RT}{LQ}$

14. Yes; the angles are all right angles, and the sides are in proportion.

15. yes

16. 1

17.

1. $\triangle ABC \cong \triangle LMN$	1. Given
2. $\angle A \cong \angle L$; $\angle B \cong \angle M$; $\angle C \cong \angle N$; $\overline{AB} \cong \overline{LM}$; $\overline{BC} \cong \overline{MN}$; $\overline{AC} \cong \overline{LN}$	2. Definition of congruent triangles
3. $AB = LM$, $BC = MN$, $AC = LN$	3. Definition of congruent segments
4. $\frac{LM}{AB} = \frac{AB}{AB} = 1$, $\frac{MN}{BC} = \frac{BC}{BC} = 1$, $\frac{LN}{AC} = \frac{AC}{AC} = 1$	4. Multiplication property of equality
5. $\frac{LM}{AB} = \frac{MN}{BC} = \frac{LN}{AC} = 1$	5. Transitive property of equality
6. $\triangle ABC \sim \triangle LMN$	6. Definition of similarity
7. If two triangles are congruent, then they are also similar	7. Law of Deduction

18.

1. $\triangle ABC$	1. Given
2. $\triangle ABC \cong \triangle ABC$	2. Reflexive property of congruence
3. $\triangle ABC \sim \triangle ABC$	3. If two triangles are congruent, then they are similar (#17)

19. Perimeter of $\triangle ABC = 14$ units; $\triangle XYZ = 42$ units; yes; they are in the same ratio as the sides.

20.

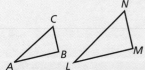

1. $\triangle ABC \sim \triangle LMN$	1. Given
2. $\frac{LM}{AB} = \frac{MN}{BC} = \frac{LN}{AC} = k$	2. Definition of similar triangles
3. $LM = (AB)k$; $MN = (BC)k$; $LN = (AC)k$	3. Multiplication property of equality
4. $LM + MN + LN = (AB)k + (BC)k + (AC)k$	4. Addition property of equality
5. $LM + MN + LN = (AB + BC + AC)k$	5. Distributive property
6. $\frac{LM + MN + LN}{AB + BC + AC} = k$	6. Multiplication property of equality

21. [12.3]

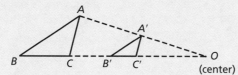

22. $\frac{1}{2}$ [12.3]

23. 1 [12.3]

24. $k > 1$ enlargement (expansion)
$k = 1$ identity
$0 < k < 1$ reduction (contraction) [12.3]

25. [12.3]

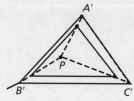

Geometry Around Us

Geometry and Art

Objectives

1. To identify geometric concepts useful to artists.
2. To identify how artists use similarity.

GEOMETRY AND ART

Math is rational—figures, theorems, formulas, strict rules. Art is creative—visual effects, interpretations, feelings. So art and math have nothing in common, right? Wrong. Of course artists are not mathematicians; they often lay out their drawings or sculptures freehand without following specific rules or formulas. But there are some mathematical principles that artists follow to make their creations beautiful. Still doubtful? Come along.

Egyptian painting

Have you ever seen Egyptian art? To most of us it looks a little crude: the people stand in awkward positions, and sizes seem to be all mixed up. What makes this art look peculiar? Well, the Egyptians did not follow the laws of perspective. They felt that important people should be drawn large, and unimportant people should be drawn smaller, no matter where they were in the picture. Due to studies by artists during the Renaissance, modern artists know that a drawing without perspective, like Egyptian art, will not look realistic. Since the Renaissance, artists have tended to use the geometric principle of proportion. First the artist establishes a vanishing point somewhere on (or even slightly off) the canvas. All the objects in the picture are drawn in relation to this point. The artist draws people in the foreground larger than people in the background. Thus a person standing ten feet from the viewer

Presentation

Have students find examples of art with geometric designs or that show the use of similarity (such as perspective). Some students may prefer to do original art that makes use of geometry.

Motivational Idea. Invite the art teacher or a professional artist to class as a guest speaker. Ask that the guest discuss how artists use math (especially geometry). Encourage the guest to bring and show some examples of his own work. ∎

appears twice as large as a person standing twenty feet away. Artists use this method to make the painting more realistic. The use of proportions to make similar figures enables the painting to portray depth.

Photographers also deal with similarity every day. When developing and enlarging pictures, photographers rely on equipment that uses the principles of similarity. For example, when a picture is enlarged or reduced, the final print is similar to the negative—only the size changes. In like manner, a slide projector produces an image on the screen similar to but much larger than the image on the slide.

Proportion also determines what forms we consider beautiful. Some artists use geometric shapes to design pottery and beautiful vases. Artists who draw or sculpt the human body also recognize the proportions in God's design. Leonardo da Vinci wrote down proportions for artists to use that he thought reflected God's perfect design.

There are some mathematical principles that artists follow to make their creations beautiful.

The Last Supper by Leonardo da Vinci.

Similar Triangles

Objectives

1. To identify and illustrate the basic similarity postulate for triangles (angle-angle).

2. To illustrate, state, and prove the Side-Side-Side Similarity Theorem for triangles.

3. To identify the Side-Angle-Side Similarity Theorem for triangles.

4. To apply the similarity postulate and theorems to pairs of triangles to establish their similarity.

Vocabulary

AA Similarity Postulate
SAS Similarity Theorem
SSS Similarity Theorem

Assignment

- Intuitive: 1-12
- Standard: 1-11, 13-19 odd, 21-25
- Rigorous: 1-11 odd, 13-26, Mind over Math

Resources

- *Activities Manual,* Bible Activity: Man— The Battleground of the Truth
- *Test Packet,* Quiz 1, Chapter 13 covers Sections 13.1 and 13.2.

13.2 Similar Triangles

Let's review the characteristics of similar triangles mentioned in Section 13.1. Look at figure 13.2.

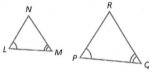

Scale model airplane

Figure 13.2

$\triangle ABC \sim \triangle XYZ$. This means that $\angle A \cong \angle X$, $\angle B \cong \angle Y$, $\angle C \cong \angle Z$, and $\frac{XY}{AB} = \frac{YZ}{BC} = \frac{XZ}{AC}$.

In this lesson you will be learning ways of proving that two triangles are similar. Many of the similarity theorems resemble the congruence theorems that you learned in Chapter 6. The theorems that will be developed are based on the AA (Angle-Angle) Postulate.

Postulate 13.1

AA Similarity Postulate. **If two angles of one triangle are congruent to two angles of another triangle, then the two triangles are similar.**

Why can we say that two triangles are similar if only two pairs of corresponding angles are congruent? Recall the earlier theorem: If two angles of a triangle are congruent to two angles of another triangle, the third angles are congruent.

Figure 13.3

Since two pairs of angles are congruent in the diagram, $\angle N$ and $\angle R$ are also congruent. Furthermore, according to the AA Similarity Postulate, $\triangle LMN \sim \triangle PQR$. Let's experiment to discover some similarity theorems.

Motivational Idea. To help students visualize similar triangles, cut out several cardboard triangles having various shapes. Project the light from an overhead projector onto a wall or screen. Place the triangles in the path of the light, making shadows similar to the original triangles on the wall. Point out that this is a dilation producing a figure in which distance is not preserved but angle measure is.

Show the students how to apply the AA Postulate, and explain the paragraphs below it. Have them do the experiment before Theorem 13.1. Students should obtain the same measurements for angles that correspond. This illustrates the SSS similarity theorem (since the

sides were constructed proportionally to those in the given triangle).

The proof of SSS for similarity is long, but it is not difficult. Go over it carefully to justify this key theorem, to provide practice with similarity proofs, and to review previous concepts. The plan of the proof is to construct a triangle similar to the smaller of the given triangles (steps 2-7) while making one side of the constructed triangle congruent to a side of the larger triangle. Next, show that the new triangle is congruent to the larger given triangle (steps 8-14). The original triangles will then be similar by AA (steps 15-17).

One-on-one. Some students struggle to make the transition from proofs involving congruent

triangles to similar triangles. Since AA is easier than proving triangles congruent, they think it is too easy and that they must have missed something. One way to help is to emphasize what establishes the *shape* of a triangle. Use physical objects (dowels or folding carpenter's rule) or constructions to show why AA, SSS, and SAS establish the shape of triangles.

Call attention to the table that summarizes the methods of showing triangles similar. Point out that there is no ASA or SAA method because AA covers both. A more in-depth table is in the Visual Packet. Note that the SAS Similarity Theorem is not proved in the text or exercises because its proof is beyond the scope of this text.

Experiment

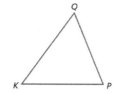

Figure 13.4

1. Copy △KPQ onto your paper.
2. With a compass, measure the length of $\overline{KP}$. Construct a segment that is twice as long as $\overline{KP}$; call the segment $K'P'$.
3. Measure $\overline{PQ}$ and construct a segment twice as long as $\overline{PQ}$. Using P' as an endpoint, mark an arc with radius equal to $2PQ$.
4. Construct a segment that equals $2KQ$. Using K' as center and using a radius equal to $2KQ$, form an arc that intersects the arc you made in step 3. Call the intersection point Q'.
5. Connect Q', K', and P' to form a triangle.

Look at △K'P'Q' and △KPQ. Measuring the corresponding angles with a protractor will convince you that although the triangles are not congruent, they are similar since the corresponding angles are congruent. What is the ratio of the side lengths of the two triangles? These measurements suggest the next theorem.

Theorem 13.1

SSS Similarity Theorem. If the three sides of one triangle are proportional to the corresponding three sides of another triangle, then the triangles are similar.

 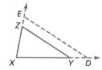

Figure 13.5

Given: In △ABC and △XYZ,
$$\frac{XY}{AB} = \frac{YZ}{BC} = \frac{XZ}{AC}$$

Prove: △ABC ~ △XYZ

Reading and Writing Mathematics

Have the students consult an encyclopedia on the subject of projection as related to mapmaking. Have them write a paragraph on "stereographic projection" of the earth onto a flat surface. They should be sure to address projections of latitudes, longitudes, and poles.

A globe is set on a plane with the South Pole as the point of tangency. Lines are determined by the North Pole and a point on the earth. Where that line intersects the plane is its point of projection. Thus, longitude lines appear straight, but latitude lines appear curved. The South Pole projects to the point of tangency, but the North Pole has no projection.

Additional Problems

Can each of the following be sides of similar triangles? Explain.

1. 8, 5, 7 and 24, 15, 21 **yes, $k = 3$**
2. 2, 3, 1 and 3, 4.5, 1.5 **no, points are collinear; no triangle could be formed**
3. 6, 12, 16 and 3, 6, 8 **yes, $k = \frac{1}{2}$**
4. What criteria for similar triangles are immediate consequences of AA? **AAA, ASA, SAA**

Ex. 2, 5. False. Even though two pairs of sides are proportional, the other pair does not have the same proportion.

Ex. 16-17. These complete the proof of Theorem 13.3 because students proved that similarity is reflexive in #18 of Section 13.1. ■

5. Give a postulate, theorem, or property to justify why the triangles are similar. Assume *ABCD* is a parallelogram. *a) SAS; b) The two smaller triangles are similar to the large triangle by AA; the two small triangles are similar to each other by the transitive property of congruence (#16). c) AA (If triangles are congruent, they are similar [#17, p. 539].)*

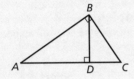

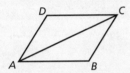

STATEMENTS	REASONS
1. $\frac{XY}{AB} = \frac{YZ}{BC} = \frac{XZ}{AC}$	1. Given
2. Draw a segment congruent to $\overline{AB}$ by extending $\overline{XY}$ and call it $\overline{XD}$; $\overline{AB} \cong \overline{XD}$	2. Auxiliary lines
3. $AB = XD$	3. Definition of congruent segments
4. $\frac{XY}{XD} = \frac{YZ}{BC}$	4. Substitution (step 3 into 1)
5. Construct $\overleftrightarrow{DE}$ parallel to $\overleftrightarrow{YZ}$	5. Auxiliary line
6. $\angle XYZ \cong \angle XDE$; $\angle XZY \cong \angle XED$	6. Corresponding Angle Theorem
7. $\triangle XDE \sim \triangle XYZ$	7. AA
8. $\frac{XY}{XD} = \frac{YZ}{DE} = \frac{XZ}{XE}$	8. Definition of similar triangles
9. $\frac{YZ}{DE} = \frac{YZ}{BC}$	9. Transitive property of equality (steps 4 and 8)
10. $\frac{XZ}{XE} = \frac{XZ}{AC}$	10. Substitution (steps 8 and 1 into 9)
11. $(YZ)(BC) = (YZ)(DE)$ $(XZ)(AC) = (XZ)(XE)$	11. Multiplication property of equality (cross multiplication; see steps 9, 10)
12. $BC = DE$, $AC = XE$	12. Multiplication property of equality
13. $\overline{BC} \cong \overline{DE}$, $\overline{AC} \cong \overline{XE}$	13. Definition of congruent segments
14. $\triangle ABC \cong \triangle XDE$	14. SSS
15. $\angle B \cong \angle XDE$; $\angle C \cong \angle XED$	15. Definition of congruent triangles
16. $\angle B \cong \angle XYZ$; $\angle C \cong \angle XZY$	16. Transitive property of congruent angles (see step 6)
17. $\triangle ABC \sim \triangle XYZ$	17. AA
18. If the three sides of one triangle are proportional to the corresponding three sides of another triangle, then the triangles are similar	18. Law of Deduction

You should know two other theorems on similar triangles.

Theorem 13.2

SAS Similarity Theorem. If two sides of a triangle are proportional to the corresponding two sides of another triangle and the included angles between the sides are congruent, then the triangles are similar.

Theorem 13.3

Similarity of triangles is an equivalence relation.

The table summarizes three quick ways to prove that two triangles are similar.

	Given	Result
AA	$\angle A \cong \angle X, \angle B \cong \angle Y$	$\triangle ABC \sim \triangle XYZ$
SSS	$\dfrac{XY}{AB} = \dfrac{YZ}{BC} = \dfrac{XZ}{AC}$	$\triangle ABC \sim \triangle XYZ$
SAS	$\dfrac{XY}{AB} = \dfrac{YZ}{BC}; \angle B \cong \angle Y$	$\triangle ABC \sim \triangle XYZ$

► A. Exercises

State whether the lengths (in units) below could be sides of similar triangles.

1. 3, 8, 7, and 12, 32, 28
2. 2, 6, 7 and 10, 30, 42
3. 12, 15, 9 and 4, 5, 3
4. 2, 3, 4 and 3, 4.5, 6
5. 7, 4, 9 and 14, 10, 18
6. $\dfrac{1}{5}, \dfrac{4}{9}, \dfrac{1}{3}$ and $\dfrac{1}{10}, \dfrac{2}{9}, \dfrac{1}{6}$

Which pairs of triangles are similar? Why?

7.

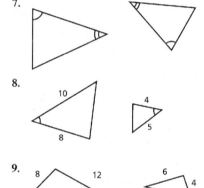

8.

9.

13.2 SIMILAR TRIANGLES **545**

Answers

1. yes
2. no
3. yes
4. yes
5. no
6. yes
7. similar, AA
8. similar, SAS
9. similar, SSS

10. not similar, sides not proportional

11. similar, AA

12. similar, SAS

13.

1. *WXYZ* is a parallelogram	1. Given
2. $\overleftrightarrow{ZY} \parallel \overleftrightarrow{WX}$; $\overleftrightarrow{ZW} \parallel \overleftrightarrow{YX}$	2. Definition of parallelogram
3. $\angle ZYW \cong \angle YWX$; $\angle ZWY \cong \angle XYW$	3. Parallel Postulate
4. $\triangle WXY \sim \triangle YZW$	4. AA

14.

1. $\overleftrightarrow{MN} \parallel \overleftrightarrow{OQ}$	1. Given
2. $\angle PQO \cong \angle PMN$; $\angle POQ \cong \angle PNM$	2. Corresponding Angle Theorem
3. $\triangle MNP \sim \triangle QOP$	3. AA

15.

1. $\triangle MNP \sim \triangle QOP$	1. Given
2. $\angle PQO \cong \angle PMN$	2. Definition of similar triangles
3. $\overleftrightarrow{MN} \parallel \overleftrightarrow{QO}$	3. Corresponding Angle Theorem

16.

1. $\triangle ABC \sim \triangle LMN$; $\triangle LMN \sim \triangle PQR$	1. Given
2. $\angle A \cong \angle L$; $\angle L \cong \angle P$; $\angle B \cong \angle M$; $\angle M \cong \angle Q$	2. Definition of similar triangles
3. $\angle A \cong \angle P$; $\angle B \cong \angle Q$	3. Transitive property of congruent angles
4. $\triangle ABC \sim \triangle PQR$	4. AA

17.

1. $\triangle ABC \sim \triangle DEF$	1. Given
2. $\angle A \cong \angle D$, $\angle B \cong \angle E$	2. Definition of similar triangles
3. $\angle D \cong \angle A$, $\angle E \cong \angle B$	3. Symmetric property of congruent angles
4. $\triangle DEF \sim \triangle ABC$	4. AA

10.

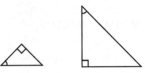

11.

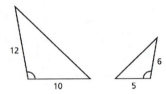

12.

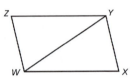

▶ **B. Exercises**

Prove the following statements.

13. *Given:* *WXYZ* is a parallelogram

   Prove: $\triangle WXY \sim \triangle YZW$

Use the figure below for the proofs in exercises 14-15.

14. *Given:* $\overleftrightarrow{MN} \parallel \overleftrightarrow{OQ}$

   Prove: $\triangle MNP \sim \triangle QOP$

15. *Given:* $\triangle MNP \sim \triangle QOP$

   Prove: $\overleftrightarrow{MN} \parallel \overleftrightarrow{QO}$

16. *Prove:* Similarity of triangles is transitive (If $\triangle ABC \sim \triangle LMN$, and $\triangle LMN \sim \triangle PQR$, then $\triangle ABC \sim \triangle PQR$.)

17. *Prove:* Similarity of triangles is symmetric

Use the following figure for the proofs in exercises 18-19.

18. *Given:* $\overrightarrow{DB} \perp \overrightarrow{DE}$; $\overrightarrow{DB} \perp \overrightarrow{AB}$
    Prove: $\triangle ABC \sim \triangle EDC$
19. *Given:* $\overrightarrow{DB} \perp \overrightarrow{DE}$; $\overrightarrow{DB} \perp \overrightarrow{AB}$
    Prove: $\dfrac{DE}{AB} = \dfrac{CE}{AC}$

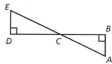

▶ C. Exercises

20. *Given:* $\overleftrightarrow{KI} \perp \overleftrightarrow{HJ}$; $\triangle HJK$ is an isosceles triangle
    Prove: $(JI)(HK) = (HI)(JK)$

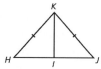

■ Cumulative Review

21. What is a relation that is reflexive, symmetric, and transitive?
22. List three symbols that represent equivalence relations.
23. Does the set of rotations with a given center P form an equivalence relation?
24. Suppose two regions are related if they have the same area. Is this an equivalence relation? Why?
25. Suppose two solids with the same volume are related. Is this an equivalence relation? Why?

Use the ideas in this chapter to show that $x = \sqrt{a}$. Make a construction that represents the square root of 5.

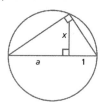

Figure 13.6

18.

1. $\overrightarrow{DB} \perp \overrightarrow{DE}$; $\overrightarrow{DB} \perp \overrightarrow{AB}$	1. Given
2. $\angle CDE$ and $\angle CBA$ are right angles	2. Definition of perpendicular
3. $\angle CDE \cong \angle CBA$	3. All right angles are congruent
4. $\angle DCE \cong \angle ACB$	4. Vertical Angle Theorem
5. $\triangle ABC \sim \triangle EDC$	5. AA

19.

1. $\overrightarrow{DB} \perp \overrightarrow{DE}$; $\overrightarrow{DB} \perp \overrightarrow{AB}$	1. Given
2. $\triangle ABC \sim \triangle EDC$	2. Exercise 18
3. $\dfrac{DE}{AB} = \dfrac{CE}{AC}$	3. Definition of similar triangles

20.

1. $\overleftrightarrow{KI} \perp \overleftrightarrow{HJ}$; $\triangle HJK$ is an isosceles triangle	1. Given
2. $\angle KIH$ and $\angle KIJ$ are right angles	2. Definition of perpendicular
3. $\angle KIH \cong \angle KIJ$	3. All right angles are congruent
4. $\angle KHI \cong \angle KJI$	4. Isosceles Triangle Theorem
5. $\triangle HIK \sim \triangle JIK$	5. AA
6. $\dfrac{JI}{HI} = \dfrac{JK}{HK}$	6. Definition of similar triangles
7. $(JI)(HK) = (HI)(JK)$	7. Multiplication property of equality

21. equivalence relation [3.1]
22. $=$, $\cong$, $\sim$ [6.3]
23. yes [12.2]
24. yes, since the Area Postulate (and Congruent Regions Postulate) guarantees that areas are well-defined numbers that satisfy the equivalence relation $=$ [8.1]
25. yes, the Volume Postulate and Congruent Solids Postulate [11.1]

Mind over Math

See Appendix B.

Similar Right Triangles

Objectives

1. To prove that the altitude to the hypotenuse of a right triangle divides it into two right triangles, each similar to the original.
2. To define and apply geometric means.
3. To compute lengths of sides and related segments for right triangles by using proportions.

Vocabulary

geometric mean

Assignment

- Intuitive: 1-15, 21-25
- Standard: 1-18, 21-25
- Rigorous: 1-15 odd, 16-25

Flash

Sailboats are classified by the number of masts and sails. Catboats have one mast in front with one sail. Sloops have one mast in the middle of the boat and two sails. Ketches and yawls each have an extra mast and sail in the stern (mizzenmast with mizzensail) and are distinguished by whether the mizzenmast stands behind or in front of the rudderpost. In a schooner, the extra mast is in the bow (front) and supports the jib and a foresail. Only the mainsail flies from the mainmast in the middle of the schooner. Interested students should look up sailboats in an encyclopedia.

13.3 Similar Right Triangles

Right triangles have some peculiar characteristics: they satisfy the Pythagorean theorem and also form the basis of trigonometric ratios (in Chapter 14). Right triangles also have some special characteristics related to similarity.

A sloop, such as this one on Chesapeake Bay, Virginia, has one mast with two sails (mainsail and jib) that are both right triangles.

Theorem 13.4

An altitude drawn from the right angle to the hypotenuse of a right triangle separates the original triangle into two similar triangles, each of which is similar to the original triangle.

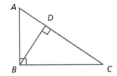

Figure 13.7

Theorem 13.4 means that if $\overline{BD}$ is an altitude of $\triangle ABC$, then 1) $\triangle BCD$, $\triangle ACB$, 2) $\triangle ABD$, $\triangle ACB$, and 3) $\triangle ABD$, $\triangle BCD$. The proof of the second case is shown here, and the other two cases are exercises.

> *Given:* $\overline{BD}$ is the altitude of right $\triangle ABC$
> *Prove:* $\triangle ABD$, $\triangle ACB$

Presentation

Common Student Error. Students often mix up the corresponding parts of a right triangle. Help them by drawing the triangles in figure 13.7 separately (as in the Visual Packet) or label the congruent angles with numbers and apply the principle that corresponding sides lie opposite congruent angles.

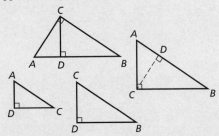

Cover the concept of a geometric mean. After presenting examples 1 and 2, have students solve several others to make sure they understand. This concept is central to Theorems 13.5 and 13.6. Use example 3 to illustrate its use.

Review the construction of the square root of a number. If you assigned the Mind over Math on page 547, you can discuss the answer now. The fact that the altitude to the hypotenuse of a right triangle is the geometric mean between 1 and *a* lets us find the square root of *a* by construction techniques.

Tips

Ex. 4. Cross multiply to get $x - 1 = 12$.

Ex. 5. Cross multiplying obtains a quadratic equation: $x^2 - 3x = 4$. Subtract four from both sides and factor: $(x - 4)(x + 1) = 0$.

Ex. 19-20. Case II was proved in the text. ∎

STATEMENTS	REASONS
1. $\overline{BD}$ is the altitude of right $\triangle ABC$	1. Given
2. $\overline{BD} \perp \overline{AC}$	2. Definition of altitude
3. $\angle BDA$ is a right angle	3. Definition of perpendicular
4. $\angle ABC \cong \angle BDA$	4. All right angles are congruent
5. $\angle A \cong \angle A$	5. Reflexive property of congruent angles
6. $\triangle ABD \sim \triangle ACB$	6. AA

In the proportion $\frac{a}{x} = \frac{x}{b}$, notice that the denominator of one ratio is the same as the numerator of the other ratio. When this happens, x is called the *geometric mean*. So 8 is the geometric mean between 16 and 4 because

$$\frac{16}{8} = \frac{8}{4}.$$

Solving for a geometric mean involves the use of a quadratic equation, which you studied in algebra.

EXAMPLE 1 Find the geometric mean between 3 and 27.

Answer
1. Set up a proportion; let x represent the geometric mean.
$\frac{3}{x} = \frac{x}{27}$

2. Cross multiply.
$x^2 = 81$

3. Solve by finding the square root of both sides.
$\sqrt{x^2} = \pm\sqrt{81}$

4. Use the principal square root.
$x = 9$

Although there are two answers ($\pm$), we select the positive root (or principal root) because the context demands a result between 3 and 27.

Resources
- *Visual Packet,* Similar Right Triangles. This poster shows each pair of similar triangles formed from an altitude to the hypotenuse.
- *Test Packet,* Quiz 2, Chapter 13 covers Section 13.3.

Reading and Writing Mathematics
Have the students look up the definition of an arithmetic progression and answer the following questions.
1. Write the next four terms in the arithmetic progression: 5, 9, . . . **13, 17, 21, 25**
2. Write the next four terms of this arithmetic progression: $\frac{1}{4}, \frac{3}{4}, \dots$ **$\frac{5}{4}, \frac{7}{4}, \frac{9}{4}, \frac{11}{4}$**
3. Write the general form of an arithmetic progression. **$A_n = A_1 + d(n - 1)$**
4. Identify A_1 and d in problems 1 and 2. **In problem 1, $A_1 = 5$ and $d = 4$; in problem 2, $A_1 = \frac{1}{4}$ and $d = \frac{1}{2}$**

Additional Problems

1. Find the geometric mean between 5 and 25.
   $\sqrt{125} = 5\sqrt{5} \approx 11.2$

2. Find the geometric mean between 12 and 20.
   $\sqrt{240} = 4\sqrt{15} \approx 15.5$

3. Name each using correct notation.

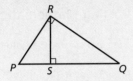

   a) legs of $\triangle PRS$ $\overline{PS}$, $\overline{RS}$
   b) altitude of $\triangle PQR$ $\overline{RS}$
   c) hypotenuse of $\triangle PQR$ $\overline{PQ}$
   d) segment of the hypotenuse adjacent to leg $\overline{PR}$ $\overline{PS}$
   e) segment of the hypotenuse adjacent to leg $\overline{RQ}$ $\overline{QS}$
   f) hypotenuse of $\triangle QRS$ $\overline{RQ}$
   g) angle congruent to $\angle P$; to $\angle Q$
      $\angle QRS$; $\angle PRS$

4. Using the same diagram, give the similarity statements for each pair of triangles.
   $\triangle PRS \sim \triangle RQS$
   $\triangle RQS \sim \triangle PQR$
   $\triangle PRS \sim \triangle PQR$

5. Using the same diagram, identify each segment as a geometric mean between two other segments.
   a) $\overline{RS}$ $\overline{PS}$; $\overline{QS}$
   b) $\overline{PR}$ $\overline{PQ}$; $\overline{PS}$
   c) $\overline{QR}$ $\overline{PQ}$; $\overline{QS}$

6. *Given:* Right $\triangle JKL$ with altitude to the hypotenuse, $\overline{MK}$
   a) $LJ = 20$, $MJ = 4$, find KM. **8**
   b) $MJ = 4$, $KJ = 6$, find LJ. **9**
   c) $LJ = 16$, $ML = 8$, find LK. **8√2**
   d) $LJ = 25$, $MJ = 5$, find MK. **10**

EXAMPLE 2 Find the geometric mean between 6 and 9.

Answer 1. Write the proportion.
   $\frac{6}{x} = \frac{x}{9}$

2. Cross multiply.
   $x^2 = 54$

3. Solve.
   $x = \pm\sqrt{54}$

4. Simplify your answer.
   $x = 3\sqrt{6}$

The geometric mean was presented here because it is used in the next theorem.

Theorem 13.5

In a right triangle, the altitude to the hypotenuse cuts the hypotenuse into two segments. The length of the altitude is the geometric mean between the lengths of the two segments of the hypotenuse.

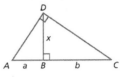

Figure 13.8

Given: Right $\triangle ACD$; $\overline{DB}$ is an altitude of $\triangle ACD$
Prove: $\frac{a}{x} = \frac{x}{b}$, or $\frac{AB}{DB} = \frac{DB}{BC}$

STATEMENTS	REASONS
1. Right $\triangle ACD$; $\overline{DB}$ is an altitude of $\triangle ACD$	1. Given
2. $\triangle ABD \sim \triangle DBC$	2. The altitude divides a right triangle into two similar triangles
3. $\frac{AB}{DB} = \frac{DB}{BC}$	3. Definition of similar triangles

Another theorem about right triangles and similarity involves a geometric mean.

Theorem 13.6

In a right triangle, the altitude to the hypotenuse divides the hypotenuse into two segments such that the length of a leg is the geometric mean between the hypotenuse and the segment of the hypotenuse adjacent to the leg.

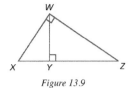

Figure 13.9

$$\frac{XZ}{WX} = \frac{WX}{XY}$$
$$\frac{XZ}{WZ} = \frac{WZ}{YZ}$$

You will prove this theorem as an exercise.

EXAMPLE 3 Given the measurements in $\triangle HIJ$, find x, y, and z.

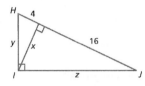

Figure 13.10

Answer According to Theorem 13.6

$$\frac{4}{x} = \frac{x}{16}$$
$$x^2 = 64$$
$$x = 8$$

According to Theorem 13.6

$$\frac{4}{y} = \frac{y}{20} \quad \text{and} \quad \frac{16}{z} = \frac{z}{20}$$
$$y^2 = 80 \quad \text{and} \quad z^2 = 320$$
$$y = 4\sqrt{5} \quad \text{and} \quad z = 8\sqrt{5}$$

Answers
1. $x = 34$
2. $x = \frac{12}{11}$
3. $x = 6$
4. $x = 13$
5. $x = 4$
6. $5\sqrt{3}$ units
7. $10\sqrt{3}$ units
8. 10 units
9. $2\sqrt{39}$ units
10. $8\sqrt{3}$ units
11. $2\sqrt{6}$ units
12. $\sqrt{33}$ units
13. $4\sqrt{11}$ units
14. $\sqrt{xy}$ units
15. $6\sqrt{3}$ units

▶ A. Exercises

Solve each proportion; assume that x is positive.

1. $\dfrac{x}{6} = \dfrac{17}{3}$

2. $\dfrac{x}{4} = \dfrac{3}{11}$

3. $\dfrac{x}{9} = \dfrac{4}{x}$

4. $\dfrac{x - 1}{3} = \dfrac{4}{1}$

5. $\dfrac{x - 3}{2} = \dfrac{2}{x}$

▶ B. Exercises

Given that $\triangle ABC$ is a right triangle and $\overline{DC}$ is an altitude to the hypotenuse, $\overline{AB}$, find the length of the indicated sides.

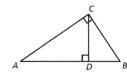

6. $AD = 15$ units; $DB = 5$ units; find CD
7. $AD = 15$ units; $DB = 5$ units; find AC
8. $AD = 15$ units; $DB = 5$ units; find BC
9. $AB = 32$ units; $DB = 6$ units; find CD
10. $AB = 32$ units; $DB = 6$ units; find BC
11. $AD = 6$ units; $AB = 10$ units; find CD
12. $AD = 8$ units; $DB = 3$ units; find BC
13. $AD = 11$ units; $DB = 5$ units; find AC
14. $AD = x$ units; $DB = y$ units; find CD
15. $AD = 12$ units; $AB = 18$ units; find CB

Prove exercises 16-17 using the figure.

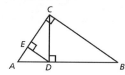

16. *Given:* Right $\triangle ABC$ with altitude $\overline{CD}$; $\overline{DE} \perp \overline{AC}$
    Prove: $\triangle AED \sim \triangle ACB$
17. *Given:* Right $\triangle ABC$ with altitude $\overline{CD}$
    Prove: $(CD)^2 = (AD)(BD)$
18. *Given:* Right $\triangle LMN$ with altitude $\overline{NO}$; $(LM)(NO) = (NM)^2$
    Prove: $MO = NO$

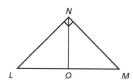

▶ **C. Exercises**

Prove the other two cases of Theorem 13.4.
19. $\triangle BCD \sim \triangle ACB$ (Case I)
20. $\triangle ABD \sim \triangle BCD$ (Case III)

■ **Cumulative Review**

Which pairs of figures are similar? For each pair of similar figures, give the scale factor, k.
21. Two circles with radii 3 and 6
22. Two rectangles: 6 by 9 and 8 by 12
23. Two rectangles: 6 by 8 and 16 by 18
24. Two regular tetrahedra with sides of length 9 and 6 respectively
25. Two squares with sides of length s and t respectively

16.

1. $\triangle ABC$ is a right triangle with altitude $\overline{CD}$; $\overline{DE} \perp \overline{AC}$	1. Given
2. $\angle DEA$ is a right angle	2. Definition of perpendicular
3. $\angle ACB$ is a right angle	3. Definition of right triangle
4. $\angle DEA \cong \angle ACB$	4. All right angles are congruent
5. $\angle A \cong \angle A$	5. Reflexive property of congruent angles
6. $\triangle AED \sim \triangle ACB$	6. AA

17.

1. $\triangle ABC$ is a right triangle with altitude $\overline{CD}$	1. Given
2. $\dfrac{AD}{CD} = \dfrac{CD}{BD}$	2. Altitude is geometric mean of two parts of hypotenuse
3. $(CD)^2 = (AD)(BD)$	3. Multiplication property of equality

18.

1. $\triangle LMN$ is a right triangle with altitude $\overline{NO}$; $(LM)(NO) = (NM)^2$	1. Given
2. $\dfrac{LM}{NM} = \dfrac{NM}{MO}$	2. Right Triangle Proportion (Theorem 13.6)
3. $(NM)^2 = (LM)(MO)$	3. Multiplication property of equality
4. $(LM)(NO) = (LM)(MO)$	4. Transitive property of equality
5. $NO = MO$	5. Multiplication property of equality

19.

1. $\triangle ABC$ is a right triangle with altitude $\overline{BD}$	1. Given
2. $\angle C \cong \angle C$	2. Reflexive property of congruent angles
3. $\overline{BD} \perp \overline{AC}$	3. Definition of altitude
4. $\angle BDC$ is a right angle	4. Definition of perpendicular
5. $\angle ABC$ is a right angle	5. Definition of right triangle
6. $\angle ABC \cong \angle BDC$	6. All right angles congruent
7. $\triangle ACB \sim \triangle BCD$	7. AA

20.

1. $\triangle ABC$ is a right triangle with altitude $\overline{BD}$	1. Given
2. $\triangle ABD \sim \triangle ACB$	2. Proof of Case II (see p. 549)
3. $\triangle ACB \sim \triangle BCD$	3. Proof of Case I (#19)
4. $\triangle ABD \sim \triangle BCD$	4. Transitive property of equality

21. similar, $k = 2$ [13.1]
22. similar, $k = \frac{4}{3}$ [13.1]
23. not similar [13.1]
24. similar, $k = \frac{2}{3}$ [13.1]
25. similar, $k = \frac{t}{s}$ [13.1]

Slopes of Perpendicular Lines

Objectives

1. To prove that perpendicular lines have slopes that are negative reciprocals.
2. To derive the equations of lines that are perpendicular to given lines.
3. To show that two lines are perpendicular.

Vocabulary
negative reciprocals

Assignment
- Intuitive: 1-4
- Standard: 1-5
- Rigorous: 1-5

Analytic Geometry

Slopes of Perpendicular Lines

You can use similar triangles to show that the product of the slopes of perpendicular lines is -1.

Theorem
If two distinct nonvertical lines are perpendicular, then their slopes are negative reciprocals.

Given: $l_1 \perp l_2$
Prove: $m_1 \cdot m_2 = -1$

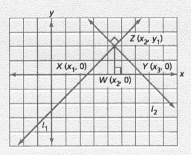

STATEMENTS	REASONS
1. $l_1 \perp l_2$	1. Given
2. Draw the altitude $\overline{ZW}$ of right $\triangle XYZ$	2. Auxiliary line
3. $\frac{XW}{ZW} = \frac{ZW}{WY}$	3. The altitude is the geometric mean between the two segments of the hypotenuse
4. $XW = x_2 - x_1$ $ZW = y_1$ $WY = x_3 - x_2$	4. Distance formula for number lines
5. $\frac{x_2 - x_1}{y_1} = \frac{y_1}{x_3 - x_2}$	5. Substitution (step 4 into 3)
6. $m_1 = \frac{y_1}{x_2 - x_1}$ $\quad m_2 = \frac{-y_1}{x_3 - x_2} = -\left(\frac{y_1}{x_3 - x_2}\right)$	6. Definition of slope
7. $m_1 \cdot m_2 = \frac{y_1}{x_2 - x_1} \cdot -\left(\frac{y_1}{x_3 - x_2}\right)$	7. Multiplication property of equality
8. $m_1 \cdot m_2 = \frac{y_1}{x_2 - x_1} \cdot -\left(\frac{x_2 - x_1}{y_1}\right)$	8. Substitution (step 5 into 7)
9. $m_1 \cdot m_2 = -1$	9. Inverse property of multiplication

Presentation

The theorem in this feature is used repeatedly in algebra and higher math classes; however, algebra books never present the proof. Go through the proof now since this may be the only time that students see a proof of this key theorem.

Guide the students through the proof. It makes use of Theorem 13.5 (step 3), which you should point out. They should be surprised that similar triangles are used to prove a basic theorem about the slopes of lines. Step 9 is a rare use in proofs of the inverse property of multiplication for real numbers. Students may not recall the property but will find it easy if you explain. Point out that step 9 is obtained by canceling expressions in step 8 and remind them that cancellation is the same as multiplying a

number by its reciprocal (as shown in the table on p. 85).

Name several numbers as slopes of lines (such as $\frac{5}{11}$, $\frac{-4}{3}$, 8, -17, and $\frac{1}{14}$). Have students call out the slope of a perpendicular line ($-\frac{11}{5}$, $\frac{3}{4}$, $-\frac{1}{8}$, $\frac{1}{17}$, and -14 respectively).

This proof is algebraic in nature, and students who like algebra will find it easier than other geometry proofs. Draw attention to this fact. This will again show the relation between geometry and algebra. Use the opportunity to emphasize the order and harmony in God's creation. The fact that algebra and geometry relate in an orderly fashion is a reflection of the order in God's creation.

Review the following forms of lines and their slopes.
Slope Formulas
$m = \frac{y_2 - y_1}{x_2 - x_1}$ (definition)
$m_2 = m_1$ (parallel lines)
$m_2 = \frac{-1}{m_1}$ (perpendicular lines)
Equations of Lines
$ax + by = c$ (general or standard form)
$y = mx + b$ (slope-intercept form)
$y - y_1 = m(x - x_1)$ (point-slope form)

Therefore if the slope of one line is $\frac{3}{7}$, the slope of a perpendicular line is $-\frac{7}{3}$. You often use this relationship to find equations of lines in algebra.

▶ Exercises

Give the equation of the line perpendicular to the line described and satisfying the given conditions.

1. $y = -\frac{4}{3}x + 5$ with y-intercept $(0, -8)$

2. $y = 2x - 1$ and passing through $(1, 4)$

3. the line containing $(2, 5)$ and $(3, 4)$ at the first point

4. $y = \frac{1}{2}x + 5$, if their point of intersection occurs when $x = 2$

5. *Prove:* The diagonals of a rhombus are perpendicular to each other. (*Hint:* Find a in terms of b and c.)

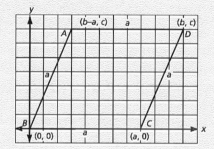

Answers

1. $y = \frac{3}{4}x - 8$

2. $y = \frac{-1}{2}x + \frac{9}{2}$

3. $y = x + 3$

4. $y = -2x + 10$

5.

Statement	Reason
1. $m_{AC} = \frac{c}{b-2a}$ $m_{BD} = \frac{c}{b}$	1. Definition of slope
2. $d_{AB} = d_{BC}$	2. Definition of rhombus
3. $d_{AB} = \sqrt{(b-a)^2 + c^2}$ $d_{BC} = \sqrt{a^2}$	3. Distance formula
4. $\sqrt{(b-a)^2 + c^2} = \sqrt{a^2}$	4. Substitution
5. $(b-a)^2 + c^2 = a^2$	5. Square both sides
6. $b^2 - 2ab + a^2 + c^2 = a^2$	6. FOIL
7. $b^2 - 2ab + c^2 = 0$	7. Addition property of equality
8. $b^2 + c^2 = 2ab$	8. Addition property of equality
9. $\frac{b^2+c^2}{2b} = a$	9. Multiplication property of equality
10. $m_{AC} = \frac{c}{b-2a}$ $= \frac{c}{b - 2(\frac{b^2+c^2}{2b})}$ $= \frac{c}{\frac{b^2-b^2-c^2}{b}}$ $= \frac{c}{\frac{-c^2}{b}}$ $= \frac{cb}{-c^2}$ $= \frac{-b}{c}$	10. Substitution
11. $m_{AC} \cdot m_{BD} =$ $\frac{-b}{c} \cdot \frac{c}{b} = -1$	11. Multiplicative inverse property
12. $\overleftrightarrow{AC} \perp \overleftrightarrow{BD}$	12. Slopes of perpendicular lines

Tips

Ex. 1. $m_1 = \frac{-4}{3}$ from slope-intercept form, so $m_2 = \frac{3}{4}$. Substitute this and $b = -8$ into the slope-intercept form.

Ex. 2. $m_1 = 2$, so $m_2 = \frac{-1}{2}$. Substitute this and $(1, 4)$ into point-slope form.

Ex. 3. $m_1 = \frac{4-5}{3-2} = -1$ by the definition of slope. Use $m_2 = 1$ and $(2, 5)$ in the point-slope form.

Ex. 4. $m_1 = \frac{1}{2}$, so $m_2 = -2$. When $x = 2$, $y = 6$. Use point-slope form.

Ex. 5. You may have proved this crucial proof without algebra (Additional Problem 2 in Section 7.2), and the algebraic proof offers an opportunity to show how different two proofs of the same theorem can be. ■

Similar Triangles and Proportions

Objectives

1. To prove theorems relating altitudes, medians, angle bisectors, perimeters, and areas of pairs of similar triangles.
2. To compute lengths of related segments in similar triangles.

Assignment

- Intuitive: 1-10, 21-26
- Standard: 1-15, 20-26
- Rigorous: 1-9 odd, 11-26

Resources

- *Activities Manual,* Math History Activity. Focuses on Felix Klein.
- *Test Packet,* Quiz 3, Chapter 13 covers Section 13.4.

Reading and Writing Mathematics

Have the students look up the definition of a geometric progression and answer the following questions.

1. Give the next four terms of the geometric progression: 5, 15, . . . **45, 135, 405, 1215**
2. Give the next four terms of the geometric progression: $1, \frac{1}{5},$ . . . $\frac{1}{25}, \frac{1}{125}, \frac{1}{625}, \frac{1}{3125}$
3. Write the general form of a geometric progression. $A_n = A_1 r^{(n-1)}$
4. Identify A_1 and r for problems 1 and 2. **For problem 1, $A_1 = 5$ and $r = 3$; for problem 2, $A_1 = 1$ and $r = \frac{1}{5}$**

13.4 Similar Triangles and Proportions

This section presents some of the many proportions associated with similar triangles. Theorem 13.10 was proved in exercise 20 of Section 13.1, and the rest are exercises in this section.

St. Louis Cathedral in New Orleans, Louisiana, has similar pyramids for steeples. Built in 1794, it is the oldest cathedral in the United States.

Theorem 13.7

In similar triangles the lengths of the altitudes extending to corresponding sides are in the same ratio as the lengths of the corresponding sides.

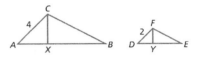

Figure 13.11

In figure 13.11, if $\triangle ABC \sim \triangle DEF$ and $\frac{AC}{DF} = 2$, then $\frac{CX}{FY} = 2$. If $CX = 3$ units, then $FY = \frac{3}{2}$ or 1.5 units.

Theorem 13.8

In similar triangles the lengths of the medians extending to corresponding sides are in the same ratio as the lengths of the corresponding sides.

Do you remember that a median extends from a vertex to the midpoint of the opposite side?

Presentation

The basic plan for proving the theorems in this section is to use the division of each of the similar triangles into two new triangles and to show that the corresponding triangles that result are also similar.

Most of the exercises in this section involve expressing proportions. Remind students to compare the correct corresponding parts. You can highlight the corresponding sides of the similar triangles with colored chalk. (You can even use dashed colored lines in one triangle and solid colored lines in the other to help set up ratios within or between triangles.)

Tips

Ex. 8-10, 14. These involve area and so require the square of the side for correct proportions. (Since area is in square units, this should be easy to remember.)

Ex. 20. Similar to the above, the volumes will require the cube of the side (cubic units). ∎

EXAMPLE Since △ABC ~ △XYZ, find AD.

Answer By Theorem 13.8, $\frac{AC}{XZ} = \frac{AD}{XW}$. Substituting numbers from the figure, $\frac{12}{8} = \frac{AD}{6}$; so AD = 9 units.

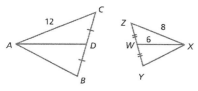

Figure 13.12

Draw a diagram to illustrate Theorem 13.9.

Theorem 13.9
In similar triangles the lengths of the corresponding angle bisectors from the vertices to the points where they intersect the opposite sides are in the same ratio as the lengths of the corresponding sides of the triangles.

Theorem 13.10
In similar triangles the perimeters of the triangles are in the same ratio as the lengths of the corresponding sides.

So far, you have seen that altitudes, medians, angle bisectors, and perimeters are all proportional to the sides. What do you predict for the ratio of the areas? Does the next theorem surprise you?

Theorem 13.11
In similar triangles the ratio of the areas of the triangles is equal to the square of the ratio of the lengths of corresponding sides.

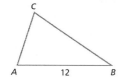

Figure 13.13

Additional Problems

1. Given △ABC ~ △GEF, $\overline{AD}$ and $\overline{GH}$ are altitudes. Find AB. **x = 7, AB = 8**

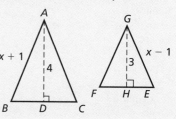

2. Given △MOP ~ △RAG, $\overline{OK}$ and $\overline{AT}$ are medians. Find TG. **MP = 2(MK) = 20; $\frac{8}{10} = \frac{20}{RG}$; RG = 25; TG = $\frac{1}{2}$ (25) = 12.5**

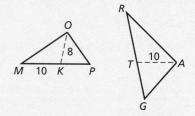

3. Given △TOP ~ △BAG, $\overline{OD}$ and $\overline{AR}$ are angle bisectors. Find OD. **OD = 8**

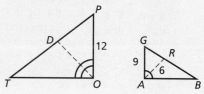

4. Given △ARP ~ △HOT, H, O, and T are midpoints, and the area of △HOT is 24 units². Find the area of △ARP.

   HO = $\frac{1}{2}$ AR, so $\frac{HO}{AR} = \frac{1}{2}$;

   $\frac{\text{Area } \triangle HOT}{\text{Area } \triangle ARP} = \left(\frac{1}{2}\right)^2$;

   Area of △ARP = 96 units²

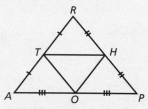

5. Given △ABC ~ △DEF, perimeter of △ABC = 144 and perimeter of △DEF = 16, AB = 12. Find DE. **DE = $1\frac{1}{3}$**

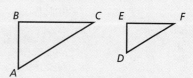

Answers

1. 3 units
2. 18 units
3. 5 units
4. 20 units
5. 4 units
6. 35 units
7. 40 units
8. 9 sq. units
9. 45 sq. units
10. 6 units
11. Answers will vary. $\frac{AB}{MN} = \frac{AE}{MQ}$
12. Answers will vary. $\frac{AC}{MO} = \frac{DC}{PO}$
13. Answers will vary. $\frac{AC}{MO} = \frac{BF}{NR}$
14. $\left(\frac{AC}{MO}\right)^2 = \frac{\text{Area of } \triangle ABC}{\text{Area of } \triangle MNO}$
15. Answers will vary; $\frac{AC}{MO} = \frac{\text{perimeter } \triangle ABC}{\text{perimeter } \triangle MNO}$

16.

1. $\triangle ABC \sim \triangle DEF$; $\overline{CX}$ and $\overline{FY}$ are the corresponding altitudes	1. Given
2. $\angle B \cong \angle E$	2. Definition of similar triangles
3. $\angle CXB$ and $\angle FYE$ are right angles	3. Definition of altitude (and perpendicular)
4. $\angle CXB \cong \angle FYE$	4. All right angles are congruent
5. $\triangle CXB \sim \triangle FYE$	5. AA
6. $\frac{FE}{CB} = \frac{FY}{CX}$; $\frac{FE}{CB} = \frac{DE}{AB}$	6. Definition of similar triangles
7. $\frac{FY}{CX} = \frac{DE}{AB}$	7. Substitution (see step 6)

17.

1. $\triangle ABC \sim \triangle EFG$; $\overline{CD}$ and $\overline{GH}$ are medians	1. Given
2. $\angle B \cong \angle F$; $\frac{EF}{AB} = \frac{FG}{BC}$	2. Definition of similar triangles
3. D and H are the midpoints of $\overline{AB}$ and $\overline{EF}$	3. Definition of median
4. $DB = \frac{1}{2}AB$; $HF = \frac{1}{2}EF$	4. Midpoint Theorem
5. $AB = 2DB$; $EF = 2HF$	5. Multiplication property of equality
6. $\frac{2HF}{2DB} = \frac{FG}{BC}$	6. Substitution (step 5 into 2)
7. $\frac{HF}{DB} = \frac{FG}{BC}$	7. Cancellation property
8. $\triangle CDB \sim \triangle GHF$	8. SAS
9. $\frac{GH}{CD} = \frac{FG}{BC}$	9. Definition of similar triangles

If $\triangle ABC \sim \triangle DEF$ and the sides have lengths as indicated, then the ratio of the areas of the triangles is $\left(\frac{12}{4}\right)^2 = 3^2 = 9$ or 9 to 1.

If the area of $\triangle DEF$ is 6 square units, then the area of $\triangle ABC$ is 54 square units.

▶ A. Exercises

Find the indicated lengths in exercises 1-10. Assume that $\triangle ABC \sim \triangle MNO$.

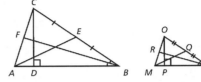

1. $AC = 8$ units; $MO = 4$ units; $CD = 6$ units; find OP
2. $AB = 15$ units; $MN = 5$ units; $NR = 6$ units; find BF
3. $BC = 24$ units; $NO = 12$ units; $AE = 10$ units; find MQ
4. $FB = 16$ units; $RN = 12$ units; $NO = 15$ units; find BC
5. $CD = 9$ units; $OP = 3$ units; $AE = 12$ units; find MQ
6. $MO = 9$ units; $AC = 18$ units; perimeter of $\triangle ABC = 70$ units; find the perimeter of $\triangle MNO$
7. $FB = 10$ units; $RN = 7$ units; perimeter of $\triangle MNO = 28$ units; find the perimeter of $\triangle ABC$
8. $AC = 8$ units; $MO = 4$ units; Area of $\triangle ABC = 36$ square units; find the Area of $\triangle MNO$
9. $BC = 9$ units; $NO = 6$ units; Area of $\triangle MNO = 20$ square units; find the Area of $\triangle ABC$
10. Area of $\triangle ABC = 81$ square units; Area of $\triangle MNO = 9$ square units; $AB = 18$ units; find MN

▶ B. Exercises

Use the same triangles in exercises 1-10 to answer exercises 11-15.

11. State a proportion involving the medians in the triangles.
12. State a proportion involving the altitudes in the triangles.
13. State a proportion involving the angle bisectors in the triangles.
14. State a proportion involving the area of the triangles.
15. State a proportion involving the perimeters of the triangles.

Prove each theorem.
16. Theorem 13.7
17. Theorem 13.8
18. Theorem 13.9
19. Theorem 13.11

▶ C. Exercises

20. Prove that if two regular tetrahedra are similar, then the ratio of the volumes is equal to the cube of the ratio of the sides.

■ Cumulative Review

Give the name of each shaded figure. Classify each as convex or concave.

21.
23.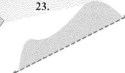
25.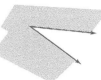
22.
24.
26.

18.

1. $\triangle ABC \sim \triangle PQR$ AK and PL are angle bisectors	1. Given
2. $\angle BAC \cong \angle QPR$, $\angle B \cong \angle Q$	2. Definition of similar triangles
3. $\angle BAK \cong \angle QPL$	3. Congruent Angle Bisector Theorem
4. $\triangle ABK \sim \triangle PQL$	4. AA
5. $\frac{PQ}{AB} = \frac{PL}{AK}$	5. Definition of similar triangles

19.

1. $\triangle ABC \sim \triangle EFG$ with altitudes $\overline{CD}$ and $\overline{GH}$ respectively	1. Given
2. $\frac{EF}{AB} = \frac{GH}{CD} = k$	2. The altitudes of similar triangles are in the same ratio as the corresponding sides
3. $A_1 =$ Area $\triangle ABC$ $= \frac{1}{2}(AB)(CD);$ $A_2 =$ Area $\triangle EFG$ $= \frac{1}{2}(EF)(GH)$	3. Area of a triangle
4. $\frac{A_2}{A_1} = \frac{\frac{1}{2}(EF)(GH)}{\frac{1}{2}(AB)(CD)}$	4. Multiplication property of equality
5. $\frac{A_2}{A_1} = \frac{(EF)(GH)}{(AB)(CD)} = \frac{EF}{AB} \cdot \frac{GH}{CD}$	5. Cancellation property
6. $\frac{A_2}{A_1} = k \cdot k = k^2$	6. Substitution (step 2 into 5)

20.

1. Similar tetrahedra of edge lengths s and e	1. Given
2. The scale of factor $k = \frac{e}{s}$	2. Definition of similar (and scale factor)
3. $V_2 = \frac{\sqrt{2}}{12} e^3;$ $V_1 = \frac{\sqrt{2}}{12} s^3$	3. Volume of tetrahedron
4. $\frac{V_2}{V_1} = \frac{\frac{\sqrt{2}}{12} e^3}{\frac{\sqrt{2}}{12} s^3}$ $= \frac{e^3}{s^3} = \left(\frac{e}{s}\right)^3$	4. Multiplication property of equality
5. $\frac{V_2}{V_1} = k^3$	5. Substitution (step 2 into 4)

21. hexagonal region, convex [2.5]
22. annular region, concave [11.5]
23. half-plane, convex [2.5]
24. interior of triangle, convex [2.5]
25. angle and its exterior, concave [2.5]
26. quadrilateral region, concave [2.5]

Section 13.5

Similar Triangles and Problem Solving

Objectives

1. To apply the proportions from similar triangles to solve word problems.
2. To apply scale proportions to compute mileage or distances on a scale drawing or map.

Assignment

- Intuitive: 1-15, 21-25
- Standard: 1-25
- Rigorous: 1-25

Additional Problems

1. If a vertical yardstick casts a 5-foot shadow, how high is a building that casts a 170-foot shadow? **102 ft.**
2. Scott's dog Rusty is two feet high and casts a 15-inch shadow. How long is Scott's shadow if he is 5' 11"? $\frac{x}{15} = \frac{71}{24}$; $x = 44\frac{3}{8}$ **in. long or 4' $8\frac{3}{8}$"**
3. The scale on a map shows one inch = 60 feet. Using the scale factor, find the required values.
   a) $3\frac{3}{4}$ in. represents _____ ft. **225**
   b) $\frac{5}{8}$ in. represents _____ ft. **37.5**
   c) To represent 540 ft., use _____ in. **9**
   d) To represent 45 ft., use _____ in. **$\frac{3}{4}$**

You should apply new material that you learn whenever possible. A Christian should also glean biblical principles and learn to apply them to his life (Prov. 2:1-5; 23:12). In this lesson you will see several applications of similar triangles.

EXAMPLE 1   Suppose that you are standing in front of the Capitol in Washington, D.C., and that you want to know the building's height above the street level but cannot measure it directly. How can you find the height of the building?

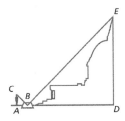

Figure 13.14

Answer 1. If you place a mirror on the ground 345 feet from the center of the rotunda in the Capitol and stand at a distance of 6 feet from the mirror, you can see the top of the Capitol reflected in the mirror. The angle at which the image reflects is the same in both directions, so $\angle ABC \cong \angle DBE$.

2. If your eye height from the ground is 5 feet, you can find the height of the dome by using similar triangles. Notice that $\triangle ABC \sim \triangle DBE$ because of AA. The corresponding sides are therefore proportional.

$$\frac{DE}{AC} = \frac{DB}{AB} \qquad\qquad \frac{DE}{5} = \frac{345}{6}$$

Continued ▶

Work through example 1. Ask why $\triangle ABC \sim \triangle DBE$. (*by AA since all right angles are congruent, and the angles at B are congruent since the angle of incidence is equal to the angle of reflection*). Students may be able to answer this even if you did not cover Chapter 12 (it was covered in *Basic Science,* BJU Press).

Some students will think that example 1 is unrealistic because you would not be able to measure the distance *BD* as 345 feet. Generate discussion about whether this is possible. Measuring wheels (such as those used by writers of guidebooks for hiking trails), however, could measure the flat areas and the step widths could be measured with rulers and added on.

Access to the blueprints would offer precise distances even without the measuring wheel.

The text asks if there could be a different way to solve example 1. The method of shadows shown in #6 would be a good possibility. Your students may see other ways. Encourage their creativity, but make sure they justify their method.

Example 2 should be easy after they have seen example 1. See if they can do it without looking in the book. This will prepare them for the exercises.

Ex. 12. The base of the larger right triangle is 8 + 3 or 11 feet, which corresponds to the length x of the rope (hypotenuse). $\frac{x}{5} = \frac{11}{3}$

Ex. 16. Let x be the new side corresponding to the 5-foot leg. The areas are proportional to the squares of the sides, $\frac{A_{new}}{A_{old}} = (\frac{x}{5})^2 = \frac{x^2}{25}$. Since the new area will be 9 times the old, the left side is equal to 9, so $x^2 = 9 \cdot 25$, or $x = 15$. Similarly, the other leg will be 3 times longer, or 21 feet.

Ex. 24. Although each digit is a curve, the two-digit number is not because you must lift up the pen between digits. ∎

3. From the computations below, the dome of the Capitol, including the statue of Freedom, is 287.5 feet high.

$$6DE = 5(345)$$
$$6DE = 1725$$
$$DE = 287.5$$

You can work most of these problems in more than one way by using different similar triangles. Can you find a different way to solve example 1?

EXAMPLE 2 A state park is building a boardwalk trail for visitors through a wetland. The plan calls for the trail to cross part of the pond as it winds through the surrounding marsh and bog. How long must the bridge be to cross the pond at the points indicated?

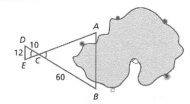

Figure 13.15

Answer To avoid wading in the pond, the rangers measure angles at D and E congruent to angles at B and A. This makes $\overleftrightarrow{DE} \parallel \overleftrightarrow{AB}$.

1. $\triangle ABC \sim \triangle EDC$ by AA
   $$\frac{AB}{ED} = \frac{BC}{DC}$$

2. The rangers measure $\overline{BC}$, $\overline{CD}$, and $\overline{ED}$: $BC = 60$ ft., $DC = 10$ ft., and $ED = 12$ ft.
   $$\frac{AB}{12} = \frac{60}{10}$$

3. Solve the proportion.
   $$10(AB) = (60)(12)$$
   $$10(AB) = 720$$
   $$AB = 72 \text{ ft.}$$

4. The pond boardwalk must span 72 ft.

4. A triangular section of a city occupies 27 acres and is divided at even intervals by Pine St. and Maple St., which are parallel to Oak St. and perpendicular to Orange Ave. Find the area of each section A, B, and C.

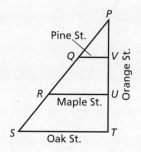

$$\frac{\text{Area } \triangle PRU}{\text{Area } \triangle PST} = (\tfrac{2}{3})^2; \text{ Area } \frac{\triangle PRU}{27} = \frac{4}{9};$$

Area $\triangle PRU$ = 12 acres

$$\frac{\text{Area } \triangle PQV}{27} = (\tfrac{1}{3})^2; \text{ Area } \triangle PQV = 3 \text{ acres}$$

Area QRUV = 12 − 3 = 9 acres;
Area RSTU = 27 − 12 = 15 acres

Answers

1. 2.5 miles
2. 30 miles
3. 17.5 miles
4. 8 inches
5. 1.2 inches
6. 120 ft.
7. 480 ft.
8. 45 ft.

▶ **A. Exercises**

The scale on a map shows 5 miles represented by 2 inches. Make a ratio as a scale factor and then answer the questions below.

1. What does one inch represent?
2. How far apart are two places if the distance on the map is twelve inches?
3. What distance corresponds to seven inches on the map?
4. What length represents twenty miles?
5. How does the map represent three miles?

▶ **B. Exercises**

6. Karen wants to find the height of the flagpole in front of the school. An 8-foot pole casts a 10-foot shadow at the same time the flagpole casts a 150-foot shadow. How high is the flagpole?

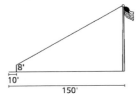

7. Al is an archaeologist and is trying to find the height of a pyramid that he is studying. If he uses the mirror technique described in example 1, he must stand 8 feet from the mirror that is placed 640 feet from the center of the pyramid. Al's eyes are approximately 6 feet from the ground. How high is the pyramid?

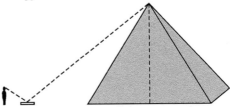

8. Find the length of the shadow that a 30-foot telephone pole casts when a 2-foot pole casts a shadow of 3 feet.

9. Dan is standing at an observation deck on top of Pine Mountain, which is 5,872 feet high. From this viewpoint Dan can see a river on the far side of Buck Ridge (as shown). If Buck Ridge is 2,936 feet high and 4,875 feet from the river, how far from the river is Pine Mountain?

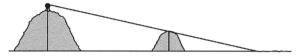

10. John and his friends have a tree house by a stream. They want to place a log across the stream as a bridge. How long must the log be in order to reach across the stream? See the figure.

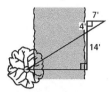

11. How tall is the Washington Monument if it casts a 185-foot shadow at the same time that a 3-foot pole casts a 1-foot shadow?

Washington Monument in Washington, D.C.

12. 18.3 ft.
13. 5.3 in.
14. 210 ft.
15. 70 yd., or 210 ft.
16. 15 by 21 ft.

12. A tent rope goes from the top of the tent to the ground and is connected to two poles, one at the top and one at the edge of the tent. How long must the rope be if the distance from the stake to the first pole is 3 feet, the distance between the two poles is 8 feet, and the distance from the stake to the top of the first pole is 5 feet?

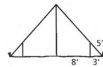

13. A flashlight shines directly on a strip of metal. How long is the strip of metal if its shadow on the wall is 16 inches long and the flashlight is 8 inches from the metal and 24 inches from the wall?

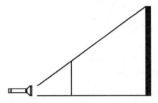

14. How tall is a tree if it casts an 84-foot shadow at the same time that a 10-foot pole casts a 4-foot shadow?

15. Find the depth of a rock quarry, using the information in the figure.

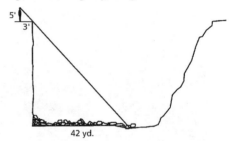

16. Mrs. Brown has a small vegetable garden. The garden forms a right triangle with legs of five and seven feet respectively. She plans to enlarge the garden to have nine times more area; how long will the legs be for the new garden?

17. Farmer Smith has a triangular pasture that is fenced. The longest side is 120 feet, and he used 300 feet of fencing. He plans to expand the pasture. The new pasture will be the same shape, and the longest side will be 180 feet. How much fencing will he use to fence it? How much more must he buy if he can still use all the old fencing?

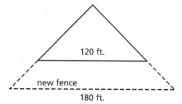

18. The scale of a map shows that one inch represents forty miles. A traveling salesman drives to Grand Island and Fargo and then returns home to Sioux City. According to the map, the perimeter of the triangular circuit was $21\frac{1}{4}$ inches. How far did he drive?

▶ **C. Exercises**

19. Mr. Cramer owns a large triangular lot. Because a river bounds two sides, he will fence only the longest side. Using 30 feet of fence, he partitioned off an area covering 80 square feet. How much fencing would he need to partition off an area covering 180 square feet?

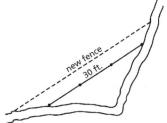

20. Suppose Mr. Cramer's triangular lot has a perimeter of 200 feet. If a portion with an 80-foot perimeter requires a fence 30 feet long on the long side, how much fence is needed on the long side of the entire lot?

Cumulative Review

Match the shape of each symbol (numeral or dash) to its classification.

21. 6   A. Simple Closed Curve
22. –   B. Simple Curve (not closed)
23. 0   C. Closed Curve (not simple)
24. 30   D. Curve (neither simple nor closed)
25. 8   E. Not a curve

17. 450 ft., buy 150 ft. more
18. 850 mi.
19. 45 ft.
20. 75 ft.
21. D [2.4]
22. B [2.4]
23. A [2.4]
24. E [2.4]
25. C [2.4]

Circles and Proportions

Objectives

1. To define segments of intersecting chords, secants, and tangents.
2. To prove theorems relating lengths of segments determined by chords, secants, and tangents of circles.
3. To apply theorems about segments formed by chords, secants, and tangents to specific circles.

Vocabulary

external secant segments
secant segments
segments of a chord

Assignments

- Intuitive: 1-10, 21-25
- Standard: 1-16, 21-25
- Rigorous: 1-15 odd, 16-25

13.6 Circles and Proportions

The Fuglevad windmill in the Netherlands has secants that intersect at the center. Note also the pyramidal base.

In Chapter 9 you studied chords, secants, and tangents. You learned how to compute the angles formed by intersections of these lines. When such lines intersect, it is also possible to find the lengths of the segments formed by using proportions.

Similar triangles provide a means of proving these proportions. Some of these relationships and proportions are basic to trigonometry, as you will see in the next chapter.

The first theorem describes a relationship between intersecting chords of a circle.

Theorem 13.12

If two chords intersect in the interior of a circle, then the product of the lengths of the segments of one chord is equal to the product of the lengths of the segments of the other chord.

Figure 13.16

This theorem states that since $\overline{AC}$ and $\overline{BD}$ intersect in the interior of $\odot O$, then $(AE)(EC) = (DE)(EB)$. Here is a proof of this theorem.

Given: $\odot O$ with chords $\overline{AC}$ and $\overline{BD}$ that intersect at E

Prove: $(AE)(EC) = (DE)(EB)$

Figure 13.17

Presentation

The plan for proving Theorems 13.12 and 13.13 is to establish similar triangles and use the resulting proportions. Once the auxiliary lines are drawn to identify the similar triangles, simply set up and solve relevant proportions.

The conclusion of Theorem 13.13 in product form may be hard to remember. Using the similar triangles and their resulting proportions may be easier for some students.

Ask students to guess formulas if a tangent is used instead of a secant (*the product of secant segments equals the square of the tangent segment*). This result can be presented three ways: proof (#20), alternate proof (Additional Problem 5, which is quick but clever), or an informal argument treating the

tangent as a secant with an interior part of length zero (apply Theorem 13.13 with $AC = AB + BC$ and $AB = 0$). If you assign #20, use the informal argument in class. You can then show the shortcut proof of Additional Problem 5 when students turn in homework. Note that if both lines are tangents, students already know that the tangent segments will be congruent.

Common Student Error. Students often use the pairs of short segments when applying Theorem 13.13. Emphasize that in both theorems, all distances in products are measured to the point of intersection of the secant lines.

Tips

Ex. 12. Equation: $3(x + 3) = 2(3 + 2)$

Ex. 13. Using Theorem 13.13, the products 7 times 4 and $(x + 12)$ times x are equal. Thus, $28 = x^2 + 12x$; $0 = x^2 + 12x - 28$; $0 = (x + 14)(x - 2)$; $x = -14$ or 2; since a length cannot be negative, 2 is the solution.

Ex. 14. Since the diameter is 10, 9 and 1 are two portions of the secant that is a diameter. The equation is $2x = 9 \cdot 1$.

Ex. 15. Using Theorem 13.13, the products 7 times 3 and $(2r + 2)$ times 2 are equal, with r being the radius of the circle. Thus, $21 = 4r + 4$; $17 = 4r$; $r = \frac{17}{4}$ or 4.25.

Ex. 16-19. These are useful in Chapter 14. You may prefer to assign only #16 and post-

STATEMENTS	REASONS
1. $\odot O$ with chords $\overline{AC}$ and $\overline{BD}$ that intersect at E	1. Given
2. Draw $\overline{AD}$ and $\overline{BC}$	2. Line Postulate
3. $\angle AED \cong \angle BEC$	3. Vertical Angle Theorem
4. $\angle ADB \cong \angle BCA$	4. Angles inscribed in the same arc are congruent
5. $\triangle AED \sim \triangle BEC$	5. AA
6. $\frac{EB}{AE} = \frac{EC}{DE}$	6. Definition of similar triangles
7. $(DE)(EB) = (AE)(EC)$	7. Multiplication property of equality
8. If $\overline{AC}$ and $\overline{BD}$ are chords intersecting at E, then $(AE)(EC) = (DE)(EB)$	8. Law of Deduction

The next theorem applies to problems in which the secants intersect in the exterior of the circle instead of the interior.

A *secant segment*, such as $\overline{AC}$ in figure 13.18, includes the chord of the circle and has as one endpoint a point in the exterior of the circle. The portion in the exterior of the circle, $\overline{BC}$, is called an *external secant segment*.

Theorem 13.13
If two secants intersect in the exterior of a circle, then the product of the lengths of one secant segment and its external secant segment is equal to the product of the lengths of the other secant segment and its external secant segment.

Given: Secants $\overleftrightarrow{AB}$ and $\overleftrightarrow{ED}$ intersect at point C in the exterior of $\odot O$

Prove: $(AC)(BC) = (EC)(DC)$

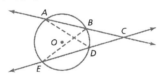

Figure 13.18

Additional Problems

Find x in the figures shown.

1.

    $2x(2x) = 5(20); x = 5$

2.

    $5(2x + 5) = x(x + 10); x = 5$

3.

    $x(x + 5) = 3(12); x = 4$

4.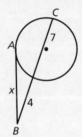

    Consider tangent $\overline{AB}$ to be a secant with internal length zero and find x using Theorem 13.13. $x(0 + x) = 4(7 + 4);$ $x \approx 6.6$

5. Prove #20 by using #18. $v^2 = t^2 + r^2$ by #18; $v^2 - r^2 = t^2$ by addition property of equality; $(v - r)(v + r) = t^2$ factoring difference of squares; $(MB)(QB) = (AB)^2$ by substitution

pone the others until the next chapter. For unit circles (radius = 1), the letters in the diagram represent important ratios in trigonometry: s, c, t, and v represent the sine, cosine, tangent, and secant ratios respectively. Note that t and v are tangent and secant segments respectively from which the ratio names derive. Thus, #18-19 prove the Pythagorean identities from trigonometry. Exercise 17 is rarely presented though it provides helpful visual aids for justifying the names of the tangent and secant ratios. This drawing is on the cover of the Visual Packet.

Ex. 21-25. Students will need resources for these and should be encouraged to research (a road atlas and an encyclopedia for Columbus).

However, if you wish to save time, the historical map for #23 is shown. The others require a map of the United States only. ∎

Answers
1. $\frac{20}{3}$ units (or $6\frac{2}{3}$)
2. 3 units
3. 4 units
4. 6 units
5. 4 units

STATEMENTS	REASONS
1. Secants $\overleftrightarrow{AB}$ and $\overleftrightarrow{ED}$ intersect at point C in the exterior of $\odot O$	1. Given
2. Draw $\overline{BE}$ and $\overline{AD}$	2. Line Postulate
3. $\angle CAD \cong \angle CEB$	3. Inscribed angles intercepting the same arc are congruent
4. $\angle ACE \cong \angle ACE$	4. Reflexive property of congruent angles
5. $\triangle DAC \sim \triangle BEC$	5. AA
6. $\frac{BC}{DC} = \frac{EC}{AC}$	6. Definition of similar triangles
7. $(AC)(BC) = (EC)(DC)$	7. Multiplication property of equality
8. If secants $\overleftrightarrow{AB}$ and $\overleftrightarrow{ED}$ intersect at C in the exterior of $\odot O$, then $(AC)(BC) = (EC)(DC)$	8. Law of Deduction

▶ **A. Exercises**

Find each length using the figure shown.

1. If $LN = 18$ units, $YN = 8$ units, and $MY = 12$ units, find YO.
2. If $LY = 4$ units, $YN = 6$ units, and $MY = 8$ units, find YO.
3. If $LY = 8$, and YN is half of MY, find YO.
4. If OY is one-third of OM, and the product of LY and YN is 8 units, find OM.

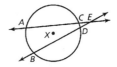

Using the diagram, find each length.
5. If $AE = 20$ units, $CE = 5$ units, and $EB = 25$ units, find ED.

6. If *EB* = 32 units, *DB* = 14 units, and *AE* = 36 units, find *AC*.

7. If *AE* = 42 units, *CE* = 12 units, and *DE* = 8 units, find *BE*.

8. If *BE* = 24 units, *DE* = 6 units, and *AE* = 36 units, find *CE*.

Find the indicated lengths.

9.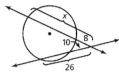

11.

10.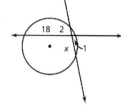

▶ B. Exercises

Find the indicated lengths.

12.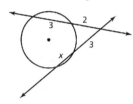

14.

13.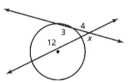

15. Find the radius.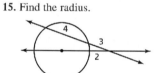

6. 20 units
7. 63 units
8. 4 units
9. $x = 32.5$
10. $x = 9$
11. $x = 2$
12. $x = \frac{1}{3}$
13. $x = 2$
14. $x = 4.5$
15. $r = \frac{17}{4}$ (or 4.25)

16.

1. $\overline{AB}$ tangent to $\odot P$ at A; $\overrightarrow{MN} \perp \overrightarrow{AP}$ at N	1. Given
2. $\overline{AP} \perp \overline{AB}$	2. Radius perpendicular to tangent at point of tangency
3. $\angle MNP$ and $\angle BAP$ are right angles	3. Definition of perpendicular
4. $\angle MNP \cong \angle BAP$	4. All right angles are congruent
5. $\angle MPN \cong \angle MPN$	5. Reflexive property of congruent angles
6. $\triangle MPN \sim \triangle BPA$	6. AA

17. $\frac{AB}{MN} = \frac{AP}{NP} = \frac{BP}{MP}$ (or $\frac{t}{s} = \frac{r}{c} = \frac{v}{r}$)

18. $\frac{t}{s} = \frac{1}{c}$, so $t = \frac{s}{c}$

19. $\frac{1}{c} = \frac{v}{1}$, so $v = \frac{1}{c}$

20.

1. $\overleftrightarrow{AB}$ is a tangent, and $\overleftrightarrow{DB}$ is a secant	1. Given
2. Draw $\overline{DA}$ and $\overline{AC}$	2. Auxiliary lines
3. $\angle 1 \cong \angle 1$	3. Reflexive property of congruent angles
4. $m\angle BAC = \frac{1}{2}m\widehat{AC}$	4. Angle formed by secant and tangent that intersect at point of tangency measures half the intercepted arc
5. $m\angle ADB = \frac{1}{2}m\widehat{AC}$	5. An inscribed angle measures half of its intercepted arc
6. $m\angle BAC = m\angle ADB$	6. Transitive property of equality
7. $\angle BAC \cong \angle ADB$	7. Definition of congruent angles
8. $\triangle BAC \sim \triangle BDA$	8. AA
9. $\frac{AB}{BC} = \frac{DB}{AB}$	9. Definition of similar triangles
10. $(AB)^2 \cong (DB)(BC)$	10. Multiplication property of equality
11. If a tangent and a secant intersect in the exterior of a circle, then the square of the length of the tangent segment equals the product of the lengths of the secant and its external secant segment.	11. Law of Deduction

Exercises 16-19 refer to the following information about the figure shown.

Given: $\overleftrightarrow{AB}$ is tangent to $\odot P$ at A

Draw: Auxiliary $\overleftrightarrow{PB}$ intersects $\odot P$ at M, and $\overleftrightarrow{MN} \perp \overline{AP}$ at N

Label: $AB = t$, $MN = s$, $PN = c$, $PB = v$, and r is the radius of $\odot P$

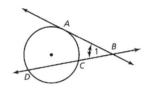

16. Prove $\triangle MPN \sim \triangle BPA$.

Use the similarity in problem 16 for exercises 17-19.

17. Write the proportion for the sides.

18. Express t in terms of s and c if the radius is 1.

19. Express v in terms of s or c if $r = 1$.

▶ **C. Exercises**

20. *Prove:* If a secant and a tangent intersect in the exterior of a circle, then the square of the length of the tangent segment equals the product of the lengths of the secant segment and the external secant segment.

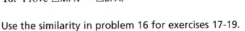

■ **Cumulative Review**

On a flat map, which curves below are simple? Which are closed?

21. The boundary of Kansas

22. The path traced by the life of a man born in Phoenix who lived for a while in Detroit and then Atlanta and died in Seattle

23. The route of Columbus's first roundtrip voyage to the New World

24. The flight path of an airplane pilot that flies from Denver via New York and Miami and back to Denver

25. The international boundary between the United States and Mexico

21. simple closed [2.4]

22. neither simple nor closed [2.4]

23. closed [2.4]

24. simple closed [2.4]

25. simple [2.4]

13.7 The Golden Ratio and Other Applications of Similarity

An interesting phenomenon appears often in the art and sculpture of the ancient world. In many of Michelangelo's and Leonardo da Vinci's paintings a special rectangular ratio occurs. This ratio is called the *Golden Ratio*. The Golden Ratio is the ratio of the length to the width of a golden rectangle. A *golden rectangle* is a rectangle with the following characteristic: if a square unit is cut from one end of the rectangle, then the resulting rectangle has the same length-to-width ratio as the original rectangle. Figure 13.19 illustrates an approximation of the golden rectangle.

Mona Lisa

Objectives

1. To define the Golden Ratio, golden rectangle, and golden spiral.
2. To identify the Golden Ratio in natural and architectural designs.

Vocabulary
Golden Ratio
golden rectangle
golden spiral

Assignment
• Intuitive: no assignment necessary
• Standard: 1-25
• Rigorous: 1-25

Resources
• *Our Christian Heritage in Art* (BJU Press, 1999). Chapter 17 discusses the golden rectangle.
• *Activities Manual*, Calculator Skills
• *Activities Manual*, Construction Skills
• *Activities Manual*, Golden Ratio in Detail
• *Test Packet*, Quiz 4, Chapter 13 covers Sections 13.5-13.7.

Reading and Writing Mathematics
Have students write the first 15 terms of the Fibonacci sequence and explain how to find successive terms. *1, 1, 2, 3, 5, 8, 13, 21, 34, 55, 89, 144, 233, 377, 610; to find a term, add the previous two together*

If you compare the lengths of the rectangles to the widths, you get a ratio of 1.619. If a 21-by-21 unit square is cut from this rectangle, a 21-by-13 unit rectangle results. The length-to-width ratio is now $\frac{21}{13} = 1.615$. Find the ratio of the length to the width of each of the resulting smaller rectangles in figure 13.19. Each time the ratio should be approximately 1.618. We can find the exact value by using algebra.

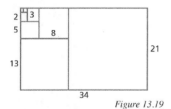

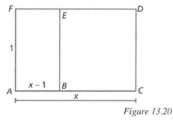

Figure 13.19

Figure 13.20

Figure 13.20 shows a general golden rectangle whose length is x units and whose width is 1 unit. Since the Golden Ratio is the ratio of the length to the width, the value of x is the value of the Golden Ratio. Because the ratio of the length to the width is the same in both the small and large rectangles, *ABEF* and *ACDF*, we can set up the proportion as follows.

13.7 THE GOLDEN RATIO AND OTHER APPLICATIONS OF SIMILARITY **571**

Presentation

With their books closed, have students draw three rectangles. Do not tell them what size. Have them put the drawings aside.

Draw a large golden rectangle on the board and show students how another golden rectangle results when you remove a square from one end of the original rectangle. Show them that this property is not true of all rectangles. Draw a rectangle that is not golden to demonstrate.

Set up the proportion for the original and the derived rectangle on the board and solve the proportion to obtain the Golden Ratio as presented in the text. Have the students use a calculator to find $\frac{1 + \sqrt{5}}{2}$ to obtain 1.618. Have them measure their rectangles to see how close they might have come to a golden rectangle. Notice that

solving the quadratic results in two answers (note ± sign). However, using the minus sign yields −0.618, which is not possible in the context of ratios of two positive lengths.

As students will discover from the Parthenon's dimensions, some ancient works display ratios that are the Golden Ratio. Since they did build accurately, many purposely chose not to use this ratio. However, since many ratios in ancient art roughly approximate the Golden Ratio, rectangles with proportions pleasing in art and architecture frequently have roughly this shape.

In figure 13.19, the sequence of numbers 1, 1, 2, 3, 5, 8, 13, 21, . . . is called the Fibonacci sequence. The ratio of any term to the previous

term approximates the Golden Ratio, and the approximation improves as the numbers get larger. References to the golden ratio in nature often involve this sequence. For instance, phyllotaxy (leaf arrangement) of plants conforms to ratios of Fibonacci numbers.

The golden ratio also relates to these mathematical ideas.

1. The ratio of the lengths of a diagonal and a side in a regular pentagon
2. The intersecting diagonals of a regular pentagon divide themselves in this ratio.
3. The ratio of the radius to a side of a regular decagon

Additional Problems

1. Is this a golden rectangle? **yes, 34 mm by 21 mm**

2. Explain why rectangle *PQRS* is not golden. **When you remove a square, you do not obtain a rectangle similar to the original. ($\frac{4}{3} \neq \frac{3}{1}$)**

3. On what percentage do you set a calculator to get a reduction to $\frac{1}{3}$ of the original size? **33%**

4. What is the scale factor if you enlarge a diagram by 100% on a copy machine? **2**

5. Use the proportion that you solved to find the Golden Ratio to prove that $\frac{1}{x} = x - 1$.
$\frac{x}{1} = \frac{1}{x - 1}$; $x^2 - x = 1$; $x(x - 1) = 1$; **and since $x \neq 0$, $x - 1 = \frac{1}{x}$ (Alternatively, recognize that the proportion to prove is equal to the one in the book by inversion.)**

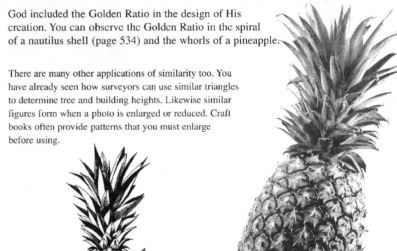

$\frac{AC}{AF} = \frac{AF}{AB}$	Golden Ratios are equal.
$\frac{x}{1} = \frac{1}{x - 1}$	
$x^2 - x = 1$	Cross multiply.
$x^2 - x - 1 = 0$	Solve this quadratic equation, using the quadratic formula.
$x = \frac{1 \pm \sqrt{1 + 4}}{2}$	
$x = \frac{1 \pm \sqrt{5}}{2}$ units	

The golden spiral is an important application of similar figures. Look at the golden spiral shown. The spiral continues to form smaller and smaller rectangles, but in the portion that is shown you should see five golden rectangles. Because their sides are proportional, all these golden rectangles are similar. What is the common ratio that shows that all the rectangles are in proportion?

God included the Golden Ratio in the design of His creation. You can observe the Golden Ratio in the spiral of a nautilus shell (page 534) and the whorls of a pineapple.

There are many other applications of similarity too. You have already seen how surveyors can use similar triangles to determine tree and building heights. Likewise similar figures form when a photo is enlarged or reduced. Craft books often provide patterns that you must enlarge before using.

Figure 13.21

This pineapple from Hawaii displays a spiral pattern.

---

4. The ratio of the leg to the base in an isosceles triangle with a vertex angle of 36° (and base angles of 72°)

5. The 12 vertices of a regular icosahedron are the 12 vertices of three mutually perpendicular golden rectangles.

You can also have students discover two other interesting properties of the Golden Ratio. These require using steps from the proof on page 572 (or setting up a similar proof). From $x^2 - x = 1$, add x to both sides to obtain $x^2 = x + 1$.

1. The Golden Ratio is equal to one more than its own reciprocal. (Divide both sides of the equation above by x to obtain $x = 1 + \frac{1}{x}$ as desired.)

2. Powers of the Golden Ratio can be written in linear form with Fibonacci numbers as coefficients. Use the formula for x^2 above to obtain
$x^2 = x + 1$
$x^3 = x(x + 1) = x^2 + x =$
$(x + 1) + x = 2x + 1$
$x^4 = x(2x + 1) = 2x^2 + x =$
$2(x + 1) + x = 3x + 2$
Similarly, $x^5 = 5x + 3$,
and $x^6 = 8x + 5$, etc.

Discuss enlargement and reduction of photographs. Bring in some photographs and their enlargements and see if the students can find the scale factor in each case. Overhead projectors also enlarge if the screen is at right angles to the overhead (otherwise the projection looks like a trapezoid instead of a rectangle, and parallelism is not preserved).

▶ A. Exercises

For each pair of photographs, find the scale factor of the dilation that would produce the second photograph.

1.

USS Constitution *at Boston, Massachusetts*

2.

USS Alabama *at Mobile, Alabama*

3.

USS Eisenhower *at sea*

Flash

The ships in the exercises also illustrate distinctive geometry necessary in the design of different kinds of ships.

The USS *Constitution (Old Ironsides)* is an old sailing ship. Sailing ships differ from sailboats in having at least three square-rigged masts; compare to the triangular sails of the sailboat in Section 13.3 (p. 548).

The USS *Alabama* is a battleship that earned nine battle stars in the Pacific theater during World War II. Its turrets have cylindrical bases.

The USS *Eisenhower* is an aircraft carrier. Note especially the large flat plane surface for landing. The *Eisenhower* is one of only seven nuclear aircraft carriers built by the U.S. These supercarriers are the largest warships in the world. (The largest is the USS *Nimitz*.)

The USS *Pintado* is a nuclear submarine (shown off the coast of San Diego). Its streamlined top designed for diving contrasts sharply with the flat top of the carrier.

Tips

Ex. 5-10. It will help to measure to the closest half millimeter.

Ex. 13. Most students will get 27 mm by 17 mm, which is within 0.03 of the Golden Ratio (but not within 0.02 as stated in #11). To obtain precise Golden Ratios requires a larger image showing rectangles with finer lines.

Ex. 14-18. Most students will not obtain Golden Ratios for any of these five. The Golden Ratios are hard to find for several reasons: 1) students will not know where to measure (outer or inner edges?); 2) the photo is not perfectly squared (left and right halves may not agree); 3) some of the figures (such as #16) are too small (even millimeters require too much

rounding to get useful ratios). You may suggest that they hunt for golden rectangles (the pediment is not a "golden triangle"). For #14, view the colonnade as framed by the end of the pediment and supporting step. For #15, use the far edges of consecutive columns (not just the space between them). For #18, use the length of the step shown. See the diagram. ■

4. $\frac{2}{3}$

5. $\frac{26.5 \text{ mm}}{15.5 \text{ mm}} = 1.71$

6. $\frac{30.5 \text{ mm}}{19 \text{ mm}} = 1.61$

7. $\frac{35.5 \text{ mm}}{10.5 \text{ mm}} = 3.0$

8. $\frac{31 \text{ mm}}{16 \text{ mm}} = 1.94$

9. $\frac{27 \text{ mm}}{16 \text{ mm}} = 1.69$

10. $\frac{22.5 \text{ mm}}{14 \text{ mm}} = 1.61$

11. 6 and 10

12. dilation

13. Answers will vary.

4.

USS Pintado *off the California coast*

Look at the series of rectangles below. Find the ratio of length to width for each. It will help to measure in millimeters.

5.   7.    9.

6.    8.    10.

▶ **B. Exercises**

11. If the ratio is within 0.02 of 1.618, then we call it a Golden Ratio. Which of the rectangles in exercises 5-10 are golden rectangles?

12. What kind of transformation takes place when a photograph is enlarged or reduced?

13. Measure the rectangles on the *Mona Lisa*. Which are golden rectangles?

Study the architecture of the Parthenon to answer exercises 14-18. The triangular part at the top is called a pediment. Find the indicated ratios. Which are golden?

Parthenon at Athens

14. Length to width of either half of the colonnade
15. Length to width of any rectangle determined by consecutive columns
16. Length to width of any small rectangle supporting the pediment
17. Base to leg of pediment
18. Length to altitude of entire building

▶ C. Exercises

19. Study the pattern in the dimensions of this series of golden rectangles: 5 by 8, 8 by 13, 13 by 21. What would be the dimensions of the next three golden rectangles?
20. If you start with a 55 by 89 golden rectangle and remove a square from one end, what size rectangle will result? Is the resulting rectangle a golden rectangle? What size is the next smaller golden rectangle of this series?

■ Cumulative Review

21. Which two conditions are theorems for proving triangles similar: SSS, ASA, SSA SAA, SAS, AAA?
22. Three of the other conditions in exercise 21 guarantee triangle similarity. Which three?
23. Why are the three similarity theorems in exercise 22 not needed?
24. Which of the six conditions does not guarantee similarity?
25. Prove (by counterexample) your answer to exercise 24.

14. Answers will vary.
15. Answers will vary.
16. Answers will vary.
17. Answers will vary.
18. Answers will vary.
19. 21 by 34, 34 by 55, 55 by 89
20. 34 by 55; yes; 21 by 34
21. SAS and SSS [13.2]
22. AAA, ASA, SAA [13.2]
23. AA covers all three [13.2]
24. SSA [13.3]
25. SSA, proportional sides, congruent angles, but triangles not similar [13.2]

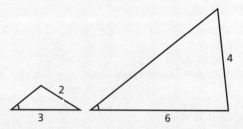

Geometry and Scripture

Objective

To survey similarity in the Bible—both the general root term (likeness) and the mathematical meaning (in artistic figures).

Answers

1. worship
2. made a golden calf as an idol
3. blue, purple, scarlet linens with cherubim
4. Bezaleel and Aholiab
5. 2 statues, engraved on walls, woven on curtains

Higher Plane

John 3:14

Geometry and Scripture

Artists use similar figures when they paint objects with the same shape but with different sizes to make one appear more distant. In the Bible, some people made figures similar to real creatures.

1. For what purpose was the fashioning of likenesses to living creatures prohibited (Exod. 20:3-5)?

2. How did Aaron break this law (Exod. 32:4)?

At other times, God commanded people to make such figures—although, of course, never to be worshiped.

3. What colors and likenesses did God want on the curtains of His tabernacle?

4. Who carried out this command (Exod. 36:2, 8; 38:21-23)?

5. Hiram (the artist for the temple) made cherubim that were similar. For what three different places did he design cherubim (II Chron. 3:7-14)?

God's restriction on art makes some people think that all art is wrong. God's commands to create images make others think that all art is good. Neither extreme is correct.

God was the first "artist" when He created the universe. He made art for good, but it can be misused. God required artistic figures (similar to real creatures) for beauty but prohibits idolizing the art.

For instance, God commanded Moses to make a brazen (bronze) statue in the likeness of a serpent (Num. 21:8-9). Later men worshiped it, and it had to be destroyed (II Kings 18:4).

> **Higher Plane:** Find the verse in John in which Jesus taught the similarity between eternal salvation by trusting His death on the cross and the physical healing found in looking on the brazen serpent.

Presentation

This study focuses on similarity. Some questions focus on the general meaning of the term *similar* (#6 and Higher Plane) to cement the root word in the students' mind. One such similarity or likeness is our likeness to God (#7-11). This similarity is only a similarity in limited ways (congruence would mean full identity with God, which men lack). These principles apply to math as seen in #8-11.

Other questions focus on mathematical similarity. Such similarity shows up in art (#2, 3, 5). Art, like music, can be a controversial subject. However, we can know that art is a good gift of God that can be misused for evil. Questions 1-5 show that some art is good (God demanded some, #1-3) but that some is bad (He also

prohibited some, when His good was misused by Aaron, #1-2). Such likenesses involve similar figures. We do not know if they were exactly life-size (congruent figures) or on a larger or smaller scale, but all three are types of mathematical similarities. So the figures were similar regardless of whether they were congruent. ■

Read Genesis 1:26-31, which teaches us about similarity, art, math, and God. God, as the first designer, made man *similar* to Himself.

6. Give the phrases in the passage that refer to this.

God made us like Himself with the ability to reason. Art, language, and math all involve reasoning since they permit us to express ideas and experiences. All three skills are essential to architecture, physics, aviation, chemistry, and medicine. Such skills help man exercise dominion over the earth as God commanded (vv. 26, 28).

7. What does *dominion* mean?

Identify the reason from Genesis 1:26-31 that shows why we should learn math. Use each once.

8. Math was created good.

9. Math reflects God's creativity and reasoning.

10. Math is a tool for fulfilling God-given responsibility.

11. Similar figures were part of God's design.

A. "let them have dominion" (v. 26)

B. "it was very good" (v. 31)

C. "Let us make man . . . after our likeness" (v. 26)

D. "God created man in his own image" (v. 27)

Art, language, and even math also require creativity. As you learn new theorems and formulas, you creatively apply them to problems you've never seen before. It also takes great creativity to design new technology like Archimedes did, prove new theorems like Euclid and Heron did, or open new fields of knowledge like Hilbert and Riemann did.

> ### Line upon Line
>
> And God said, Let us make man in our image, after our likeness: and let them have dominion over the fish of the sea, and over the fowl of the air, and over the cattle, and over all the earth, and over every creeping thing that creepeth upon the earth. 🙢
>
> **Genesis 1:26**

6. in our image, after our likeness, in His own image, in the image of God
7. authority, rule
8. B
9. D
10. A
11. C

Objective

To help students prepare for evaluation.

Vocabulary
See Appendix A.

Assignment
• Intuitive: 1-30
• Standard: 1-30
• Rigorous: 1-30

Resources
• *Activities Manual,* Cumulative Review
• *Activities Manual,* Terms and Symbols
• *Activities Manual,* Practice
• *Test Packet,* Chapter 13 Exam

Answers
1.
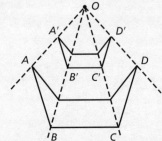

2.
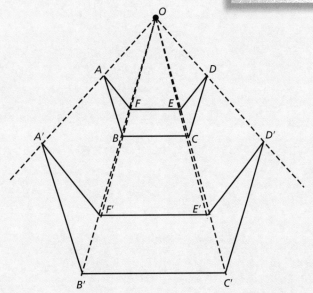

Chapter 13 Review

Use the diagram and perform the indicated dilation, given the scale factor. Use O as the center of dilation.

1. $\frac{1}{2}$
2. 4

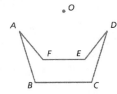

In a given dilation, O is the center, A is mapped onto A', B is mapped onto B', and C is mapped onto C'. Find the indicated measures using a factor of $\frac{1}{4}$.

3. If $AO = 16$ units, find $A'O$
4. If $AB = 12$ units, find $A'B'$
5. If $OC = 60$ units, find OC'

Solve each proportion.

6. $\frac{x}{9} = \frac{18}{54}$ 7. $\frac{15}{9} = \frac{x}{2}$ 8. $\frac{1}{9} = \frac{12}{x}$

State whether the following pairs are similar figures. Explain why they are similar or why they are not similar.

9.

10.

11.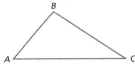

12. *Given:* △AED ~ △CEB
    Prove: ABCD is a trapezoid

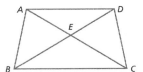

3. 4 units
4. 3 units
5. 15 units
6. 3
7. $\frac{10}{3}$ (or $3\frac{1}{3}$)
8. 108
9. similar: SSS
10. not similar; sides are not in proportion
11. not similar; figures are not the same shape
12.

1. △AED ~ △CEB	1. Given
2. ∠EDA ≅ ∠EBC	2. Definition of similar triangles
3. $\overrightarrow{AD} \parallel \overrightarrow{BC}$	3. Parallel Postulate
4. ABCD is a trapezoid	4. Definition of trapezoid

13. *Given:* $\triangle ABF \sim \triangle EBC$;
$\overline{GB} \perp \overline{AF}$; $\overline{BD} \perp \overline{CE}$
Prove: $\dfrac{FB}{CB} = \dfrac{GB}{DB}$

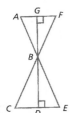

14. If $\triangle ABC \sim \triangle XYZ$, then what are the lengths of the missing sides?

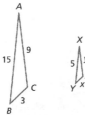

Can the lengths (in units) given here be possible side lengths of similar triangles?

15. 4, 9, 12 and 16, 36, 48
16. 2, 5, 6 and 1, $\frac{5}{2}$, 3
17. 8, 9, 11 and 4, 6, $\frac{11}{2}$
18. State three ways to prove that two triangles are similar.

If $\overline{CX}$ is the altitude to the hypotenuse of right $\triangle ABC$, find the lengths indicated.
19. $AX = 12$ units; $XB = 4$ units; find CX
20. $AX = 27$ units; $XB = 3$ units; find CX
21. $AX = 8$ units; $AB = 10$ units; find AC

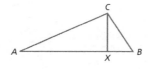

$\triangle HIJ \sim \triangle ZPQ$, $\overline{JK}$ and $\overline{QR}$ are altitudes, $\overline{HL}$ and $\overline{ZS}$ are medians, and $\overline{IM}$ and $\overline{PT}$ are angle bisectors. Find the indicated lengths.
22. $JI = 8$ units; $QP = 4$ units; $JK = 6$ units; find QR
23. $HJ = 15$ units; $ZQ = 3$ units; $HL = 20$ units; find ZS
24. $HI = 25$ units; $ZP = 15$ units; $MI = 20$ units; find TP
25. Perimeter of $\triangle HIJ = 26$ units; $JK = 10$ units; $QR = 5$ units; find the perimeter of $\triangle ZPQ$
26. $HL = 18$ units; $ZS = 8$ units; Area $\triangle HIJ = 42$ square units; find Area $\triangle ZPQ$
27. If a telephone pole casts a 110-foot shadow at the same time that a 4-foot pole casts a 10-foot shadow, how tall is the telephone pole?
28. Explain what the Golden Ratio and the golden rectangle are.
29. Name three occupations that use the idea of similar figures.
30. Explain the mathematical significance of Genesis 1:26.

13.

1. $\triangle ABF \sim \triangle EBC$; $\overline{GB} \perp \overline{AF}$; $\overline{BD} \perp \overline{CE}$	1. Given
2. $\overline{BG}$ and $\overline{BD}$ are altitudes to $\overline{AF}$ and $\overline{CE}$ respectively	2. Definition of altitude
3. $\dfrac{FB}{CB} = \dfrac{GB}{DB}$	3. Altitudes proportional to sides

14. $x = 1$ unit; $y = 3$ units
15. yes
16. yes
17. no
18. AA, SSS, and SAS
19. $4\sqrt{3}$ units
20. 9 units
21. $4\sqrt{5}$ units
22. 3 units
23. 4 units
24. 12 units
25. 13 units
26. 8.3 square units
27. 44 ft.
28. The Golden Ratio is approximately 1.618, which corresponds to the ratio of the length to the width of a golden rectangle. A golden rectangle is a rectangle with dimensions such that when a square is taken from one end, the result is another golden rectangle.
29. Answers will vary.
30. God created all things, but man in particular is similar to God in important ways (reason, spirit). In math, the term *similar* also refers to likeness, but the likeness is based on having the same shape (though not necessarily the same size).

Presentation

Another way to review is to read (or at least skim) the entire chapter, taking notes on the things that are important. Make special note of theorems and definitions and any other principles. Next, students should go back over their notes, looking for points stressed by the teacher or things that they missed while skimming the text. Students who are permitted to write in their books and have underlined or highlighted key points should review those key points as well.

Tips

Ex. 29. Several occupations that use the idea of similar figures are photography, surveying, mapmaking, engineering, and carpentry. ■

14 Trigonometry

Trigonometry

This plane of blue pyramids absorbs microwaves. It lines an anechoic chamber used for electronic measurements.

An anechoic chamber is a chamber in which no echoes exist. Because it eliminates echoes, this chamber improves the accuracy of measurements that are made in it. Triangles, such as the ones that form the sides of these pyramids, were chosen to design the microwave absorption material essential for this device. Even high technology uses geometric shapes.

The sound waves in an anechoic chamber (as well as in nature) are also related to a geometric concept. Sound waves, which form echoes, travel in concentric spheres in all directions from their source. When the edge of a sphere of sound hits a surface more than thirty feet away, the sound bounces back, creating an echo.

Like sound waves that move out in all directions from their source, the words people speak and the effects of those words spread in all directions. Once someone makes a remark, he cannot stop its influence on other people. That is why Christians must guard their words. A carelessly spoken word may create harmful waves before it echoes to its origin.

After this chapter you should be able to

1. define six trigonometric ratios.

2. evaluate trigonometric ratios.

3. state and apply exact trigonometric ratios for 30°, 45°, and 60° angles.

4. use tables or calculators to approximate trigonometric ratios.

5. solve right triangles.

6. prove trigonometric identities.

7. apply trigonometry to surveying and other word problems.

8. derive and apply formulas for regular polygons using trigonometry.

581

Overview

After defining the three basic trig ratios, students apply them to find angle measures and side lengths. The chapter also covers the special 45-45 and 30-60 right triangles. These ideas provide a foundation for the reciprocal ratios, solving right triangles, and proving identities. Word problems using right triangle trigonometry are included. The chapter climaxes by applying trig to regular polygons to develop formulas for the apothem and radius.

Bulletin Board Idea

An alternate approach to the trig ratio definitions can be shown by placing a unit circle on the board with a ray intersecting the circle at point *P* with the coordinates of *P* shown to be (cos θ, sin θ), and the ray extended to show tan θ as well (as on the cover of the Visual Packet). The board could be titled *Unit Circle Trig*.

Flash

The blue pyramids absorb sound waves. Companies cover the interior of buildings that hold aircraft with this anechoic material.

Resource

• *Visual Packet*, cover. Shows the geometric interpretation of all six trig functions.

Presentation

A tuning fork vibrates to create sound at a certain pitch or note. Notes differ because different tuning forks vibrate at different frequencies (greater or fewer vibrations each second). If a pencil is attached to the tuning fork, the cycle of vibrations is recorded on paper as a wavy line. The higher the note, the more oscillations in a given space.

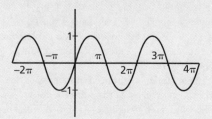

The values of the sine function cycle in this manner, and the graph of the sine function shows the same pattern. The sine function is the most important of the six trig functions because it is always the first trig function defined and all the other trig functions can be defined from it. Students can see from this example how it is useful in the study of sound. Ask students to name some areas in which the study of sound is applied. (*acoustics for buildings and amplification; radio and TV signal transmission; recorded music; telephones*) ∎

Trigonometric Ratios

Objectives

1. To identify and define three trigonometric ratios.
2. To find trigonometric ratios for specific right triangles.
3. To prove that the trigonometric ratios for corresponding angles of similar triangles are equal.
4. To find sides of triangles, given certain trig ratios.

Vocabulary

adjacent side
cosine of an angle
hypotenuse
opposite side
sine of an angle
tangent of an angle
trigonometric ratios
trigonometry

Assignment

- Intuitive: no assignment necessary
- Standard: 1-20, 24-28
- Rigorous: 1-19 odd, 21-28

Resources

- *Activities Manual,* Math History Activity: Regiomontanus
- *Test Packet,* Quiz 1, Chapter 14 covers Section 14.1.

Reading and Writing Mathematics

Have the students use a protractor and metric ruler to draw a large right triangle on paper. Have them measure the sides (in millimeters) and angles (in degrees) and compute the three trig ratios for the acute angles. Have them check their accuracy by comparing their work with the true values (table or calculator). ***Answers will vary.***

Additional Problems

Find the sine, cosine, and tangent of angle θ in each triangle given.

1.

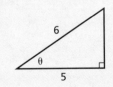

$$\sin \theta = \frac{\sqrt{11}}{6}, \cos \theta = \frac{5}{6}, \tan \theta = \frac{\sqrt{11}}{5}$$

14.1 Trigonometric Ratios

A ratio is a comparison of two numbers. When you think of a comparison, you probably think of the similarities and differences between two things. In our spiritual lives we are to make sure that our spiritual conditions measure up to the standards of the Bible. First Corinthians 2:13 states, "Which things also we speak, not in the words which man's wisdom teacheth, but which the Holy Ghost teacheth; comparing spiritual things with spiritual." Make sure that you compare your spiritual condition to the truths found in the Bible and not to the condition of your friends or other people. Keep your eyes on Jesus Christ.

In Chapter 13, while studying similar figures and triangles, you learned that there are many ratios and proportions associated with these figures. In this chapter we will study some special ratios of right triangles. These ratios are called *trigonometric ratios.* Trigonometry is the name given to the field of mathematics that deals with triangles, their angles, and the ratios of their side measurements. The word *trigonometry* is derived from the Greek words *trigonon* and *metrica* and means "triangle measure." So trigonometry is the study of triangle measurement.

Look at $\triangle ABC$ and $\triangle XYZ$.

Since $\triangle ABC$ and $\triangle XYZ$ are similar, the sides are proportional.

$$\frac{XY}{AB} = \frac{YZ}{BC} = \frac{XZ}{AC}$$

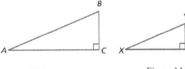

Figure 14.1

From this you can easily obtain the following proportions.

$$\frac{BC}{AB} = \frac{YZ}{XY}, \frac{AC}{AB} = \frac{XZ}{XY}, \frac{BC}{AC} = \frac{YZ}{XZ}$$

As an example, to derive the first proportion, cross multiply and then divide both sides by $(XY)(AB)$.

$$\frac{XY}{AB} = \frac{YZ}{BC}$$
$$(BC)(XY) = (AB)(YZ)$$
$$\frac{BC}{AB} = \frac{YZ}{XY}$$

The proportions above show that for similar triangles, the ratio of any two sides of one triangle is the same as the ratio of the corresponding sides of the other triangle. In other words, the ratio will be the same regardless of the size of the triangles. This is important as the basis of the entire field of trigonometry.

Presentation

Discuss the first paragraph and review ratios. Continue through the presentation, stressing the stability of the ratios of corresponding sides for similar triangles.

Define the trig functions (sine, cosine, and tangent) using right triangles and summarize them with the table on page 584. Go through example 2 to be sure that students understand how to find these ratios. Also cover example 1, which shows that sometimes you must first apply the Pythagorean theorem to get the length of the third side before forming the ratio.

Emphasize that the trig ratios are the ratios of particular side lengths and that $\sin 32°$ or $\tan 15°$ are constants like π or $\sqrt{2}$.

Students should understand that these numbers do not depend upon the size of the triangle in which they are found because the ratios do not change as long as the triangles are similar. You may wish to use #25 in class to stress this.

Since the acute angles of a right triangle are complementary, there is a relationship between the sine and cosine functions. In the drawing, $\sin A = \frac{a}{c}$ and $\cos B = \frac{a}{c}$. The sine of an angle and the cosine of its complement are equal. This is handy for understanding trig tables (section 3).

Your students will need to memorize the trig ratios in terms of the sides (opposite, adjacent, and hypotenuse) as shown in the

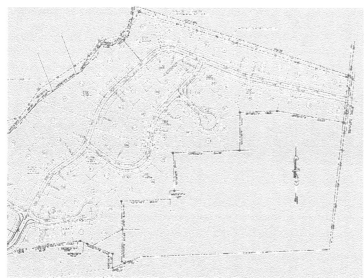

Gray Engineering used trigonometry to prepare this layout for a subdivision in South Carolina.

Notice that if the corresponding acute angles of the two right triangles are congruent, the triangles will always be similar by AA. Therefore, the measures of the acute angles determine the right triangle and thus the ratios of the triangle. If you can find the ratio of particular sides of a right triangle that is determined by a given acute angle, then the ratio remains constant for all triangles determined by this acute angle. Since the ratios remain constant, mathematicians have given them names.

In $\triangle ABC$ the side opposite the right angle is called the hypotenuse. The sides are labeled with lowercase letters corresponding to their opposite angles. The side opposite $\angle A$ is a.

The ratio of the side opposite $\angle A$ to the hypotenuse is $\frac{a}{c}$. This ratio is called the *sine* of $\angle A$. The sine of $\angle A$ is abbreviated sin A. So sin A = opposite side over hypotenuse = $\frac{a}{c}$.

Another common ratio is the *cosine* ratio. The cosine of an angle is the ratio of the adjacent side to the hypotenuse. The cosine of $\angle A$ is $\frac{b}{c}$. In trigonometry this relationship is symbolized by cos A = adjacent side over hypotenuse = $\frac{b}{c}$.

Figure 14.2

2.

$$sin\ \theta = \frac{\sqrt{21}}{5},\ cos\ \theta = \frac{2}{5},\ tan\ \theta = \frac{\sqrt{21}}{2}$$

3.

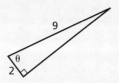

$$sin\ \theta = \frac{\sqrt{77}}{9},\ cos\ \theta = \frac{2}{9},\ tan\ \theta = \frac{\sqrt{77}}{2}$$

4. If sin $\theta = \frac{1}{7}$, find cos θ. $\frac{4\sqrt{3}}{7}$

5. If tan $\theta = 8$, find sin θ. $\frac{8\sqrt{65}}{65}$

table. One memory device to use is Sohcahtoa, an imaginary chieftain. Each syllable provides the initials for a trig function definition: Soh indicates that sin A = opposite over hypotenuse. Another is "Ollie had a heavy old anchor," where one remembers separately that each pair of letters corresponds to sine, cosine, and tangent respectively.

One-on-one. Some students get confused over which is the adjacent side (since the hypotenuse is also adjacent). Remind them that the adjacent side refers to the adjacent leg whereas the hypotenuse is opposite the right angle. ■

The last ratio that we will look at in this brief introduction to trigonometry is the *tangent* ratio. The tangent of $\angle A$, abbreviated tan A, is the ratio of the opposite side to the adjacent side. These three basic trigonometric ratios are summarized in the following table. You should remember that the lowercase letters represent lengths of the sides of the triangle, so the ratios are always numbers.

Trigonometric Ratios			
Name	Abbreviation	Meaning	Side ratio
sine of $\angle A$	sin A	opposite over hypotenuse	$\frac{a}{c}$
cosine of $\angle A$	cos A	adjacent over hypotenuse	$\frac{b}{c}$
tangent of $\angle A$	tan A	opposite over adjacent	$\frac{a}{b}$

Examples are given below to help you find these special ratios.

EXAMPLE 1   Find the sine of $\angle A$ and the sine of $\angle B$.

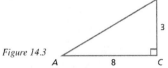

Figure 14.3

Answer   **1.**   You can find the length of the hypotenuse of this triangle by applying the Pythagorean theorem.

$$a^2 + b^2 = c^2$$
$$3^2 + 8^2 = c^2$$
$$9 + 64 = c^2$$
$$73 = c^2$$
$$\sqrt{73} = c$$

So the hypotenuse is $\sqrt{73}$.

2.   Find the required ratios, using the lengths of the sides of the triangle.
Remember from algebra that you should not leave a radical in the denominator of a fraction. Rationalize the denominator.

$$\sin A = \frac{\text{opposite}}{\text{hypotenuse}} \qquad\qquad \sin B = \frac{\text{opposite}}{\text{hypotenuse}}$$

$$= \frac{3}{\sqrt{73}} \qquad\qquad\qquad = \frac{8}{\sqrt{73}}$$

$$= \frac{3}{\sqrt{73}} \cdot \frac{\sqrt{73}}{\sqrt{73}} \qquad\quad = \frac{8}{\sqrt{73}} \cdot \frac{\sqrt{73}}{\sqrt{73}}$$

$$= \frac{3\sqrt{73}}{73} \qquad\qquad\quad = \frac{8\sqrt{73}}{73}$$

EXAMPLE 2   Find the tangent of ∠ A.

Answer $\tan A = \dfrac{\text{opposite}}{\text{adjacent}}$

$= \dfrac{a}{b}$

$= \dfrac{4}{5}$

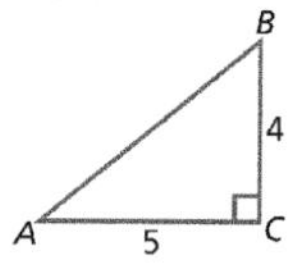

Figure 14.4

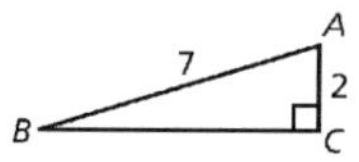

Answers

1. $\dfrac{6\sqrt{61}}{61}$

2. $\dfrac{7}{4}$

3. $\dfrac{4\sqrt{6}}{11}$

4. 1

5. $\dfrac{3\sqrt{13}}{13}$

6. $\dfrac{3\sqrt{5}}{7}$

▶ A. Exercises

Find the indicated trigonometric ratio for each triangle. Apply the Pythagorean theorem if needed.

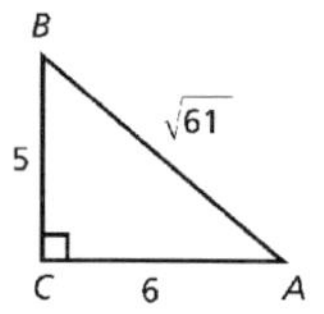

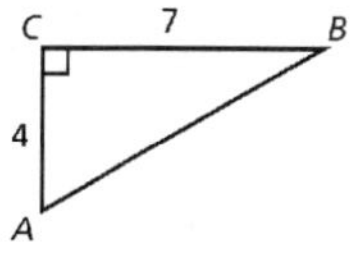

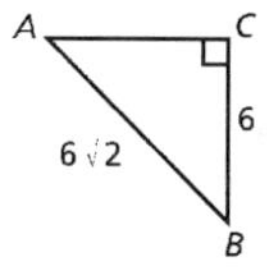

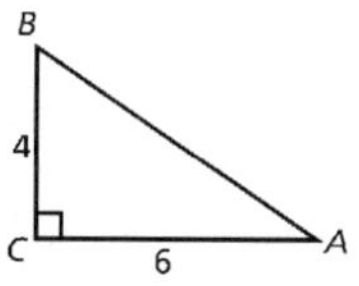

1. cos A

4. tan B

2. tan A

5. sin B

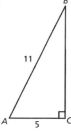

3. sin A

6. cos B

7.

8.

9.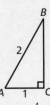

10.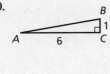

11. $\sin A = \frac{4}{5}$; $\sin B = \frac{3}{5}$; $\cos A = \frac{3}{5}$;
    $\cos B = \frac{4}{5}$; $\tan A = \frac{4}{3}$; $\tan B = \frac{3}{4}$

12. $\sin A = \frac{3\sqrt{58}}{58}$; $\cos A = \frac{7\sqrt{58}}{58}$;
    $\tan A = \frac{3}{7}$; $\sin B = \frac{7\sqrt{58}}{58}$;
    $\cos B = \frac{3\sqrt{58}}{58}$; $\tan B = \frac{7}{3}$

13. $\sin A = \frac{2\sqrt{5}}{5}$; $\sin B = \frac{\sqrt{5}}{5}$;
    $\cos A = \frac{\sqrt{5}}{5}$; $\cos B = \frac{2\sqrt{5}}{5}$;
    $\tan A = 2$; $\tan B = \frac{1}{2}$

14. $\sin A = \frac{\sqrt{7}}{4}$; $\cos A = \frac{3}{4}$;
    $\tan A = \frac{\sqrt{7}}{3}$; $\sin B = \frac{3}{4}$;
    $\cos B = \frac{\sqrt{7}}{4}$; $\tan B = \frac{3\sqrt{7}}{7}$

15. $\tan A = 2\sqrt{2}$, $\sin A = \frac{2\sqrt{2}}{3}$

16. $\cos B = \frac{5\sqrt{41}}{41}$
    $\sin B = \frac{4\sqrt{41}}{41}$

17. $\cos A = \frac{\sqrt{5}}{3}$, $\tan A = \frac{2\sqrt{5}}{5}$

18. $\sin A = \frac{4\sqrt{6}}{11}$
    $\tan A = \frac{4\sqrt{6}}{5}$

19. $\frac{\sqrt{7}}{4}$

20. $\frac{4\sqrt{41}}{41}$

Sketch a right triangle that has the given trigonometric ratio.

7. $\cos A = \frac{2}{5}$

8. $\tan A = \frac{4}{3}$

9. $\sin B = \frac{1}{2}$

10. $\tan B = 6$

▶ **B. Exercises**

Find the sine, cosine, and tangent of each acute angle of the right triangles below.

11.

13.

12.

14.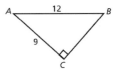

In each problem below, a trigonometric ratio for a certain angle in right △ABC is given. Find the other two trigonometric ratios for the angle.

15. $\cos A = \frac{1}{3}$

16. $\tan B = \frac{4}{5}$

17. $\sin A = \frac{2}{3}$

18. $\cos A = \frac{5}{11}$

Find the indicated trigonometric ratios. (*Hint:* Draw a picture of a triangle that would correspond to the given ratio in each problem.)

19. If $\sin A = \frac{3}{4}$, find $\cos A$.

20. If $\tan B = \frac{4}{5}$, find $\sin B$.

21. If $\sin A = \frac{2}{5}$, find $\tan B$.

22. If $\cos B = \frac{7}{9}$, find $\cos A$.

▶ C. Exercises

23. Use the Pythagorean theorem to prove $\sin^2 A + \cos^2 A = 1$ in right $\triangle ABC$, where $\angle C$ is the right angle.

■ Cumulative Review

24. Find x if $\triangle ABC \sim \triangle DEF$.

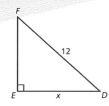

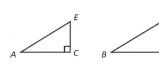

Use the diagrams below for the proofs in exercises 25-27. Angles A and B have the same measure, and $\angle C$ and $\angle D$ are right angles.

25. If $m\angle A = m\angle B$, prove that $\triangle ACE \sim \triangle BDF$.

26. Prove $\sin A = \sin B$.

27. Using exercise 25 show that $\cos A = \cos B$ and $\tan A = \tan B$. Write a proportion; do not write a proof.

28. Why do you always get the same number for the trigonometric ratios no matter how far you extend the angle?

---

21. $\frac{\sqrt{21}}{2}$

22. $\frac{4\sqrt{2}}{9}$

23. By definition $\sin A = \frac{a}{c}$ and $\cos A = \frac{b}{c}$

$\sin^2 A + \cos^2 A =$

$\left(\frac{a}{c}\right)^2 + \left(\frac{b}{c}\right)^2 = \frac{a^2}{c^2} + \frac{b^2}{c^2} = \frac{a^2 + b^2}{c^2}$

Now, by the Pythagorean theorem $c^2 = a^2 + b^2 = c^2$, so substitute into the last step.

$\therefore \sin^2 A + \cos^2 A = \frac{c^2}{c^2} = 1$

24. $x = 9$ [13.1]

25. [13.2]

1. $m\angle A = m\angle B$, $\angle C$ and $\angle D$ are right angles	1. Given
2. $\angle A \cong \angle B$	2. Definition of congruent angles
3. $\angle C \cong \angle D$	3. All right angles congruent
4. $\triangle ACE \sim \triangle BDF$	4. AA

26. [14.1]

1. $m\angle A = m\angle B$, $\angle C$ and $\angle D$ are right angles	1. Given
2. $\triangle ACE \sim \triangle BDF$	2. Exercise 25
3. $\frac{BF}{AE} = \frac{DF}{CE}$	3. Definition of similar triangles
4. $(BF)(CE) = (DF)(AE)$	4. Multiplication property of equality
5. $\frac{CE}{AE} = \frac{DF}{BF}$	5. Multiplication property of equality
6. $\sin A = \sin B$	6. Definition of sine

27. [14.1] $\frac{BF}{AE} = \frac{BD}{AC}$, $(BF)(AC) = (BD)(AE)$, $\frac{AC}{AE} = \frac{BD}{BF}$, $\cos A = \cos B$, $\frac{BD}{AC} = \frac{FD}{EC}$, $(BD)(EC) = (FD)(AC)$, $\frac{EC}{AC} = \frac{FD}{BD}$, $\tan A = \tan B$

28. The ratios are the same because the triangles are similar. [13.5]

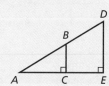

14.2

Special Triangles

Objectives

1. To develop theorems to give the relationships between the sides and hypotenuse of 45-45 and 30-60 right triangles.
2. To establish the trig ratios for the 45-45 and 30-60 right triangles.
3. To find missing sides or angles of specific 45-45 and 30-60 right triangles.

Vocabulary
45-45 right triangles
30-60 right triangles

Assignment
• Intuitive: no assignment necessary
• Standard: 1-22, 24-28
• Rigorous: 1-21 odd, 23-28

Resource
• *Activities Manual,* Cevians in Principle

Reading and Writing Mathematics.
Have the students compare sin 60° and sin 30°. Why isn't the second one-half of the first? **sin 60 = 0.866 and sin 30° = .5000, which is not 0.433 (half of sin 60). The relationship is not linear (see the sine curve in the introduction to this chapter).**

Additional Problems
Given the following measures of the sides of a right triangle, determine which are 45-45, 30-60, or neither.

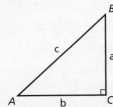

1. $5, \sqrt{5}, \sqrt{30}$ *neither*
2. $6, 2\sqrt{3}, 4\sqrt{3}$ *30-60*
3. $4, 4, 4\sqrt{2}$ *45-45*
4. $9, 12, 15$ *neither*
5. $\sqrt{3}, \sqrt{5}, 2\sqrt{2}$ *neither*
6. $11, 11\frac{\sqrt{3}}{3}, 22\frac{\sqrt{3}}{3}$ *30-60*

14.2 Special Triangles

Two special triangles are used frequently in trigonometry. These two triangles are singled out as "distinct among the set of triangles." Therefore, *special* triangles are both "distinctive" and "useful." Christians are special in the eyes of God. They should also be useful in the hands of God. If you are a Christian, you should be willing to be used as God directs you. If you trust the Lord and let Him lead you, He will give you wisdom and understanding (Prov. 3:1-13).

All the property lines in this subdivision had to be surveyed and mapped before construction could begin.

The first special triangle is the 45-45 right triangle. Since the sides opposite congruent angles in a triangle are congruent, this triangle is an isosceles triangle.

Suppose that $CB = 1$ unit; then $AC = 1$ unit. To find AB, use the Pythagorean theorem.

$$(AC)^2 + (CB)^2 = (AB)^2$$
$$1^2 + 1^2 = (AB)^2$$
$$2 = (AB)^2$$
$$\sqrt{2} = AB$$

If $CB = 2$ units, then $AC = 2$ units.

$$(AC)^2 + (CB)^2 = (AB)^2$$
$$2^2 + 2^2 = (AB)^2$$
$$8 = (AB)^2$$
$$2\sqrt{2} = AB$$

Figure 14.5

Do you see the pattern? Repeat the process with x.

If $CB = x$, then $AC = x$ units.

$$(AC)^2 + (CB)^2 = (AB)^2$$
$$x^2 + x^2 = (AB)^2$$
$$2x^2 = (AB)^2$$
$$x\sqrt{2} = AB$$

This proves the following theorem.

Presentation

Study the first paragraph and Proverbs 3:1-13 with your students. Discuss the fact that they need to be teachable Christians.

Cover the material on 45-45 right triangles. On the chalkboard, draw a triangle with legs one unit long and show that the hypotenuse is $\sqrt{2}$ using the Pythagorean theorem. Draw a larger 45-45 right triangle with one side given, point out that the two triangles are similar by AA, and find the other two sides by proportions. Using the original triangle, find the sine, cosine, and tangent of 45°.

The 30-60 right triangle can be presented by dropping an altitude to the base of an equilateral triangle. Point out that the altitude of an equilateral triangle bisects the angle and the opposite base. This produces two 30-60 right triangles. If the side opposite the 30° angle is one unit long, the hypotenuse (side of the original equilateral triangle) is 2, and by the Pythagorean theorem the third side of the 30-60 right triangle is $\sqrt{3}$.

The 45-45 and 30-60 right triangles are special because we can determine the relations between the sides using only the Pythagorean theorem. In other triangles, such as a 20-70 right triangle, if the short side is one unit long, you cannot apply the Pythagorean theorem until you know the length of the long leg (which requires trig). Using trig, the exact length (an irrational number) can be expressed as tan 70, which is approximately 2.7474774195. ■

Theorem 14.1

If the length of a leg of an isosceles right triangle (45-45 right triangle) is x, then the length of the hypotenuse is $x\sqrt{2}$.

From this theorem you can find the trigonometric ratios and the lengths of all the sides of a 45-45 right triangle if you are given one side of the triangle. Notice that the three sides are always in the ratio of $1:1:\sqrt{2}$.

EXAMPLE 1 Find the three trigonometric ratios for a 45° angle and the lengths of the sides of the triangle.	

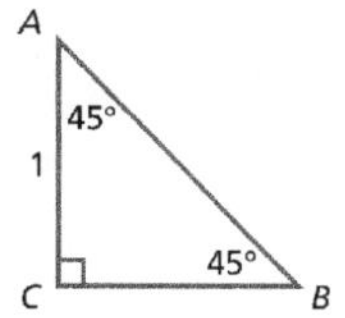

Answer   From Theorem 14.1 you can find each side length.

$$b = 1 \qquad a = 1 \qquad c = \sqrt{2}$$

Figure 14.6

Therefore, you can find the trigonometric ratios of the 45° angle.

$$\sin 45° = \frac{\text{opposite}}{\text{hypotenuse}} = \frac{1}{\sqrt{2}} = \frac{\sqrt{2}}{2}$$

$$\cos 45° = \frac{\text{adjacent}}{\text{hypotenuse}} = \frac{1}{\sqrt{2}} = \frac{\sqrt{2}}{2}$$

$$\tan 45° = \frac{\text{opposite}}{\text{adjacent}} = \frac{1}{1} = 1$$

Consider the equilateral triangle in figure 14.7. Since an equilateral triangle is equiangular, all of its angles measure 60°. The altitude bisects the vertex angle into two angles that measure 30° each. Thus the altitude divides the equilateral triangle into two 30-60 right triangles. The 30-60 right-triangle is the other special triangle.

Thus, $\triangle ABC$ is a 30-60 right triangle. If BC is 1 unit, then DB is 2 units because the altitude of an equilateral triangle intersects the opposite side at the midpoint. Since $\triangle ABD$ is an equilateral triangle, AB is 2 units also. Now that we know $BC = 1$ unit and $AB = 2$ units, we can find AC by using the Pythagorean theorem.

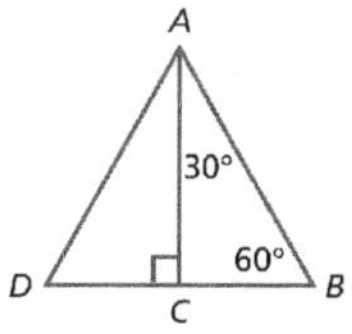

$$(BC)^2 + (AC)^2 = (AB)^2$$
$$1^2 + (AC)^2 = 2^2$$
$$1 + (AC)^2 = 4$$
$$(AC)^2 = 3$$
$$AC = \sqrt{3} \text{ units}$$

Figure 14.7

Once you know the length of each side of a right triangle, you can find the trigonometric ratios for the angles. Now we will derive the pattern for the 30-60 right triangle as a theorem.

If $BC = x$ units, then $DB = 2x$ units and $AB = 2x$ units. By the Pythagorean theorem,

$$(BC)^2 + (AC)^2 = (AB)^2$$
$$x^2 + (AC)^2 = (2x)^2$$
$$(AC)^2 = 4x^2 - x^2$$
$$(AC)^2 = 3x^2$$
$$AC = x\sqrt{3} \text{ units}$$

Theorem 14.2 summarizes these findings about the 30-60 right triangle.

Theorem 14.2

If the length of the leg opposite the 30° angle of a 30-60 right triangle is x, then the length of the leg opposite the 60° angle is $x\sqrt{3}$, and the length of the hypotenuse is $2x$.

Notice the sides are always in the ratio $1:\sqrt{3}:2$.

EXAMPLE 2   Find the side lengths and the trigonometric ratios for the acute angles of the following 30-60 right triangle.

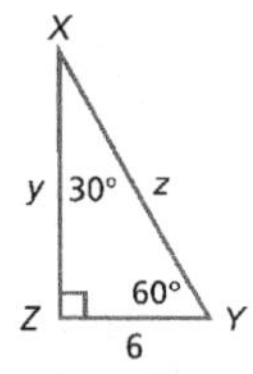

Answer   By Theorem 14.2, $y = 6\sqrt{3}$ units and $z = 12$ units. After you find these values, you can easily find the trigonometric ratios.

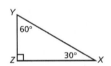

Figure 14.8

$\sin 30° = \frac{1}{2}$ $\sin 60° = \frac{\sqrt{3}}{2}$

$\cos 30° = \frac{\sqrt{3}}{2}$ $\cos 60° = \frac{1}{2}$

$\tan 30° = \frac{\sqrt{3}}{3}$ $\tan 60° = \sqrt{3}$

▶ **A. Exercises**

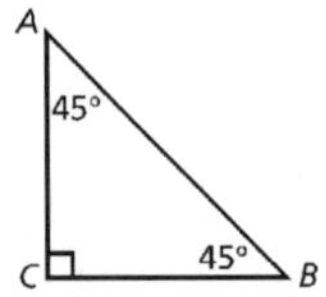

For each of the given measures, find the lengths of the sides of the triangles.

	AB	AC	BC
1.			18 units
2.		9 units	
3.			12 units
4.	5 units		
5.	4 units		

	XY	XZ	YZ
6.			5 units
7.	12 units		
8.		24 units	
9.			2 units
10.		15 units	

▶ B. Exercises

Given the following side lengths, determine which of these triangles are special and give the name of each special right triangle.

11. $6, 6, 6\sqrt{2}$ 14. $8, 8\sqrt{2}, 16$

12. $1, 1, \sqrt{2}$ 15. $12, 12, 12\sqrt{3}$

13. $7, 7\sqrt{3}, 14$ 16. $4, 4\sqrt{3}, 8$

Give the following trigonometric ratios. Draw pictures if necessary.

17. $\sin 45°$ 20. $\tan 45°$

18. $\cos 30°$ 21. $\cos 60°$

19. $\tan 60°$ 22. $\sin 30°$

▶ C. Exercises

23. For acute $\triangle ABC$, show that Area $\triangle ABC = \frac{1}{2}bc \sin A$. (*Hint:* Let $\overline{CD}$ be the altitude from vertex C and use the resulting right triangles.)

■ Cumulative Review

Give the dimensions of the figure with the following areas.

24. A square with area of 20 square units

25. An equilateral triangle with an area of $100\sqrt{3}$ square units

26. A regular hexagon with an area of $50\sqrt{3}$ square units

27. A circle with an area of 5π square units

28. A cube with a surface area of $\frac{8}{3}$ square units

Answers

1. $AB = 18\sqrt{2}$ units, $AC = 18$ units
2. $AB = 9\sqrt{2}$ units, $BC = 9$ units
3. $AB = 12\sqrt{2}$ units, $AC = 12$ units
4. $AC = BC = \frac{5\sqrt{2}}{2}$ units
5. $AC = BC = 2\sqrt{2}$ units
6. $XY = 10$ units, $XZ = 5\sqrt{3}$ units
7. $XZ = 6\sqrt{3}$ units, $YZ = 6$ units
8. $XY = 16\sqrt{3}$ units, $YZ = 8\sqrt{3}$ units
9. $XY = 4$ units, $XZ = 2\sqrt{3}$ units
10. $XY = 10\sqrt{3}$ units, $YZ = 5\sqrt{3}$ units
11. 45-45
12. 45-45
13. 30-60
14. neither
15. neither
16. 30-60
17. $\frac{\sqrt{2}}{2}$
18. $\frac{\sqrt{3}}{2}$
19. $\sqrt{3}$
20. 1
21. $\frac{1}{2}$
22. $\frac{1}{2}$
23.

1. $\triangle ABC$ is acute	1. Given
2. $\overline{CD}$ is the altitude from vertex C of length h	2. Auxiliary line
3. $A = \frac{1}{2} ch$	3. Area of triangle
4. $\sin A = \frac{h}{b}$	4. Definition of sine
5. $h = b \sin A$	5. Multiplication property of equality
6. $A = \frac{1}{2} c(b \sin A)$	6. Substitution (step 5 into 3)
7. $A = \frac{1}{2} bc \sin A$	7. Associative and commutative properties of multiplication

24. side is $2\sqrt{5}$ units [8.1]
25. side is 20 units [8.3]
26. side is $\frac{10\sqrt{3}}{3}$ units [8.4]
27. radius is $\sqrt{5}$ [8.5]
28. edge is $\frac{2}{3}$ units [8.6]

Geometry Around Us

Surveying

GEOMETRY
AROUND
US

Objectives

1. To identify geometric and trigonometric concepts used in surveying.
2. To identify the purpose and value of surveying.

The surveyor uses a standard elevation as a reference point for the measurements so that he can draw a contour map.

Surveyors sight on ruled rods to determine vertical distance above a base point.

SURVEYING

While driving by a highway construction site, most of us have seen surveyors at work. One man holds an orange pole upright while his partner peers through an object resembling a telescope and waves his arms back and forth. Although we can describe their actions, we might have trouble explaining what they are doing. But surveyors would explain that they are measuring plots of land using trigonometry.

Engineers often need to know the topography of an area of land to design roads, buildings, ditches, and dikes. Surveyors can determine vertical changes in the property by standing a calibrated pole on the ground and observing it through the telescope of a level instrument. The surveyor uses a standard elevation as a reference point for the measurements so that he can draw a contour (topographic) map. Also called a benchmark, the standard elevation was established by the United States Geological Survey (USGS) and is relative to

---

Bring a USGS topographic map to class and have the students study the information it contains. Have them contrast contour lines in steep areas and flat areas. Bring the USGS quadrangle of your location so that students can relate the contours to familiar terrain.

Motivational Idea. Have a professional surveyor as a guest speaker (or take a field trip to visit one). Ask him to demonstrate his survey work and instruments and to explain how he uses trigonometry.

Questions for Discussion

1. Why would rectangular coordinates of each corner or turning point for a piece of property be valuable for a surveyor? **to calculate distances in order to use them to find lengths of sides and area**

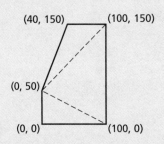

2. Since surveyors measure boundaries in an imaginary horizontal plane just above the highest point, how does this affect the owners of steep, hilly property compared to owners of relatively flat property? **Owners of hilly property actually have more land than it appears.**

3. Name the principal tools of a surveyor. Which of these are presently incorporated into one instrument because of modern technology? **Transit, steel tape (or chain), compass, rod, plumb bob, flagging, stakes (steel and wood). Some student may also mention an axe or machete. A total station combines the transit, steel tape, compass, and data book.** ■

mean sea level. The surveyor shows the elevations on a drawing by labeling a contour line with a number, thus indicating that any point on that line is at a certain elevation above or below the mean sea level.

All of the land in the United States has been mapped on topographic maps. The maps are so detailed that mapping North Carolina requires over 900 maps. These maps were made with steel tape and transits. The tapes (called chains) were used to measure horizontal distance. When steep slopes prohibited the surveyor from holding the tape horizontally, he used trigonometry. By measuring the distance along the sloped ground and using the transit to find the angle (A) of the incline, he could use the cosine to find the horizontal distance:

$$\cos A = \frac{\text{horizontal distance}}{\text{distance along the slope}}$$

Surveyors once measured angles by turning the telescope on their transit from one side of the angle to the other. They then read the angle measure from the base. Surveyors call this method "turning an angle."

Modern technology has greatly improved the methods of measuring distances and turning angles. The transit and steel tape as well as the compass and data notebook have all been combined into one instrument called a *total station.* An electronic distance meter sends a laser beam to a reflector at the other end of the distance to be measured. This beam reflects back to the meter, which converts the time of travel into decimal units of length and stores the information electronically. Measuring angles is also done electronically. The surveyor later downloads the data into a computer at his office, which performs the calculations and drawings.

The USGS topographic map of Mt. Whitney, California, uses contours representing 20 meters (65.62 ft.).

Electronic total station for surveying

GEOMETRY AROUND US   593

Flash
Have students find Mt. Whitney (the highest peak in the contiguous U.S.) on the map. Notice that the east slopes are very steep (many contour lines close together). Rock climbers ascend that side with ropes. Notice that the trail follows a much more gradual ascent route. Even still, the trail is not protected by forest (green) because it is far above the tree line.

Flash
The Nikon DTM-300 (total station pictured) is used by civil engineers, architects, and map survey teams. It runs over 7 hours on one battery and includes data storage and programs.

Solving Right Triangles

14.3 Solving Right Triangles

The height of a lighthouse, such as this one at Portland, Maine, is known to the keeper. By sighting a ship and measuring the angle below the horizontal, the keeper can solve the triangle to determine the distance of a distressed ship from the shore.

Objectives

1. To find the trigonometric ratios for angles using a calculator or tables.
2. To find missing sides or angles of right triangles.

Vocabulary
trigonometric tables

Assignment
- Intuitive: no assignment necessary
- Standard: 1-10, 11-25 odd, 27-31
- Rigorous: 1-10 odd, 11-31, and Mind over Math

Resources
- *Activities Manual,* Construction Skills
- *Activities Manual,* Golden Rectangle in Detail
- *Test Packet,* Quiz 2, Chapter 14 covers Sections 14.2 and 14.3.

Flash

Captains of ships identify lighthouses based on lighthouse lists that distinguish designs from brick or stone towers to metal frameworks or wooden houses on metal platforms. In areas with lighthouses of similar design, colored stripes are used for distinction. At night, captains recognize lighthouses by their light patterns (steady beam, short flashes, or short dark spans at regular intervals; flashes and dark periods can be single or in groups).

In the last section you used a method for finding the ratio values of several of the more common angle measures, such as 30, 45, and 60. But what do you do when you need the trigonometric ratio for angles other than these special angles? You could draw a triangle that has an acute angle congruent to the angle you are interested in. By measuring the sides and finding the appropriate ratios, you could find the trigonometric ratios for any acute angle. But this method is both time consuming and imprecise.

Georg Rhaeticus (1514-76), a German mathematical astronomer, spent twelve years of his life developing two very accurate trigonometric tables, which were published after his death in 1613. These tables made computations using trigonometric ratios consistent. These tables also saved much time for later mathematicians. Rhaeticus was the first mathematician to relate trigonometric ratios to the sides of a right triangle.

Calculators have made finding trigonometric ratios even easier. You may use a calculator or the trigonometric table in the back of this book to solve triangles. However, you must learn to recognize the special angles and ratios. Whenever a special angle is involved, the exact answer is expected. Calculators and trigonometric tables provide only approximate answers, and an approximate answer will not be accepted for the special angles.

Solving a right triangle means finding all the angle measures and all the side lengths of the triangle from the information given. By using trigonometric ratios, the Pythagorean theorem, and the sum of the angles of a triangle, you should be able to solve the triangles in this section. If you take a more advanced class in trigonometry, you will study other methods of solving triangles. Study the following examples.

Presentation

Have a student tell the class the value of sin 45° ($\frac{\sqrt{2}}{2}$); then have the students look it up in the table in the back of the book. Use a calculator and compare the values, pointing out that the table gives an approximation to four decimal places (0.7071). Point out once again that this number is a constant because all right triangles containing a 45-degree angle are similar.

Using a calculator is the easiest and most accurate method for obtaining trig ratios. (You may want students to compare the value of sin 45 obtained from a calculator with the value from the table.) For instance, to find cos 43°, enter 43 in the calculator and press cos. On a calculator that carries 12 digits, cos 43° =

0.731353701619. (On a few calculators, cos is pressed before 43.) If you already know a particular ratio and need the angle, enter the ratio as a decimal, and then press arc cos (some are labeled cos^{-1}; others require you to press INV and then cos or 2ndF and then cos). For example, to find the angle measure for cos A = 0.4895, $m\angle A$ = 60.6922766761°, which would usually be rounded to 61°.

The trigonometric table (p. 616) has values only for those angles that are whole numbers between 0° and 90°. This keeps the table small but requires you to round angle measures to the nearest degree. For angles between 45 and 90 degrees, you must use the list on the right margin and select your column from the bottom

margin. Explain this to students and illustrate the process of reading up from the bottom with sin 71 to obtain 0.9455.

Occasionally we want the angle in degrees, minutes, and seconds. For the earlier problem in which cos A = 0.4895 and $m\angle A$ = 60.6922766761°, subtract 60 and multiply 0.6922766761 times 60 (minutes) to get 41.53′. Subtract the 41 minutes and multiply 0.536600566 times 60 (seconds) to get 32.196′. The final answer is 60° 41′ 32″.

Explain that "solving a triangle" means determining the measures of all the angles and all the sides. The three main tools are

EXAMPLE 1 Given right $\triangle ABC$, find the measures of each side and angle.

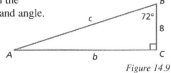

Figure 14.9

Answer

1. Since the tangent is the ratio of the opposite side to the adjacent side, you can set up an equation in one variable for b.

$$\tan 72° = \frac{b}{8}$$

2. Find $\tan 72° = 3.0777$ using a calculator or the table on page 616. Solve for b.

$$3.0777 \approx \frac{b}{8}$$
$$(3.0777)(8) \approx b$$
$$25 \approx b$$

3. $\angle A$ must be the complement of $\angle B$ since this is a right triangle.

$$m\angle A = 90° - m\angle B = 90° - 72° = 18°$$

4. The hypotenuse is the only side remaining. Find c by using either the Pythagorean theorem or another trigonometric ratio.

$$a^2 + b^2 = c^2 \qquad \cos 72° = \frac{8}{c}$$
$$8^2 + (25)^2 = c^2 \qquad 0.3090 \approx \frac{8}{c}$$
$$64 + 625 = c^2 \qquad 0.3090c \approx 8$$
$$689 = c^2 \qquad c \approx \frac{8}{0.3090}$$
$$26 \approx c \qquad c \approx 26$$

The complete solution to this triangle is given below.

$$m\angle A = 18° \qquad a = 8 \text{ units}$$
$$m\angle B = 72° \qquad b \approx 25 \text{ units}$$
$$m\angle C = 90° \qquad c \approx 26 \text{ units}$$

Often there is more than one way to solve a right triangle. Use the method that seems easiest for you.

Reading and Writing Mathematics

Have the students find tan 40° 17′ 28″ and explain their procedure. *Convert the minutes and seconds into degrees. Divide 28 by 60 to get a fraction of a minute, and add to 17. Divide the result by 60 to get a fraction of a degree. The total number of degrees is 40.291111°. Press the tan button to get tan 40.291111° = 0.8478.*

Additional Problems

Find the following using a calculator. Your answers should be accurate to four decimal places.

1. cos 72°   *0.3090*
2. tan 9°   *0.1584*
3. sin 59°   *0.8572*
4. tan 61°   *1.8040*

Find $m\angle A$ to the nearest degree given the following trig ratios.

5. tan A = 1.3250   *53°*
6. cos A = 0.9455   *19°*
7. sin A = 0.9130   *66°*

1) trig ratios
2) complementary angles
3) Pythagorean theorem

Go over the three examples and point out the use of each method and why it was needed for a particular step. In example 1, the first step requires the use of a trig ratio to get another side. Of course step 3 could have been done first since the second acute angle is the complement of the given one. Notice that step 4 can be done by using either a trig ratio or the Pythagorean theorem. Note that the trig ratios do not require knowing b (found in step 1), which is needed for the Pythagorean theorem.

Some students may notice that the table includes 0 and 90 degrees and question how

you can form a triangle to calculate trig ratios in these cases. This question will be studied fully in future courses. To explain briefly, show students the pattern on the table. As angle measure x decreases from 45 to 0°,

sin x approaches 0,
cos x approaches 1, and
tan x approaches 0.

Thus, sin 0° = 0, cos 0° = 1, and tan 0° = 0.

Similarly, as angle measure x increases from 45 to 90°,

sin x approaches 1,
cos x approaches 0, and
tan x increases without bound.

Thus, sin 90° = 1, cos 90° = 0, and tan 90° cannot be defined.

Tips

Ex. 3, 5. Those using the table must be careful to use the angle measures on the right margin and the headings at the bottom.

Ex. 6, 8, 10. These also require the right and bottom headings of the table.

Ex. 26. First find PQ from $\sin 28 = \frac{PQ}{20}$.

$PQ = 20 \sin 28 = 20 (0.4695) = 9.39$.

Then solve $\sin 50 = \frac{PQ}{PS}$. $PS \sin 50 = PQ$ and

$PS = \frac{PQ}{\sin 50} = \frac{9.39}{\sin 50} = \frac{9.39}{(0.7660)} = 12.26$ cm. ∎

EXAMPLE 2 Solve right $\triangle ABC$ if $\angle C$ is
the right angle, $m\angle A = 38°$,
and $c = 26$ units.

Answer Draw a picture of $\triangle ABC$.
A picture will often help
you figure out the rest of
the triangle.

Figure 14.10

1. To find b, use the cosine ratio. $\cos 38° = \frac{b}{26}$

2. Find $\cos 38°$. $0.7880 \approx \frac{b}{26}$

   $20.5 \approx b$ *(nearest tenth)*

3. To find a, use the sine ratio. $\sin 38 = \frac{a}{26}$

   $0.6157 \approx \frac{a}{26}$

   $16.0 \approx a$

4. To find $m\angle B$, find the $m\angle B = 90° - 38° = 52°$
   complement of $\angle A$.

EXAMPLE 3 Solve right $\triangle ABC$.

Answer We know that $m\angle C = 90°$.

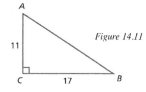

Figure 14.11

1. To find $m\angle A$, use the tangent ratio. $\tan A = \frac{17}{11}$

2. Find the closest number to 1.5455 in $\tan A \approx 1.5455$
   the tangent column in the table. $m\angle A \approx 57°$
   Identify the angle.

3. To find $m\angle B$, find the complement
   of $\angle A$ or use the tangent ratio again.

   $m\angle B = 90° - m\angle A$ $\tan B = \frac{11}{17}$

   $m\angle B \approx 90° - 57°$ $\tan B \approx 0.6471$

   $m\angle B \approx 33°$ $m\angle B \approx 33°$

Continued ▶

4. To find c, use the Pythagorean theorem or a trigonometric ratio.

$$a^2 + b^2 = c^2 \qquad \sin 57° = \frac{17}{c}$$

$$11^2 + 17^2 = c^2 \qquad 0.8387 \approx \frac{17}{c}$$

$$410 = c^2 \qquad c \approx \frac{17}{0.8387}$$

$$20 \approx c \qquad c \approx 20$$

▶ A. Exercises

Find the indicated trigonometric ratios. See the table on page 616.

1. sin 41°
2. cos 12°
3. tan 82°
4. tan 16°
5. cos 59°

Find $m\angle A$, given the following trigonometric ratios. See the table on page 616. Find the angle to the nearest degree.

6. tan A = 9.514
7. cos A = 0.8746
8. sin A = 0.9925
9. sin A = 0.2079
10. tan A = 4.000

▶ B. Exercises

Use the triangles shown. Name the ratio or theorem that you would use to find the indicated measurement and then calculate it.

11. DF
12. GH
13. EF
14. $m\angle G$
15. $m\angle E$

Solve each right triangle. Round your answers to the nearest tenth or to the nearest degree.

16.
17.
18.

Answers

1. 0.6561
2. 0.9781
3. 7.1154
4. 0.2867
5. 0.5150
6. 84°
7. 29°
8. 83°
9. 12°
10. 76°
11. cosine, $DF \approx 19.1$
12. Pythagorean theorem, $GH = \sqrt{146} \approx 12.1$
13. sine, $EF \approx 5.8$
14. tangent, $m\angle G \approx 66°$
15. complement, $m\angle E = 90° - 17° = 73°$
16. $m\angle B = 43°$; $b = 8.4$ units; $c = 12.3$ units
17. $m\angle Z = 51°$; $m\angle X = 39°$; $y = 19.2$ units
18. $b = 7.4$ units; $c = 8.0$ units; $m\angle A = 22°$

19. $n = 4.5$ units; $l = 2.2$ units; $m\angle N = 64°$
20. $m\angle P = 32°$; $m\angle O = 58°$; $q = 49.4$ units
21. $m\angle A = 26°$; $m\angle B = 64°$; $b = 30.5$ units
22. $m\angle A = 8°$; $b = 241.9$ units; $c = 244.3$ units
23. $m\angle B = 43°$; $a = 19.3$ units; $c = 26.4$ units
24. $m\angle A = 63°$; $m\angle B = 27°$; $c = 37.1$ units
25. $m\angle A = 12°$; $a = 5.8$ units; $b = 27.4$ units
26. 12.26 cm
27. similar, AA [13.2]
28. congruent, HL ($\overline{PQ} \cong \overline{PQ}$) or HA ($\angle R \cong \angle S$) [7.1]
29. similar, theorem on altitude of right triangle [13.3]
30. neither [13.2]
31. congruent, SAS [6.6]

Mind over Math

See Appendix B.

19.

20.

Solve right $\triangle ABC$ if $\angle C$ is the right angle. Round your answers to the nearest tenth or to the nearest degree.

21. $a = 15$ units; $c = 34$ units
22. $m\angle B = 82°$; $a = 34$ units
23. $m\angle A = 47°$; $b = 18$ units

24. $a = 33$ units; $b = 17$ units
25. $c = 28$ units; $m\angle B = 78°$

▶ **C. Exercises**

26. Find *PS* using the diagram.

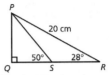

■ **Cumulative Review**

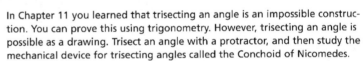

Which are congruent, similar, or neither? Why?

27.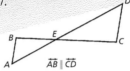

$\overleftrightarrow{AB} \parallel \overleftrightarrow{CD}$

30.

28.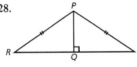

31.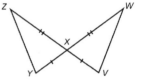

29.

MIND OVER MATH

In Chapter 11 you learned that trisecting an angle is an impossible construction. You can prove this using trigonometry. However, trisecting an angle is possible as a drawing. Trisect an angle with a protractor, and then study the mechanical device for trisecting angles called the Conchoid of Nicomedes.

Measurement

A surveyor needs to use a variety of calculation methods because direct measurements may be hindered by trees or cliffs. For distances he may need the distance formula, the Pythagorean theorem, or a trigonometric ratio. For finding areas of plots of land he may need $A = \frac{1}{2}ab \sin C$, or Heron's formula. Using such calculations would be foolish if they had not been proved correct. Analytic geometry provides the simplest means for proving many of the useful formulas. The following example proves a method used by builders to check that a foundation is precisely rectangular.

EXAMPLE Prove that the diagonals of a rectangle are congruent (Theorem 7.18) using analytic geometry.

Answer Locate the rectangle on a Cartesian graph in an appropriate position. Place one vertex at the origin and label the other vertices with arbitrary ordered pairs.

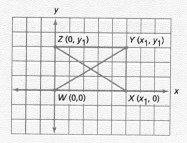

Given: Quadrilateral WXYZ is a rectangle

Prove: $\overline{ZX} \cong \overline{WY}$

STATEMENTS	REASONS
1. Quadrilateral WXYZ is a rectangle	1. Given
2. $XZ = \sqrt{(x_1-0)^2 + (0-y_1)^2} = \sqrt{x_1^2 + y_1^2}$ $WY = \sqrt{(x_1-0)^2 + (y_1-0)^2} = \sqrt{x_1^2 + y_1^2}$	2. Distance formula applied to $\overline{XZ}$ and $\overline{WY}$
3. $WY = XZ$	3. Transitive property of equality
4. $\overline{WY} \cong \overline{XZ}$	4. Definition of congruent segments

ANALYTIC GEOMETRY **599**

Analytic Geometry

Measurement

Objectives

1. To prove properties of polygons using analytic geometry.
2. To apply analytic geometry to perimeter, area, slope, and other problems.
3. To relate analytic geometry concepts to trigonometry.

Assignment

- Intuitive: no assignment necessary
- Standard: 1-5
- Rigorous: 1-5

Presentation

This unit provides a good review of many of the previous concepts of analytic geometry. The students will need to use the distance formula, slope, Heron's formula, midpoint formula, slopes of parallel lines, and slopes of perpendicular lines.

Analytic geometry proofs generally follow the pattern of setting down coordinates for the figure, usually as simply as possible. For instance, let one vertex be the point (0,0) in the plane; then apply one or two concepts that relate to what is being proved. For example, to show two segments perpendicular, the slopes are found and checked to see if they are negative reciprocals. Care must be taken to keep the notation correct and to watch out for negative signs, but generally these proofs are easy.

Tips

Ex. 2. Use Heron's formula:
$$\sqrt{8.17(1.77)(4.56)(1.85)} = \sqrt{121.99} \approx$$
11 sq. units

Ex. 3. This requires both the slope formula (p. 127) and the midpoint formula (p. 296). You may want to review these before assigning this one. ■

Answers

1. $\sqrt{41} + \sqrt{13} + 2\sqrt{10} \approx 16.3$ units
2. $\sqrt{121.99} \approx 11$ sq. units
3. The midpoint of $\overline{AB}$ is M, and the midpoint of $\overline{AC}$ is N.

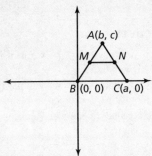

The coordinates of M and N are $M\left(\frac{b}{2}, \frac{c}{2}\right)$ and $N\left(\frac{a+b}{2}, \frac{c}{2}\right)$. The slope of $\overline{MN}$ is 0; thus $\overline{MN}$ is horizontal and parallel to the base $\overline{BC}$ on the x-axis.

4. The coordinates of the midpoints M and N are $M\left(\frac{b}{2}, \frac{c}{2}\right)$, $N\left(a + \frac{b}{2}, \frac{c}{2}\right)$.
   The distance between M and N and between B and C is found by the distance formula.

$$d_{MN} = \sqrt{\left(\frac{a+b}{2} - \frac{b}{2}\right)^2 + \left(\frac{c}{2} - \frac{c}{2}\right)^2}$$

$$d_{MN} = \sqrt{\left(\frac{a}{2}\right)^2 + 0^2}$$

$$d_{MN} = \sqrt{\left(\frac{a}{2}\right)^2}$$

$$d_{MN} = \frac{a}{2}$$

$$d_{BC} = \sqrt{(a - 0)^2 + (0 - 0)^2}$$

$$d_{BC} = \sqrt{a^2 + 0^2}$$

$$d_{BC} = \sqrt{a^2}$$

$$d_{BC} = a$$

So $MN = \frac{1}{2}(BC)$

5. The slope is rise over run, which is tangent.
   $m = \tan 40° = 0.8391$

▶ Exercises

Use the figure for exercises 1-2.

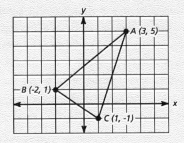

1. Find the perimeter of the triangle.
2. Find the area of the triangle.

Prove the following theorems.
3. The segment joining the midpoints of two sides of a triangle is parallel to the third side.
4. The length of the segment joining the midpoints of two sides of a triangle is one-half the length of the third side.

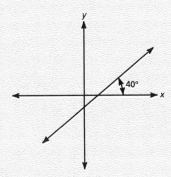

5. Use trigonometry to find the slope of the line.

14.4 Trigonometric Identities

Three *reciprocal ratios* are multiplicative inverses of the sine, cosine, and tangent ratios respectively. The abbreviations for the reciprocal ratios are csc A, meaning *cosecant* of $\angle A$; sec A, meaning *secant* of $\angle A$; and cot A, meaning *cotangent* of $\angle A$. So in all there are six trigonometric ratios, and they are related in pairs. The definitions of the three reciprocal ratios follow.

$\csc A = \dfrac{1}{\sin A}$	$\sec A = \dfrac{1}{\cos A}$	$\cot A = \dfrac{1}{\tan A}$

The most important relationship between two trigonometric ratios is proved below.

> **Theorem 14.3**
> **Sum of Squares Identity.** For any angle x,
> $\sin^2 x + \cos^2 x = 1$.

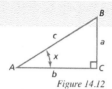
Figure 14.12

Notice the form of notation used for the square of sine x. In trigonometry we write $\sin^2 x$ rather than $(\sin x)^2$ to save writing parentheses. By contrast, $\sin x^2$ means that you square the angle measure before finding the sine.

STATEMENTS	REASONS
1. $m\angle A = x$ and $\triangle ABC$ is right	1. Given
2. $\sin x = \dfrac{a}{c}$	2. Definition of sine
3. $\cos x = \dfrac{b}{c}$	3. Definition of cosine
4. $a = c \sin x$ and $b = c \cos x$	4. Multiplication property of equality
5. $a^2 + b^2 = c^2$	5. Pythagorean theorem
6. $(c \sin x)^2 + (c \cos x)^2 = c^2$	6. Substitution (step 4 into 5)
7. $c^2 \sin^2 x + c^2 \cos^2 x = c^2$	7. Power of product property
8. $\sin^2 x + \cos^2 x = 1$	8. Multiplication property of equality

Trigonometric Identities

Objective

To prove trigonometric identities.

Assignment

- Intuitive: no assignment necessary
- Standard: 1-16, 21-25
- Rigorous: 1-25

Resources

- *Visual Packet,* Unit Circle (cover). This poster shows the geometry of trig functions.
- *Activities Manual,* Calculator Skills
- *Test Packet,* Quiz 3, Chapter 14 covers Sections 14.3 and 14.4.

Additional Problems

1. Find the exact value of sec 30°. $\dfrac{2\sqrt{3}}{3}$
2. Find csc 14° by using a calculator. **4.134**
3. Find cot x if $\sin x = \dfrac{2}{7}$. $\dfrac{3\sqrt{5}}{2}$

Prove or disprove each statement.

4. $\sin x \cos x = 1$ **Answers will vary; let $x = 45°$, $(\sin 45)(\cos 45) = (\dfrac{\sqrt{2}}{2})(\dfrac{\sqrt{2}}{2})$ $= \dfrac{2}{4} = \dfrac{1}{2}$; $\dfrac{1}{2} \neq 1$, not an identity.**

5. $\sin x \tan x = \sec x - \cos x$

$$\sin x \tan x = \sin x \, \frac{\sin x}{\cos x}$$
$$= \frac{\sin^2 x}{\cos x}$$
$$= \frac{1 - \cos^2 x}{\cos x}$$
$$= \frac{1}{\cos x} - \frac{\cos^2 x}{\cos x}$$
$$= \sec x - \cos x$$

Presentation

This section introduces the remaining three trigonometric ratios. Define secant, cosecant, and cotangent as shown on page 601. Emphasize that these reciprocal identities work both ways. That is, you can solve for the denominators to obtain $\sin A = \dfrac{1}{\csc A}$, and this is sometimes handy in proving identities. Likewise, $\cos A = \dfrac{1}{\sec A}$ and $\tan A = \dfrac{1}{\cot A}$.

Common Student Error. Students may mix up the definitions for secant and cosecant. You can tell them that a function beginning with s is the reciprocal of one that starts with c.

Next, go through the discussion leading up to the identity $\sin^2 x + \cos^2 x = 1$. Define a trigonometric identity and emphasize that it must be true in all cases. A comparison to one

of the properties of algebra such as the commutative property will help. Tell them that if they can find one case in which it is not true, then it is not an identity.

Explain the method of proving identities and work through the three examples in the text. Stress that students must start with something known to be true. A useful starting statement can be found by identifying the most complicated side and making a true statement from it. You can do this either by applying the reflexive property of equality (set it equal to itself) or by applying an identity or algebraic property. Once you have a true statement, apply algebraic properties and identities step-by-step until you obtain the desired expression (i.e., the

other side of the original identity to be proved). The transitive property (multiple uses) gives the desired identity.

Usually, when an identity is proved, one simply shows the chain of equalities (as in example 3). In the first two examples, we explained the reasons as we presented the identity. However, you can emphasize the fact that these really are proofs by having students write out the reasons for their steps in two-column form. You can also tell students the value of these skills since trig identities are used in integral calculus to transform functions into more workable forms. Example 3 will be difficult if students are rusty on the FOIL method from algebra. You can review it by doing an easy

Answers

1.
$$\frac{\sec x}{\csc x} = \frac{\sec x}{\csc x}$$
$$= \frac{\frac{1}{\cos x}}{\frac{1}{\sin x}}$$
$$= \frac{1}{\cos x} \cdot \frac{\sin x}{1}$$
$$= \frac{\sin x}{\cos x}$$
$$= \tan x$$

2.
$$1 + \tan^2 x = 1 + \tan^2 x$$
$$= 1 + \frac{\sin^2 x}{\cos^2 x}$$
$$= \frac{(\cos^2 x + \sin^2 x)}{\cos^2 x}$$
$$= \frac{1}{\cos^2 x}$$
$$= \sec^2 x$$

3.
$$\cot x = \cot x$$
$$= \frac{1}{\tan x}$$
$$= \frac{1}{\frac{\sin x}{\cos x}}$$
$$= 1 \cdot \frac{\cos x}{\sin x}$$
$$= \frac{\cos x}{\sin x}$$

4.
$$\sec x \cot x = \sec x \cot x$$
$$= \frac{1}{\cos x} \cdot \frac{1}{\tan x}$$
$$= \frac{1}{\cos x} \cdot \frac{1}{\frac{\sin x}{\cos x}}$$
$$= \frac{1}{\cos x} \cdot \frac{\cos x}{\sin x}$$
$$= \frac{1}{\sin x}$$
$$= \csc x$$

5.
$$\cos x \csc x = \cos x \csc x$$
$$= \cos x \left(\frac{1}{\sin x}\right)$$
$$= \frac{\cos x}{\sin x}$$
$$= \cot x$$

6.
$$\csc x \cos^2 x + \sin x = \csc x \cos^2 x + \sin x$$
$$= \frac{1}{\sin x}(\cos^2 x) + \sin x$$
$$= \frac{\cos^2 x}{\sin x} + \frac{\sin^2 x}{\sin x}$$
$$= \frac{\cos^2 x + \sin^2 x}{\sin x}$$
$$= \frac{1}{\sin x}$$
$$= \csc x$$

7.
$$\cot^2 x + 1 = \cot^2 + 1$$
$$= \frac{\cos^2 x}{\sin^2 x} + 1$$
$$= \frac{\cos^2 x + \sin^2 x}{\sin^2 x}$$
$$= \frac{1}{\sin^2 x}$$
$$= \csc^2 x$$

A trigonometric property that is true for all values of the variable is called a *trigonometric identity*. Like theorems, identities must be proved. When doing so, you must start with one side of the equation and transform it to the other side without working on both sides of the equation. If you work on both sides of the equation, you have assumed the truth of the statement you want to prove. Remember that this is the fallacy called circular argument.

To avoid this error, you must begin with a known truth. Even though you do not have to prove identities in two-column format, you should still have a reason in your mind for each step. One good way to get started is to select one side to work on and then apply the reflexive property to this expression. Study the examples below.

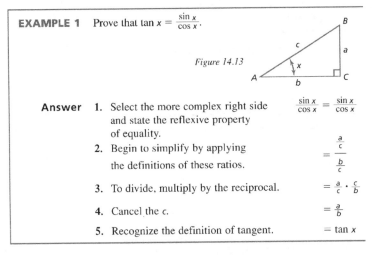

EXAMPLE 1   Prove that $\tan x = \frac{\sin x}{\cos x}$.

Figure 14.13

Answer
1. Select the more complex right side and state the reflexive property of equality. $\frac{\sin x}{\cos x} = \frac{\sin x}{\cos x}$
2. Begin to simplify by applying the definitions of these ratios. $= \frac{\frac{a}{c}}{\frac{b}{c}}$
3. To divide, multiply by the reciprocal. $= \frac{a}{c} \cdot \frac{c}{b}$
4. Cancel the c. $= \frac{a}{b}$
5. Recognize the definition of tangent. $= \tan x$

The identity is now proved. Notice that by the transitive property of equality the top and bottom lines in the proof are equal: $\frac{\sin x}{\cos x} = \tan x$.

EXAMPLE 2   Prove that $\sin x \sec x = \tan x$.

Answer
1. Start with the more complicated side, the left side. $\sin x \sec x = \sin x \sec x$
2. The reciprocal identity states that $\sec x = \frac{1}{\cos x}$. $= \sin x \cdot \frac{1}{\cos x}$
3. The identity proved in example 1 can now be used to prove this identity. $= \frac{\sin x}{\cos x}$ $= \tan x$

---

example similar to typical algebra problems. Multiply $(x + 2)(x + 5)$. Multiplying First-Outer-Inner-Last, we get $x^2 + 5x + 2x + 10$, or $x^2 + 7x + 10$.

Common Student Error. Many students start with the identity to be proved and work on both sides until they get a true statement like $5 = 5$. This process is more of a check than a proof. Students should understand proofs well enough by now to see that such checks are backwards (the final equality is obvious, while the first statement was not justified). Ask whether they ever begin a proof with the *Prove* statement (*no, that would result in circular reasoning*). In the same way, an identity cannot be proved by using it as the first step.

Tips

Ex. 3. This crucial exercise helps with several later ones. You may wish to do it in class.

Ex. 5, 7, 11, 15, 16, 19. These use #3.

Ex. 10. The shortest proof uses #2. ■

God's intricate order provides many interesting relationships among these ratios. The following example shows how to use the Sum of Squares Identity (Theorem 14.3) in proofs. By subtracting from both sides, $\sin^2 x + \cos^2 x = 1$ has two other forms: $\sin^2 x = 1 - \cos^2 x$ and $\cos^2 x = 1 - \sin^2 x$.

EXAMPLE 3 Prove that $(1 + \cos x)(1 - \cos x) = \sin^2 x$.

Answer Begin with the left side. Simplify using the FOIL method. The last step uses the Sum of Squares Identity.

$$(1 + \cos x)(1 - \cos x) = (1 + \cos x)(1 - \cos x)$$

$$= 1 + \cos x - \cos x - \cos^2 x$$

$$= 1 - \cos^2 x$$

$$= \sin^2 x$$

Notice that this identity could also have been proved by substituting $1 - \cos^2 x$ for $\sin^2 x$ on the right side and factoring the difference of two squares.

Finally, remember that $\sec^2 x$ means $(\sec x)^2$. This enables you to substitute reciprocal ratios even when a quantity is squared. For instance, $\sec^2 x = \frac{1}{\cos^2 x}$ since $\sec x = \frac{1}{\cos x}$.

▶ A. Exercises
Prove each identity.

1. $\tan x = \frac{\sec x}{\csc x}$

2. $1 + \tan^2 x = \sec^2 x$

3. $\cot x = \frac{\cos x}{\sin x}$

4. $\sec x \cot x = \csc x$

5. $\cos x \csc x = \cot x$

▶ B. Exercises

6. $\csc x \cos^2 x + \sin x = \csc x$
7. $\cot^2 x + 1 = \csc^2 x$
8. $\csc^2 x (1 - \cos^2 x) = 1$
9. $\cot x + \tan x = \csc x \sec x$
10. $\cos^2 x(1 + \tan^2 x) = 1$
11. $\sin x \sec x \cot x = 1$
12. $(\sin x + \cos x)^2 = 1 + 2\sin x \cos x$

13. $1 - \sin x \cos x \tan x = \cos^2 x$
14. $\sec x - \sin x \tan x = \cos x$
15. $\csc x - \cos x \cot x = \sin x$
16. $\csc x - \sin x = \cos x \cot x$
17. $\sec^2 x (1 - \sin^2 x) = 1$
18. $(\cos x + \sin x)^2 + (\cos x - \sin x)^2 = 2$

▶ C. Exercises

19. $\frac{1 + \tan x}{1 + \cot x} = \tan x$

20. $\sin x \cos x - \sec x \sin x = -\sin^2 x \tan x$

---

12. $(\sin x + \cos x)^2 = (\sin x + \cos x)^2$
$= \sin^2 x + 2 \sin x \cos x + \cos^2 x$
$= \sin^2 x + \cos^2 x + 2 \sin x \cos x$
$= 1 + 2 \sin x \cos x$

13. $1 - \sin x \cos x \tan x$
$= 1 - \sin x \cos x \tan x$
$= 1 - \sin x \cos x \cdot \frac{\sin x}{\cos x}$
$= 1 - \sin^2 x$
$= \cos^2 x$

14. $\sec x - \sin x \tan x = \sec x - \sin x \tan x$
$= \frac{1}{\cos x} - \sin x \cdot \frac{\sin x}{\cos x}$
$= \frac{1 - \sin^2 x}{\cos x}$
$= \frac{\cos^2 x}{\cos x}$
$= \cos x$

15. $\csc x - \cos x \cot x = \csc x - \cos x \cot x$
$= \frac{1}{\sin x} - \cos x \cdot \frac{\cos x}{\sin x}$
$= \frac{1}{\sin x} - \frac{\cos^2 x}{\sin x}$
$= \frac{1 - \cos^2 x}{\sin x}$
$= \frac{\sin^2 x}{\sin x}$
$= \sin x$

16. $\csc x - \sin x = \csc x - \sin x$
$= \frac{1}{\sin x} - \sin x$
$= \frac{1 - \sin^2 x}{\sin x}$
$= \frac{\cos^2 x}{\sin x}$
$= \cos x \cdot \frac{\cos x}{\sin x}$
$= \cos x \cot x$

17. $\sec^2 x (1 - \sin^2 x) = \sec^2 x (1 - \sin^2 x)$
$= \sec^2 x (\cos^2 x)$
$= \frac{1}{\cos^2 x} \cdot \cos^2 x$
$= \frac{\cos^2 x}{\cos^2 x}$
$= 1$

18. $(\cos x + \sin x)^2 + (\cos x - \sin x)^2$
$= (\cos x + \sin x)^2 + (\cos x - \sin x)^2$
$= (\cos^2 x + 2 \cos x \sin x + \sin^2 x) +$
$(\cos^2 x - 2 \cos x \sin x + \sin^2 x)$
$= (\cos^2 x + \sin^2 x) + (\cos^2 x + \sin^2 x)$
$= 1 + 1$
$= 2$

19. $\frac{1 + \tan x}{1 + \cot x} = \frac{1 + \tan x}{1 + \cot x}$
$= \frac{1 + \frac{\sin x}{\cos x}}{1 + \frac{\cos x}{\sin x}}$
$= \frac{\frac{\cos x + \sin x}{\cos x}}{\frac{\sin x + \cos x}{\sin x}}$
$= \frac{\cos x + \sin x}{\cos x} \cdot \frac{\sin x}{\sin x + \cos x}$
$= \frac{\sin x}{\cos x}$
$= \tan x$

(continued) see Answer section

---

8. $\csc^2 x (1 - \cos^2 x) = \csc^2 x (1 - \cos^2 x)$
$= \csc^2 x \cdot (\sin^2 x)$
$= \frac{1}{\sin^2 x} \cdot (\sin^2 x)$
$= \frac{\sin^2 x}{\sin^2 x}$
$= 1$

9. $\cot x + \tan x = \cot x + \tan x$
$= \frac{\cos x}{\sin x} + \frac{\sin x}{\cos x}$
$= \frac{\cos^2 x + \sin^2 x}{\sin x \cos x}$
$= \frac{1}{\sin x \cos x}$
$= \frac{1}{\sin x} \cdot \frac{1}{\cos x}$
$= \csc x \sec x$

10. $\cos^2 x (1 + \tan^2 x) = \cos^2 x (1 + \tan^2 x)$
$= \cos^2 x (\sec^2 x)$
$= \cos^2 x \cdot \frac{1}{\cos^2 x}$
$= \frac{\cos^2 x}{\cos^2 x}$
$= 1$

11. $\sin x \sec x \cot x = \sin x \sec x \cot x$
$= \sin x \cdot \frac{1}{\cos x} \cdot \frac{1}{\tan x}$
$= \frac{\sin x}{\cos x} \cdot \frac{1}{\tan x}$
$= \tan x \cdot \frac{1}{\tan x}$
$= 1$

$$= \sin x \cos x - \sec x \sin x$$

$$= \sin x(\cos x - \sec x)$$

$$= \sin x\left(\cos x - \frac{1}{\cos x}\right)$$

14.5

Applications of Trigonometry

Objectives

1. To apply trigonometric ratios to solve right triangles.
2. To apply trigonometry to solve word problems.

Vocabulary
angle of depression
angle of elevation

Assignment
- Intuitive: no assignment necessary
- Standard: 1-14, 21-25
- Rigorous: 1-13 odd, 15-25

Resource
- *Activities Manual,* Ellipses in Brief

Reading and Writing Mathematics
Give the students the figure shown, which is a unit circle (radius = 1) with two triangles. Point out that there are two triangles shown and that contained within the figure are three segments whose lengths exactly correspond to the sine, cosine, and tangent of ∠*DOA*. Ask them to identify them. ***sin ∠DOA = BC,*** ***cos ∠DOA = OC, tan ∠DOA = AD***

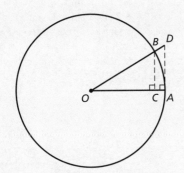

Additional Problems
1. A ramp is to be constructed with an angle of inclination of 15° that must reach the top of a 4-foot-high truck dock. How long is the incline of the ramp? ***15.5 ft.***

Match to each description the letter of the most specific term that applies.

21. Any composite of two reflections across concurrent lines
22. Any mapping with a scale factor greater than one
23. Any one-to-one correspondence from the plane onto the plane
24. Any mapping that preserves distance
25. Any mapping that preserves shape

A. translation
B. enlargement
C. isometry
D. reduction
E. reflection
F. rotation
G. similarity
H. transformation

14.5 Applications of Trigonometry

Builders translate mathematically made blueprints into architecture such as the state capitol at Providence, Rhode Island.

One definition of *apply* is "to put into practice." It is good to know and understand different areas of study, but if you do not put your knowledge into practice, it does not benefit you. It is important, then, that you not only learn material but that you also apply it. Likewise, a Christian needs to search the Word of God and apply its principles to his life. "Be ye doers of the word and not hearers only" (James 1:22). Do you apply the principles you learn from math and from Scripture?

604 CHAPTER 14 TRIGONOMETRY

Presentation

Several of the applications in this section involve determining heights of mountains, property boundaries, or sizes of lakes or swamps. You can help your students see that these are realistic applications by discussing the feature on surveying.

Define and illustrate the angles of elevation and depression on the board. Students often have difficulty with the angle of depression since it is usually not in the triangle drawn for a problem, though its complement is. Review the Parallel Postulate and alternate interior angles to help them understand.

Have the students read example 1; then apply the general rules that follow for solving application problems with your students. After reading the problem, ask some questions to get them to focus on the information presented. When completed, discuss example 2.

1. What is the unknown to be found?

2. What information is known and what parts of the sketch will it represent?

3. Identify a trig ratio that connects the unknown to known information such as angle measures and distances.

Since the textbook table is in whole degrees, use a scientific calculator. When dealing with longer distances, fractions of an angle can have a significant impact on distances. Rounding an angle of 56.6° to 57° gives an error of 5.9 feet for a 1000-foot distance.

In this lesson you will see some simple applications of trigonometry. There are many other advanced applications of trigonometry in surveying work, engineering, navigation, and astronomy. But in this lesson we will concentrate on problems such as finding the height of a mountain without climbing it or the distance across a deep river. You must understand the next two terms before you can solve the problems.

Definitions

The **angle of elevation** is the angle formed by a horizontal line and the line of sight toward an object that is above the horizontal. The measure of this angle is the *inclination*.

The **angle of depression** is the angle formed by a horizontal line and the line of sight toward an object that is below the horizontal. The measure of this angle is the *declination*.

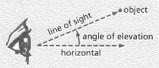
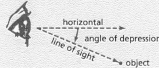

Figure 14.14

EXAMPLE 1   The KVLY-TV antenna near Blanchard, North Dakota, is the tallest structure in the world. Standing a distance of 1006 feet from the base of the antenna, you find the measure of the angle of elevation to the top of the antenna to be 64°. Find the height of the antenna.

Answer

1. Draw a diagram and label it.

2. Label the unknown height a.

3. Use a trigonometric ratio to write an equation involving a.

$$\tan 64° = \frac{a}{1006}$$

$$2.0503 \approx \frac{a}{1006}$$

$$2063 \approx a$$

4. The antenna is 2063 feet high.

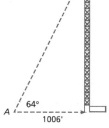

Figure 14.15

---

2. A ranger on a 260-foot-high lookout tower spots a forest fire at an angle of depression of 5°. How far away from the base of the tower is the fire?   **2971.8 ft. (over 0.5 mile)**

3. Silver Cascade, Colorado, flows 200 ft. along a slope inclined at 40°. How long is the vertical drop?   **128.6 ft.**

4. A plane is traveling at an altitude of 3100 ft. A wind is blowing hard enough to cause a paratrooper to fall at an angle of 11° east of straight down. If he wants to land in a certain field, how far west of the field must he jump?   **602.6 ft.**

5. When two sides of a right triangle are given, what is the best way to calculate the third side and why?   **the Pythagorean theorem because it gives an exact answer (in radical form) rather than an approximation**

Flash

KVLY-TV was formerly called KTHI-TV. The tower was assembled in 33 working days with no casualties. It broadcasts NBC (local channel 11) to over 240,000 homes in the Red River Valley along the Minnesota-North Dakota state line. The beacon at the top sways 10 feet in 70 mph winds. A higher structure, a radio tower built in 1974 at Warsaw, Poland, collapsed in 1991, leaving KVLY the highest in the world.

Tips

Ex. 16. Since $\frac{2400}{\tan 82.5} \approx 316$, Mt. Mitchell is 316 feet below the plane, or $7000 - 316 = 6684$ feet above sea level.

Ex. 20. First, find the area of the base: $V = BH = B \cdot 30 = 9000$, so $B = 300$. Next, substitute your result into $B = \frac{1}{2} ap = \frac{1}{2} a(6s) = 300$ and divide both sides by 3 to obtain $as = 100$. Since $\cos 30 = \frac{a}{s}$, solve for a to obtain $a = s \cos 30$. Substitute this into the previous formula to get $s \cos 30(s) = 100$, or $s^2 = \frac{100}{\cos 30}$. Thus, $s^2 = 115.47$ and $s = \sqrt{115.47} \approx 10.7$ ft. ∎

There are some general rules to follow when solving these kinds of problems.

1. Read the problem carefully.
2. Plan your solution by sketching the problem, labeling it correctly, and identifying the appropriate trigonometric ratio.
3. Solve an equation using the trigonometric ratio.
4. Check to see that you answered the question and that your answer is reasonable.

EXAMPLE 2   A surveyor must find the distance between two particular points that are on opposite sides of a river. He is unable to measure it directly. He measures a distance of 180 feet from point B to another point A on the same side of the river, directly across the river from C. With his instrument at B, he turns the angle, looking first at A, then at C. He finds that this angle is 43 degrees. What is the distance from B to C?

Figure 14.16

Answer

1. Label the desired distance a.

2. The adjacent side of the given angle is known and the hypotenuse to be found. Select the cosine ratio since it involves these two sides.

$$\cos 43° = \frac{180}{a}$$

3. Solve the equation resulting from this trigonometric ratio.

$$0.7314 \approx \frac{180}{a}$$
$$0.7314a \approx 180$$
$$a \approx \frac{180}{0.7314}$$
$$a \approx 246$$

4. The distance across the river from B to C is 246 feet.

▶ A. Exercises

1. A 40-foot guy wire is connected to a telephone pole, forming a 21° angle with the pole. How far from the pole is the guy wire anchored to the ground?

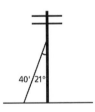

2. An observer from a lighthouse sees a boat that is at an angle of depression of 8°. If the lighthouse is 140 feet above sea level, how far is the boat from the lighthouse?

Answers
1. 14.3 ft.
2. 996 ft.
3. 1026.6 ft.
4. 131.5 yd.
5. 60°
6. 1.5 mi.
7. 59°
8. 670.0 ft.
9. 376.8 ft.
10. 1673.8 ft.

▶ B. Exercises

Round your answers to the nearest tenth or to the nearest degree.

3. Dan finds the angle of depression from his location at the top of a mountain to a stream below to be 78°. The height of the mountain is 4830 feet above the stream. Find the horizontal distance from Dan to the stream.

4. Scientists can estimate the height of objects on different planets and on the moon by measuring the shadows of the objects. If a crater rim casts a 127-yard shadow when the sun shines on it at a 46° angle of elevation from the moon's surface to the sun, what is the height of the crater rim?

5. Karen has an exotic tropical bird that escaped from its cage. The bird is now on a tree branch 13 feet above the ground. If Karen places a 15-foot ladder against the tree branch, what angle does the ladder make with the ground?

6. An airplane takes off from Harrisburg Airport at an angle of elevation of 4°. If the plane is traveling at 215 miles per hour and maintains a constant speed and rate of climb, how high is the plane after 6 minutes?

7. The slope of a line is defined by the ratio of the vertical change to the horizontal change. If the slope of a line is $\frac{5}{3}$, what angle does the line make with the horizontal?

8. A hot-air balloon rises and moves away from you. The total distance it travels is 1382 feet. The angle of elevation from you to the balloon is 29°. How high is the balloon?

9. Donna needs to find the distance across a pond from point A to point B (see illustration). The distance from A to C is 500 feet, and $m\angle C = 37°$. What is the distance from A to B?

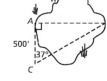

10. A submarine makes a dive after being on the surface of the ocean. The angle of the dive with the surface is 12°. If the submarine levels off at a depth of 348 feet, how far does the submarine travel to get to this depth?

11. 17 feet
12. 62.1 miles
13. 1142.5 ft. (about 0.2 mile)
14. 1656.3 ft.
15. about 30 mi. east (157,689 ft.)
16. 6684 ft.
17. 54.7 ft.
18. 21°
19. 34°
20. $s = \sqrt{115.47} \approx 10.7$ ft.
21. 40° [8.4]
22. 84 [3.4]
23. $\frac{25\sqrt{3}}{4} \approx 10.8$ [8.3]
24. $\frac{75\sqrt{3}}{2} \approx 65$ [8.4]
25. 98.4 [8.4]

11. Rob is installing a 15-foot TV antenna on the flat roof of an apartment building. The guy wires will be attached eight feet from the base of the antenna. How long should the guy wires be?

12. Happytown is 60 miles due west of Parkville. Welcome is due south of Happytown. Two planes depart from Parkville with an angle of 46° between their flight paths, one for Happytown and one for Welcome. How far is it from Welcome to Happytown?

13. A balloonist floats 800 feet above Barker Park. He observes his house at a declination of 35°. How far is his house from the park?

14. You measure an inclination of 25° to a cloud 700 feet above ground. How far is the cloud from you?

15. Mauna Kea is 13,796 feet above sea level. A westbound ship first sights the summit at an angle of elevation of 5°. How far from land is the ship?

16. An air survey team is flying at 7000 feet above sea level. They measure a declination to the summit of Mt. Mitchell at $7\frac{1}{2}°$. After flying another 2400 feet, they are directly above the summit. How high is Mt. Mitchell?

17. Ribbon Falls, Colorado, flows 140 feet along a slope inclined 23° above the horizontal. How far does it drop vertically?

18. If Sliding Rock, North Carolina, drops 50 feet in a horizontal distance of 130 feet, how steep is the slide?

19. Chuck found an old cabin far from the trails in the woods. His map shows that he is six miles from Tadmor and five miles south of a pond that is due west of Tadmor. How many degrees east of north should he face on his compass to head for Tadmor?

▶ C. Exercises

20. A city water tower is to be constructed in the shape of a prism with a regular hexagon as base. How long should an edge of the base be if the height is to be 30 feet and the tower must hold 9000 cubic feet of water?

■ Cumulative Review

21. Give the measure of a central angle of a regular nonagon.
22. Give the perimeter of a regular heptagon with a side of length 12.
23. Give the area of a regular triangle with side of length 5.
24. Give the area of a regular hexagon with side of length 5.
25. Give the area of a regular octagon with side of length 6 and apothem of length 4.1.

14.6 Trigonometry and Regular Polygons

An aerial view of the Pentagon (U.S. military headquarters) reveals the regular polygon.

Consider the regular pentagon below.

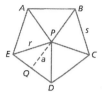

Figure 14.17

Recall that the 5 central angles, being congruent, measure $\frac{360}{5} = 72°$ each. Since the radii are congruent, the triangles are isosceles. This means that each apothem ($\overline{PQ}$) bisects the central angles into two 36° angles. Also, it is the perpendicular bisector of the side to which it is drawn. This means that we can focus on the right triangle thus formed.

Figure 14.18

Using trigonometry, $\tan 36° = \frac{\frac{1}{2}s}{a}$ and $\sin 36° = \frac{\frac{1}{2}s}{r}$. If the length of a side is known, $a = \frac{s}{2 \tan 36°}$ and $r = \frac{s}{2 \sin 36°}$.

EXAMPLE 1 Find the apothem and radius of a regular pentagon with a side of length 12.

Answer $a = \frac{12}{2 \tan 36°} = 6 \cot 36° \approx 8.3$

$r = \frac{12}{2 \sin 36°} = 6 \csc 36° \approx 10.2$

Remember that to find reciprocal ratios on a calculator, you will probably need to use the definition. For instance, to find $\cot 36°$, use the definition $\cot 36° = \frac{1}{\tan 36°}$. Find $\tan 36°$ and then press the reciprocal $\left(\frac{1}{x}\right)$ button.

14.6

Trigonometry of Regular Polygons

Objectives

1. To identify and apply the relation between the apothem and side of a regular polygon.
2. To apply trigonometry to regular polygons.

Assignment
- Intuitive: no assignment necessary
- Standard: 1-10, 21-25
- Rigorous: 1-20 odd, 21-25

Resources
- *Activities Manual,* Bible Activity: God's Work
- *Test Packet,* Quiz 4, Chapter 14 covers Sections 14.5 and 14.6.

Reading and Writing Mathematics

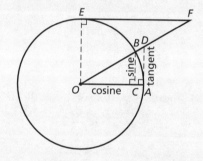

As a continuation of the Reading and Writing Math section from 14.5, consider the figure shown with the answers labeled for 14.5 and

---

Presentation

The trigonometry of a regular polygon is easier than you might think. Consecutive radii of the polygon and the side adjacent to both radii form an isosceles triangle with the apothem as its altitude. Therefore, the trigonometry of a polygon reduces to a right triangle. Students have calculated apothems for squares, equilateral triangles, and regular hexagons (since Chapter 8). However, apothems for other regular polygons require trigonometry. The table shows the measure of the angle (see figure) essential to each calculation. Notice in each case it is half of the central angle.

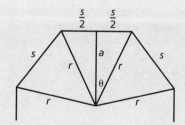

Polygon	Central Angle	θ
equ. triangle	120	60
square	90	45
pentagon	72	36
hexagon	60	30
heptagon	$51\frac{3}{7}$	$25\frac{5}{7}$
octagon	45	$22\frac{1}{2}$
nonagon	40	20
decagon	36	18
hendecagon	$32\frac{8}{11}$	$16\frac{4}{11}$
dodecagon	30	15

the additions $\overline{EO}$, $\overline{EF}$, and the extension of $\overline{OD}$ to point F. The secant, cosecant, and cotangent ratios of $\angle DOA$ are each represented exactly by the length of a segment. Two of them are found in $\triangle OEF$ and the other in $\triangle OAD$. Ask the students to find the segments.

$cot \angle DOA = cot \angle F = \overline{EF}$, $csc \angle DOA =$
$csc \angle F = \overline{OF}$, $sec \angle DOA = \overline{OD}$

Additional Problems

Using a regular heptagon of side s, give the
  1. measure of the central angle.   **51.4°**
  2. apothem in terms of a side.
     $a = \frac{s}{2 \tan 25.7°} = \frac{s}{2} \cot 25.7°$
  3. radius in terms of the side.
     $r = \frac{s}{2 \sin 25.7°} = \frac{s}{2} \csc 25.7°$
  4. area between the regular heptagon and the circumscribed circle in terms of a side.
     $A = \frac{\pi s^2}{4} \csc^2 25.7° - 7 \frac{s^2}{4} \cot 25.7°$ or
     $A \approx 0.54 \, s^2$
  5. If the area is 40 square inches, find the radius. $r \approx 3.8$ in. (since $s^2 = 11$ and $s \approx 3.32$)

Answers
  1. 72°, 36°
  2. 54°
  3. 4.1, 5.1
  4. 61.5
  5. 36°, 18°
  6. $a = \frac{s}{2 \tan 18°} = \frac{s}{2} \cot 18°$
  7. $r = \frac{s}{2 \sin 18°} = \frac{s}{2} \csc 18°$
  8. $a \approx 15.4$, $r \approx 16.2$ mm
  9. $s = 24 \sin 18° \approx 7.4$ m
  10. $A = \frac{1}{2} ap = \frac{1}{2} (10.77) \, 70 \approx 377$ ft.^{2}
  11. $a = \frac{s}{2 \tan 22.5°} = \frac{s}{2} \cot 22.5°$

      $r = \frac{s}{2 \sin 22.5°} = \frac{s}{2} \csc 22.5°$
  12. $A = \frac{1}{2} \cdot \frac{s}{2} \cot 22.5° \cdot 8s = 2s^2 \cot 22.5°$
      or $A \approx 4.828 \, s^2$
  13. $7 = \frac{s}{2 \tan 22.5}$
      $s = 14 \tan 22.5 \approx 5.8$

EXAMPLE 2   If the radius of a circle is 10 cm, find the length of the side of an inscribed regular pentagon.

    Answer $r = \frac{s}{2 \sin 36°}$

            $10 = \frac{s}{2 \sin 36°}$

            $s = 20 \sin 36° \approx 11.8$ cm

You should be able to derive similar formulas for other regular polygons.

▶ A. Exercises

Refer to the regular pentagon to find the following.

  1. $m\angle CPD$ and $m\angle CPM$
  2. $m\angle PCM$
  3. PM and PD
  4. area of the pentagon

▶ B. Exercises

Using a regular decagon of side s, find
  5. the measures of the central angle and its bisected angle.
  6. the apothem in terms of the side.
  7. the radius in terms of the side.
  8. the apothem and radius if the side is 10 mm.
  9. the side if the circumscribed circle has a radius of 12 m.
  10. the area if the side is 7 feet.

Use a regular octagon of side s. Find formulas for the
  11. apothem and radius.
  12. area.
  13. If the apothem is 7 in., how long is the side?

Go through the section where a regular pentagon is used showing the use of trig to find the apothem and radius. Use the Additional Problems to help the students apply the concept before they do the exercises.

Students may need review on simplifying complex fractions. Remind them that to divide fractions, you invert and multiply.

Therefore, $\frac{\frac{a}{b}}{\frac{c}{d}}$ is the same as $\frac{a}{b} \cdot \frac{d}{c}$, or $\frac{ad}{bc}$.

This explains why (p. 609)

$\frac{\frac{1}{2}s}{a} = \frac{\frac{s}{2}}{\frac{a}{1}} = \frac{s}{2a}$.

Tips

Ex. 24. The printed answer assumes that the golden rectangles are horizontal (5 cm as the long side). If the 5 cm represents the short side, the heights of the lateral sides will be 8.09. Thus, $A = 2(25) + 4(5)(8.09) = 211.8$ cm^2. ∎

Part of a regular *n*-gon with side *s* units long is shown.

14. Express AM, $m\angle APM$, and the perimeter in terms of *n* and *s*.

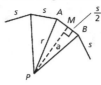

► C. Exercises

Find a formula for each part of the *n*-gon.
15. apothem
16. radius
17. area
18. Prove your formula for the apothem.

Find a formula for the volume of the solid with height *H* and a regular *n*-gon of side *s* as a base.
19. prism
20. pyramid

■ Cumulative Review

Find the dimensions of each.
21. Cube with a volume of 64 cu. in.
22. Sphere with a volume of 36π cu. ft.
23. Regular octahedron with a volume of $72\sqrt{2}$ cubic inches

Find the volume of each.
24. A rectangular solid has a square base with edges 5 cm long. The lateral faces are golden rectangles.
25. A pyramid is 11 units high and has a regular polygon as its base. The polygon has 20 sides each 4 units long. (*Hint:* Use trigonometry to find the apothem first.)

14. $AM = \frac{s}{2}$, $m\angle APM = \frac{1}{2}\left(\frac{360}{n}\right) = \frac{180}{n}$, $p = ns$

15. $a = \frac{s}{2}\cot\frac{180}{n}$

16. $\sin\frac{180}{n} = \frac{\frac{s}{2}}{r}$, so $r = \frac{2}{2\sin\frac{180}{n}}$

$\frac{s}{2}\csc\frac{180}{n}$

17. $A = \frac{1}{2}ap$
$= \frac{1}{2}\left(\frac{s}{2}\cot\frac{180}{n}\right)ns$
$= n \cdot \frac{s^2}{4}\cot\frac{180}{n}$

18.

1. regular *n*-gon of side *s*	1. Given
2. $m\angle APB = \frac{360}{n}$	2. Central angles of a regular *n*-gon are congruent and measure $\frac{360}{n}$
3. $\overline{PM} \perp \overline{AB}$	3. Definition of apothem
4. $\angle PMB$ and $\angle PMA$ are right angles	4. Definition of perpendicular
5. $\triangle BMP \cong \triangle AMP$	5. Exercise 16 (Sec. 7.1)
6. $\overline{BM} \cong \overline{AM}$; $\angle BPM \cong \angle APM$	6. Definition of congruent triangles
7. $\overrightarrow{PM}$ bisects $\angle APB$	7. Definition of angle bisector
8. $m\angle APM = \frac{180}{n}$	8. Angle Bisector Theorem
9. *M* is midpoint of $\overline{AB}$	9. Definition of midpoint; definition of congruent segments
10. $AM = \frac{s}{2}$	10. Midpoint Theorem
11. $\tan\frac{180}{n}$ $= \frac{\frac{s}{2}}{a} = \frac{s}{2a}$	11. Definition of tangent
12. $2a\tan\left(\frac{180}{n}\right) = s$	12. Multiplication property of equality
13. $a = \frac{s}{2}\tan\frac{180}{n}$	13. Multiplication property of equality
14. $a = \frac{s}{2}\cot\frac{180}{n}$	14. Reciprocal identity

19. $V = BH = \frac{1}{4}nHs^2\cot\frac{180}{n}$

20. $V = \frac{1}{3}BH = \frac{1}{12}nHs^2\cot\frac{180}{n}$

21. edge of 4 in. [11.1]
22. radius of 3 ft. [11.6]
23. edge of 6 inches [11.5]
24. $5 \cdot 5 \cdot \left(\frac{1+\sqrt{5}}{2}\right) \cdot 5 = 202.25$ cu. cm [13.7]
25. $\tan 9° = \frac{2}{a}$, $a \approx 12.6$, $B = 504$ sq. units $V = 1848$ cu. units [11.4]

Geometry and Scripture

Answers

1. Exod. 27:1 and Rev. 21:16
2. to divide day and night, for signs, seasons, days and years (v. 14), and to give light (vv. 15, 17)
3. 0° (sunrise)
4. 90° (noon)
5. 0° (sundown)
6. third hour (9 A.M.) 45°
7. sixth hour (noon) 90°
8. ninth hour (3 P.M.) 45°
9. beginning of the watches, middle watch, morning watch

Geometry and Scripture

Trigonometry means triangle measure. You know that each trigonometric function is a ratio of lengths that depend on the size of the given angle. Angles are basic to trigonometry. Let's look at angles mentioned in Scripture.

1. What Line upon Line verses contained references to the concept of right angles?

You know that the angle of inclination of the sun enables us to tell time and also to find elevations using shadows.

2. According to Genesis 1, why did God make the sun?

In Chapter 10 we saw that sunrise and sunset are figures of speech that draw on the language of appearance. Give the apparent angle of elevation of the sun in each of these verses.

3. Mark 16:2   5. Judges 19:14
4. Acts 26:13

The day from sunrise to sunset is divided into twelve hours. Give the time of day and determine the approximate angle of elevation of the sun for each event in the Crucifixion.

6. Jesus is crucified (Mark 15:25).
7. God darkens the sun (Luke 23:44).
8. Jesus' death (Luke 23:44-47)

For the Hebrews in the Old Testament, the night was divided into three watches, or guard duties.

9. Judges 7:19, I Samuel 11:11, and Lamentations 2:19 refer to these three watches. Give the names of the watches in order from dusk to dawn.

Presentation

This study focuses on measures of angles. The main examples of angle measure in Scripture relate to keeping time. The angle of elevation of the sun determines lengths of shadows as measured on sun dials. Since the ancient society did not depend on schedules and appointments down to the minute, they commonly divided the daylight at the third, sixth, and ninth hour and also divided the night into watches. Students will find references to each of these divisions.

The most interesting of these references is the Line upon Line verse because it mentions both the time-keeping device (dial) and the miracle of making the shadow shorten (to set the clocks back, as it were). ∎

Romans divided the night into four watches. These watches could be referred to in different ways. Sometimes they were just numbered first watch, second watch, third watch, and fourth watch.

> **HIGHER PLANE:** Find three verses in the Gospels that refer to the night watches by number.

The watches could also be referred to by name: even (dusk until 9 P.M.); midnight (until 12 A.M.); cockcrowing (until 3 A.M.); morning (until dawn).

10. Which of these four watches are mentioned by name in Mark 13:35?

The third, sixth, and ninth hours split the day into four parts based on the angle of inclination of the sun. Shadows could be measured for greater accuracy. Two major types of dials were used: a traditional sundial and a series of steps. Either way, the dial measured an angle: the angle of elevation of the sun.

11. The dial of Ahaz in II Kings 20 probably consisted of steps down which the shadow would fall. How did God use this dial to reverse His created order (v. 11)?

Line upon Line

AND ISAIAH THE PROPHET cried unto the Lord: and he brought the shadow ten degrees backward, by which it had gone down in the dial of Ahaz. 🙢

II KINGS 20:11

Chapter 14

Review

Chapter 14 Review

Objective

To help students prepare for evaluation.

Vocabulary

See Appendix A.

Assignment

- Intuitive: no assignment necessary
- Standard: 1-14, 21-25
- Rigorous: 1-30

Resources

- *Activities Manual,* Cumulative Review
- *Activities Manual,* Terms and Symbols
- *Activities Manual,* Practice
- *Test Packet,* Chapter 14 Exam; Fourth-Quarter Quiz, Analytic Geometry: Fourth-Quarter Exam

Answers

1. $\sin A = \frac{7\sqrt{149}}{149}$; $\sin B = \frac{10\sqrt{149}}{149}$;

   $\cos A = \frac{10\sqrt{149}}{149}$; $\cos B = \frac{7\sqrt{149}}{149}$;

   $\tan A = \frac{7}{10}$; $\tan B = \frac{10}{7}$

2. $\sin Z = \frac{5\sqrt{34}}{34}$; $\sin X = \frac{3\sqrt{34}}{34}$;

   $\cos Z = \frac{3\sqrt{34}}{34}$; $\cos X = \frac{5\sqrt{34}}{34}$;

   $\tan Z = \frac{5}{3}$; $\tan X = \frac{3}{5}$

3. $\sin A = \frac{12\sqrt{193}}{193}$; $\tan A = \frac{12}{7}$

4. $AB = 9\sqrt{2}$ units; $BC = 9$ units
5. $AC = 6\sqrt{2}$ units; $BC = 6\sqrt{2}$ units
6. $MO = 7\sqrt{3}$ units; $MN = 14$ units
7. $MO = 13\sqrt{3}$ units; $NO = 13$ units

8. $\frac{\sqrt{3}}{2}$ (or 0.8660)

9. 1.000
10. 0.6293
11. 0.0698
12. 0.1908
13. 3.078
14. 47°
15. 28°
16. 66°
17. $c = 9\sqrt{13}$ units ≈ 32.4; $m\angle B = 34°$;
    $m\angle A = 56°$
18. $m\angle X = 32°$; $y = 14.4$ units; $z = 17.0$ units

Find the three basic trigonometric ratios for each acute angle of each right triangle below.

1.

2.

3. Find the other two trigonometric ratios for $\angle A$ if $\cos A = \frac{7\sqrt{193}}{193}$.

Given that $\triangle ABC$ is a 45-45 right triangle, and $\triangle MNO$ is a 30-60 right triangle, find the measures of the other two sides.

4. $AC = 9$ units

5. $AB = 12$ units

6. $NO = 7$ units

7. $MN = 26$ units

Give the following trigonometric ratios.

8. cos 30°   10. sin 39°   12. sin 11°

9. tan 45°   11. cos 86°   13. tan 72°

Find the measure of $\angle A$.

14. sin $A = 0.7314$ 15. cos $A = 0.8828$ 16. tan $A = 2.246$

Solve each right triangle.

17.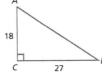

18.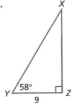

Presentation

Have students return to the opening page of the chapter (p. 581) and look over the objectives. All eight points should seem easy for them. By looking over these, they should see that the main points to review are the definitions of the six trig functions, the relations between sides of special right triangles, proving an identity, and solving a word problem. ∎

Prove the following trigonometric identities.

19. $\sec x - \cos x = \sin x \tan x$

20. $\sin x (\csc x - \sin x) = \cos^2 x$

21. Meteorologists can find the height of a cloud ceiling by shining a light vertically and then finding the angle of elevation to the spot where the light meets the clouds. Find the height of the cloud ceiling by the information given in the illustration.

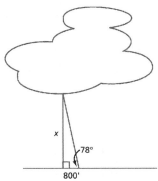

Write the three reciprocal identities.

22. $\sec x$

23. $\cot x$

24. $\csc x$

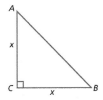

25. Solve the isosceles right triangle shown.

26. Solve the special triangle shown.

27. Give the three basic trigonometric ratios for angle A in exercise 25.

28. Give the three basic trigonometric ratios for angles A and B in exercise 26.

29. If $\triangle ABC \sim \triangle DEF$ and $\cos B = 0.3657$, what is $\cos E$?

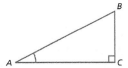 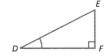

30. Explain the mathematical significance of II Kings 20:11.

19. $\sec x - \cos x = \sec x - \cos x$

$= \dfrac{1}{\cos x} - \cos x$

$= \dfrac{1}{\cos x} - \dfrac{\cos^2 x}{\cos x}$

$= \dfrac{1 - \cos^2 x}{\cos x}$

$= \dfrac{\sin^2 x}{\cos x}$

$= \sin x \cdot \dfrac{\sin x}{\cos x}$

$= \sin x \tan x$

20. $\sin x (\csc x - \sin x) = \sin x (\csc x - \sin x)$

$= \sin x \cdot (\dfrac{1}{\sin x} - \sin x)$

$= \dfrac{\sin x}{\sin x} - \sin^2 x$

$= 1 - \sin^2 x$

$= \cos^2 x$

21. 3763.7 ft.

22. $\sec x = \dfrac{1}{\cos x}$

23. $\cot x = \dfrac{1}{\tan x}$

24. $\csc x = \dfrac{1}{\sin x}$

25. $c = x\sqrt{2}, m\angle A = m\angle B = 45°, m\angle C = 90°$

26. $q = x\sqrt{3}, r = 2x, m\angle Q = 60°, m\angle R = 90°$

27. $\sin 45° = \dfrac{\sqrt{2}}{2}, \cos 45° = \dfrac{\sqrt{2}}{2}, \tan 45° = 1$

28. $\sin P = \dfrac{1}{2}, \cos P = \dfrac{\sqrt{3}}{2}, \tan P = \dfrac{\sqrt{3}}{3}$

$\sin Q = \dfrac{\sqrt{3}}{2}, \cos Q = \dfrac{1}{2}, \tan Q = \sqrt{3}$

29. 0.3657

30. Angle measurements are used in this verse for telling time and to display the Lord's power to perform a miracle.

Trigonometric Table

DEGREES	sin	cos	tan	cot	sec	csc	
0	.0000	1.0000	.0000		1.000		90
1	.0175	.9998	.0175	57.290	1.000	57.299	89
2	.0349	.9994	.0349	28.636	1.001	28.654	88
3	.0523	.9986	.0524	19.081	1.001	19.107	87
4	.0698	.9976	.0699	14.301	1.002	14.336	86
5	.0872	.9962	.0875	11.430	1.004	11.474	85
6	.1045	.9945	.1051	9.514	1.006	9.567	84
7	.1219	.9925	.1228	8.144	1.008	8.206	83
8	.1392	.9903	.1405	7.115	1.010	7.185	82
9	.1564	.9877	.1584	6.314	1.012	6.392	81
10	.1736	.9848	.1763	5.671	1.015	5.759	80
11	.1908	.9816	.1944	5.145	1.019	5.241	79
12	.2079	.9781	.2126	4.705	1.022	4.810	78
13	.2250	.9744	.2309	4.331	1.026	4.445	77
14	.2419	.9703	.2493	4.011	1.031	4.134	76
15	.2588	.9659	.2679	3.732	1.035	3.864	75
16	.2756	.9613	.2867	3.487	1.040	3.628	74
17	.2924	.9563	.3057	3.271	1.046	3.420	73
18	.3090	.9511	.3249	3.078	1.051	3.236	72
19	.3256	.9455	.3443	2.904	1.058	3.072	71
20	.3420	.9397	.3640	2.747	1.064	2.924	70
21	.3584	.9336	.3839	2.605	1.071	2.790	69
22	.3746	.9272	.4040	2.475	1.079	2.669	68
23	.3907	.9205	.4245	2.356	1.086	2.559	67
24	.4067	.9135	.4452	2.246	1.095	2.459	66
25	.4226	.9063	.4663	2.145	1.103	2.366	65
26	.4384	.8988	.4877	2.050	1.113	2.281	64
27	.4540	.8910	.5095	1.963	1.122	2.203	63
28	.4695	.8829	.5317	1.881	1.133	2.130	62
29	.4848	.8746	.5543	1.804	1.143	2.063	61
30	.5000	.8660	.5774	1.732	1.155	2.000	60
31	.5150	.8572	.6009	1.664	1.167	1.942	59
32	.5299	.8480	.6249	1.600	1.179	1.887	58
33	.5446	.8387	.6494	1.540	1.192	1.836	57
34	.5592	.8290	.6745	1.483	1.206	1.788	56
35	.5736	.8192	.7002	1.428	1.221	1.743	55
36	.5878	.8090	.7265	1.376	1.236	1.701	54
37	.6018	.7986	.7536	1.327	1.252	1.662	53
38	.6157	.7880	.7813	1.280	1.269	1.624	52
39	.6293	.7771	.8098	1.235	1.287	1.589	51
40	.6428	.7660	.8391	1.192	1.305	1.556	50
41	.6561	.7547	.8693	1.150	1.325	1.524	49
42	.6691	.7431	.9004	1.111	1.346	1.494	48
43	.6820	.7314	.9325	1.072	1.367	1.466	47
44	.6947	.7193	.9657	1.036	1.390	1.440	46
45	.7071	.7071	1.0000	1.000	1.414	1.414	45
	cos	sin	cot	tan	csc	sec	DEGREES

Symbols

{ }	set braces or empty set	$\vec{AB}$	vector AB	∥	is parallel to
{x|x}	set builder notation	$\angle ABC$	angle ABC	⊥	is perpendicular to
∈	is an element of	$m\angle ABC$	measure of angle ABC	∨	or
∉	is not an element of	$\triangle ABC$	triangle ABC	∧	and
⊆	is a subset of	$\angle A\text{-}BC\text{-}D$	dihedral angle with edge BC	~	not or is similar to
⊄	is not a subset of	⊙ P	circle P	$p \to q$	p implies q
⊂	is a proper subset of	$m\overarc{AB}$	measure of arc AB	$p \leftrightarrow q$	p if and only if q
∅	empty set	$\|x\|$	absolute value of x	∀	for all
U	universal set	=	is equal to	∃	there exists
ℝ	set of real numbers	≠	is not equal to	$\cos A$	cosine of angle A
∪	union	≈	is approximately equal to	$\sin A$	sine of angle A
∩	intersection	>	is greater than	$\tan A$	tangent of angle A
AB	distance between A and B	<	is less than	π	pi
$\overline{AB}$	segment AB	≥	is greater than or equal to	°	degree
$\overleftrightarrow{AB}$	line AB	≤	is less than or equal to	$\sqrt{}$	square root
$\overrightarrow{AB}$	ray AB	≅	is congruent to		
$\overleftrightarrow{AB}$	half-line AB	≇	is not congruent to		

Postulates and Theorems

Postulate 1.1 *Expansion Postulate.* A line contains at least two points. A plane contains at least three noncollinear points. Space contains at least four noncoplanar points.

Postulate 1.2 *Line Postulate.* Any two points in space lie in exactly one line.

Postulate 1.3 *Plane Postulate.* Three distinct noncollinear points lie in exactly one plane.

Postulate 1.4 *Flat Plane Postulate.* If two points lie in a plane, then the line containing these two points lies in the same plane.

Postulate 1.5 *Plane Intersection Postulate.* If two planes intersect, then their intersection is exactly one line.

Theorem 1.1 If two distinct lines intersect, they intersect in one and only one point.

Theorem 1.2 A line and a point not on that line are contained in one and only one plane.

Theorem 1.3 Two intersecting lines are contained in one and only one plane.

Theorem 1.4 Two parallel lines are contained in one and only one plane.

Postulate 2.1 *Line Separation Postulate.* Every point divides any line through that point into three disjoint sets: the point and two half-lines.

Postulate 2.2 *Plane Separation Postulate.* Every line divides any plane containing the line into three disjoint sets: the line and two half-planes.

Theorem 2.1 *Jordan Curve Theorem.* Any simple closed curve divides a plane into three disjoint sets: the curve itself, its interior, and its exterior.

Postulate 3.1 *Ruler Postulate.* Every point of a line can be placed in correspondence with a real number.

Postulate 3.2 *Completeness Postulate.* Given a ray, $\vec{AB}$, and any positive real number r, there is exactly one point C on the ray so that $AC = r$.

Distance Formula The distance, d, between two points $A(x_1, y_1)$ and $B(x_2, y_2)$ is $d = \sqrt{(x_1 - x_2)^2 + (y_1 - y_2)^2}$.

Theorem 3.1 *Midpoint Theorem.* If M is the midpoint of $\overline{AB}$, then $AM = \frac{1}{2}AB$.

Theorem 3.2 The perimeter of a regular n-gon with sides of length s is $n \cdot s$.

Postulate 4.1 *Protractor Postulate.* For every angle A there corresponds a positive real number less than or equal to 180. This is symbolized $0 < m\angle A \le 180$.

Postulate 4.2 *Continuity Postulate.* If k is a half-plane determined by $\vec{AC}$, then for every real number, $0 < x \le 180$, there is exactly one ray, $\vec{AB}$, that lies in k such that $m\angle BAC = x$.

Postulate 4.3 *Angle Addition Postulate.* If K lies in the interior of $\angle MNP$, then $m\angle MNP = m\angle MNK + m\angle KNP$.

Theorem 4.1 All right angles are congruent.

Theorem 4.2 If two angles are adjacent and supplementary, then they form a linear pair.

Theorem 4.3 Angles that form a linear pair are supplementary.

Theorem 4.4 If one angle of a linear pair is a right angle, then the other angle is also a right angle.

Theorem 4.5 *Vertical Angle Theorem.* Vertical angles are congruent.

Theorem 4.6 Congruent supplementary angles are right angles.

Theorem 4.7 *Angle Bisector Theorem.* If $\overrightarrow{AB}$ bisects $\angle CAD$, then $m\angle CAB = \frac{1}{2}m\angle CAD$.

Theorem 5.1 The conditional $p \rightarrow q$ is equivalent to the disjunction $\sim p \lor q$.

Theorem 5.2 *Contrapositive Rule.* A conditional statement is equivalent to its contrapositive. In other words, $p \rightarrow q$ is equivalent to $\sim q \rightarrow \sim p$.

Postulate 6.1 *Parallel Postulate.* Two lines intersected by a transversal are parallel if and only if the alternate interior angles are congruent.

Historic Parallel Postulate Given a line and a point not on the line, there is exactly one line passing through the point that is parallel to the given line.

Postulate 6.2 *SAS Congruence Postulate.* If two sides and an included angle of one triangle are congruent to the corresponding two sides and included angle of another triangle, then the two triangles are congruent.

Postulate 6.3 *ASA Congruence Postulate.* If two angles and an included side of one triangle are congruent to the corresponding two angles and included side of another triangle, then the two triangles are congruent.

Theorem 6.1 *Congruent Segment Bisector Theorem.* If two congruent segments are bisected, then the four resulting segments are congruent.

Theorem 6.2 Segment congruence is an equivalence relation.

Theorem 6.3 Supplements of congruent angles are congruent.

Theorem 6.4 Complements of congruent angles are congruent.

Theorem 6.5 Angle congruence is an equivalence relation.

Theorem 6.6 *Adjacent Angle Sum Theorem.* If two adjacent angles are congruent to another pair of adjacent angles, then the larger angles formed are congruent.

Theorem 6.7 *Adjacent Angle Portion Theorem.* If two angles, one in each of two pairs of adjacent angles, are congruent, and the larger angles formed are also congruent, then the other two angles are congruent.

Theorem 6.8 *Congruent Angle Bisector Theorem.* If two congruent angles are bisected, the four resulting angles are congruent.

Theorem 6.9 Triangle congruence is an equivalence relation.

Theorem 6.10 Circle congruence is an equivalence relation.

Theorem 6.11 Polygon congruence is an equivalence relation.

Theorem 6.12 *Alternate Exterior Angle Theorem.* Two lines intersected by a transversal are parallel if and only if the alternate exterior angles are congruent.

Theorem 6.13 *Corresponding Angle Theorem.* Two lines intersected by a transversal are parallel if and only if the corresponding angles are congruent.

Theorem 6.14 If a transversal is perpendicular to one of two parallel lines, then it is perpendicular to the other also.

Theorem 6.15 If two coplanar lines are perpendicular to the same line, then they are parallel to each other.

Theorem 6.16 The sum of the measures of the angles of any triangle is 180°.

Theorem 6.17 If two angles of one triangle are congruent to two angles of another triangle, then the third angles are also congruent.

Theorem 6.18 The acute angles of a right triangle are complementary.

Theorem 6.19 *SAA Congruence Theorem.* If two angles of a triangle and a side opposite one of the two angles are congruent to the corresponding angles and side of another triangle, then the two triangles are congruent.

Theorem 6.20 *Isosceles Triangle Theorem.* In an isosceles triangle the two base angles are congruent.

Theorem 6.21 If two angles of a triangle are congruent, then the sides opposite those angles are congruent, and the triangle is an isosceles triangle.

Theorem 6.22 A triangle is equilateral if and only if it is equiangular.

Theorem 6.23 *SSS Congruence Theorem.* If each side of one triangle is congruent to the corresponding side of a second triangle, then the two triangles are congruent.

Theorem 7.1 *HL Congruence Theorem.* If the hypotenuse and a leg of one right triangle are congruent to the hypotenuse and corresponding leg of another right triangle, then the two triangles are congruent.

Theorem 7.2 *LL Congruence Theorem.* If the two legs of one right triangle are congruent to the two legs of another right triangle, then the two triangles are congruent.

Theorem 7.3 *HA Congruence Theorem.* If the hypotenuse and an acute angle of one right triangle are congruent to the hypotenuse and corresponding acute angle of another right triangle, then the two triangles are congruent.

Theorem 7.4 *LA Congruence Theorem.* If a leg and one of the acute angles of a right triangle are congruent to the corresponding leg and acute angle of another right triangle, then the two triangles are congruent.

Theorem 7.5 Any point lies on the perpendicular bisector of a segment if and only if it is equidistant from the two endpoints.

Theorem 7.6 *Circumcenter Theorem.* The perpendicular bisectors of the sides of any triangle are concurrent at the circumcenter, which is equidistant from each vertex of the triangle.

Theorem 7.7 *Incenter Theorem.* The angle bisectors of the angles of a triangle are concurrent at the incenter, which is equidistant from the sides of the triangle.

Theorem 7.8 *Orthocenter Theorem.* The lines that contain the three altitudes are concurrent at the orthocenter.

Theorem 7.9 *Centroid Theorem.* The three medians of a triangle are concurrent at the centroid.

Theorem 7.10 *Exterior Angle Theorem.* The measure of an exterior angle of a triangle is equal to the sum of the measures of its two remote interior angles.

Theorem 7.11 *Exterior Angle Inequality.* The measure of an exterior angle of a triangle is greater than the measure of either remote interior angle.

Theorem 7.12 *Longer Side Inequality.* One side of a triangle is longer than another side if and only if the measure of the angle opposite the longer side is greater than the measure of the angle opposite the shorter side.

Theorem 7.13 *Hinge Theorem.* Two triangles have two pairs of congruent sides. If the measure of the included angle of the first triangle is larger than the measure of the other included angle, then the opposite (third) side of the first triangle is longer than the opposite side of the second triangle.

Theorem 7.14 *Triangle Inequality.* The sum of the lengths of any two sides of a triangle is greater than the length of the third side.

Theorem 7.15 The opposite sides of a parallelogram are congruent.

Theorem 7.16 SAS Congruence for Parallelograms

Theorem 7.17 A quadrilateral is a parallelogram if and only if the diagonals bisect one another.

Theorem 7.18 Diagonals of a rectangle are congruent.

Theorem 7.19 The sum of the measures of the four angles of every convex quadrilateral is 360°.

Theorem 7.20 Opposite angles of a parallelogram are congruent.

Theorem 7.21 Consecutive angles of a parallelogram are supplementary.

Theorem 7.22 If the opposite sides of a quadrilateral are congruent, then the quadrilateral is a parallelogram.

Theorem 7.23 A quadrilateral with one pair of parallel sides that are congruent is a parallelogram.

Midpoint Formula If M is the midpoint of $\overline{AB}$ where $A(x_1, y_1)$ and $B(x_2, y_2)$, then $M\left(\frac{x_1 + x_2}{2}, \frac{y_1 + y_2}{2}\right)$.

Postulate 8.1 *Area Postulate.* Every region has an area given by a unique positive real number.

Postulate 8.2 *Congruent Regions Postulate.* Congruent regions have the same area.

Postulate 8.3 *Area of Square Postulate.* The area of a square is the square of the length of one side: $A = s^2$.

Postulate 8.4 *Area Addition Postulate.* If the interiors of two regions do not intersect, then the area of the union is the sum of their areas.

Theorem 8.1 The *area of a rectangle* is the product of its base and height: $A = bh$.

Theorem 8.2 The *area of a right triangle* is one-half the product of the lengths of the legs.

Theorem 8.3 The *area of a parallelogram* is the product of the base and the altitude: $A = bh$.

Theorem 8.4 The *area of a triangle* is one-half the base times the height: $A = \frac{1}{2}bh$.

Theorem 8.5 The *area of a trapezoid* is one-half the product of the altitude and the sum of the lengths of the bases: $A = \frac{1}{2}h\,(b_1 + b_2)$.

Theorem 8.6 The *area of a rhombus* is one-half the product of the lengths of the diagonals: $A = \frac{1}{2}d_1 d_2$.

Theorem 8.7 *Pythagorean Theorem.* In a right triangle, the sum of the squares of the lengths of the legs is equal to the square of the length of the hypotenuse: $a^2 + b^2 = c^2$.

Theorem 8.8 The *area of an equilateral triangle* is $\frac{\sqrt{3}}{4}$ times the square of the length of one side: $A = s^2 \frac{\sqrt{3}}{4}$.

Heron's Formula If $\triangle ABC$ has sides of lengths a, b, c, and semiperimeter s, then the area of the triangle is $A = \sqrt{s(s - a)(s - b)(s - c)}$.

Theorem 8.9 The central angles of a regular n-gon are congruent and measure $\frac{360°}{n}$.

Theorem 8.10 The *area of a regular polygon* is one-half the product of its apothem and its perimeter: $A = \frac{1}{2}ap$.

Theorem 8.11 The *apothem of an equilateral triangle* is one-third the length of the altitude: $a = \frac{1}{3}h$.

Theorem 8.12 The apothem of an equilateral triangle is $\frac{\sqrt{3}}{6}$ times the length of the side: $a = \frac{\sqrt{3}}{6}s$.

Theorem 8.13 The *area of a circle* is pi times the square of the radius: $A = \pi r^2$.

Theorem 8.14 The *surface area of a prism* is the sum of the lateral surface area and the area of the bases: $S = L + 2B$. The lateral surface area of a right prism is the product of its height and the perimeter of its base: $L = pH$.

Theorem 8.15 The *surface area of a cylinder* is the sum of the lateral surface area and the area of the bases: $S = L + 2B$. The lateral surface area of a right cylinder is the product of its circumference and height: $L = cH$.

Theorem 8.16 The *surface area of a pyramid* is the sum of the lateral surface area and the area of the base: $S = L + B$. For a regular pyramid, the lateral surface area is the sum of n equal triangular areas or $L = \frac{1}{2}pl$, and the total surface area is given by: $S = \frac{1}{2}p(L + a)$, where p is the perimeter of the base, L is the slant height, and a is the length of the apothem.

Theorem 8.17 The *surface area of a cone* is the sum of the lateral surface area and the area of the base: $S = L + B$; the lateral surface area of a circular cone is half the product of the circumference and slant height: $L = \frac{1}{2}cl$.

Theorem 8.18 The *surface area of a sphere* is 4π times the square of the radius: $S = 4\pi r^2$.

Theorem 8.19 The *surface area of a regular polyhedron* is the product of the number of faces and the area of one face: $S = nA$.

Postulate 9.1 *Chord Postulate.* If a line intersects the interior of a circle, then it contains a chord of the circle.

Postulate 9.2 *Arc Addition Postulate.* If B is a point on $\overset{\frown}{AB}$, then $m\overset{\frown}{AB} + m\overset{\frown}{BC} = m\overset{\frown}{AC}$.

Theorem 9.1 In a circle, if a radius is perpendicular to a chord of a circle, then it bisects the chord.

Theorem 9.2 In a circle or in congruent circles, if two chords are the same distance from the center(s), the chords are congruent.

Theorem 9.3 In a circle or in congruent circles, if two chords are congruent, then they are the same distance from the center(s).

Theorem 9.4 If a line is tangent to a circle, then it is perpendicular to the radius drawn to the point of tangency.

Theorem 9.5 *Law of Contradiction.* If an assumption leads to a contradiction, then the assumption is false and its negation is true.

Theorem 9.6 If a line is perpendicular to a radius at a point on the circle, then the line is tangent to the circle.

Theorem 9.7 Tangent segments extending from a given exterior point to a circle are congruent.

Theorem 9.8 *Major Arc Theorem.* $m\overset{\frown}{ACB} = 360 - m\overset{\frown}{AB}$

Theorem 9.9 Chords of congruent circles are congruent if and only if they subtend congruent arcs.

Theorem 9.10 In congruent circles, chords are congruent if and only if the corresponding central angles are congruent.

Theorem 9.11 In congruent circles, minor arcs are congruent if and only if their corresponding central angles are congruent.

Theorem 9.12 In congruent circles, two minor arcs are congruent if and only if the corresponding major arcs are congruent.

Theorem 9.13 The measure of an inscribed angle is equal to one-half the measure of its intercepted arc.

Theorem 9.14 If two inscribed angles intercept congruent arcs, then the angles are congruent.

Theorem 9.15 An angle inscribed in a semicircle is a right angle.

Theorem 9.16 The opposite angles of an inscribed quadrilateral are supplementary.

Theorem 9.17 The measure of an angle formed by two lines that intersect in the exterior of a circle is one-half the difference of the measures of the intercepted arcs.

Theorem 9.18 The measure of an angle formed by two lines that intersect in the interior of a circle is one-half the sum of the measures of the intercepted arcs.

Theorem 9.19 The measure of an angle formed by two lines that intersect at a point on a circle is one-half the measure of the intercepted arc.

Theorem 9.20 If the degree measure of an arc is θ and the circumference of the circle is c, then the length of the arc is given by $\frac{1}{c} = \frac{\theta}{360}$, or $1 = \frac{c\theta}{360}$.

Theorem 9.21 The area of a sector is given by the proportion $\frac{A}{\pi r^2} = \frac{\theta}{360}$ or $A = \frac{\pi r^2 \theta}{360}$ where A is the area of the sector of a circle with radius r and θ is the arc measure of the sector in degrees.

Postulate 10.1 *Space Separation Postulate.* Every plane separates space into three disjoint sets: the plane and two half-spaces.

Theorem 10.1 If the endpoints of a segment are equidistant from two other points, then every point between the endpoints is also equidistant from the two other points.

Theorem 10.2 A line perpendicular to two intersecting lines in a plane is perpendicular to the plane containing them.

Theorem 10.3 If a plane contains a line perpendicular to another plane, then the planes are perpendicular.

Theorem 10.4 If intersecting planes are each perpendicular to a third plane, then the line of intersection of the first two is perpendicular to the third plane.

Theorem 10.5 If $\overleftrightarrow{AB}$ is perpendicular to plane p at B, and $\overline{BC} \cong \overline{BD}$ in plane p, then $\overline{AC} \cong \overline{AD}$.

Theorem 10.6 Every point in the perpendicular bisecting plane of segment $\overline{AB}$ is equidistant from A and B.

Theorem 10.7 The perpendicular is the shortest segment from a point to a plane.

Theorem 10.8 Two lines perpendicular to the same plane are parallel.

Theorem 10.9 If two lines are parallel, then any plane containing exactly one of the two lines is parallel to the other line.

Theorem 10.10 A plane perpendicular to one of two parallel lines is perpendicular to the other line also.

Theorem 10.11 Two lines parallel to the same line are parallel.

Theorem 10.12 A plane intersects two parallel planes in parallel lines.

Theorem 10.13 Two planes perpendicular to the same line are parallel.

Theorem 10.14 A line perpendicular to one of two parallel planes is perpendicular to the other also.

Theorem 10.15 Two parallel planes are everywhere equidistant.

Theorem 10.16 Opposite edges of a parallelepiped are parallel and congruent.

Theorem 10.17 Diagonals of a parallelepiped bisect each other.

Theorem 10.18 Diagonals of a right rectangular prism are congruent.

Euler's Formula $V - E + F = 2$ where V, E, and F represent the number of vertices, edges, and faces of a convex polyhedron respectively.

Theorem 10.19 The intersection of a sphere and a secant plane is a circle.

Theorem 10.20 Two points on a sphere that are not on the same diameter lie on exactly one great circle of the sphere.

Theorem 10.21 Two great circles of a sphere intersect at two points that are endpoints of a diameter of the sphere.

Theorem 10.22 All great circles of a sphere are congruent.

Theorem 10.23 A secant plane of a sphere is perpendicular to the line containing the center of the circle of intersection and the center of the sphere.

Theorem 10.24 A plane is tangent to a sphere if and only if it is perpendicular to the radius at the point of tangency.

Postulate 11.1 *Volume Postulate.* Every solid has a volume given by a positive real number.

Postulate 11.2 *Congruent Solids Postulate.* Congruent solids have the same volume.

Postulate 11.3 *Volume of Cube Postulate.* The volume of a cube is the cube of the length of one edge: $V = e^3$.

Postulate 11.4 *Volume Addition Postulate.* If the interiors of two solids do not intersect, then the volume of their union is the sum of the volumes.

Postulate 11.5 *Cavalieri's Principle.* For any two solids, if all planes parallel to a fixed plane form sections having equal areas, then the solids have the same volume.

Theorem 11.1 The *volume of a rectangular prism* is the product of its length, width, and height: $V = lwH$.

Theorem 11.2 A cross section of a prism is congruent to the base of the prism.

Theorem 11.3 The *volume of a prism* is the product of the height and the area of the base: $V = BH$.

Theorem 11.4 The *volume of a cylinder* is the product of the area of the base and the height: $V = BH$. In particular, for a circular cylinder $V = \pi r^2 H$.

Theorem 11.5 The *volume of a pyramid* is one-third the product of the height and the area of the base: $V = \frac{1}{3}BH$.

Theorem 11.6 The *volume of a cone* is one-third the product of its height and base area: $V = \frac{1}{3}\pi r^2 H$.

Theorem 11.7 The *volume of a sphere* is four-thirds π times the cube of the radius: $V = \frac{4}{3}\pi r^3$.

Theorem 12.1 *Isometry Theorem.* Every isometry can be expressed as a composition of at most three reflections.

Postulate 13.1 *AA Similarity Postulate.* If two angles of one triangle are congruent to two angles of another triangle, then the two triangles are similar.

Theorem 13.1 *SSS Similarity Theorem.* If the three sides of one triangle are proportional to the corresponding three sides of another triangle, then the triangles are similar.

Theorem 13.2 *SAS Similarity Theorem.* If two sides of a triangle are proportional to the corresponding two sides of another triangle and the included angles between the sides are congruent, then the triangles are similar.

Theorem 13.3 Similarity of triangles is an equivalence ratio.

Theorem 13.4 An altitude drawn from the right angle to the hypotenuse of a right triangle separates the original triangle into two similar triangles, each of which is similar to the original triangle.

Theorem 13.5 In a right triangle, the altitude to the hypotenuse cuts the hypotenuse into two segments. The length of the altitude is the geometric mean between the lengths of the two segments of the hypotenuse.

Theorem 13.6 In a right triangle, the altitude to the hypotenuse divides the hypotenuse into two segments such that the length of a leg is the geometric mean between the hypotenuse and the segment of the hypotenuse adjacent to the leg.

Slopes of Perpendicular Lines If two distinct nonvertical lines are perpendicular, then their slopes are negative reciprocals.

Theorem 13.7 In similar triangles the lengths of the altitudes extending to corresponding sides are in the same ratio as the lengths of the corresponding sides.

Theorem 13.8 In similar triangles the lengths of the medians extending to corresponding sides are in the same ratio as the lengths of the corresponding sides.

Theorem 13.9 In similar triangles the lengths of the corresponding angle bisectors from the vertices to the points where they intersect the opposite sides are in the same ratio as the lengths of the corresponding sides of the triangles.

Theorem 13.10 In similar triangles the perimeters of the triangles are in the same ratio as the lengths of the corresponding sides.

Theorem 13.11 In similar triangles the ratio of the areas of the triangles is equal to the square of the ratio of the lengths of corresponding sides.

Theorem 13.12 If two chords intersect in the interior of a circle, then the product of the lengths of the segments of one chord is equal to the product of the lengths of the segments of the other chord.

Theorem 13.13 If two secants intersect in the exterior of a circle, then the product of the lengths of one secant segment and its external secant segment is equal to the product of the lengths of the other secant segment and its external secant segment.

Theorem 14.1 If the length of a leg of an isosceles right triangle (45-45 right triangle) is x, then the length of the hypotenuse is $x\sqrt{2}$.

Theorem 14.2 If the length of the leg opposite the 30° angle of a 30-60 right triangle is x, then the length of the leg opposite the 60° angle is $x\sqrt{3}$, and the length of the hypotenuse is $2x$.

Theorem 14.3 *Sum of Squares Identity.* For any angle x, $\sin^2 x + \cos^2 x = 1$.

Glossary

Acute angle An angle with a measure less than 90° or a triangle with three acute angles.

Adjacent angles Two coplanar angles that have a common side and a common vertex but no common interior points.

Alternate exterior angles Angles on opposite sides of the transversal and outside the other two lines.

Alternate interior angles Angles on opposite sides of the transversal and between the other two lines.

Altitude A perpendicular segment that extends from a vertex to the opposite side of a triangle, or the vertex to the plane of the base of a cone (or pyramid), or the parallel sides of a trapezoid, or the parallel bases of a cylinder (or prism).

Angle The union of two distinct rays with a common endpoint.

Angle bisector A ray that (except for its origin) is in the interior of an angle and forms congruent adjacent angles.

Apothem The perpendicular segment that joins the center with a side of a regular polygon.

Arc A curve that is a subset of a circle.

Arc measure The same measure as the degree measure of the central angle that intercepts the arc.

Area The number of square units needed to cover a region completely.

Between A point M is between A and B (A-M-B) if $AM + MB = AB$.

Biconditional A statement of the form "p if and only if q" ($p \leftrightarrow q$), which means $p \to q$ and $q \to p$.

Bisector Any curve that intersects a segment only at the midpoint.

Central angle An angle that is in the same plane as a circle and whose vertex is the center of the circle.

Centroid The point of intersection of the medians of a triangle.

Chord A segment having both endpoints on a circle (or sphere).

Circle The set of all points that are a given distance from a given point in a given plane.

Circumcenter The point of intersection of the perpendicular bisectors of the sides of a triangle.

Circumference The distance around a circle (i.e., perimeter).

Circumscribed The outside figure when a polygon is positioned with all vertices on a circle or when a circle is tangent to each side of a polygon.

Closed A curve that begins and ends at the same point or a surface that has a finite size and divides the other points in space into an interior and an exterior.

Collinear points Points that lie on the same line.

Complementary angles The sum of two angle measures is 90°.

Concentric circles Circles with the same center but radii of different lengths.

Concurrent Lines that intersect at a single point.

Conditional A statement of the form "If p then q" ($p \rightarrow q$).

Cone The union of a region and all segments that connect the boundary of the region with a specific noncoplanar point.

Congruent angles Angles that have the same measure.

Congruent arcs Arcs on congruent circles that have the same measure.

Congruent circles Circles whose radii are congruent.

Congruent polygons Polygons that have three properties: 1) same number of sides, 2) congruent corresponding sides, and 3) congruent corresponding angles.

Congruent segments Segments that have the same length.

Congruent triangles Triangles in which corresponding angles and corresponding sides are congruent.

Construction A drawing made with the aid of only two instruments: an unmarked straightedge and a compass.

Convex The property that any two points of a set determine a segment contained in the set.

Corresponding angles Angles on the same side of the transversal and on the same side of their respective lines.

Cosine (cos A) The right triangle ratio adjacent over hypotenuse.

Cylinder The union of two regions of the same size and shape in different parallel planes, and the set of all segments that join corresponding points on the boundaries of the regions.

Diagonal A segment that connects two vertices of a polygon but is not a side of the polygon or that connects two vertices of a polyhedron that are not on the same face.

Diameter A chord that passes through the center of a circle or sphere.

Distance The distance between two points A and B is the absolute value of the difference of their coordinates. Distance between points A and B is denoted by AB, given by $AB = |a - b|$.

Edge One of the segments that defines a face of a polyhedron (or a line that divides half-planes).

Equiangular polygon A convex polygon in which all angles have the same degree measure.

Equilateral polygon A polygon in which all sides have the same length.

Equivalence relation A relation that is reflexive, symmetric, and transitive.

Exterior angle An angle that forms a linear pair with one of the angles of a triangle.

Face One of the polygonal regions that form the surface of a polyhedron (or either half-plane that defines a dihedral

angle, or a plane that divides half-spaces).

Great circle The intersection of a sphere and a secant plane that contains the center of the sphere.

Greater than A real number a is greater than a real number b ($a > b$) if there is a positive real number c so that $a = b + c$.

Half-line The set of all points on a line on a given side of a given point of the line.

Incenter The point of intersection of the angle bisectors of a triangle.

Inscribed A polygon inscribed in a circle has all its vertices on the circle; an angle inscribed in a circle is one whose vertex is on a circle and whose sides each contain another point of the circle.

Isometry A transformation that preserves distance.

Isosceles triangle A triangle with at least two congruent sides.

Law of Deduction A method of proving a conditional statement by temporarily assuming the hypothesis and deducing the conclusion.

Linear pair A pair of adjacent angles whose noncommon sides form a straight angle (are opposite rays).

Measure of an angle The real number that corresponds to a particular angle.

Median of a triangle A segment extending from a vertex to the midpoint of the opposite side.

Midpoint The midpoint of $\overline{AB}$ is M if A-M-B and $AM = MB$.

Obtuse An angle with a measure greater than 90° or a triangle with an obtuse angle.

Opposite Collinear rays with only the origin in common, or disjoint half-planes with a common edge, or (in a quadrilateral) sides with no common vertex or angles with no common side, or (in a hexahedron) faces with no common edge or edges on opposite faces not joined by an edge.

Orthocenter The point of intersection of the altitudes of a triangle.

Parallel Coplanar lines that do not intersect, planes that do not intersect, or a line and a plane that do not intersect.

Parallelepiped A hexahedron in which all faces are parallelograms.

Parallelogram A quadrilateral with two pairs of parallel opposite sides.

Perimeter The distance around a closed curve.

Perpendicular Two lines that intersect to form right angles, or two planes that intersect to form right dihedral angles, or a line that intersects a plane and is perpendicular to every line in the plane that passes through the point of intersection.

Platonic solids The five regular polyhedra.

Polygon A simple closed curve that consists only of segments.

Polyhedron A closed surface made up of polygonal regions

Prism A cylinder with polygonal regions as bases.

Pyramid A cone with a polygonal region as its base.

Radius A segment that connects a point on the circle or sphere with the center or that connects a vertex of a regular polygon to its center (plural: radii).

Ray The union of a half-line and its origin. It extends infinitely in one direction from a point.

Rectangle A parallelogram with four right angles.

Region The union of a simple closed curve and its interior.

Regular A polygon that is both equilateral and equiangular, a right pyramid or right prism with a regular polygon as base, or a polyhedron with congruent regular polygons as faces so that the same number of faces intersect at each vertex.

Remote interior angles The two angles of a triangle that do not form a linear pair with a given exterior angle.

Rhombus A parallelogram with four congruent sides.

Right An angle that measures 90°, a triangle with a right angle, a prism with lateral edges perpendicular to the base, or a pyramid with an altitude from the vertex that passes through the center of the base.

Scalene triangle A triangle with no congruent sides.

Secant A line that is in the same plane as the circle and intersects the circle in exactly two points.

Sector of a circle A region bounded by two radii and the intercepted arc.

Segment The set consisting of two points A and B and all the points in between.

Segment of a circle A region bounded by a chord and its intercepted arc.

Side One of the segments that forms a polygon or either ray that forms an angle.

Similar polygons Polygons having corresponding angles that are congruent and corresponding sides that are proportional.

Sine (sin A**)** The right triangle ratio opposite over hypotenuse.

Skew lines Lines that are not coplanar.

Slant height The distance on the surface of a cone or pyramid from the vertex to the base.

Solid The union of a closed surface and its interior.

Sphere A surface in space consisting of the set of all points at a given distance in space from a given point.

Square A rectangle with four congruent sides (or a rhombus with four congruent angles).

Supplementary angles The sum of two angle measures is 180°.

Symmetry An isometry (other than the identity) that maps a figure onto itself. A reflection results in line symmetry; a rotation, in rotational symmetry; a rotation of 180°, in point symmetry.

Tangent (tan A**)** The right triangle ratio opposite over adjacent.

Tangent line (or *tangent***)** A line in the plane of a circle that intersects the circle in exactly one point.

Transversal A line that intersects two or more distinct coplanar lines in two or more distinct points.

Trapezoid A quadrilateral with a pair of parallel opposite sides.

Triangle The union of segments that connect three non-collinear points.

Trichotomy property For any two real numbers a and b, exactly one of the following is true: $a = b$, $a < b$, or $a > b$.

Vertex A point at the intersection of segments or rays in angles, polygons, cones, prisms, pyramids, and polyhedra.

Vertical angles Angles adjacent to the same angle and forming linear pairs with it.

Volume The number of cubic units needed to fill up the interior of a solid completely.

Index

Photo Credits

Cover
Unusual Films: shell, turtle; George R. Collins: mimosa; PhotoDisc, Inc.: bridge, bubbles, wood grain, staircase; NASA: galaxy

Title Page, Introduction
Unusual Films ii (top); PhotoDisc, Inc. ii (bottom), iii (all); Greek National Tourist Office viii (top); Dr. Margene Ranieri viii (bottom), Aramco World Magazine ix; PhotoDisc, Inc. x; Unusual Films xi

Chapter 1
Unusual Films 1, 2, 27; Corel Corporation 3; PhotoDisc, Inc. 6, 22; National Zoological Park, Smithsonian Institution 9; Digital Stock 11, 32; The Field Museum (#GEO 85827c) 16; Brian Johnson 25

Chapter 2
Harry Ward 40–41; Unusual Films, Courtesy of Six Flags over Georgia 42; George R. Collins 43; Digital Stock 45, 68; PhotoDisc, Inc. 48, 54; Planet Art 52; Corel Corporation 53 (all); Kay Shaw Photography 55; Susan Day/Daybreak Imagery 56; Greater Quebec Area Tourism and Convention Bureau 62; M. C. Escher's *Möbius Strip II* © 1998 Cordon Art B. V. – Baarn – Holland. All rights reserved. 70; National Park Service 73

Chapter 3
PhotoDisc, Inc. 84 (top), 95, 106; Corel Corporation 84 (bottom); Jack Dill 89; Digital Stock 97, 99; Planet Art 109

Chapter 4
Stephen Christopher 116–17; Colonel Kemp Moore 118; The Biltmore Company 121 (top); Used with permission from the Biltmore Company, *A Guide to Biltmore Estate* 121 (bottom); PhotoDisc, Inc. 131, 143; Courtesy of Pacific Design Center 135; Winston Fraser 142; Digital Stock 146; Central Office of Information, Wales 150

Chapter 5
Courtesy of IBM Corporation 158–59; PhotoDisc, Inc. 160, 166, 176, 189; Digital Stock 172; M. C. Escher's *Ascending and Descending* © 1998 Cordon Art B. V. – Baarn – Holland. All rights reserved. 199

Chapter 6
Stephen Christopher 206–7; Brian Johnson 208, 220 (top); PhotoDisc, Inc. 214, 233, 240; Eastman Chemicals Division 220 (bottom), 245; BJU Press files 226; Ted Rich 238; Corel Corporation 239, 252

Chapter 7
M. C. Escher's *Transitional System IA–IA* © 1998 Cordon Art B. V. – Baarn – Holland. All rights reserved. 260–61; Andersen Windows, Inc. 262, 273, 281, 298; PhotoDisc, Inc. 267; Jack Dill 279, 280, 291; Digital Stock 287

Chapter 8
PhotoDisc, Inc. 308–9, 341 (top), 348; Unusual Films 311; Ward's Natural Science Est. 316 (top), 355; © 1998 Dr. E. R. Degginger 316 (bottom), 333, 341 (middle, bottom); Digital Stock 323; George R. Collins 332; USDA 338

Chapter 9
Unusual Films, Courtesy of Six Flags over Georgia 364–65, 405; Corel Corporation 366, 389; Ford Motor Company 374; PhotoDisc, Inc. 381, 388, 394; Fred E. Mang Jr., Courtesy of National Park Service 390; Brian Johnson 399

Chapter 10
NASA 414–15, 428, 434, 440, 448; Corel Corporation 416; PhotoDisc, Inc. 420; J. Norman Powell 423; U.S. Naval Observatory 439; USDA 451

Chapter 11
PhotoDisc, Inc. 458–59, 471 (top), 488, 489; Unusual Films 461, 464, 495; USDA 471 (bottom); Corel Corporation 475; National Radio Astronomy Observatory 481; Gaffney Board of Public Works 482; Ward's Natural Science Est. 490

Chapter 12
Creation Science Foundation Ltd. 498–99; Kenya Tourist Office 500; PhotoDisc, Inc. 501, 515, 525; Cedar Point, photo by Dan Feicht, 506; M. C. Escher's *Circle Limit 3* © 1998 Cordon Art B. V. – Baarn – Holland. All rights reserved. 512; J. Norman Powell 522; Brian Johnson 526

Chapter 13
Unusual Films 534–35, 542; Ron Tagliapietra 536; Planet Art 540, 541; Jack Dill 548; Digital Stock 556, 563, 566, 573 (top), 575; Corel Corporation 571, 572, 574 (bottom); USS *Alabama* Battleship Commission 573 (middle); Naval Historical Foundation 573 (bottom); U.S. Navy 574 (top)

Chapter 14
Photo courtesy of Emerson & Cuming Microwave Products Inc. 580–81; Gray Engineering Consultants Inc. 583; PhotoDisc, Inc. 588, 594; Unusual Films 592; Nikon Inc. 593 (bottom); USGS 593 (top); Providence/Warwick Convention & Visitors Bureau 604 (left); KVLY–TV 605; BJU Press files 609

Appendix A

Vocabulary

Chapter 8 Vocabulary

altitude (cone, pyramid)

apothem of a regular polygon

Area Addition Postulate

area of a region

Area of a Square Postulate

Area Postulate

center of a regular polygon

central angle of a regular polygon

Congruent Regions Postulate

great circle

*Heron's formula

lateral surface area

lune

Platonic solid

Pythagorean theorem

radius (circle, regular polygon, sphere)

regular (polygon, polyhedron, prism, pyramid)

*semiperimeter

slant height

surface area

Chapter 9 Vocabulary

arc (major, minor)

arc measure

center (circle, regular polygon)

central angle (circle, regular polygon)

common tangent (external, internal)

congruent arcs

congruent circles

corollary

externally tangent circles

inscribed angle

internally tangent circles

point of tangency

secant

sector of a circle

segment of a circle

semicircle

*standard form (equation of circle)

tangent (lines, circles)

*Term from Analytic Geometry section

Chapter 10 Vocabulary

closed surface

cube

diagonal (parallelepiped, hexahedron)

dihedral angle

edge (dihedral angle)

equator

face (dihedral angle)

great circle

half-space

hemisphere

horizon

interior of a dihedral angle

international date line

latitude

line parallel to a plane

line perpendicular to a plane

longitude

measure of a dihedral angle

non-Euclidean geometry

opposite edges of a parallelipiped

opposite faces of a parallelipiped

parallelepiped

perpendicular bisecting plane

perpendicular lines in space

perpendicular planes

perspective drawing (one, two, three point)

plane angle

prime meridian

Riemannian geometry

secant plane

solid

spherical geometry

tangent (circles, lines, planes, segments)

vanishing point

Chapter 11 Vocabulary

annulus

*axis of a conical surface

Cavalieri's principle

concentric circles

Congruent Solids Postulate

*conical surface

*conic section

cross section

cubic unit

*elements of a conical surface

*equation of a parabola

*generating curve

oblique prism

section

volume

Volume Addition Postulate

Volume of Cube Postulate

Volume Postulate

Chapter 12 Vocabulary

angle of rotation

axis of symmetry

center of rotation

composition

dilation

enlargement

fixed point

identity transformation

image

invariance

isometry

line of reflection

line symmetry

magnitude of a rotation

mapping

orientation

point symmetry

preimage

preserved

reduction

reflection

rotation

rotational symmetry

scale factor

similar figures

transformation

translation

Chapter 13 Vocabulary

AA Similarity Postulate

cross multiplication

external secant segment

geometric mean

Golden Ratio

golden rectangle

golden spiral

*negative reciprocals

proportion

ratio

SAS Similarity Theorem

secant (line, plane, segment)

segment (chord, circle)

similar (figures, polygons)

SSS Similarity Theorem

Chapter 14 Vocabulary

adjacent side

angle of depression

angle of elevation

cosine of an angle

45-45 right triangles

opposite side

sine of an angle

tangent of an angle

30-60 right triangles

trigonometric ratios

trigonometric tables

trigonometry

Appendix B

Mind over Math

Chapter 8

1. No, it would quadruple. Double just one side.
2. Gets 9 times larger
3. Gets 25 times larger
4. 141% ($\sqrt{2}$ = 1.414)

Chapter 9

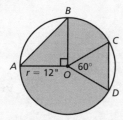

Perimeter:

Since the arc measures $360 - 90 - 60 = 210°$, its length is $\frac{210}{360} 2\pi (12) = 14\pi$.

For the hypotenuse, $c^2 = 12^2 + 12^2$, or $c = 12\sqrt{2}$

p = circle part + hypotenuse + base of equilateral triangle

$p = 14\pi + 12\sqrt{2} + 12 \approx 73$ in.

Area:

$A_{\text{lg. segment}} = A_{\text{sector}} - A_{\text{triangle}}$
$= \frac{1}{4}(\pi r^2) - \frac{1}{2}bh$
$= \frac{1}{4}\pi \cdot 12^2 - \frac{1}{2} \cdot 12 \cdot 12$
$= 36\pi - 72$

$A_{\text{sm. segment}} = A_{\text{sector}} - A_{\text{triangle}}$
$= \frac{1}{6}(\pi r^2) - s^2 \frac{\sqrt{3}}{4}$
$= \frac{1}{6}(\pi 12^2) - (12)^2 \frac{\sqrt{3}}{4}$
$= 24\pi - 36\sqrt{3}$

$A_{\text{circle}} = \pi r^2 = \pi \cdot 12^2 = 144\pi$

A_{shaded}
$= A_{\text{circle}} - A_{\text{lg. segment}} - A_{\text{sm. segment}}$
$= 144\pi - (36\pi - 72) - (24\pi - 36\sqrt{3})$
$= 84\pi + 72 + 36\sqrt{3}$ sq. in. ≈ 398.2 sq. in.

Chapter 10

Cubes can be truncated two ways so that all the faces of the new solid will still be regular polygons. The simplest way is to cut a small pyramid from each corner. Since a corner will be cut from each of the 6 square faces, a smaller regular octagon will remain in place of each square. The 8 corners removed will leave faces that are equilateral triangles. Thus, the truncated cube has 14 faces: 6 regular octagons and 8 equilateral triangles.

The other way to truncate a cube is to slice off the largest pyramids possible, extending from midpoint to midpoint of the edges of the cube. This leaves a smaller square on each of the original faces and again leaves an equilateral triangle at each of the original corners. This truncated figure has 14 faces: 6 squares and 8 equilateral triangles. (This solid is called a *cuboctohedron* because it is obtained by truncating either the cube or the octahedron; see Solids poster in the Visual Packet.)

In the final question none of the removed tetrahedra are regular for either solid. Notice that three faces are right triangles (2 equal parts of the original cube edges and the hypotenuse forming the slice), so three of the faces are not regular triangles. Also, since the bottom face (at slice) is equilateral, it is not congruent to the other three.

You can extend this exploration to other truncated polyhedra. Only 13 semiregular polyhedra (or Archimedean solids) exist that have all faces regular and all faces of the same type congruent. Of these, 7 are simple truncations of regular polyhedra. Besides the 2 formed from cubes, students can fill in the table for the other 5.

Polyhedron	From Original Faces	From Original Corners	Total Faces
truncated tetrahedron	4 reg. hexagons	4 eq. triangles	8
truncated octahedron	8 reg. hexagons	6 squares	14
truncated dodecahedron	12 reg. decagons	20 eq. triangles	32
truncated icosahedron	20 reg. hexagons	12 reg. pentagons	32
icosidodecahedron	12 reg. pentagons	20 eq. triangles	32

The last row is obtained by truncating a dodecahedron at the midpoints. However, it can also be obtained by truncating the icosahedron at the midpoints (the 20 triangles remain from the original faces and the pentagons are formed at the sliced corners). The name comes from this 20-and-12-hedron fact.

Chapter 11

What happens to the volume of each figure, if
1. 9 times larger
2. 8 times larger
3. $2\sqrt{2}$ times larger
4. 125 times larger

Chapter 12

Properties of transformations:
1. not commutative; $R \circ S \neq S \circ R$
2. associative; $(R \circ S) \circ T = R \circ (S \circ T)$
3. identity; $R \circ I = R$ and $I \circ R = R$
4. inverse; R^{-1} reverses the transformation R so that $R \circ R^{-1} = I$ and $R^{-1} \circ R = I$

In higher math, a set with an associative operation has an identity element and inverses and is called a *group*. Composition of transformations is an important group since it is not commutative.

Chapter 13

The altitude (x) of a right triangle is the geometric mean between the portions into which it divides the hypotenuse. Therefore,

$$\frac{a}{x} = \frac{x}{1} \qquad\qquad x^2 = a \qquad\qquad x = \sqrt{a}$$

To make a construction that represents the $\sqrt{5}$, a circle with a diameter of six units is needed. Copy the one-unit segment repeatedly to obtain a segment six units long. Set the compass at the midpoint to draw the circle of radius three. Construct the perpendicular to the diameter one unit from either endpoint. The distance from the diameter to the circle along the perpendicular represents $\sqrt{5}$.

The end result should look exactly like figure 13.6 but larger. Check with a ruler that a is 5 times longer than the segment marked 1. Since $x = \sqrt{a}$, x represents the square root of 5.

This problem is important because it shows students that the square root is a length that can be constructed with a straightedge and compass. If you have them do $\sqrt{9}$, they can check for themselves that the 3-unit altitude is three times the length of the unit segment.

Chapter 14

Check the students' trisection with a protractor to be sure that all three portions have the same measure, each one-third of the original angle.

A conch is a shell, and a conchoid is a shell-shaped curve. Nicomedes (fl. 180 B.C.) developed his conchoid specifically for trisecting angles and doubling cubes. For the diagram and details of the trisection, see *History of Mathematics,* Vol. 2, pp. 298-300, by D. E. Smith.

Heron's Formula

Heron's formula can be proved primarily by algebraic methods. It is stated here, followed by its proof.

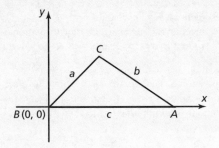

Heron's Formula

Theorem: The area of $\triangle ABC$ with side lengths a, b, and c and semiperimeter s is

$$A = \sqrt{s(s - a)(s - b)(s - c)}.$$

In this theorem $s = \frac{a + b + c}{2}$.

Given: $\triangle ABC$ with side lengths a, b, and c; $s = \frac{a + b + c}{2}$

Prove: $A = \sqrt{s(s - a)(s - b)(s - c)}$

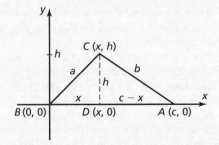

First draw the altitude from C to AB and label it h. CD cuts AB into two segments having lengths x and $c - x$. The area of this triangle can be found by the formula $A = \frac{1}{2}ch$, but h is unknown.

1. Apply the Pythagorean theorem to $\triangle BDC$.
$$a^2 = h^2 + x^2$$

2. Solve for h^2.
$$a^2 - x^2 = h^2$$

3. Apply the Pythagorean theorem to $\triangle ADC$.
$$b^2 = h^2 + (c - x)^2$$

4. Substitute for h^2.
$$b^2 = (a^2 - x^2) + (c - x)^2$$

5. Solve for x.
$$b^2 = a^2 - x^2 + c^2 - 2cx + x^2$$
$$b^2 = a^2 + c^2 - 2cx$$
$$a^2 - b^2 + c^2 = 2cx$$
$$\frac{a^2 - b^2 + c^2}{2c} = x$$

6. Factor your equation from step 2.
$$h^2 = a^2 - x^2; \; h^2 = (a - x)(a + x)$$

7. Substitute x (step 5) into your equation (step 6) and simplify leaving the numerator factored.

$$h^2 = \left[a - \left(\frac{a^2 - b^2 + c^2}{2c}\right)\right]\left[a + \left(\frac{a^2 - b^2 + c^2}{2c}\right)\right]$$

$$h^2 = \frac{[2ac - (a^2 - b^2 + c^2)]}{2c} \cdot \frac{[2ac + (a^2 - b^2 + c^2)]}{2c}$$

$$h^2 = \frac{[2ac - (a^2 - b^2 + c^2)][2ac + (a^2 - b^2 + c^2)]}{4c^2}$$

$$h^2 = \frac{(2ac - a^2 + b^2 - c^2)(2ac + a^2 - b^2 + c^2)}{4c^2}$$

8. Write the factor as $[b^2 - (\;)][(\;) - b^2]$.
$$h^2 = \frac{[b^2 - (a^2 - 2ac + c^2)][(a^2 + 2ac + c^2) - b^2]}{4c^2}$$

9. Write each parenthesis as a square.
$$h^2 = \frac{[b^2 - (a - c)^2][(a + c)^2 - b^2]}{4c^2}$$

10. Factor each bracket as a difference of squares.
$$h^2 = \frac{[b - (a - c)][b + (a - c)][(a + c) - b][(a + c) + b]}{4c^2}$$

$$h^2 = \frac{(b - a + c)(b + a - c)(a + c - b)(a + c + b)}{4c^2}$$

Leaving this equation momentarily, look at the equation for the semiperimeter.

$$s = \frac{a + b + c}{2}$$

$$2s = a + b + c$$

$$2s - 2a = a + b + c - 2a$$
$$2s - 2b = a + b + c - 2b$$
$$2s - 2c = a + b + c - 2c$$

$$2(s - a) = b + c - a$$
$$2(s - b) = a + c - b$$
$$2(s - c) = a + b - c$$

11. Substitute these quantities in your equation from step 10.
$$h^2 = \frac{[2(s - a)][2(s - c)][2(s - b)][2s]}{4c^2}$$

12. Reduce the fraction by canceling.
$$h^2 = \frac{16s(s - a)(s - c)(s - b)}{4c^2}$$

$$h^2 = \frac{4s(s - a)(s - c)(s - b)}{c^2}$$

13. Now, $c^2 h^2 = \frac{4s(s - a)(s - c)(s - b)}{c^2} \cdot c^2$

$$= 4s(s - a)(s - c)(s - b)$$

14. So, $ch = \sqrt{4s(s - a)(s - c)(s - b)}$
$$= 2\sqrt{s(s - a)(s - c)(s - b)}$$

Remember that the formula for the area of the triangle is

$$A = \frac{1}{2}ch.$$

15. Substitute for ch:
$$A = \frac{1}{2} \cdot 2\sqrt{s(s - a)(s - c)(s - b)}$$
$$A = \sqrt{s(s - a)(s - c)(s - b)}$$

Did you obtain Heron's formula? **yes**

Appendix K

Two Proofs

Theorem 10.8 Two lines perpendicular to the same plane are parallel.

This theorem would be easy to prove if the lines were coplanar. However, proving them coplanar is hard. In the following proof, the lines are not proved coplanar until step 14. Only two steps are needed to complete the proof from there.

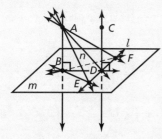

Given: Plane *m* contains points *B* and *D*; $\overleftrightarrow{AB} \perp m$; $\overleftrightarrow{CD} \perp m$

Prove: $AB \parallel CD$

1. Plane *m* contains points *B* and *D*; $\overleftrightarrow{AB} \perp m$; $\overleftrightarrow{CD} \perp m$
   1. Given
2. Draw $\overleftrightarrow{AD}$ and $\overleftrightarrow{BD}$, $l \perp \overleftrightarrow{BD}$ in plane *m*, points *E* and *F* on *l* so that $DE = DF$, then draw $\overleftrightarrow{BF}$, $\overleftrightarrow{AF}$, $\overleftrightarrow{BE}$, $\overleftrightarrow{AE}$; plane *n* determined by points *A*, *B*, and *D*
   2. Auxiliary lines and planes
3. $\overline{DE} \cong \overline{DF}$
   3. Definition of congruent segments
4. $\overleftrightarrow{BD}$ is the perpendicular bisector of $\overline{EF}$
   4. Definition of bisector
5. $BE = BF$
   5. Points of perpendicular bisector are equidistant from endpoints
6. $\overline{AE} \cong \overline{AF}$
   6. If the foot of a perpendicular to a plane is equidistant from two other points in the plane, then so is every other point on the perpendicular (Theorem 10.5)

7. $\overline{AD} \cong \overline{AD}$
   7. Reflexive property of congruent segments
8. $\triangle ADE \cong \triangle ADF$
   8. SSS
9. $\angle ADE \cong \angle ADF$
   9. Definition of congruent triangles
10. $\angle ADE$ and $\angle ADF$ are supplementary
    10. A linear pair forms supplementary angles
11. $\angle ADE$ and $\angle ADF$ are right angles
    11. Congruent supplements form right angles
12. $\overleftrightarrow{AD} \perp \overleftrightarrow{EF}$
    12. Definition of perpendicular
13. $\overleftrightarrow{EF} \perp n$
    13. A line perpendicular to two intersecting lines is perpendicular to the plane containing them (Theorem 10.2)
14. $\overleftrightarrow{CD}$ lies in plane *n*
    14. Exactly one plane through *A* is perpendicular to *l*
15. $\overleftrightarrow{AB} \perp \overleftrightarrow{BD}$, $\overleftrightarrow{CD} \perp \overleftrightarrow{BD}$
    15. Definition of line perpendicular to a plane
16. $\overleftrightarrow{AB} \parallel \overleftrightarrow{CD}$ in plane *n*
    16. Lines perpendicular to the same line are parallel

Theorem 10.15 Two parallel planes are everywhere equidistant.

This is another theorem that may sound simple but is not. To prove that the planes are equidistant, we must construct auxiliary perpendiculars at two arbitrary points and show that the segments joining the two planes along these perpendiculars have the same length.

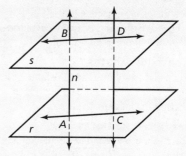

Given: Planes *r* and *s*; $r \parallel s$

Draw: $\overleftrightarrow{AB} \perp r$ at *A*, $\overleftrightarrow{CD} \perp r$ at *C*, $\overleftrightarrow{AC}$, $\overleftrightarrow{BD}$ where $B \in s$ and $D \in s$

Prove: $AB = CD$

1. Planes *r* and *s*; $r \parallel s$
   1. Given
2. Draw lines $\overleftrightarrow{AB} \perp r$ at *A*, $\overleftrightarrow{CD} \perp r$ at *C*, $\overleftrightarrow{AC}$, $\overleftrightarrow{BD}$ where $B \in s$ and $D \in s$
   2. Auxiliary lines
3. $\overleftrightarrow{AB} \perp s$, $\overleftrightarrow{CD} \perp s$
   3. A line perpendicular to one of two parallel planes is perpendicular to the other (Theorem 10.14)
4. $\overleftrightarrow{AB} \parallel \overleftrightarrow{CD}$
   4. Lines perpendicular to same plane are parallel (Theorem 10.8)
5. $\overleftrightarrow{AB}$ and $\overleftrightarrow{CD}$ are coplanar, lie in plane *n*
   5. Definition of parallel lines
6. $\overleftrightarrow{AC} \parallel \overleftrightarrow{BD}$
   6. A plane intersects parallel planes in parallel lines (Theorem 10.12)
7. $\overleftrightarrow{AB} \perp \overleftrightarrow{AC}$, $\overleftrightarrow{AB} \perp \overleftrightarrow{BD}$; $\overleftrightarrow{CD} \perp \overleftrightarrow{AC}$, $\overleftrightarrow{CD} \perp \overleftrightarrow{BD}$
   7. Definition of line perpendicular to plane
8. $\angle ABD$, $\angle ACD$, $\angle CAB$, $\angle CDB$ are right angles
   8. Definition of perpendicular lines
9. *ABCD* is a parallelogram (rectangle)
   9. Definition of parallelogram (rectangle)
10. $\overline{AB} \cong \overline{CD}$
    10. Opposite sides of a parallelogram are congruent
11. $AB = CD$
    11. Definition of congruent segments

Appendix L

Postulate Summary

The postulates have been classified in this book. The classification is a convenient memory device or summarization tool.

Incidence Postulates (5)
Expansion Postulate, Line Postulate, Plane Postulate, Flat Plane Postulate, and Plane Intersection Postulate (Chapter 1)

Separation Postulates (3)
Line Separation Postulate, Plane Separation Postulate, Space Separation Postulate (Chapters 2 and 10)

Measurement Postulates (5)
for segments: Ruler and Completeness Postulates (Chapter 3)
for angles: Protractor, Continuity, and Angle Addition Postulates (Chapter 4)

Parallel Postulates (2)
Parallel Postulate and Historic Parallel Postulate (Chapter 6)

Congruence Postulates (2)
SAS and ASA (Chapter 6)

Area Postulates (4)
Area Postulate, Congruent Regions Postulate, Area of Square Postulate, Area Addition Postulate (Chapter 8)

Circle Postulates (2)
Chord Postulate and Arc Addition Postulate (Chapter 9)

Volume Postulates (5)
Volume Postulate, Congruent Solids Postulate, Volume of Cube Postulate, Volume Addition Postulate, Cavalieri's Principle (Chapter 11)

Similarity Postulates (1)
AA Similarity Postulate (Chapter 13)

Appendix M

Leonardo da Vinci

Variety was the most distinguishing characteristic of the life of Leonardo da Vinci. He was a master in many areas, including art, architecture, military engineering, biology, science, optics, geology, and mathematics. Da Vinci is probably best known for his famous paintings. Some of his most well known works are *Mona Lisa*, *Virgin of the Rocks*, and *The Last Supper*. He also drew diagrams and sketches for both anatomical and mathematical textbooks. He thought mathematics was a key element of his art and once wrote, "Let no one read me who is not a mathematician."

Da Vinci had a humble beginning. He was born on April 15, 1452, the son of a young lawyer and a peasant girl near the Tuscan village of Vinci, Italy. He lived with his father, Ser Piero da Vinci, who noticed his son's talent in drawing when Leonardo was very young. At the age of eighteen, Leonardo apprenticed in painting and sculpture with Andrea del Verrocchio, a famous artist and sculptor of Florence. The knowledge and skills he learned from Verrocchio aided da Vinci throughout his life. When the apprenticeship ended in 1477, he began working as an engineer—a profession that was then involved primarily in military strategy.

Da Vinci's mathematical discoveries and inventive designs varied as much as his interests. He designed his own adjustable compass, which was similar to the ones we use today. He also invented a device based on trigonometry to determine the height of a mountain. He drew the technical diagrams for a math book called *On Divine Proportion*, which was written by his friend Luca Pacioli. To da Vinci, mathematics was the basis of his work.

In 1517 da Vinci became the royal painter and architect for King Francis I of France. He settled in Cloux, France, in semiretirement and died two years later on May 2, 1519.

Da Vinci used mathematics in every form of his artwork from mechanical drawings to portrait paintings. He received his advanced mathematical training from Luca Pacioli. He saw and appreciated geometry for its visualization of abstract thought. He also used precise measuring instruments and construction techniques for his technical drawings.

You may want students to study *The Last Supper* to find further examples of golden rectangles, reflections, or symmetry. The painting appears on page 541. Another alternative is his painting *Virgin of the Rocks*, which may be found in books on art.

Answers

Chapter 9—Circles

9.4

25.

1. Trapezoid *ABCD* inscribed in ⊙*L*
   1. Given
2. $\overleftrightarrow{AB} \parallel \overleftrightarrow{DC}$
   2. Definition of trapezoid
3. ∠*BDC* ≅ ∠*ABD*
   3. Parallel Postulate
4. *m*∠*BDC* = *m*∠*ABD*
   4. Definition of congruent angles
5. *m*∠*BDC* = $\frac{1}{2}m\widehat{BC}$; *m*∠*ABD* = $\frac{1}{2}m\widehat{AD}$
   5. Inscribed angle measures half the intercepted arc
6. $\frac{1}{2}m\widehat{BC} = \frac{1}{2}m\widehat{AD}$
   6. Substitution (step 5 into 4)
7. $m\widehat{BC} = m\widehat{AD}$
   7. Multiplication property of equality
8. $\widehat{BC} \cong \widehat{AD}$
   8. Definition of congruent arcs
9. $\overline{BC} \cong \overline{AD}$
   9. Chords congruent if and only if arcs congruent
10. *ABCD* is an isosceles trapezoid
    10. Definition of isosceles trapezoid
11. If a trapezoid is inscribed in a circle, then it is isosceles
    11. Law of Deduction

26. Definition of perpendicular [4.3]
27. Longer Side Inequality [7.4]
28. Exterior Angle Theorem [7.3]
29. Triangle Inequality [7.5]
30. 180° in triangle [6.5]

9.5

21.

1. $\overleftrightarrow{AB}$ is a secant, and $\overleftrightarrow{BC}$ is a tangent to ⊙*P* at *B*
   1. Given
2. Draw diameter $\overline{BD}$
   2. Auxiliary line
3. $m\widehat{DAB} = 180$
   3. Degree measure of a semicircle
4. $\overleftrightarrow{BD} \perp \overleftrightarrow{BC}$
   4. Radius is perpendicular to tangent at point of tangency
5. ∠*CBD* is a right angle
   5. Definition of perpendicular
6. *m*∠*CBD* = 90 = $\frac{1}{2}$(180)
   6. Definition of right angle
7. *m*∠*CBD* = $\frac{1}{2}(m\widehat{DAB})$
   7. Substitution (step 3 into 6)
8. *m*∠*ABD* = $\frac{1}{2}m\widehat{AD}$
   8. Inscribed angle measures half of intercepted arc
9. *m*∠*ABC* + *m*∠*ABD* = *m*∠*CBD*
   9. Angle Addition Postulate
10. *m*∠*ABC* + $\frac{1}{2}m\widehat{AD}$ = $\frac{1}{2}m\widehat{DAB}$
    10. Substitution (steps 7 and 8 into 9)
11. *m*∠*ABC* = $\frac{1}{2}m\widehat{DAB}$ − $\frac{1}{2}m\widehat{AD}$
    11. Addition property of equality
12. *m*∠*ABC* = $\frac{1}{2}(m\widehat{DAB} − m\widehat{AD})$
    12. Distributive property
13. $m\widehat{AD} + m\widehat{AB} = m\widehat{DAB}$
    13. Arc Addition Postulate
14. $m\widehat{AB} = m\widehat{DAB} − m\widehat{AD}$
    14. Addition property of equality
15. *m*∠*ABC* = $\frac{1}{2}m\widehat{AB}$
    15. Substitution (step 14 into 12)

22. rhombus [4.5]
23. perpendicular bisectors of each other [7.6]
24. $4\sqrt{34}$ [3.4]
25. 30 [8.2]
26. pentahedron [2.7]

14.

1. $\overleftrightarrow{AB}$ is tangent to ⊙*C* at *A*; $\overleftrightarrow{AN} \perp \overleftrightarrow{AB}$
   1. Given
2. *C* ∉ $\overleftrightarrow{AN}$
   2. Assumed
3. Draw $\overline{CA}$
   3. Auxiliary line
4. $\overline{CA} \perp \overleftrightarrow{AB}$
   4. Radius perpendicular to tangent at point of tangency
5. ∠*BAN* is a right angle, ∠*CAB* is a right angle
   5. Definition of perpendicular
6. ∠*BAN* ≅ ∠*CAB*
   6. All right angles congruent
7. *m*∠*BAN* = *m*∠*CAB*
   7. Definition of congruent angles
8. *m*∠*BAN* = *m*∠*CAN* + *m*∠*CAB*
   8. Angle Addition Postulate
9. *m*∠*BAN* > *m*∠*CAB*
   9. Greater than property
10. *C* ∈ $\overleftrightarrow{AN}$
    10. Law of Contradiction (steps 7, 9)

29.

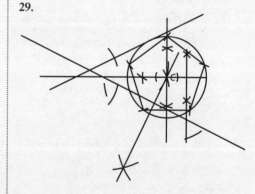

30. The dimensions given include the circumference of the sea and the diameter from brim to brim. If the width of the brim is considered (one handbreadth according to a parallel passage), the resulting approximation of π provides the most accurate approximation of π known from the ancient world.

Chapter 10—Space

10.6

20.

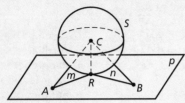

1. Sphere *S* with center *C* and plane *p* tangent at *R*	1. Given
2. Draw $\overline{CR}$ and $\overline{RA}$ and $\overrightarrow{RB}$ in *p*	2. Auxiliary lines
3. *C*, *R*, and *A* determine a plane *m*; *C*, *R*, and *B* determine plane *n*	3. Plane Postulate
4. $m \cap S$ = great circle₁, $n \cap S$ = great circle₂	4. Definition of great circle
5. $\overleftrightarrow{RA}$ is tangent to great circle₁; $\overleftrightarrow{RB}$ is tangent to great circle₂	5. Definition of tangent
6. $\overline{CR} \perp \overleftrightarrow{RA}$, $\overline{CR} \perp \overleftrightarrow{RB}$	6. Radius of circle is perpendicular to a tangent line at the point of tangency
7. $\overline{CR} \perp p$	7. A line perpendicular to two lines in a plane is perpendicular to the plane containing them
8. If a plane is tangent to a sphere, then it is perpendicular to a radius of the sphere at the point of tangency	8. Law of Deduction
9. Sphere *S* with center *C* has a radius $\overline{CR}$ perpendicular to a plane *p* at *R*	9. Given
10. Assume $S \cap p$ at $B \neq R$	10. Assumption
11. $\overleftrightarrow{RB}$ is a secant	11. Definition of secant line
12. *R*, *B*, *C* determine a plane *m*	12. Plane Postulate

13. $\overleftrightarrow{CR} \perp \overleftrightarrow{RB}$	13. A line perpendicular to a plane is perpendicular to every line in the plane through the point of intersection
14. *m* intersects *S* in a great circle	14. Definition of a great circle
15. $\overleftrightarrow{RB}$ is a tangent	15. A line perpendicular to a radius at a point of a circle is a tangent line
16. *S* intersects *p* at exactly one point *R*	16. Law of Contradiction (see steps 11 and 15)
17. If a radius is perpendicular to a plane at a point of the sphere, then the plane is a tangent plane	17. Law of Deduction (steps 9, 16)
18. A plane is tangent to a sphere if and only if it is perpendicular to the radius at the point of tangency	18. Definition of biconditional

Chapter 10 Review

24.

  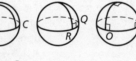

25.

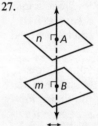

1. Sphere *S* with center *C* and chord $\overline{AB}$	1. Given
2. A great circle *E* contains *A* and *B*	2. Two points on a sphere lie on a great circle
3. Draw $\overline{CP}$ perpendicular to $\overline{AB}$ $(P \in S)$	3. Auxiliary line
4. $\overline{CP}$ bisects $\overline{AB}$	4. The radius of a circle perpendicular to a chord of the circle bisects the chord

26.

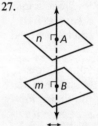

1. $\overrightarrow{PQ} \perp p$ at *P*, $A \in p, A \neq P$	1. Given
2. *A*, *P*, *Q* determine plane *n*	2. Plane Postulate
3. $\overrightarrow{PQ} \perp \overleftrightarrow{PA}$	3. Definition of line perpendicular to plane
4. $\angle QPA$ is a right angle	4. Definition of perpendicular
5. $m\angle QPA > \angle QAP$	5. In a right triangle, two angles are acute (See 7.3 #17)
6. $AQ > PQ$	6. Longer Side Inequality

27.

1. $n \perp \overleftrightarrow{AB}$ at *A*, $m \perp \overleftrightarrow{AB}$ at *B*	1. Given
2. Assume *n* and *m* intersect in at least one point *C*	2. Assumption
3. $\angle ABC$ and $\angle BAC$ are right angles	3. Definition of perpendicular
4. $\triangle ABC$ is a right triangle with a right angle at *A*	4. Definition of right triangle
5. $\angle BAC$ is acute	5. In a right triangle, two angles are acute
6. Planes *n* and *m* are parallel	6. Law of Contradiction (see steps 3 and 5)

28.

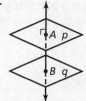

1. $\overleftrightarrow{AB}$ is perpendicular to plane p at A; $\overleftrightarrow{AB}$ intersects plane q at B; $p \parallel q$	1. Given
2. Plane q contains two other noncollinear points C and D	2. Expansion Postulate
3. Points A, B, C determine plane m; points A, B, D determine plane n	3. Plane Postulate
4. m intersects p in $\overleftrightarrow{AF}$; n intersects p in $\overleftrightarrow{AG}$	4. Plane Intersection Postulate
5. $\overleftrightarrow{AB}$ is perpendicular to $\overleftrightarrow{AF}$ and $\overleftrightarrow{AG}$	5. Definition of line perpendicular to plane
6. $\overleftrightarrow{BC} \parallel \overleftrightarrow{AF}$ in plane m, $\overleftrightarrow{BD} \parallel \overleftrightarrow{AG}$ in plane n	6. A plane intersects parallel planes in parallel lines
7. $\overleftrightarrow{AB} \perp \overleftrightarrow{BC}$, $\overleftrightarrow{AB} \perp \overleftrightarrow{BD}$	7. A line perpendicular to one of two parallel lines is perpendicular to the other
8. $\overleftrightarrow{AB} \perp$ plane q	8. A line perpendicular to two intersecting lines is perpendicular to plane containing them

29.

1. $\overleftrightarrow{AB} \parallel \overleftrightarrow{CD}$, $m \cap n = \overleftrightarrow{AB}$, $n \cap p = \overleftrightarrow{CD}$, $m \cap p = \overleftrightarrow{EF}$	1. Given
2. $\overleftrightarrow{AB}$ intersects $\overleftrightarrow{EF}$ at Q	2. Assumption
3. $Q \in n$ since $\overleftrightarrow{AB} \subset n$, $Q \in p$ since $\overleftrightarrow{EF} \subset p$	3. Flat Plane Postulate
4. $Q \in n \cap p$	4. Definition of intersection (step 3)
5. $Q \in \overleftrightarrow{CD}$	5. Substitution (step 1 into 4)
6. $\overleftrightarrow{AB} \parallel \overleftrightarrow{EF}$	6. Law of Contradiction (steps 1, 2, and 5)
7. $\overleftrightarrow{CD} \parallel \overleftrightarrow{EF}$	7. Two lines parallel to same line are parallel

30. Exodus 27:1 contains God's commands for building the altar. The base is square, and the three dimensions specified describe a rectangular solid. These facts are important in discussing whether the created universe is Euclidean (also the Law of Dimensions from Chapter 7).

Chapter 11—Volume

11.6

5.

8.

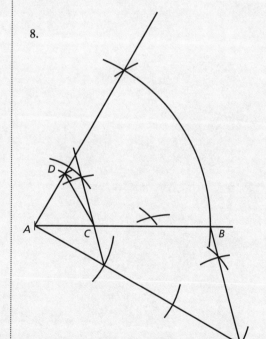

9.

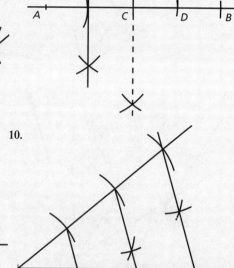

10.

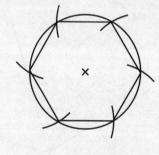

radius of circum. circle

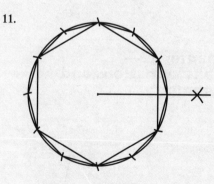

11.

12.

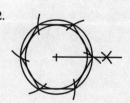

19. [6.9]

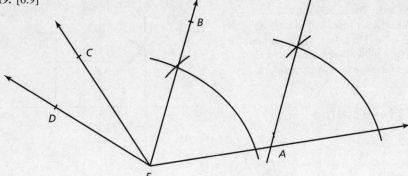

20. [7.7

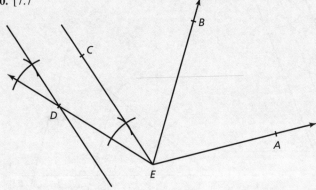

21. [3.7]

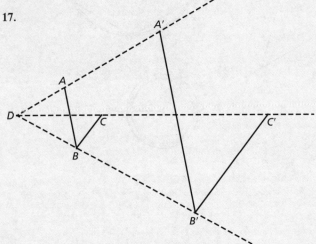

20. $\sin x \cos x - \sec x \sin x$

$$= \sin x \cos x - \sec x \sin x$$

$$= \sin x(\cos x - \sec x)$$

$$= \sin x \left(\cos x - \frac{1}{\cos x} \right)$$

$$= \frac{\sin x \cdot (\cos^2 x - 1)}{\cos x}$$

$$= \frac{\sin x \cdot [\cos^2 x - (\sin^2 x + \cos^2 x)]}{\cos x}$$

$$= \frac{\sin x \cdot [-\sin^2 x]}{\cos x}$$

$$= \frac{-\sin^2 x \cdot \sin x}{\cos x}$$

$$= -\sin^2 x \tan x$$

Chapter 12—
Transformations and
Symmetry

12.3

17.

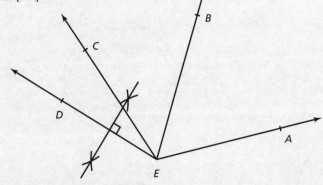

18.

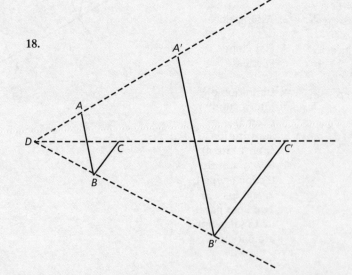